Persian Literature as World Literature

Literatures as World Literature

Can the literature of a specific country, author, or genre be used to approach the elusive concept of "world literature"? **Literatures as World Literature** takes a novel approach to world literature by analyzing specific constellations—according to language, nation, form, or theme—of literary texts and authors in their own world-literary dimensions.

World literature is obviously so vast that any view of it cannot help but be partial; the question then becomes how to reduce the complex task of understanding and describing world literature. Most treatments of world literature so far either have been theoretical and thus abstract, or else have made broad use of exemplary texts from a variety of languages and epochs. The majority of critical work, the filling in of what has been traced, lies ahead of us. **Literatures as World Literature** fills in the devilish details by allowing scholars to move outward from their own areas of specialization, fostering scholarly writing that approaches more closely the polyphonic, multiperspectival nature of world literature.

Series Editor:
Thomas O. Beebee

Editorial Board:
Eduardo Coutinho, Federal University of Rio de Janeiro, Brazil
Hsinya Huang, National Sun-yat Sen University, Taiwan
Meg Samuelson, University of Cape Town, South Africa
Ken Seigneurie, Simon Fraser University, Canada
Mads Rosendahl Thomsen, Aarhus University, Denmark

Volumes in the Series
German Literature as World Literature, edited by Thomas O. Beebee
Roberto Bolaño as World Literature, edited by Nicholas Birns and Juan E. De Castro
Crime Fiction as World Literature, edited by David Damrosch, Theo D'haen, and Louise Nilsson

Persian Literature as World Literature

Edited by
Mostafa Abedinifard, Omid Azadibougar, and
Amirhossein Vafa

BLOOMSBURY ACADEMIC
NEW YORK • LONDON • OXFORD • NEW DELHI • SYDNEY

BLOOMSBURY ACADEMIC
Bloomsbury Publishing Inc
1385 Broadway, New York, NY 10018, USA
50 Bedford Square, London, WC1B 3DP, UK
29 Earlsfort Terrace, Dublin 2, Ireland

BLOOMSBURY, BLOOMSBURY ACADEMIC and the Diana logo are
trademarks of Bloomsbury Publishing Plc

First published in the United States of America 2021
This paperback edition published 2023

A catalog record for this book is available from the Library of Congress.

ISBN: HB: 978-1-5013-5422-9
         PB: 978-1-5013-7454-8
         ePDF: 978-1-5013-5420-5
         eBook: 978-1-5013-5421-2

Series: Literatures as World Literature

Typeset by Integra Software Services Pvt. Ltd.

To find out more about our authors and books visit www.bloomsbury.com
and sign up for our newsletters.

In memory of
Fatemeh Sayyah (1902–48),
pioneering polyglot, literary critic, and comparatist

Contents

Acknowledgments

We have had the good fortune to work with many wonderful people in the process of preparing this volume and would like to thank each and every one of them.

We are grateful to the Series Editor, Thomas Oliver Beebee, who welcomed the proposal in the first place and accepted it for inclusion in this impressive collection. We hope similar spaces will open in the future to move the study of Persian and other Iranian literatures to comparative literary studies in order to increase exchanges with wider scholarly communities.

We would like to express our appreciation to Katherine De Chant, our first point of contact with Bloomsbury. Katherine was very helpful and encouraging in the initial steps of our work on the volume. We then kept working with Haaris Naqvi and Amy Martin. We especially thank them for their patience and constant support throughout the stages of the preparation of the manuscript. Sarah McNamee and her wonderful typesetting team were superbly professional and accommodating in getting the Persian segments right. We warmly thank you all for the great work done.

This work would not have been complete without the professional contribution of the three reviewers who read the manuscript at our request during a time when work and life routines were interrupted, and provided us with detailed and constructive assessments. On behalf of ourselves and the contributors to the volume, we thank them for their time and dedication to sustaining excellent scholarly standards in the discipline. Likewise, we thank the readers who reviewed the manuscript on Bloomsbury's behalf for their time and insightful suggestions.

We appreciate the work of the contributors to this volume. You have all been very patient with our constant inquiries during the past two years, and your collegial cooperation allowed the work to progress smoothly and seamlessly. It has been a pleasure for us to share a vision with you. This work will hopefully have a part in shaping the future of Persian, Iranian, and world literary studies, tackling some of the shortcomings we have occasionally discussed.

Last but not least, we thank our families for their unwavering support and encouragement during this fairly long process.

Notes on Transliteration, Translation, and Dates

The presence of a combination of classical and modern Persian, and other West Asian languages posed a major challenge to a systemic and coherent transliteration of non-English words. Our intention has been to facilitate the reading of the text for students and scholars uninitiated in Persian and Iranian literary studies. Therefore, we chose the simplified transliteration scheme once used by the *Iranian Studies* journal. However, where Arabic or (Ottoman) Turkish words and phrases are cited, some adjustments have been made to the scheme. In addition, where titles or words in other sources use a different transliteration scheme, they have been quoted as they appear (particularly in the bibliography).

Translations are rendered by each chapter's author unless otherwise specified. Where an author's translation of a title or passage is different from published translated versions of the original material, available versions are mentioned but the author's rendering is kept intact.

Where Persian sources are referenced, the Iranian calendar year is provided followed by the Gregorian calendar year (e.g., 1400/2021). This is to allow the locating of sources for those who might need to access and consult the original texts.

Introduction: Decolonizing a Peripheral Literature

Amirhossein Vafa, Omid Azadibougar, and Mostafa Abedinifard

The idea of this volume began with a call for papers that warned of an existing crisis in Persian literary studies, and called for an urgent need for the reassessment of research aims and methods to redress the crisis. We claimed that "Persian literary studies have, more often than not, been prevailed by nationalistic, nativist and isolationist scholarship at the cost of neglecting the worldliness of the texts studied," and to overcome the status quo made a case for reading Persian literary texts *as* world literature, "as transnational, worldly texts that expand beyond local and national penchants, sometimes through circulation beyond their local and national origins, yet—more importantly—also through their rarely explored transactions, negotiations, and confrontations with other worlds and world literatures." This, we proposed, was the only way to change the field of literary criticism to confront "parochial and exclusivist interpreting practices" in Persian literary scholarship.

Three years past this starting point, the editors still stand by their claims. This volume opens with assumptions that Persian literature, its historiography, and its study as national and world literature within and beyond Persian-speaking societies and their diasporas need reassessment. The papers collected in this volume respond to this need and advance critical approaches that, we believe, can tackle the crisis—however partially. We take it that admitting *crisis*, in contrast to claiming stability, can be a sign of disciplinary well-being if engaged critically and constructively—to safeguard the survival of the discipline and what it represents. Our insistence on a crisis of literature in this Introduction, therefore, signifies the hope for a *dynamic*, rather than a stagnant and self-perpetuating, field of scholarship.

In the case of postrevolutionary Iran, which has also happened to become the primary focus of this volume, multiple factors—from the cultural priorities of the population at large to state censorship—have caused the crisis during the past decades, significantly disturbing, often utterly interrupting, literary production and consumption. The decline of literature in the contemporary (postcolonial and developing) societies of the Persian-speaking world, and in particular Iran, is reflected in the rapidly declining number of literary publications' print-runs and their respective readership, despite the increasing number of private publishers (see Nanquette's contribution to this volume). Ironically, this is happening exactly as literacy has increased unprecedentedly during the past decades. And while as a global phenomenon the dominance of visual media has marginalized literature,[1] their effects in developing societies remain far more radical and unpredictable.[2] At the same time, the significant role of digital technologies and the social media has only worsened the impact of "massified culture" on literature through the erosion of a sense of aesthetic beauty, since, as Antonio Candido reminds us, in an analysis applicable to contemporary Iranian situation, "literacy would then not increase the number of readers of literature, as conceived here, proportionally; but would fling the literate together with the illiterate, directly from the phase of folklore into this kind of urban folklore that is massified culture."[3]

Moreover, the study of Persian literature, especially at departments of national literature where Persian is the *lingua franca*, almost exclusively remains focused on philology and classical aesthetics; as such, criticism rarely broaches the relevance and significance of literature to contemporary social and political conditions—except perhaps in vague, symbolic terms that only limit the literary act to the national experience. Even then, such literary studies fall short of offering new readings that can revive the study of classical texts from bracing and radical perspectives.[4]

Even when deploying interpretive methods that welcome the pertinence of literature to sociopolitical conditions, scholars of Persian literature have more often than not been emulating and reproducing Eurocentric theories. In the past few decades, for instance, a fervent interest in translating texts (mostly from English) on literary/critical theory and criticism has been all the rage in Iran. This theoretical interest is allegedly also being carried forward to Afghanistan and Tajikistan.[5] Nonetheless, the majority of such rendered texts are no more than "textbooks" aimed at undergraduate and/or early graduate-level students in North American universities, that is, at best secondhand summary accounts of primary texts in exclusively European critical and literary theory.[6] The availability of such texts in Persian has made them accessible to scholars

[1] For instance, see Jan Baetens, "Novelization, a Contaminated Genre?" *Critical Inquiry* 32, no. 1 (2005), 43–60.
[2] Antonio Candido, "On Literature and Society," in *Literature and Underdevelopment*, trans. and ed. Howard S. Becker (Durham: Duke University Press, 1995), 119–41.
[3] Ibid., 123.
[4] For an effective critique of this brand of nationalist and parochial aesthetics, see Aria Fani, "The Allure of Untranslatability: Shafiʻi-Kadkani and (Not) Translating Persian Poetry," *Iranian Studies* 54, no. 1–2 (2020), 95–125. Commenting on the idea of "untranslatability," proposed by a leading scholar of Persian Language and Literature, Fani argues that the "notion of a monolith called 'all Persian readers' or 'all Muslim readers' who carry in their veins the literary lore of their poetic tradition may be enchanting, but it is nebulous and unquantifiable at best, and culturally chauvinistic at worst" (110). Such essentialist ethnocentrism is neither uncommon nor an isolated case; indeed, it represents the mainstream discourse that has constructed Persian literary studies for decades. Most interestingly, translation is *the* phenomenon that exposes it.
[5] Recently scholars of English and Persian literature teaching at Iranian universities have been invited to universities in Afghanistan to deliver talks on how to apply, say, Lacan and Freud to literary texts. Even when such regional networks are formed, they merely reproduce the monologic practice of reading non-European texts through the reductive lens of Western theory.
[6] For two instances of such widely read and applied translations into Persian, see Charles Bressler, *An Introduction to Literary Theory and Criticism*, 1st ed., trans. Mostafa Abedinifard (Tehran: Niloufar, 2007); Lois Tyson, *Critical Theory Today: A User-Friendly Guide*, 2nd ed., trans. Maziyar Hossen-Zadeh and Fatemeh Hosseini (Tehran: Hekayat-e Qalam-e Novin, 2015).

in departments of Persian literature, who often fill their scholarship with references to such entry-level theoretical *toolboxes* and develop mechanical applications of theory to a plethora of literary texts.[7]

The result is a reinforcement of the authoritative status of the perceived theory rather than any new knowledge or critical insight on the texts under discussion, on Persian literature or in comparative literary studies. A look at the publications of different journals on (comparative) literary studies in Persian—as well as graduate dissertations coming from nation-based institutions of higher education—reveals that rather than engaging extant theories in a dialogical and creative manner in the hope of providing new concepts and insights, many scholars are mere *consumers* of theory, unproblematically and subserviently *applying* (a code name for enforcing) simplified accounts of Western canonical theories to Persian texts; what ensues is predictable, acontextual and often contradictory results of the sort that we can at best call *colonial knowledge*.

Furthermore, while the ascendance of marketplace capitalism with a neoliberal logic in contemporary global economy is rendering the so-called "impractical" fields, such as literary studies, more difficult to justify and financially sustain in the corporate university, in postcolonial institutions of learning, a similar trend is happening under the logic of "development." In the Iranian context, it comes with a nativist ideology that tends to prioritize classical aesthetics over contemporary—and potentially secular—literature. One outcome of this sea change (and the discourse vacuum it creates) is the hegemony of mainstream literature, branded as World Literature, which exerts influence on non–Euro-American literatures, not only serving as a gatekeeper of literatures *as* world literature but also shaping readerly taste and authorial standards, hence limiting the scope of creative work in what the late Pascale Casanova called "the world republic of letters."

This restricted perspective on world literature is further exacerbated in a context where the political will to control the market and the publishing industry advocates censorship and interrupts an already volatile system of literary production and consumption. Combined with the spread of globalization in media and political discourse, as well as the rise to prominence of multiculturalism and the return of World Literature, Persian literature is therefore under unprecedented pressure to redefine its social, cultural, and political relevance in Iran, the wider Persian-speaking world, and across the globe. This precarious condition, due in part to a lack of any indigenous theoretical mindset, or what Revathi Krishnaswamy calls "world literary knowledge" to theorize Persian literary worldliness, threatens not only literature, but the entire field of cultural production.[8]

---

[7] Other than Arabic, students of Persian Language and Literature are not institutionally required to learn other languages. Due to its ubiquity in classical Persian literature, Arabic is not, strictly speaking, a "foreign" language as such. In the absence of foreign language training, the majority of scholars of Persian literature rely on translated texts. Given the assumptions of the institution of Persian Language and Literature (e.g., the sole national language and source of culture and cultural identity), this is quite ironic.

[8] See Revathi Krishnaswamy, "Toward World Literary Knowledges: Theory in the Age of Globalization." *Comparative Literature* 62, no. 4 (Fall 2010), 399–419. The situation may not be as dire in the cases of literature in Persian translation and global Iranian cinema, yet similar trends could be identified.

Whether the present state of cul-de-sac, as we see it, is due to state intervention in literary production, cultural developments of the past decades and/or the increasing marginalization of Persian as a "peripheral" language and literature in the contemporary world order, we are convinced that Persian literature and its study should be redefined, and methodologically recast. Departments of national literature, comparative literature and even Area Studies from within Persian-speaking societies to their respective diasporas, are in dire need of a "new" Persian literary studies that promotes a radical rethinking of the sociopolitical aspects of the discipline. This is where the integration of the public and cultural realms, and the aesthetic and the political, can lead to a reconciliation—and decolonization—of the Persian-speaking world.

Focusing on such diverse issues as nationality, race, gender, sexuality and the environment, revisionary readings of Persian literature, contextualized within the broader frame of the region and of the world itself, would be part of the new democratic process in the Persian literary and cultural studies we envision. Not all such *revisionary interventions* occur in the chapters that follow in this volume, but as a declaration of our editorial stance they help to negotiate new opportunities of transnational cooperation to oppose literary and cultural sites of ethnocentrism, economic inequality, and gender-based violence: for instance, decentering the racially fraught divides that undermine networks of cross-cultural exchange, or tackling the formation and consolidation of monolingual nationalism that neglects non-Persian languages in common use in Iran, and the Persianate world.

***

The contemporary epoch of World Literature, which gained currency with multiculturalism and globalization, could well be under siege with the resurgence of far-right nationalism across Europe and the United States, alongside the consequences of the Covid-19 pandemic and the climate crisis, at the time of this writing. Nevertheless, we still live and breathe in the era of US-led globalization, and despite the ever-growing influence of China and other developing economies on the global stage, the logic of modernity/coloniality, as conceived by Aníbal Quiano and Walter D. Mignolo, is still built on a dichotomy that has rendered Persian a peripheral language and literature. We therefore maintain that an exploration of Persian literature as world literature must be carried out in the light of the "worldliness" of Persianate societies within the modern postcolonial world, and the particular conditions of their literary and cultural participation in this world.

The contribution of Persian literature and theory to contemporary discourses on World Literature is unfortunately slim. Furthermore, with a few notable exceptions,[9] the contribution of Area Studies experts throughout the Persian diaspora to anthologies of World Literature, and to the scholarship on the subject, has been relatively small.

---

[9]   See, for instance, M. R. Ghanoonparvar, "The Blind Owl," in *The Novel: History, Geography and Culture*, vol. 1, ed. Franco Moretti (Princeton, NJ: Princeton University Press), 794–801; Hamid Dabashi, *The Shahnameh: The Persian Epic as World Literature* (New York: Columbia University Press, 2019).

While such minimal involvement can be primarily blamed on scholarly inertia, it is also important to note the significant role of Western epistemic dominance and the colonial structures underlying production and circulation of knowledge around the globe.[10] A case in point for the doggedness of this epistemic dominance and violence is the great lengths Dick Davis goes to, in the introduction to his own translation of *Vis and Ramin*, in order to demonstrate—despite obvious intertextualities and circumstantial evidence in favor—that the Persian text has most likely been a source for many subsequent European romances, particularly the strand of tales known as *Tristan and Isolde*[11] (see Alexandra Hoffmann's chapter in this volume for a confident counterexample in response to the said colonial structure of knowledge production).

In the face of the above challenges, to conceive as World Literature a literature—here, Persian—that has conventionally been perceived as *national*, will be an essential, albeit insufficient, solution. From Goethe and Marx to Damrosch and Moretti, the core driving idea of World Literature has been the insufficiency of national frames for understanding literary and cultural transformation; intercultural exchange is a given and has to be accounted for, which is particularly where the concept of World Literature diverges from conventional ways of doing Comparative Literature: the latter is based in national literary historiography (an invention of European modernity), whereas the former examines the dissemination of texts that may not be essentially nationally based. World Literature has, therefore, been a promising field, creating spaces where the asymmetrical relations in literary scholarship—resulting from differences between national cultures—are critiqued in favor of inclusive approaches, where wider and more complex literary and cultural exchanges are imagined and studied. The very book series the present volume appears in, *Literatures as World Literature*, is an example of such a space, given that conventionally, studies of Persian literature have been categorized under area studies (Persian/Iranian Studies, Middle East Studies, or—although to a lesser extent—Islamic Studies and Asian Studies), which institutionally restrict interaction with literary and cultural traditions beyond regionally imagined ones (e.g., Arabic and Turkish).

Despite the significance of World Literature as a scholarly project, however, the challenges the concept is facing are numerous. When Marx and Engels wrote that "[i]n place of the old local and national seclusion and self-sufficiency, we have intercourse in every direction, universal inter-dependence of nations," they probably imagined a global economy in which the supply chains would be distributed among nations, making national independence as such irrelevant and impossible. Such a worldly organization would presume a similar, if not equal, permeation of capitalism in national economies, integrating them into an international system they all create, contribute to, and depend on. Under such circumstances, Marx and Engels imagined,

---

[10] For two pertinent sources, albeit with a focus on social sciences, see Raewyn Connell, *Southern Theory: The Global Dynamics of Knowledge in Social Science* (Crows Nest, N.S.W.: Allen & Unwin, 2007); Fran Collyer et al., *Knowledge and Global Power: Making New Sciences in the South* (Clayton, Australia: Monash University Publishing, 2019).

[11] Fakhraddin Gorgani, *Vis and Ramin*, trans. Dick Davis (New York: Penguin, 2008), xxxviii.

"[n]ational one-sidedness and narrowmindedness become more and more impossible, and from the numerous national and local literatures, there arises a world literature."[12] This ideal, however, still remains elusive.

The uneven development of capitalism and globalization has meant constricted access to the world, both as material and as idea: not all nations participate in shaping and sharing the material conditions of the world equally, nor do they gain identical access to the cultural apparatuses that form and represent the global culture. As a consequence, differing conceptualizations of the literary persist, challenging the idea that World Literature—despite the existence of translation—is representative of this diversity. Whether it is access to mainstream publishers and literary markets for creative writers, or to scholarly publishing networks, globalization has, more often than not, intensified the status of previously canonical literatures.[13] In this sense, the promises of World Literature have only been nominal: the immense capacity of Western institutions for publication, coupled with almost immediate access to primary materials (including linguistic training where needed) and methodologies, has meant that the majority of works debated in World Literature are still from conventionally dominant cultures.

Complicating this picture and adding to the problem are also self-colonizing and self-Orientalist attitudes, for instance, in the Iranian cultural milieux, where the literary translation market can be shown to have barely been *globalized* or *worlded*.[14] A brief survey of this market shows it to be dominated by works that reveal their translators' and publishers' internalization of the Western, and particularly a traditional North American, mainstream literary taste and an outrageously comparative lack of interest in translating works that reflect the social experiences of the historically marginalized, or works written by authors from the "Global South." This taste, itself informed by and in turn informing the popular taste, has predictably led to a constricted view of world literature, represented as a collection of "masterpieces from a few 'major cultures'";[15] even when welcoming of *othered* literatures, this paradigm acts in a reductionist manner, for instance by representing a whole country or even continent by, mainly or merely, a particular number of works. Drawing on the basic modes of world literature

---

[12] Karl Marx and Friedrich Engels, *The Communist Manifesto* (New York: The Seabury Press, 1967), 137.

[13] See David Damrosch, "World Literature in a Postcanonical, Hypercanonical Age," in *Comparative Literature in an Age of Globalization*, ed. Haun Saussy (Baltimore: Johns Hopkins University Press, 2006), 43–53. The increase of debates on World Literature has further pushed the "shadow canon" into the shadows of literary studies.

[14] On self-colonization, see Alexander Kiossev, "The Self-Colonizing Metaphor," *Atlas of Transformtion*, 22 October 2017, http://monumenttotransformation.org/atlas-of-transformation/html/s/self-colonization/the-self-colonizing-metaphor-alexander-kiossev.html. On self-Orientalism, with special attention to modern Iranian history, see Reza Zia-Ebrahimi, *The Emergence of Iranian Nationalism: Race and the Politics of Dislocation* (New York: Columbia University Press, 2016). According to what he deems *dislocative nationalism*, Zia-Ebrahimi shows, Arabs have become implacable others in modern Iran.

[15] David Damrosch, "Major Cultures and Minor Literatures," in *Teaching World Literature*, ed. David Damrosch (New York: MLA, 2009), 193.

Damrosch introduces (i.e., as classics, as masterpieces, and as windows on the world), one could easily show that the majority of the works rendered in each and all of these categories, as published in modern Iran, would barely go "beyond the boundaries of Western Europe."[16]

At the same time, a combination of global and regional geopolitical issues might further jeopardize domestic aspirations for World Literature. There is increasing cynicism toward globalization on both sides of the Atlantic—the engines of globalization—as well as elsewhere: the vocal "America First" idea in the United States is one sign of the return of nationalism; Brexit and similar trends across the European continent imply that transnational projects such as the EU are being challenged. In this environment, nationalist projects such as the Iranian Revolution of 1979, sidelined during the formation of liberal globalization and intensified capital mobility in the last decades of the twentieth century, find confirmation for renewed interest in nationalism, particularly in the aftermath of international sanctions that have crippled the national economy. For literature, this may not necessarily mean a return to national canons, but it might signify that the ideals of World Literature could remain elusive, particularly if nationalist interest in politics is coupled with pedagogical plans.

On the other hand, since the problems of Iranian nationalism are embedded in the history of Iranian modernity/coloniality, the participation of Persian literature in world literature could ironically exacerbate them. The effects of a deeply flawed process of nation-building are only becoming more visible in the current century. For instance, large populations eliminated from the nation-building project—romantically invested in the hegemony of Persian as national culture—now demand linguistic and cultural recognition beyond their locality. In an intellectual environment that is historically and theoretically unprepared to tackle this challenge, the stakes are high, so the successful transplantation of Persian Literature into World Literature could also lead to intensified nationalism and further endorse and prolong the elimination of other Iranian and non-Persian cultures and languages in the region. In the Persian literary field, therefore, World Literature remains an attractive and precarious temptation.

***

This collection of essays comes with a number of limitations. First, Persianate literatures from Central Asia and the Indian subcontinent are not represented in this volume. While part of this aspect, especially Persian in the Indian subcontinent, has often previously appeared in postcolonial debates, such examinations often place Persian and its circulation vis-à-vis European languages. Therefore, although significant, the postcolonial approach remains shy of the decolonizing project we envision. While we are conscious of this absence, we believe in the "new" Comparative Literature, as conceived by Spivak to foreground *area expertise*, and the "collaborative" practice of

---

[16] David Damrosch, "Introduction: All the World in the Time," in *Teaching World Literature*, ed. David Damrosch (New York: MLA, 2009), 7.

World Literature, as conceived by Damrosch to encourage *collectivity*. We therefore encourage fellow scholars in the region to expand the horizons set by this volume. Dick Davis's recently published translation *The Mirror of My Heart: A Thousand Years of Persian Poetry by Women,* itself based on a larger anthology published in Persian in prerevolutionary Iran, is interesting as an attempt toward further inclusivity, as it includes poems by poets from "Iran of course, but also India, Afghanistan, and areas of central Asia that are now Uzbekistan, Turkmenistan, and Tajikistan."[17]

Moreover, non-Persian Iranian languages and literatures are not included in this book either, despite the fact that important texts have been written in these languages, including, to name only a few, *Kateeny the Great* in Assyrian (by William D. S. Daniel); *Kurdish Shahnameh* in Gorani oral tradition, compiled by Ahmadkhani, also known as Sarhang Almas Khan; *Nazani/Mzgani* in Hawrami by Saeid Khan Kurdistani; poems by Magtymguly Pyragy in Turkmen; *Ma'zun's Divan* in Qashqai Turkish; Amir Pazevari's *amiri*s in Mazandarani; a plethora of unexplored texts of Bhuddhist Sogdian and Baluchi literature; transregional narratives and musical traditions of Arabic-speaking communities in southern Iran, including the descendants of Africans in the south and south-west.[18] While we are privileged to contain in the present collection transregional studies of Persian literary worldliness (see Abdulla Rexhepi's contribution on the reception of Persian poetry in the Balkans, and Gay Jennifer Breyley's chapter on an Iranian novel in English and an Azeri-speaking writer who publishes in Persian), this volume claims neither to cover the entirety of the Persian-speaking world, nor the multiplicity of languages and cultures in Iran, under the Persian hegemony.[19]

The fact that an absolute majority of students doing Persian Literature graduate without having ever heard of the above texts or read them in an institutional context is indicative of the prevalence of an aesthetic totalitarianism that marginalizes other-oriented thinking by subjecting a large body of poetic and narrative texts in multiple languages to an already discriminatory canon of Persian literature: Vahshi Bafqi's *Nazer and Manzur*, for instance, is as much a love story as *Leily and Majnun*, yet it remains underrated due to the homoerotic element in the story; this further confirms that the current ideologies that govern Persian literary studies are broken, obsolete, and regressive.

By the same token, we are also conscious, and wary, of the fact that the editors of this volume are cisgender, heterosexual, male Iranians who, despite originating from varied Iranian ethnicities, enjoy a certain range of "Persian" privileges by virtue of

[17] The hardcover edition was published in 2019 by Mage Publishers, and the paperback edition was published in 2021 by Penguin Classics.
[18] Some of the above texts have been translated into Persian (e.g., *Kateeny the Great* and collections of Amir Pazvari's poems), yet they have remained unstudied. Of these, no translations into other languages are available, though the first volume of *Kateeny the Great* has been rendered into English by Rameil Sayyad and should become internationally available before long.
[19] A main reason behind the absence of these texts from our collection might be the lack of current active research on them, in part due to an epistemological limit imposed by institutional requirements. Whether located in departments of national literature (e.g., Persian, English, French, or German), or at Area Studies or (Comparative) Literary Studies programs, students find themselves in programs that make these texts unavailable and research on them discouraged, if not almost impossible.

being academics and literary scholars within and outside the region. We are conscious of such identity politics and hope to pave the way for a radical worldliness in this, and forthcoming, studies of Persian literature as world literature.

Beyond the region, studies of diasporic literature are, with the exception of Naghmeh Esmaeilpour's contribution, also absent from our volume. Especially in the case of the Iranian diaspora, the diasporic literary output is relatively huge and diverse (e.g., genre-wise), covering a wide political spectrum with regard to foreign policy, or domestic politics in Iran and across the region. *Persepolis* (Marjane Satrapi, 2000), *My Father's Notebook* (Kader Abdollah, 2000), *Reading Lolita in Tehran* (Azar Nafisi, 2003), and *No Friend but the Mountains* (Behrouz Boochani, 2018) are only some of the texts that will have to be accommodated in Persian-as-world literary thinking if the canon is to be expanded and globalized. Adding the work of writers such as Atiq Rahimi (the author of *The Patient Stone*, among other works) and Khaled Hosseini (the author of *The Kite-Runner, A Thousand Splendid Suns, And the Mountains Echoed*) who are originally from Afghanistan but who write in, respectively, French and English, drawing on Persian literary heritage, indicates the complexity of the task. Yet our conscious (but temporary) departure from the diaspora is rooted in our effort to recast the "world canon" of Persian literature, which today mostly includes translations of classical poetry, or diasporic memoirs and novels from Iran and Afghanistan.

History (and literary history) is more an act of forgetting than of remembering. In processing collective memory for selection and canonization, ideologies that sift the mass data shape literary historiography, creating a narrative that supports the ends of the agent(s) that participate in the writing of literary history. Even in the eighth-century Fars, in southern Iran, a remarkably prolific and influential poetic figure like Jahan Malek Khatun is marginalized in favor of her male counterparts, in particular Hafez and Ubeyd.[20] This marginalization is reflected even today, both in literary anthologies and course syllabi.[21] Our hope is that this volume can shed light on the forgotten and less studied aspects of Persian literary history—including its pre-national sense of worldliness—to reimagine contemporary literary historiography beyond the Eurocentric colonial logic that has defined it to date.

∗∗∗

The chapters throughout this volume are organized in three sections. The four papers in the first section address the issue of Persian literary worldliness or the circumstantial realities that, in the Saidian sense of the term, have informed the significance, or peripherality, of Persian literature on the global stage. In the second section, contributors address the broad implications of global mobility as an inevitable

---

[20] See Dominic Parviz Brookshaw, *Hafiz and His Contemporaries: Poetry, Performance, and Patronage in Fourteenth-Century Iran* (London: I.B.Tauris, 2019).

[21] In 2018, while preparing a syllabus for an undergraduate survey course titled "Classical Persian Literature in English Translation," one of us noted the conspicuous absence of female poets as well as literary figures, male or female, that normally fall outside accepted canons, from almost all extant course syllabi on the topic, as found on the internet.

force in history whereby Persian (among other) cultural artifacts and traveling texts have either been lost in translation or, more frequently, gained in circulation. The third section marks a transnational turn toward a new Persian literary studies, whereby the classics are reimagined from a global perspective and in turn lesser known texts are restored from the margins. From this critical vantage point, the leap of faith to read Persian literature as world literature is also a quest in search of justice, and sites of solidarity, within and beyond the world literary system.

Within the above structure, we present the chapters and the historical periods they address thematically rather than chronologically, focusing not so much on an episodic history of Persian literature as processes of canon formation as essentially contemporary phenomena. Opening the first section, "Literary Worldliness," Amir Irani-Tehran, in "The Birth of the German *Ghazal* out of the Spirit of World Literature," focuses on the formative phase of the conception of World Literature, examining the reception of Hafez in the tradition of German Romanticism. At the center stage, of course, is not Goethe and his exhausted—and much exoticized—link to Hafez, but the poet and dramatist August von Platen who sought to transplant the Hafezian *ghazal* form into the German literary polysystem. Irani-Tehrani first articulates the reasons as to why the Persian *ghazal* did not fully take root in Germany, and he rightly maintains that Platen's "proto-world literary gesture" deserves theoretical inspection in order to reimagine the possibility of what an engagement between the German and Persian literary polysystems could do today.

The motif throughout this volume to queer the space of World Literature, evident in Irani-Tehrani's study of a less-explored link in the network of Perso-German literary exchange, continues in Sam Lasman's "Otherworld Literature: Parahuman Pasts in Classical Persian Historiography and Epic." Medieval Persianate writers, notes Lasman, encountered both ideological pitfalls and creative opportunities in crafting narratives out of a contested pre-Islamic past. Central to their accounts was the depiction of primordial relations between the human realm and otherworldly terrains inhabited by beings such as *div*, *jinn*, and *pari*. Such parahuman entities and their homelands became key sites for exploring the relationship between conflicting sources of historical truth and ideological legitimacy. The ensuing foundation myths in the works of al-Tabari and Ferdowsi, amongst others, would then juxtapose periods of sexual and spatial mixing with the violent enforcement of boundaries between human civilization and demonic wilderness. Lasman's intriguing exploration of what can be called "otherworldly cosmopolitanism" not only resists our present-day discourses of reality but also sheds light on the uncanny underpinnings of modern world systems, including the concrete foundations of World Literature itself.

The focus of the first part on Persian literary worldliness narrows down, with the final two chapters, to contemporary Iran. In "Globalization in Pre- and Post-revolutionary Iranian Literature: A Comparative Study of Authors Inside and Outside Iran," Naghmeh Esmaeilpour examines selected works by Iranian novelists Hushang Golshiri, Simin Daneshvar (writing from inside the country), Shahrnush Parsipur, and Shahriar Mandanipour (writing from the diaspora) to demonstrate how the emergent discourse of globalization is manifest through codes, signs, and grammatical structures of their narratives. Whereas studies of contemporary Iranian literature as world literature are mired down in geopolitics, due particularly to Iran's international isolation following the 1979 Revolution, Esmaeilpour is more broadly concerned with issues of "transfictionality" and "transmediality," and how the authors employ literature as a medium of expression to communicate with other world cultures by indicating the interconnectivity of textual interactions and transformation.

In line with Esmaeilpour's attempt to reimagine Persian literary worldliness beyond the limits of nation thinking, Laetitia Nanquette contributes to recent developments in Digital Humanities and book history in studies of contemporary Iranian literature. Nanquette's originality, in "Contemporary Persian Literature and Digital Humanities," lies not simply in the novelty of integrating world literary studies and Digital Humanities but, more importantly, in the way the findings of her quantitative research help to debunk certain misconceptions about the state of the literary market in postrevolutionary Iran. This chapter provides us with precise figures to phenomena that are often sketchy and readily accepted by outside observers. For instance, while Nanquette does confirm such facts as the ebb and flow of publication according to the political situation, she convincingly contradicts the myth that government publishers produce a higher quantity of texts than independent publishers.

Marie Ostby's "Genres without Borders: Global Readings of Modern Iranian Literature beyond 'Center' and 'Periphery'" begins the second part of the volume, "Traveling Texts." Ostby argues that despite the impact of political entrenchment, and escalation of tension between Iran the United States at the time of writing, a deep and wide network of connections exists between Persian and Euro-American literary cultures that has only grown richer since the early twentieth century. Ostby's rigorous critique, which occurs outside the purview of the conception of World Literature along the "East-West" axis, builds on a network of cross-cultural exchange that is rather sustained and expanded by experimentation with genre and the creation of new literary forms. Thus, in defying and expanding genre categorization, contemporary Iranian writers and poets, Simin Behbahani chief amongst them, have not only resisted a global hegemony in which forms are too often seen to move only from a Euro-American "center" to a series of "peripheral" literary communities and markets, but they have also effectively resisted the reductive and potentially racist typologies and classifications that are endemic to World Literature Inc., conceived through the logic of US-led globalization and imperialism.

As mentioned earlier, alongside decentering the World Literature canon, another chief intention of this volume is to decolonize Persian literature in terms of its own local hegemony. Abdulla Rexhepi, in "Persian Epistemes in Naim Frashëri's Albanian Poetry," offers a bracing perspective on Persian literature as world literature that is defiantly regional, irrespective of the German Romantic past and the US multicultural present of the discipline. Focusing on the Albanian poet Naim Frashëri, who conceived a Balkan national imaginary through the medium of Persian literature, Rexhepi notes that in the Albanian-populated regions of the Ottoman Empire, an intellectual elite began to appropriate, and write, literature in the Persian language. At the forefront of this literary movement was Frashëri who would go on to use many epistemic elements of the Persian mystical and epic tradition in his own Albanian-language poetry. Borrowing from the concepts and archetypes of Persian literature, Naim Frashëri, Rexhepi argues, succeeded in connecting Albanian literature to world literature, while also enriching Albanian creativity with concepts such as mystical love and patriotism.

Not unlike Rexhepi's case of the Persian texts traveling the Balkans, Olga M. Davidson's reading of the "Baysonqori Preface" to the *Shahnameh* is historically situated in the pre-European world system. The lengthy introduction to Ferdowsi's epic poem, commissioned by the Timurid Prince Baysonqor in 1426 CE, appropriates the global proportions of the edited text, making the totalizing claim that the edition, in its inherent expansiveness, is worthy of acceptance by all Iranians regardless of their backgrounds. Reminiscent of the formation of the modern Iranian canon, and Ferdowsi's position at its core, the "Baysonqori Preface" manifests an imperial "ecumenism" for the princely project of presenting the *Shahnameh* as the homogenizing expression of Iranian identity. Both Davidson and Rexhepi, therefore, shed light on the conceptions of national imaginaries via world literature, which preceded Goethe's aspirations for a German cosmopolitan identity via *Weltliteratur*.

Alexandra Hoffmann's contribution, "Cats and Dogs, Manliness and Misogyny: On the *Sindbad-nameh* as World Literature," falls in the same category of de-Europeanizing world literary theory. By integrating gender politics into her critique, Hoffmann offers a timely corrective to Orientalist readings of *Sindbad-nameh* as an essentially sexist master text, which was thought to have informed the misogyny of the Seven Sages tradition in Medieval Europe. In her comparative examination of the tale "Canis" ("The Faithful Greyhound"), from its European variation to the oldest extant Persian edition by Zahiri Samarqandi (1160–4 CE), Hoffmann argues that the misogynist moral that attributes the blame for the rash killing of an animal to women was, in fact, introduced in the European adaptations of *Sindbad-nameh*, as opposed to the Persian original in which developments on the level of individual tales work against such broad conclusions. Hoffmann maintains that the analysis of the Islamicate versions of one of the most widespread tales in the global Middle Ages challenges the picture of a simplistic "misogynist import" of the Seven Sages tradition into the European literary system.

Adineh Khojastehpour, in "Cinema Joins Forces with Literature to Form Canon: The Cinematic Afterlife of Sa'edi's 'The Cow' as World Literature," brings our appreciation of traveling texts to global Iranian cinema. Khojastehpour takes up the frequently debated case of cinematic adaptation in Iran, that of Gholamhossein Sa'edi's short story "The Cow" (1964) into Dariush Mehrjui's eponymous film (1969), in order to bring new insights to the interconnectedness of World Cinema and World Literature. The author–director bond between Sa'edi and Mehrjui, and the unique consequences of that collaboration post-Iranian Revolution (1979), Khojastehpour argues, not only helped Iranian cinema to travel beyond the borders of the modern nation-state by projecting *The Cow* into, and securing its place in, World Cinema, but, due to the constantly evolving afterlives of the adaptation, this literary-artistic partnership also significantly contributed to the globalization of modern Persian literature, as attested to by the fate of Sa'edi's "The Cow."

The third and final part of the volume, "The Transnational Turn," begins with Levi Thompson's "Until a Shirt Blossoms Red: Proto-Third Worldism in Ahmad Shamlou's *Manifesto*." Thompson focuses on Shamlou's relatively under-studied poetry collection to recast the poet not as the revolutionary icon of modern Persian poetry per se, but as a world poet whose work manifests sites of transnational solidarity among diverse political imaginaries in Korea, Germany, Spain, and of course Iran. Thompson views *Manifesto* (1951) as a catalyst in Shamlou's poetics and politics, for it grants his body of work a global consciousness without which our understanding of his literary career, including the poems that focus on Iran, will be incomplete. Taking a decisive step toward a reading of Persian poetry as world literature, Thompson argues that while Shamlou's poetry has an undeniable planetary dimension in its openness to shared humanity, nature, and time, the political realities it negotiates cannot escape the transnational tensions of the mid twentieth century.

By the same token, Gay Jennifer Breyley, in "Translocal Dreams of Justice and Mobility: Fariba Vafi's *Tarlan* and Ali Mirdrekvandi's *No Heaven for Gunga Din*," examines the ways two Iranian novels—the former produced in Iran and the latter written in English, in Iran, and posthumously published in London—reflect on unjust power relations and the desire for various forms of personal mobility as they present localized narratives in their contexts of historic world events, and transnational structures of authority. Breyley demonstrates that the different ways in which Vafi and Mirdrekvandi wrote and published their respective novels echo the power relations that made the texts, especially their content, possible. As the chapter considers the roles of family, police, military and colonial structures, war and political conflict, and the local effects of world events, it also analyzes the nature of the popularity of the two samples under scrutiny. Another aspect of Breyley's contribution, which is definitive to new readings of Persian literature as world literature, is her focus on Mirdrekvandi's *No Heaven for Gunga Din* (1965), perhaps the only example of Anglophone literature written, if not also produced, in Iran. This under-studied novel, then, is a unique example of the postcolonial world Englishes that must be accounted for as a significant work of world literature.

Whereas Thompson and Breyley explore cases of the transnational turn in Persian literary studies as liberating and decolonial projects, Amy Motlagh, in "The Purloined *Letter*: Reconsidering Simin Daneshvar's *Dagh-e Nang* and the Politics of Translation in the Landscape of World Literature," makes a different argument. In her thorough interrogation of Jeffrey Einboden's critique of Simin Daneshvar's translation of Nathaniel Hawthorne's *The Scarlet Letter* (1850), published as *Dagh-e Nang* (1334/1955), Motlagh exposes the pitfalls of the "transnational turn" in American Studies. The chapter not only considers the tacit imperialism and exceptionalism that characterize Einboden's project but also unearths the way in which the growing interest in translation has ironically facilitated misreading practices and academic imperialism. Einboden's misapprehension of Daneshvar's translation, Motlagh contends, is not unique but more broadly encapsulates the limits of the American project of World Literature.

In the concluding chapter of the volume, the title of which reads as a prologue, Navid Naderi ponders the disruptive possibilities of reading "World Literature as Persian Literature." Naderi's intention, needless to say, is not so much a cross-essentializing recourse to the East–West binary thinking, but a dialectical inversion of the title of this volume, bringing it to a close. This chapter argues for an understanding of "world literature" and "national literature" as dialectically opposite concepts, as each historically, and irremediably, depend on the other in order to perform its particular abstract work. Focusing on the cultural work of philology in its relation to the planetary economy of translation at the time of the emergence of the concept of world literature, Naderi argues that, on the one hand, World Literature as a paradigm of literary study and creation cannot be understood as superseding the paradigm of national literature and, on the other hand, peripheral national literatures (in our case, Persian) cannot but be world literature. In other words, peripheral literatures could not have been conceived either as "national" or as "literature" were it not for the abstract work performed by the concept, and institution, of World Literature.

As the papers in this collection imply, addressing the crisis of Persian literary studies is possible through critically engaging the self-aggrandizing celebration of already canonized texts that contribute to the perpetuation of a false sense of the self and nation inherited from colonial processes. In order to fill this knowledge gap, and move toward a radical critique of the logic of modernity/coloniality that has to date constructed literary studies in Iran (and in Persian), it is therefore essential to develop research projects focused on introducing and examining a variety of non-Persian literary and cultural texts. Persian Language and Literature departments should also transform into something broader—such as literary studies—to accommodate non-Persian literary traditions. In addition, while it is significant to begin reading the classics in new noncanonical ways, Persian literature curricula and linguistic training programs must be updated and expanded to equip each student with a wider mix of languages than merely European or west-Asian languages (which is presently common). Through this epistemological shift, modern literary studies can counter narratives that, energized by the logocentrism of monolingual romantic nationalism, justify orientalism abroad and oppression at home. Moreover, it is from this perspective that the Eurocentrism of both literary studies and literary translation into Persian—which has been debated quite often—can be revisited to ponder the diverse reasons as to why the relationship between Persian and other world languages have so long been limited to a few European *lingua franca*s, significantly constricting the possibilities for growth and regeneration. We hope the papers in this volume will be a step toward the ends of decolonizing a literary tradition that has been, unbeknownst to itself, pushed to and positioned in the periphery of World Literature.

Part One

Literary Worldliness

1

The Birth of the German *Ghazal* out of the Spirit of World Literature

Amir Irani-Tehrani

> *Die Schenke, die du dir gebaut,*
> *Ist größer als jedes Haus.*
> *Die Tränke, die du drin gebraut,*
> *Die trinkt die Welt nicht aus.*
> F. Nietzsche

In the fall of 1820, forty-two poems in the style of Persian mystical poet Rumi were published by Friedrich Rückert, the editor of a literary pocket almanac, *Taschenbuch für Damen: auf das Jahr 1821*. These would be the first German *ghazal*s, heralding a two-year *ghazal*-publishing frenzy by Rückert and his younger friend and erstwhile collaborator, August von Platen, whose *Neue Ghaselen* two years later put an end to the literary duel with this epigram: "Der Orient ist abgetan, / Nun seht die Form als unser an" (The orient is done, / now behold the form as ours).[1] While Rückert's Rumi "replicas" were the first *ghazal*s in German, it was Platen who was first to publish original German *ghazal*s and who became "Gaselendichter κατ᾽ ἐξοχήν," *ghazal*-poet, par excellence![2]

Despite the intensity and relative prosodic success of Platen's campaign to make *ghazal* German, save for some limited application by a few notable poets, the form was largely not used, even when Orientalizing was smart. For example, Friedrich von Bodenstedt's 1851 *Lieder des Mirza Schaffy* saw at least one hundred forty editions and many translations, but it seldom uses the *ghazal* form.[3] In fact, today there is little trace of the German *ghazal*. Judith Ryan's *The Cambridge Introduction to German Poetry* (2012) only mentions Platen once, and then in relation to the sonnet, with no

---

[1]   August von Platen, *Werke*, ed. Kurt Wölfel and Jürgen Link (Munich: Winkler, 1982), 285.
[2]   Friedrich Veit, *Platens Nachbildungen aus dem Diwan des Hafis* (Berlin: Alexander Duncker, 1908), 265.
[3]   Arthur Frank Remy, *The Influence of India and Persia on the Poetry of Germany* (New York: AMS Press, 1966), 64.

mention of Rückert or the *ghazal* at all. Reflecting on this transient phenomenon we may wonder why the *ghazal* form did not take root in German literary soil, and what *primo loco* spurred Platen to not just transfer the *ghazals'* contents into German, but also their form.

The post-Napoleonic German national crisis, instead of being resolved by the Congress of Vienna (1815), was extenuated by it, leading to the nobility's further fall from grace as an agent of brutal repression. The crisis mirrored a spiritual and sensual conflict in Platen's own subjectivity, provoking his existential need to reflect on what is noble. As courtly love poetry, the Persian *ghazal* offered Platen something for which he had found no precedent in the Western literary tradition: an anagogic form that could subsume his homoerotic disposition while *performatively* reframing for the era what the nobility signified beyond rank and wealth.[4] That the new transplant wilted on the alternate route taken through bourgeois sentimentality, proletarian class struggle, and aristocratic militarism toward German unification by the century's end only casts Platen's project in starker relief.

While comprehensive engagement of Platen's *ghazal* oeuvre far exceeds this chapter's latitude, to highlight the existential importance of this project to him, a line can be traced from Platen's originary search for a tradition that weds sensuality and spirituality, through the labor of his Persian studies, his painful delivery of the *ghazal* for his fatherland, and his subsequent death in exile. This quest is nowhere more pronounced than in the infamous Heine–Platen affair, which while liable to be the only thing an average Germanist would know about Platen today, is seldom viewed with an appreciation of its *prima causa*: an unwitting attack on the *ghazal* as form. Equally important is to highlight the merit of revisiting these largely forgotten *ghazals* now as the academic zephyr promises more than ever the sort of polytropic, multidisciplinary research and collaboration that their reception warrants, to make them available to a Persian readership inscribed in them at their birth:

Du, der nie gewagt zu fliegen	تو که هرگز نکرده ای جرأت
Nach dem Orient, wie wir,	که کئی سوی خاوران پرواز
Laß dies Büchlein, Laß es liegen,	بگذر از این کز آن تو نیست
Denn Geheimnis ist es dir.	وز برایت بود دفتری پُر راز
Wenn einst Perser deutsche Verse	آنگه که فارسی‌زبانان خوانند شعر ما را
Lesen, wie wir ihre jetzt,	چون ما آلمانی ها اکنون شعرشان را
Dann geschieht's, daß ein Perser	خوشا گر که باشد در بین ایشان کسی
Diese Lieder übersetzt.[5]	کو کند ترجمه این ترانه‌های آلمانی

---

[4] The Persian *ghazal* has been noted as inherently "performative." Dominic Brookshaw, for example, says: "It accomplished (or sought to accomplish, perhaps through repeated evocation) what it described" (Dominic Parviz Brookshaw, *Hafiz and His Contemporaries* [London: I.B.Tauris, 2019], 3).

[5] Platen, *Werke*, 242. To my knowledge there exists no Persian translation of Platen. I can only hope that my wanting one would spur more graceful ones. I am responsible for all uncited German and Persian translations.

You, who never dared to fly
To the Orient like we
Let this booklet, let it be
For secret it shall be to thee.
When once Persians German verses
Read, like we do theirs of late,
Then it shall be that a Persian,
These German songs will translate.

In his polysystem theory, Itamar Even-Zohar argues that literary translations introduce into the home literature features that include not just "a new (poetic) language, or compositional patterns and techniques" but also possibly "new models of reality."[6] As we will see, the notion of acquiring a new model of reality is essential to Platen's project. The degree of such translations' impact, Even-Zohar argues, is inversely related to the maturity, strength, centrality, or stability of the home literary polysystem. Translations have the greatest impact, he says, when the home literary polysystem is experiencing a turning point, crisis, or a vacuum; and the younger, weaker, and more peripheral it is within the larger literary polysystem wherein it lies.[7]

Starting in the early eighteenth century, translations from the classical and the more established Romance languages had strengthened the German literary polysystem such that by Rückert and Platen's time, its position within the European polysystem had already become more central. By 1819, when Goethe published his *Divan*, the German literary polysystem, while still not as strong as the French, was not anymore young, weak, or peripheral. And yet, the German system experienced a pivotal and existential crisis both on the political and the literary level.

The French Revolution, then the Napoleonic Wars, and the subsequent "German wars of liberation" (1813–14) stirred a sense of unity, fraternity, and hope, only to be crushed at the Conference of Vienna (1814–15) which restored the pre-Napoleonic order and formed a loose German confederation, *Deutscher Bund*. The *Burschenschaften* (university fraternities), formed at this time, became centers of political agitation by Platen's first semester at university when the *Bund* ratified the Carlsbad Decrees (1819) to limit political activity. There was a ubiquitous murmur: whither Germany?

Spiritually, for a century, the Enlightenment had impelled a gradual secularization that many in Platen's time experienced as spiritual dearth. By the end of Weimar Classicism in 1805, the humanist wells of inspiration seemed sapped; and the initially theoretical and later literary German Romantic movement had similarly bled their medieval resources dry in a quest for homespun organic spirituality. Now, by the late 1820s, all had coalesced into a lethargic world of *ennui* and melancholic *Weltschmerz*. This is where Rückert and Platen found themselves when they started writing *ghazals*.

---

[6]   Itmar Even-Zohar, "The Position of Translated Literature within the Literary Polysystem," *Poetics Today* 11, no. 1 (1990): 47.
[7]   Ibid.

It is ironic that the prodigious Goethe, a culprit in this exhaustion, would also show a way forward by his practical engagements with extra-European literature, and in time, his concept of *Weltliteratur*.[8]

The two sides of the German national crisis, the fading aristocracy and the rising bourgeoisie are remarkably well personified by the two erstwhile collaborating *ghazal*-smiths. The future Professor Rückert who would translate from some forty-four languages, was a patriot and a family man with a strong sense of community and fraternity.[9] But his famous motto, *Weltpoesie allein ist Weltversöhnung* (world-poetry alone is world-reconciliation), distinguishes him from Platen, for whom reconciliation with the world was not quite as easy.[10]

Platen: Poros and Penia

It would be misleading to say that Karl August Georg Maximilian Count of Platen-Hallermünde's lineage reached three major European royal houses, since both he and his father were products of second marriages, and thus doubly removed from principal inheritance.[11] His mother had moreover raised him on the proto-Romantic and republican precepts of Rousseau's *Émile*, and introduced him early to the French and other Romance-language literary traditions. Platen's diary, which he kept in some twelve languages, was modeled after Rousseau's *Les Confessions*.

Prussia had just ceded Platen's hometown of Ansbach, to Bavaria, when the insolvent aristocrat youth, with no prospect but to enter the service of a prince, was enrolled at the Bavarian Military Academy. The estrangement and displacement felt by the north-German-accented Prussian-Lutheran boy in the ghastly barracks in Catholic Munich would only multiply soon thereafter when he would come to recognize in himself what we today call homosexuality and try to reconcile it with the prevalent conventional Christian mores of his age, which reduced his feelings to their crassest expression. Inspired by Rousseau, he always favored over rationality the truth of subjective feelings, the expression of whose reconciliation with faith, through his poetic temperament, would ever override public prudence.[12]

---

[8]   While a fateful conversation with his secretary, Johann Peter Eckermann on January 27, 1827 (first published only a decade later) is cited as the programmatic inaugural event in world literature, Goethe's *Divan* prefigured it, and it was the primary progenitor of the German *ghazal*. As such, the *Divan*'s practical impact frames our discussion of World Literature as a "spirit" of what is yet to come.

[9]   For Rückert's vita see, Annemarie Schimmel, *Friedrich Rückert* (Göttingen: Wallstein Verlag, 2015).

[10] Friedrich Rückert, *Gesammelte Gedichte* (Erlangen: Carl Heyder Verlag, 1837), 34.

[11] For Platen's vita, see Peter Bumm, *August Graf von Platen* (Paderborn: Schöningh, 1990); Rudolf Schlösser, *August Graf v. Platen* (Munich: Piper, 1910).

[12] For Platen and the homoerotic see Hans Mayer, "Die Platen-Heine-Konfrontation" in *Akzente* (1973, vol. 3), 273–88; Frank Busch, *August Graf von Platen, Thomas Mann: Zeichen und Gefühle* (Munich: Fink, 1987), 52–125; Paul Derks, *Die Schande der heiligen Päderastie* (Berlin: Winkel, 1990), 79–117; Heinrich Detering, *Das offene Geheimnis* (Göttingen: Wallstein, 1994), 479–611.

Early on, fellow cadets were the Erato for Platen's poetic finger practices. In time, alongside his change in stations, cadet-muses turned to courtiers, officers, and later students. But a type united all of them: physical vigor and splendor checked with some want of literary learning and the need of a peer's loving mentorship. Most importantly, these boys and later men seldom recognized the heart-wrenching poetry they stirred in their casual acquaintance who sometimes held forth on the sacred beauty of the loving friendship among men. In conforming to a neo-Platonic convention as the most prevalent form of such expression, this early framing unwittingly flouts actual physical sensuality, and later primes a search within the Western tradition for any precedent aesthetic poesis to express Platen's inextricably tangled spiritual and sensual homoerotic sentiment. The resulting existential research soon fostered a prosodic virtuosity that traversed the German language's limits and productively engaged ever greater numbers of literary traditions. But it was not until reading Goethe's *Divan* that he finally was oriented to where he wanted to go.

As a preteen cadet, Platen could take Sunday leave, when he would often visit the Schellings, Friedrich and Caroline. The impact of the German Idealist's philosophy on Platen's poetry, the latter's critical inaptitude notwithstanding, has been well established.[13] How Friedrich Schelling received Hafez, which would further elucidate Platen's *ghazal*s, still awaits engagement, but it is beyond the scope of the present introduction. Nevertheless, besides the speculative, Schelling also figures practically in the German *ghazal*'s birth, not least by personally interceding later, to secure for Platen a precious Hafez manuscript, the Munich Codex.

In 1810, we find the fourteen-year-old Platen transferred to Das Haus der Edelknaben (House of the Noble Boys) to train and serve as a royal page until the age of eighteen. He would, for the rest of his life, depend on the personal grace of the king, as a small financial burden on the Bavarian state until his early death in 1836.[14] In 1814, partly rapt in the patriotic fervor, Platen joined the army and was swiftly deployed to fight Napoleon. The rather maladroit lieutenant's role in Germany's liberation, however, cannot be understated since Bavaria's first infantry regiment was crossing the Rhein when dusk fell on the emperor's deserted coach in Waterloo on June 18, 1815. Four years later, Platen's petition to switch service tracks met no resistance from the downsizing army, and after spending a semester at the University of Würzburg, improving his Greek and Latin in preparation for an entrance exam, he was matriculated there in the fall of 1818.

Decisive for Platen's approach to the *ghazal* was his prosodic research at this time. Beside the classics, he read the major oeuvres of at least five foreign literatures in the original and productively experimented with the Spanish Redondilla (stanzas of four lines, rhyming *abba* in consonance). On April 25, 1818, he noted in his diary the purchase of books by Horace, Theocritus, and Anacreon in an entry starting with a

---

[13] Manfred Riedel, "'Das Geheimnisvolle Wie der Dinge': Schelling und Platen," in *Leben, Werke, Wirking*, ed. Hartmut Bobzin and Gunnar Och (Paderborn: Schöningh, 1998), 21–44.

[14] Helmut Flaschendecker, "Die ungeliebte Pflicht – Platen als bayerischer Offizier," in *Leben, Werke, Wirking*, ed. Hartmut Bobzin and Gunnar Och (Paderborn: Schöningh, 1998), 1–20.

forty-one-line original German Anacreontic poem.[15] Also notable at this time is a new muse—a young fraternity boy Platen called "Adrast" until he learned his real name, Eduard Schmidtlein—who would inspire many Anacreontic Redondilla.

Anacreon–Hafez Link

Platen's serendipitous study of the Anacreontic and the Redondilla, it turned out, was the perfect preparation for tackling the *ghazal*. The poetic fragments of Anacreon—an Ionian poet who fled the Persian attack on Asia Minor in 545 BCE to Samos—inspired the later Alexandrine and Byzantine "Anacreontic" genre, some of which have survived in Constantine Kephalas's *Greek Anthology* (ca. 900), published in the late sixteenth century by the French Humanist Henri Estienne.[16] This was Platen's Greek textbook.

Joseph von Hammer, whose 1812–13 Hafez translation famously inspired Goethe's *Divan*, had already noted Anacreontic elements like wine, song, and Eros, and had employed Anacreontic meter in his translation, whenever possible. In his meticulous 1971 structural analysis, Jürgen Link has deductively uncovered a much deeper relation between the Persian *ghazal* and the Anacreontic.[17] The "Anacreontic meter" is either a catalectic iambic dimeter (u u – u – u – –) or the closely related anaclastic (in the fourth and fifth position) ionic dimeter (u u – – u u – –).[18] For the latter, the second-century Alexandrian grammarian Hephaestion has given "Persian" as an alternate name. Finn Thiesen sees the ionic corresponding to *bahr-e ramal-e makhbun*, which he says, can be reduced to two unstressed syllables followed by two stressed (u u – –).[19] The uniform meter of the Anacreontic poem, unbroken in stanzas, according to Link, creates a "row of constant elements" mirrored in the multiple recurrence of anaphora and anadiplosis, and occasionally even that of whole lines.[20] The resulting independent, alternately recurring "leitmotifs" in play within the poem create a "structure of oscillation" wherein, beside and between the repetition of the same word or phrase, different words that express aspects of the same motif create oscillation on yet another level. The poem as a whole then, according to Link, can be characterized as an ecstatic, liberating, dance-inducing "poem of oscillating image series," which also features an aesthetic cosmic lexis to include flora and avifauna.[21] The abstractness of these images within the poem's tight economy precludes a developmental narrative structure, prompting Link to observe that each individual image-row location can be shifted within the poem's structure, not at random, but within the leitmotif's framework.

[15] August von Platen, *Die Tagebücher*, 2 vols., ed. G. Laubmann and L. Scheffler (Stuttgart: Cotta, 1896–1900), vol. 2, 43–4.
[16] Foteini Spingou, "Byzantine Collections and Anthologies of Poetry," in *A Companion to Byzantine Poetry: Wolfram Hörandner, Andreas Rhoby, and Nikos Zagklas* (Leiden: Brill, 2019), 389.
[17] Jürgen Link, *Artistische Form und ästhetischer Sinn in Platens Lyrik* (Munich: Fink, 1971), 44, 60.
[18] Ibid., 43–6.
[19] Finn Thiesen, *A Manual of Classical Persian Prosody* (Wiesbaden: Harrassowitz, 1982), 132.
[20] Link, *Artistische*, 44–6.
[21] Ibid., 47–54.

The Anacreontic and the Hafezian *ghazal*'s structural similarities, Link says, also extend to a catalog of images, including the rose as the aesthetic ideal and the wind as the textual image of the oscillation. This glossary is expanded in the *ghazal* to what Link calls "a world of beauty." It includes the rose, the nightingale, the narcissus, pearls, the garden, paradise, sun, moon, the beloved, and so on.[22] Additionally, Link points out in Hafez what appears to be an audaciously abrupt switch in perspectives within the otherwise harmonious "cosmic" balance struck between the smallest and largest, the nearest and farthest, the earthly and heavenly, the particular and universal, and so on. This audacious oscillation, Link says, intensifies as it happens not just within the poem as a whole, but also within each distich and even hemistich.[23] Platen excels at creating this audacious oscillation within stand-alone distichs held together through leitmotifs and tight prosody not in mere replicas or translations, but using his own codex of beautiful images, which include classical and Judeo-Christian Western imagery, and while at times overlapping Hafez, never simply imitate it, perhaps with the exception of his *Der Spiegel des Hafis*, where he expressly sets out to do Hafez.

Goethe's *Divan*: A Light in Darkness

"Hoje, hoje," starts the journal entry on March 4, 1819, in Portuguese, "O primeiro paso he ja detraz de mi. Aindanão està certo, que entrarei em familiaridade com elle, mas he possivel ao menos. Poderei saudar-lhe outras vezes, e abordar-lhe na rua."[24] Unimpressed with Schmidtlein's bookshelf when they finally meet, Platen proceeds to try to make a case for the importance of *belles lettres*, even for law students, in recitations of poems in garden promenades and discussion of plays in dorm rooms, while refining his secret Anacreontic Redondillas.

Although similar to many others, this affair marks a caesura in Platen's work and vita, as now for the first time, he crosses a line and shares his verses with their muse. According to Frank Busch, Schmidtlein's position in the affair rests on a socially accepted conception of love as ideology, while Platen, positively misreading the clues, moves ever closer to the letter of his Anacreontic verses.[25] Bumm, who describes Platen as physically weak and ugly, shorter and thinner than average, slightly cross-eyed and hard of hearing, thinks that middle-class Schmidtlein's initial consent to the odd friendship pivots on the flattery he felt as the object of a cultured aristocrat's interest.[26]

---

[22] See Brookshaw's codex, *Hafiz*, 115–54.

[23] While generally agreeing with the oscillation principle and the Hafezian audacity in its usage, Friedrich Veit cautions that some of what the German reader experiences as oscillation may be due to poor manuscripts, deficient philology, or simple misunderstanding, and not as such in the original (Veit, *Nachbildungen*, 149).

[24] "Today, today … I have taken the first step. It is not certain that I will become more acquainted with him, but it is at least possible. I will be able to greet him in the future, and approach him in the street" (Platen, *Tagebücher II*, 219). I thank Olivia Holloway for the translation.

[25] Busch, *Zeichen und Gefühle*, 80.

[26] Bumm, *Platen*, 212.

Once shared, Schmidtlein responded to Platen's Spanish–Greek erotic verses with a terse letter expressing repulsion as well as an implicit threat of violence.[27] This sent the poet spiraling into existential self-loathing. He immediately decided to transfer to Erlangen. "Je me regarde comme un scélérat, qui se craint soi-même," he confides to his diary on October 18, 1819, in French, after copying the entire text of the received missive. "Le poids de sa malédiction et de son profond mépris pèsent sur moi. Toute occupation me tourmente. Il faut toujours lutter contre la vie."[28]

Soon after this traumatic episode, while convalescing at home ahead of his university transfer, Platen saw an auspicious oracular dispatch from the distant Olympian heights of Weimar staring at him from a local bookstore display: *Der West-oestliche Divan!*

Nord und West und Süd zersplittern,
Throne bersten, Reiche zittern,
Flüchte du, im reinen Osten
Patriarchenluft zu kosten

North and West and South splinter apart, thrones explode, kingdoms tremble: take flight to the pure East to taste the air of the Patriarchs![29]

From the opening lines of the Book of the Singer, he would have read straight through to its prose addendum, *Noten und Abhandlungen zu besserem Verständniß* (Notes and Essays for a Better Understanding), and the *Divan*'s openness to Greco-Persian homoeroticism would not have escaped him.[30] This was something for which he had found little precedent in the tradition prior to this pathbreaking expression of sovereign nonconformity: not a choice between sensual homoeroticism and metaphysical love, but both. Platen's first productive reactions ("Licht" and "Parsenlied"), however, thematize the need for spiritual redemption and seem to be responses to the *Divan*'s penultimate book, "Buch des Parsen," where Goethe addresses Iran's pre-Islamic Zoroastrian pedigree, whence the binaries of light and darkness and good and evil are derived.[31] He is not yet ready for Hafez.

The first year at Erlangen was one of recovery and distraction, outdoor activities with easy friends, and even a brief lunch *abonnement* at a fraternity. His mood improved. His productivity suffered. By July, he was ready for the *Divan* and approached Professor Johann Kanne about Persian, who could not help, but who offered him instead an

---

[27] Platen, *Tagebücher II*, 327.
[28] "I see myself as a scoundrel who fears himself. The weight of his curse and his deep contempt weigh on me. Every activity is tormenting me. One always has to struggle against life" (ibid.). Translation by Stephanie Irani-Tehrani, my sine qua non.
[29] Goethe, Johann Wolfgang von, and Eric Ormsby, *West-eastern Divan* (London: Gingko, 2019), 4–5.
[30] For Goethe's views on homosexuality, see W. Daniel Wilson and Angela Steidele, *Goethe, Männer, Knaben: Ansichten zur "Homosexualität"* (Berlin: Insel, 2012).
[31] August von Platen, "Parsenlied" (1819) in *Lyrische Blätter* (Leipzig: Brockhaus, 1821), 33; "Licht" (1819) in *Vermischte Schriften* (Erlangen: Heyder, 1822), 48; for dates, see Hubert Tschersig, *Das Gasel in der deutschen Dichtung und das Gasel bei Platen* (Leipzig: Quelle & Meyer, 1907), 17.

Arabic to Latin translation course in the fall. Save for his collaboration with Rückert, Platen learned Persian largely autodidactically.[32] In August, he met Rückert, just back from Vienna, where he had briefly studied with Hammer. With scant Persian textual material accessible, the few books Rückert had brought from Vienna were vital. The most important was Hammer's Hafez translation and a hand-copied portion of the Viennese Persian Hafez manuscript. Moving forward, the two shared their new discoveries, as Platen visited many collections and libraries near and far, looking for any Persian texts he could copy. Notably, neither fully knew what they were copying initially, and the meaning of texts was derived often through epistolary debates where they edited each other's spellings through marginalia. Only in the spring of 1822 was Friedrich Schelling finally able to procure for them the Munich Codex that compared favorably to Hammer's Viennese one. Between 1821 and 1823, Platen also copied and bound several Hafez selections, which he called "*guldasta*" (Persian for "a nosegay" or "a hand-picked bouquet"), in various sizes to carry around or take on trips, and worked on memorizing them.[33] One such *guldasta* boasts an original Persian *ghazal* by Platen as motto.[34] There is some evidence to suggest he knew what Persian sounds like.[35]

The labor that led Platen to finally deliver *ghazal*s started in early 1821 upon Friedrich Schelling's arrival in Erlangen. By April, Platen issued in rapid succession *Die Ghaselen* and *Ghaselen zweiter Sammlung*, followed in a few months by *Der Spiegel des Hafis*. In the interim between the latter and his final *ghazal* cycle, *Neue Ghaselen* (1823), he considered publishing a first European critical edition of Hafez and left for Vienna to join Hammer as an Orientalist, only to reconsider at the Austrian border and instead seclude himself for a few months to produce his remarkable Hafez translations, unpublished in his lifetime. Finally, just before Platen's death, *Vesta*, a Viennese journal, published a few more *ghazal*s he had composed in Naples in 1832.

The *Divan*'s Highest Challenge and Formal Warning

Das Alter wägt und mißt es,
Die Jugend spricht: so ist es.[36]

Old age weighs and measures it,
Youth speaks: That is it.

---

[32] Hartmut Bobzin, "Platens Studium des Persischen und seine Ghaselen-Dichtung," in *"Was er wünscht, das ist ihm nie geworden" August Graf von Platen 1796–1835*, ed. Gunnar Och (Erlangen: Universitätsbibliothek 1996), 88–130; and Hartmut Bobzin, "Platen und Rückert im Gespräch über Hafis," in *August Graf von Platen: Leben, Werk, Wirkung* (Paderborn: Schöningh, 1998), 103–21.

[33] Veit, *Nachbildungen*, 285.

[34] Ibid., 280.

[35] Journal entry for January 13, 1821 (Platen, *Tagebücher II*, 443) contains a German sentence written in Perso-Arabic, which, when transcribed back, gives evidence of this knowledge. The usage of *gh* for *g*, and *ş* for *s* may just be experimental. All soft German *chs* are transcribed as hard ones (i.e., *kh*).

[36] Platen's motto to *Der Spiegel des Hafis* (Platen, *Werke*), 266.

Beside the inspiration to orient himself to Hafez, there are two interrelated sections of the *Divan* that would have given direct impulse to Platen's project: Goethe's poetic dissertation of the *ghazal*'s formal challenge, which seems to have been received by Platen as a challenge; and Goethe's translation theory expounded in the prose section of the cycle, which not only promotes close, mirroring, translations but also instructs translators to have heart and brace themselves for public pushback if they aim high and try to cultivate a sophisticated novel taste. The possibility of having to give up the fatherland and exile are already inscribed here.

In a poem in the *Divan*'s Book of Hafez, called "Nachbildung" (Imitation), Goethe acknowledges that he does not follow Hafez in form, while subtly depicting distinctive features of the *ghazal* that proscribe such an endeavor. The poem starts with a hope: "In deine Reimart hoff' ich mich zu finden" (In the art of your rhymes I hope to find myself).[37] Like everything else that follows in the poem, this hope for finding himself can only be understood as a jaunty gesture, especially if compared with Platen, who can be said to have literally looked to find himself in the art of Hafez's rhyme. What Goethe does much more is to reproduce the effect that reading a *ghazal* would have on an uninitiated Western palate.

While the *ghazal* does not break into stanzas, Goethe's poem has three. In the Persian *ghazal*, the first two *mesra*'s (hemistiches) rhyme to make a stand-alone unit, *beyt* (distich), the first of which, the *matla*', gives the poem's *bahr* (meter). The rhyme scheme, *aa*, *za*, *ya*, *xa*, and so on connects the otherwise rather disparate *beyt*s and is sometimes supplemented by *radif*, a repeated word or phrase. This, together with the monorhyme, is often experienced by the uninitiated as repetitive. By employing a relentless iambic pentameter and the rhyme "-en" in twelve consecutive lines, Goethe connects the first two stanzas, affecting a sense of an unbroken stanza and formal monotony, which is nevertheless immediately subverted through a dissimilitude of strong imagery. While offering no independent detachable distichs, through a sudden shift in both meter and rhyme in the third and the second's narrative discontinuity, a sense of oscillation is hinted. The *ghazal*'s audacious oscillation is further implied through the image of a lowly "spark," turning into lasciviously described destructive flames reaching celestial bodies, which, in turn, kindle an inspiration in "ein deutsches Herz" (a German heart). This "German heart" in the middle stanza's final line recalls *takhallos*, the Persian *ghazal*-writer's self-referential *nom de plume*, which would normally turn up in the last *beyt*, *maqta*'. To further replicate the "note to self" aspect of the *maqta*', Goethe's third stanza shifts to the trochaic and cross-rhymes the soft German "-ch" and "-in," six times before an extra line where the poem ends on a hard *ch*-sound, "-acht"! This is Goethe's rather oblique *maqta*': "Selbst der Geist erscheint sich nicht erfreulich, / Wenn er nicht, auf neue Form bedacht, / Jener taten Form ein Ende macht" (The mind seems not to enjoy itself when, set on new form, it doesn't put an end to such dead form).[38] The poetic warning of a formal aporia, ironically, sparks in the hearts of Rückert and Platen the hope of there being something left to contribute.

[37] Goethe-Ormsby, *Divan*, 56–7.
[38] Ibid.

In performatively discussing translation's travails, "Imitation" directs the reader to an essay on translation in the cycle's prose appendix, where Goethe provides a conceptual framework and theoretical methodology for the originary impulse of Rückert's replicas and Platen's German *ghazals*. There, he names the prosaic, the parodistic, and "the highest" or the poetic, as three types of translation. While one may dominate, instances of the three exist in all translations. Yet, there is a hierarchy. The highest type, where the original and translation become identical, is also most resisted by the public. "For the translator who sticks closely to his original more or less abandons the originality of his own nation: and so, a third element comes into being for which the public must gradually develop a taste."[39] This gives heart to Platen to persevere in his cultivation of a public taste for his—to use Even-Zohar's words—"new models of reality."

Daybreak

"Ich habe ein paar herrliche Tage durchlebt, die ich zu den liebsten meines Lebens zählen darf" (I have experienced a few glorious days that shall count as the loveliest in my life), Platen confides to his diary on July 23, 1821.[40] Here, he describes an *otium* with Fritz von Fugger, an old friend from the cadet days, and Otto von Bülow, a visiting Hanoverian officer, to whom *Der Spiegel des Hafis* would be dedicated. What makes these days "loveliest" is not only the unexpected buoyancy of Bülow's retorts to Platen's teasing lines but also old Fugger's casual indulgence, who at lunch suggests that Platen and Bülow play Hafez and *saqi* (cupbearer), and himself a perplexed footman as comic relief. Platen recites all he knows of Hafez by heart before they carve out "Hafez and Saqi" on a tree in Persian calligraphy. Here, Persian appears in the diary for the first time, a Hafez line, followed by a prose translation:

چو آفتاب می از مشرق پیاله بر آید
ز باغ عارض ساق هزار لاله بر آید

Wie die Sonne des Weines aus dem Oriente des Bechers aufgeht, so aus dem
Garten der Wange des Schenkens gehen tausend Tulpen auf.

As the sun-wine in orient's cup comes up; so, a thousand tulips in the
Garden of the cupbearer's countenance come up.

Platen's *ghazal* project aims for a spiritual space that mirrors the regal setting of this vignette: the gardens of Schloss Weißenstein, where the three had gone to pay a visit to the oversized baroque paintings. And yet its aim is not its surface appearance of exclusivity and condescension, but ennoblement through the gospel of beauty, as

---

[39] Ibid., 498.
[40] Ibid., 469–72.

evident by his continuous efforts to exalt and elevate his muses—be it the middle-class Schmidtlein or the aristocratic von Bülow. Consider, for example, the *matla'* of the first cycle's *ghazal* 21, written for Schmidtlein:

> Dir gehorcht' ich, will'gen Ohres, ehedem,
> Gleichwie Asien dem Kores ehedem;
> Was dem schwerverschlossnen Busen Zunge leiht,
> Deine Liebe rief hervor es ehedem.[41]

> I obeyed you willingly o long ago,
> Like to Cyrus ceded Asia long ago;
> And what o lends to heavy burdened breast a tongue,
> Your love evoked o so very long ago.

Platen's rosy solution for both his existential crisis as well as the German geopolitical one: anagogic nobility. As alternative to an era that is moving from Biedermeier's mundane middle-class sensibilities toward bourgeois and proletarian revolutions to be met with brutal reactionary suppression, he is offering poems of spiritual and sensual love in a foreign form. This quixotic—to use Thomas Mann's adjective—campaign to win the *ghazal* for his fatherland, while tone-deaf to the contemporary public sentiment, boasts not only prosodic achievement but also close contextual appreciation.[42] Even-Zohar's polysystem theory can help contextualize a brief *ghazal* genealogy, which is important for understanding the world that Platen envisions and the place he sees for himself within it: unlike *Il Principe*, he wants to be a minstrel that steers the prince away from Machiavellian schemes by inspiring in him the ennobling love of beauty.

At the inception of the Umayyad Caliphate in the seventh century, the translations of imperial-scale statecraft manuals from the Persian that assumed a central position within the Arabic literary polysystem due to a vacuum they could fill also impacted poetry. The position of the *nadim* in the Caliphate court, as the "boon companion to the ruler," harkens to the Sasanian and Parthian *khorrambash* ("joy-bringer") minstrel tradition, to which figures of "Barbad" and "Sarkesh" in Platen's first cycle (17, 29) explicitly point.[43] Often chosen from among the lower ranked courtiers, *nadims* were expected not just to entertain but also to provide loving "counsel and moral guidance."[44] Through the panegyric *qasideh*, they offered not just encomium but also anagogy to the audience, noble in name, who would be reminded of what nobility of spirit entails.[45] This is similar to the function of the *grand chant courtois*, which, as

[41] Platen, *Die Ghaselen*, 19.
[42] Thomas Mann, "August von Platen," in *Schriften und Reden zur Literatur, Kunst und Philosophie*, vol. 2 (Frankfurt: Fischerei, 1968), 33–48.
[43] Julie Scott Meisami, *Medieval Persian Court Poetry* (Princeton: Princeton University Press, 1987), 3, 7. See especially the chapters "The Poet and Court in Persia" (3–39) and "*Ghazal*: The Ideals of Love" (297–98).
[44] Ibid., 7.
[45] Ibid., 269.

J. B. Allen puts it was "to teach mortal aristocratic people how to exist as the achieved personification of their roles."[46]

In the *ghazal*, the same noble project is done in a more loving and intimate setting. This love, which, Julie Meisami reminds us, "might or might not include a carnal dimension," within the milieu "was not only not condemned, but widely tolerated and frequently highly esteemed."[47] Beyond an exchange economy, the poet's nobility relies less on rank than on the love he inspires and the pain he suffers as the "mirror to the prince." True "nobility is not conferred by birth, but by the state of loving."[48]

What separates the idealized love in the *ghazal* from its European counterpart, Meisami tells us, is that in the former "the beloved, however exalted, is still a partner in a relationship that confers both rights and obligations on each member."[49] This is its principle of justice. So, the patron of the *ghazal* is not beyond reproach. However, the manner of criticism is important. And this accounts for Platen's often plaintive tone toward his unjust muses who do not fulfill their noble obligations, despite the love he provides them.

For Whose Fatherland?

As a plan of action for Platen's fatherland, however, the actual economic aspect is absent. Platen's patrons are only muses completely outside an actual exchange economy, and his existence is only possible because the king of Bavaria decides not to cut his lieutenant's retirement wage and because he has a rich aunt in Hanover who experiences occasional bouts of generosity. But for his books, he had to elicit subscriptions from his friends before the publisher would print a copy.

The *Ghazal* 30 (with the *radif* "dem Vaterland" ["for the fatherland"]), which announces the *ghazal* using the first-person accusative pronoun "verkünde mich," closes Platen's first cycle with a remarkable display of prosodic virtuosity, where thirteen-syllable hemistiches get as close as possible to the *ghazal*'s formal replication.[50] The rhyme ("-le") falls on an anaclastic between the fourth and fifth positions of the iambic heptameter, making this usually important element sound like a mere unstressed stutter. This stutter, furthermore, read together with the first syllable of the *radif* (i.e., "dem" [to-, or for-, *the*]), may be described as a pyrrhic. Considering the poem's content, the seldom used pyrrhic, literally a hollow victory, is ironically prophetic. Rhythmically, it recreates an uneven canter of a Persian merchant ("Perserkaufmann") on a heavily burdened camel ("schwerbeladenem Kameele") bringing home what he has collected abroad. The *ghazal* addresses a *you* (presumably a German), whose heart swells ("entgegenschwillt") for his fatherland, and who has won the love ("gewannst

---

[46] Ibid., 243.

[47] Ibid., 246.

[48] Ibid., 255.

[49] Ibid., 258.

[50] August von Platen, *Die Ghaselen*, ed. Ramin Shaghaghi (Hamburg: Männerschwarm, 2014), 23.

du lieb") of a Parsi-singing ("die Parsi singet") nightingale, who sings with a related throat ("verwandter Kehle") for the fatherland. Here, the "related" homelands mirror into one, as the nightingale sings to Persia *ghazals* that the poet sings, implicitly, for Germany. Platen is offering his compatriots his goods, whereby he hopes to make a living, not so much in terms of an exchange economy; rather, to fashion a world in which he, as himself, could live—a home.

Out and Away

Finally, the Heine–Platen affair that marks Platen's abandonment of his Germany project and inaugurates his terminal self-exile, is yet another illustration of the existential aspect of the *ghazal* for him.[51] In 1828, young Heinrich Heine published a few "xenia" poems (something like "bonus material") by his associate Karl Immermann, at the end of the second installment to his commercially successful travel narrative, *Reisebilder* (1827). Among other things, one of the poems ridiculed "*ghazal* poets" saying they "eat too much from the fruits of the gardens of Shiraz and vomit *ghazals*."[52] Implicated were Platen and Rückert. While the latter did not so much as acknowledge the fact, Platen's vehement reaction included composing a whole play in verse about Immermann, called *Der romantische Oedipus* (1829, *The Romantic Oedipus*), and attacking Heine in explicitly anti-Semitic terms. Heine, in turn, made a stink about Platen's homosexuality by citing, among other things, the following verses from the *matla'* of the eighth *ghazal* of Platen's second cycle:

> Ich bin wie Leib dem Geist, wie Geist dem Leibe dir!
> Ich bin wie Weib dem Mann, wie Mann dem Weibe dir![53]

> To soul a body I, like body's soul to you!
> To man a wife and like a man to wife for you.

Their scandal has been thoroughly discussed,[54] and there is little to add, save for the fact that Platen's undoubtedly unjust overreaction highlights the existential role that the *ghazal* played for him. Even before going after Platen's homoeroticism, by slighting

---

[51] For an overview of all pertinent primary source material, see Keppel, Ch., and Joachim Bartholomae, eds. "*Schlaffe Ghaselen*" *und "Knoblauchgeruch": Platen, Immermann und Heine streiten über freche Juden, warme Brüder und wahre Poesie* (Hamburg: Männerschwarm Verlag, 2012).

[52] "Von den Früchten, die sie aus dem Gartenhain von Schiras stehlen,/Essen sie zuviel, die Armen, und vomieren dann Ghaselen" (ibid., 245).

[53] Platen, *Die Ghaselen*, 33.

[54] See, for example, Frank Busch, *August Graf von Platen, Thomas Mann: Zeichen und Gefühle* (Munich: Fink, 1987); Paul Derks, *Die Schande der heiligen Päderastie: Homosexualität und Öffentlichkeit in der deutschen Literatur 1750–1850* (Berlin: Winkel, 1990); Heinrich Detering, *Das Offene Geheimnis: Zur literarischen Produktivität eines Tabus von Winckelmann bis zu Thomas Mann* (Göttingen: Wallstein, 1994); Hans Mayer, "Die Platen-Heine-Konfrontation," *Akzente* 3 (1973): 273–88.

the *ghazal* project, Heine had unwittingly pierced a nerve in Platen's existential core—the very place in Heine that Platen's subsequent riposte targeted.

Initially, Heine's attempt at arousing public indignation for Platen's homosexuality was far less effective than Platen's anti-Semitic attack. One reason was that while anti-Semitism has always been very near to the surface, there is nothing lewd anywhere in Platen's work to arouse such outrage, not even in his diaries. Scholars assume, based on a purported change in the hues of his writing, that he may have lost his virginity in Italy in 1824, but there is nothing blatantly sexual, let alone uncouth, in his work.

What differentiates the Persian *ghazal* from the Arabic homoerotic *ghazal*s of the likes of Abu Nuwas (d. 814), for example, Meisami tells us, is the "idealizing tone of the Persian homoerotic poetry." The Arabic "poetry on the love of boys," she explains, "is often salacious, if not downright obscene."[55] In contrast, while "the refined and idealistic nature of love was certainly stressed, its physical aspect was by no means ignored; even in mystical *ghazal*s, the sensual and spiritual sides of love typically coexist as analogues, rather than alternatives."[56] It was precisely this noble eroticism, the chaste quest for inspiring beauty, that Platen found so liberating about the Persian *ghazal*, also explaining why Heine's mockery was so threatening and infuriating.

Upon Platen's obstinate insistence, in the absence of Arabic movable types, his own Persian handwriting had to be carved out and molded several times for the purpose of printing the first cycle's motto, a couplet from the introduction to the fifteenth-century mystic Jami's *Yusef va Zoleykha* (*Yusuf and Zulaikha*) Platen repeats the gesture of leading with the spiritual, in the second cycle with an inscription from San Juan de la Cruz, "Entremos más adentro en la espesura," which promises to get "deeper into the thicket." The trek starts in Shiraz and goes through Andalusia as it approaches Germany. The third cycle, which contains a German motto cited in the first paragraph of this chapter, is different from all others in that there we find a most straightforward treatment of Platen's sexuality. The third cycle, in effect, is Platen's coming out as "the first self-professing homosexual of the modern world literature."[57]

Conclusion

Nobility's fall from grace and Germany's struggles toward unification both informed Platen's wistful interest in the *ghazal* form and anticipated its rejection as untimely and undesirable. Platen's quixotic expedition, spurred by an existential need to poeticize a Hafezian world of integrated spiritual and homoerotic aesthetics in which he could live as an integrated subject, failed in part due to the destined peripheral position of his translations within the newly strengthened German literary polysystem. At the same time, he could not have single-handedly recreated the world of fourteenth-century

---

[55] Meisami, *Court Poetry*, 247.
[56] Ibid., 245.
[57] Bumm, *Platen*, 320.

Shiraz in nineteenth-century Bavaria. But more significant than Platen's inability to integrate into the imminent Germany was his inability to sound an inner consonance, to which his penchant for polemics attests. And to be fair, his German *ghazal*s, splendid examples of prosodic virtuosity that they are, could not make him Hafez. As Bürgel has correctly noted, in Platen the sensual and the spiritual seem to be placed next to each other, be it in one cycle, in one poem, even in one *mesra'*, whereas in Hafez, they are inseparable.[58] Multiple factors had created a dissonance within Platen that could not be overcome just by reproducing the *ghazal* form. Nor could that form affect the course of political development in his fatherland. But these failures do not take away from the significance of what Platen has achieved in terms of world literature.

What makes the Platenic *ghazal*s important is their active call, through time and space, for Persians, not only to engage Hafez but also German verses, perhaps with the same intensity and productivity as he did theirs. His case shows that an immediate gratification cannot be the aim. Yet, here appears to be a noteworthy chiasmus: although the process that started with the decriminalization of homosexuality in the Napoleonic Code had not gained widespread cultural acceptance in Germany during Platen's time, it has by now led to the problematization of the gender-binary itself—at least in intellectual circles in the West. At the same time, in the decade of Platen's birth, the Qajar Dynasty consolidated Iran into a centralized state that would soon encounter industrial modernity in successive military defeats to the more technologically advanced Russian and English forces. The subsequent motivation to catch up with "modernity" set in motion a cultural reorientation, which in part pivoted on a rethinking of traditional Iranian gender roles and identities—a process dubbed by Afsaneh Najmabadi the "feminization of beauty."[59] The very definition of gender in terms of man/woman, Najmabadi found, was a modern move. Privileging European bourgeois values like the stigmatization of homosexuality helped establish and enforce this ascendant binary, bolstered further through dominant readings of classical texts in a purely spiritual way, cleansed of their embarrassing "oriental" homoeroticism.

Because it will always be inextricably linked to Goethe, the *ghazal* form remains more of an often-overlooked resident alien than a complete stranger within the German literary polysystem, regardless of what is included in introductory German poetry volumes. But more interestingly, the specific elements that were often cited at the time as reasons for the *ghazal*'s unpalatability in nineteenth-century Europe permeate any given pop song today: disparate oscillating verses of largely homogenous aesthetic lexis lacking apparent cohesive narrative and united through repetitious refrains and reprises. Even the concept of *takhallos* is prevalent. Most importantly, in today's pop songs one can find that space where openness to interpretation merges sensual (pan) eroticism and spirituality. In this sense, the likes of Platen may have helped preserve and transmit the *ghazal* form far more successfully than they, or we, ever imagined.

---

[58] Johann Christoph Bürgel, "Platen und Hafis," in *August Graf von Platen: Leben, Werk, Wirkung* (Paderborn: Schöningh, 1998), 85–102.

[59] Afsaneh Najmabadi, *Women with Mustaches and Men without Beards: Gender and Sexual Anxieties of Iranian Modernity* (Berkeley: University of California Press, 2005), 1–8.

Bibliography

Bobzin, Hartmut, and Gunnar Och. *August Graf von Platen: Leben, Werk, Wirkung.* Paderborn: Schöningh, 1998.

Brookshaw, Dominic Parviz. *Hafiz and His Contemporaries: Poetry, Performance and Patronage in Fourteenth-Century Iran.* London: I.B.Tauris, 2019.

Bumm, Peter. *August Graf von Platen: Eine Biographie.* Paderborn: F. Schöningh, 1990.

Busch, Frank. *August Graf von Platen, Thomas Mann: Zeichen und Gefühle.* Munich: Fink, 1987.

Derks, Paul. *Die Schande der heiligen Päderastie: Homosexualität und Öffentlichkeit in der deutschen Literatur 1750–1850.* Berlin: Winkel, 1990.

Detering, Heinrich. *Das Offene Geheimnis: Zur Literarischen Produktivität eines Tabus von Winckelmann bis zu Thomas Mann.* Göttingen: Wallstein, 1994.

Even-Zohar, Itamar. "The Position of Translated Literature within the Literary Polysystem." *Poetics Today* 11, no. 1 (1990): 45–51.

Goethe, Johann Wolfgang von, and Eric Ormsby. *West-Eastern Divan.* London: Gingko, 2019.

Kayser, Wolfgang. "Beobachtungen zur Verskunst des West-Östlichen Divans." *Publications of the English Goethe Society* 23, no. 1 (1954): 74–96.

Keppel, Christopher, and Joachim Bartholomae. "*Schlaffe Ghaselen*" und "*Knoblauchgeruch*": *Platen, Immermann und Heine Streiten über freche Juden, warme Brüder und wahre Poesie.* Hamburg: Männerschwarm Verlag, 2012.

Link, Jürgen. *Artistische Form und ästhetischer Sinn in Platens Lyrik.* Munich: Fink, 1971.

Mann, Thomas. "August von Platen." In *Schriften und Reden zur Literatur, Kunst und Philosophie*, vol. 2. Frankfurt: Fischerei, 1968. 33–48.

Mayer, Hans. "Die Platen-Heine-Konfrontation." In *Akzente: Zeitschrift für Literatur.* 273–88. Stuttgart: Metzlersche Verlagsbuchhandlung, vol. 3, 1973.

Meisami, Julie Scott. *Medieval Persian Court Poetry.* Princeton: Princeton University Press, 1987.

Najmabadi, Afsaneh. *Women with Mustaches and Men without Beards: Gender and Sexual Anxieties of Iranian Modernity.* Berkeley: University of California Press, 2005.

Och, Gunnar. *August Graf von Platen, 1796–1835: Was er wünscht, das ist ihm nie Geworden: Eine Ausstellung im 200. Geburtsjahr des Dichters, 22. Mai–16. Juni 1996.* Erlangen: Universitätsbibliothek, 1996.

Platen, August von. *Die Ghaselen.* Ed. Ramin Shaghaghi. Hamburg: Männerschwarm, 2014.

Platen, August von. *Die Tagebücher des Grafen August von Platen: Aus der Handschrift des Dichters*, 2 vols. Ed. G. Laubmann and Ludwig Scheffler. Stuttgart: Cotta, 1896–1900.

Platen, August von. *Lyrische Blätter No. 1.* Leipzig: Brockhaus, 1821.

Platen, August von. *Vermischte Schriften.* Erlangen: Heyder, 1822.

Platen, August von. *Werke Band I.* Ed Kurt Wölfel and Jürgen Link. Munich: Winkler, 1982.

Rückert, Friedrich. *Gesammelte Gedichte.* Erlangen: Carl Heyder, 1837.

Ryan, Judith. *The Cambridge Introduction to German Poetry.* Cambridge: Cambridge University Press, 2012.

Schimmel, Annemarie, and Rudolf Kreutner. *Friedrich Rückert: Lebensbild und Einführung in Sein Werk.* Göttingen: Wallstein, 2015.

Schlösser, Rudolf. *August Graf v. Platen: Ein Bild seines geistigen Entwicklungsganges und seines dichterischen Schaffens.* Munich: Piper, 1910.

Spingou, Foteini. "Byzantine Collections and Anthologies of Poetry." In *A Companion to Byzantine Poetry.* Brill's Companions to the Byzantine World, vol. 4. Ed. Wolfram Hörandner, Andreas Rhoby, and Nikos Zagklas. Leiden: Brill, 2019.

Thiesen, Finn. *A Manual of Classical Persian Prosody, with Chapters on Urdu, Karakhanidic and Ottoman Prosody.* Wiesbaden: Harrassowitz, 1982.

Tschersig, Hubert. *Das Gasel in der deutschen Dichtung und das Gasel bei* Platen. *Breslauer Beiträge Zur Literaturgeschichte* 11 vols. Vol. 1. Leipzig: Quelle & Meyer, 1907.

Veit, Friedrich. *Des Grafen von Platens Nachbildungen aus dem Diwan des Hafis und ihr persisches Original.* Berlin: Alexander Duncker, 1908.

Wilson, W. Daniel, and Angela Steidele. *Goethe, Männer, Knaben: Ansichten zur "Homosexualität."* Berlin: Insel Verlag, 2012.

2

Otherworld Literature: Parahuman Pasts in Classical Persian Historiography and Epic

Sam Lasman

What is the place of otherworlds in world literature? For paradigms that base the latter concept in modes of circulation amongst globalized cultures, on the resulting assertion or abolition of national identities, on constituting empire or dismantling it, literature that depicts interactions between human and supernatural realms seems at best an allegory for the relationship between ostensibly historical polities, at worst like a frivolous irrelevance. Yet premodern texts regularly demand that otherworlds be taken seriously. They contend that battles, sexual encounters, and other exchanges between human civilizations and their enigmatic doubles have played vital roles in shaping communal pasts. Among the richest expressions of this relationship are the historical narratives produced by Persianate writers around the turn of the first millennium CE. These texts proved foundational for the self-conception of Islamicate societies in the global Middle Ages and beyond, depicting a past in which conflicting origin narratives could be reconciled around the primordial struggles between humans and beings identified variously as *div, jinn,* or *pari* (besides a host of other terms). In centering these uncanny encounters, the works discussed in this chapter both root the heterogeneous cosmopolitanism of classical Persian literature in parahuman terms, and suggest productive avenues for considering the relationship between world and otherworld literatures.

Thus any consideration of premodern Persian literature as world literature must acknowledge that the "world" in question is not simply or transparently "our" world, the planet Earth (Persian *zamin*) according to a modern geospatial imagining. Whether describing extant worlds, conjuring literary worlds out of an assemblage of earlier traditions, or knitting together sociocultural worlds around mutual engagement with texts, classical Persian authors insist on the perceptual contingency of any single world, and the multiplicity of potential worlds. Texts as foundational as the first major work of New Persian prose, Bal'ami's *Tarikhnameh,* and the epochal cultural milestone of Ferdowsi's *Shahnameh,* depict a world bordering on otherworldly spaces and interpenetrated by otherworldly beings.

My use of "otherworld" for the home of the *div* ("demon; monster; fiend") and their associates consciously evokes the medieval European context.[1] While in many ways a problematic term, "otherworld" remains a helpful descriptor for a heterogeneous set of places united by their shared narrative functions. Geographically, they are simultaneously close and distant—*unheimliche* spaces located just underground yet also miles distant, across seas or forbidding wildernesses. They are terrifying hellscapes of monsters and ritual combats, but also arcadian lands of enchanting beauty and erotic possibility. Their inhabitants have fundamentally human features—societies, reason, speech—and more uncanny qualities, including the vast spectrum of abilities covered by the concept of "magic." Almost always, otherworlds exist in parallel not to the present moment but to an altered temporality, often resembling an imagined past. Inaccessible to the disenchanted now, they are explicitly literary spaces.

The writers discussed here—Abu Ja'far Muhammad bin Jarir al-Tabari (d. 923 CE); Abu 'Ali Mohammad Bal'ami (d. c. 997 CE); Abolqasem Ferdowsi (d. c. 1025 CE); and Abu Sa'id 'Abd al-Hayy Gardizi (d. c. 1050 CE?)—do not represent the sum of early Persianate narrators of otherworld literature. But they form an important foundational cohort that powerfully influenced later imaginations. None saw themselves as producing "literature"; no such category existed within their cultural milieu. Modern assessments have tended to distinguish "historians" such as al-Tabari, Bal'ami, and Gardizi, who wrote prose chronicles, from epic poets like Ferdowsi who composed in *moteqareb* epic verse. While this categorization does reflect important differences in their methodologies, there are indications that contemporary audiences sometimes approached all these texts with similar modes of understanding.[2] While today, the "historians" (particularly al-Tabari) are prized for their accounts of events such as the campaigns of the nascent Islamic Caliphate, their narrations of long-lost mythic eras clearly cannot be read with the same positivist aims. In contrast even to their tales of ancient prophets, which can be studied (for instance) within the context of *'ilm al-hadith*,[3] it is hard to know how to read their accounts of the Iranian otherworld except as literature.

Under this approach, otherworld literature troubles the margins of world literature, much as otherworld beings haunt the borders of the ancient kingdoms these writers depict. Unalienable to any modern nationalism and threatening all hegemonies, up to and including anthropocentrism, the parahumans of classical Persian historiography enact the transgressive embodiments that Jack Halberstam identifies as core cultural functions of monstrosity: "the disruption of categories, the destruction of boundaries, and the presence of impurities."[4] It is perhaps no accident that these terms are equally

---

[1] For a recent scholarly discussion of this concept in medieval Western Europe, see Aisling Byrne, *Otherworlds: Fantasy and History in Medieval Literature*, Oxford: Oxford University Press, 2016.

[2] An instance of such undifferentiated reception is ibn al-Athir's anecdote of the mocking question Mahmud of Ghazna asked the deposed Majd al-Dawla of Rayy: "'Haven't you read *Shahnameh*, the history of the Persians, and *al-Tabari's History*, the history of the Muslims?'" ('Ali 'Izz al-Din ibn al-Athir al-Jazari, *Al-Kamil fi al-Ta'rikh*, ed. C. Tornberg [Beirut: Dar Sadir, 1966], vol. 9, 371).

[3] The science of the study of *hadith* literature, the record of the sayings and acts of Prophet Muhammad, his family, and his close companions.

[4] Jack Halberstam, *Skin Shows: Gothic Horror and the Technology of Monsters* (Durham: Duke University Press, 1995), 27.

applicable to the process of translation, which both betrays its text and opens its passage into a wider world of reception. Themselves translated beings (interculturally as well as interlinguistically), the *div, pari,* and *jinn* considered in this chapter implant Halberstam's fundamental instabilities into the origins of cities, literary cultures, and humanity at large.

Despite often sharing names, these beings differ profoundly from the *daeuua-* and *pairika-* (Avestan) or *dēw* and *parig* (Pahlavi) of Zoroastrian texts. The ontology of such supernatural forces remained vexing within Zoroastrianism, through an equation of evil with lying and nonexistence (in contrast with the trifecta of good, truth, and existence). Evil entities are expressions of Ahrimanic will, yet they possess no real substance, since matter itself is inherently opposed to demonic forces of negation. While evil intent is a powerful force, it can only manifest by attaching itself to material agents. Thus, believers' attempts to separate *daeuua-* from their physical hosts—by lighting fires, healing the sick, slaying vermin, spreading knowledge of the truth, and keeping the body and household clean—are considered pious acts.[5]

Unlike these categorically evil, "un-created" creatures, later *div* and *pari* possess the moral complexity and free will of Islamicate *jinn,* with whom they are sometimes compared or equated.[6] Yet, any assumption of an essential ontological correspondence between *div* and the Qur'anic *jinn* obscures the radical reconceptualization that occurred when Muslim Iranians recast their pre-Islamic history and lore in monotheistic terms. In doing so, these writers presented supernatural beings that were not atavistic fossils of ancient belief systems but rather the syncretic offspring of medieval Iranian, Arabic, Muslim, Hebraic, and Central Asian conceptions, drawn from both popular and elite strata. These polyvalent origins made the *div* and their ilk ideal figures for works like al-Tabari's monumental Ta'rikh al-Rusul wa-l-Muluk (*History of Prophets and Kings,* completed 915 CE) and its Persian adaptation, Bal'ami's *Tarikhnameh,* both of which sought to combine a wide range of traditions in order to create comprehensive historical narratives for multiethnic Islamicate states (the Abbasids for al-Tabari; the Samanids, for Bal'ami).[7]

Compared to later authors writing in Persian, al-Tabari's Arabic account of Iranian otherworld dwellers in the *Ta'rikh* is brief and allusive. In his discussions of Jayumart (the Zoroastrian proto-mortal Gayumart reimagined as the first world-king), al-Tabari makes no mention of either warfare or intermingling with otherworldly creatures.

---

[5] A. V. Williams, "Dēw," *Encyclopaedia Iranica,* accessed June 7, 2019. Key Middle Persian Zoroastrian texts that refer to these creatures include the first, fourth, and fifth chapters of the *Bundahishn,* the third book of the *Denkard,* and the fifth chapter of the *Arda Wiraz Namag.* Transcriptions of all these texts can be found in the TITUS project Middle Persian database, available at http://titus.uni-frankfurt.de/indexe.htm.

[6] For normative accounts of the *jinn,* see D. B. MacDonald et al., "Djinn," in *Encyclopedia of Islam,* ed. P. Bearman et al. For *daiva/div,* see Clarisse Herrenschmidt and Jean Kellens, "Daiva," and Mahmoud Omidsalar, "Div," in *Encyclopaedia Iranica.* For *pari,* see Siamak Adhami, "Pairika," in *Encyclopaedia Iranica.*

[7] For a thorough discussion of the political aims of al-Tabari and Bal'ami, see A. C. S. Peacock, *Medieval Islamic Historiography and Political Legitimacy: Bal 'ami's Tarikhnamah* (London: Routledge, 2007), 11–12, 170.

Rather, he introduces these beings diagetically in the inauguration speech of Jayumart's grandson, King Awshhanj:

> He said that he had inherited the kingdom from his grandfather Jayumart; and that he was a punishment and a vengeance upon the rebellious among men and devils [*shayatin*]. And [the Persians] recount that he vanquished Iblis and his armies, and forbid them from mixing with humans. And he wrote for them a writing upon white paper, and in it imposed on them covenants that they not appear before [or impede: *ya'ridu li*] any human, and threatened them on that point. And he killed the rebellious among them [*maradatahum*], and a band of ghouls [*ghilan*], and they fled from fear of him into the deserts and mountains and valleys. And indeed he ruled all the climes ... And they recount that Iblis and his armies rejoiced at the death of Awshhanj; that is, at his death, they entered the dwellings of Adam's children, and descended upon them from the mountains and valleys.[8]

In its depiction of complex relations between humans and parahumans, this passage is essentially unique in the *Ta'rikh*. Al-Tabari's accounts of the subsequent reigns of Tahmurath and Jam al-Shidh (Jamshid)[9] contain brief mentions of continuing struggle, though they do not exhibit the same anxiety over "mixing with humans" (*al-ikhtilat bi-l-nas*). The historian's earlier stories of conflicts with Iblis occur largely on the celestial plane, and do not involve physical battles between Adam's children and satanic armies. While Bal'ami and Ferdowsi situate epic struggles against the *div* during Jayumart's era, describing the conflict in terms of blood feud, al-Tabari leaves unclear the origins of Awshhanj's vendetta (*naqma*) against the "rebellious among men and devils" (*maradat al-ins wa-l-shayatin*). This phrase echoes the Qur'an (6:112): "And thus We have made for every prophet an enemy—devils from mankind and jinn" (*shayatina-l-insi wa-l-jinn*).[10] Yet it is never clear why Awshhanj, whom al-Tabari equates with the obscure patriarch Mahala'il bin Qaynan[11] (the Biblical Mahalalel), should be tasked with such a crusade.

The simple answer is that al-Tabari is synchronizing Zoroastrian myth, in which the primordial Pishdadi kings are responsible for subduing the dark forces of Ahriman, with Semitic material in which the equivalent conflict is mankind's resistance to satanic wiles. Yet, al-Tabari's sources for this passage on Awshhanj are unknown. Himself a native of the Caspian region known in his day as Tabarestan and today as Mazandaran (the same region that later writers identified as a refugium of demonic powers),[12] the

---

[8]   Abu Ja'far Muhammad bin Jarir al-Tabari, *Ta'rikh al-Rusul wa-l-Muluk*, vol. 1, ed. Muhammad Abu-l-Fadl Ibrahim (Cairo: Dar al-Ma'arif, 1960), 169. This and all translations belong to the current author, unless otherwise noted.

[9]   al-Tabari, *Ta'rikh,* 172–5.

[10] The translation is from the Sahih International version (Dar Abdu-l-Qasim Publishing House: Jiddah, 1997), available at https://quran.com/6/112.

[11] al-Tabari, *Ta'rikh,* 168.

[12] Franz Rosenthal, "General Introduction," *The History of al-Tabari, Volume 1: General Introduction and from the Creation to the Flood*, trans. and ann. Franz Rosenthal (Albany: State University of New York Press, 1989), 10–11.

historian undoubtedly spoke a Persian dialect and may have acted at least partially as his own informant.[13] Yet writing of Jayumart, al-Tabari both ignores any material related to the struggle against Ahriman and offers a mockingly euhemerist take on why the Persians considered this figure, rather than Adam, to be the first man. At the end of Jayumart's life, al-Tabari writes, the king became tyrannical and demanded to be known as Adam, on the pain of mutilating anyone who called him otherwise.[14]

Sarah Bowen Savant notes that this distortion is a key example of Islamic historians' "cynical appraisals of Zoroastrian cosmogony" meant to defame pre-Islamic heritage.[15] Yet, if al-Tabari is seeking to discredit Iranian mythic history, it is hard to explain why he allots Jayumart's descendant a lead role in battle against Iblis. Rather, it is more productive to view al-Tabari's account of Awshhanj as a literary intervention, creating a character whose syncretic background leads not to a single reconciled history but rather to a vision of the past incongruous with either dualistic Iranian or prophetic Islamic views of human origins. Liminal to both traditions but beholden to neither, Awshhanj becomes a site for al-Tabari to consider the porous boundaries of humanity, history, and other allegedly comprehensive categories. It is telling that the geography of the otherworld depicted here is ever-shifting, encompassing the intransigent areas where state power struggles to exert its coercive force ("deserts and mountains and valleys"), but creeping, in uncertain times, up to and over the thresholds of human dwellings. This geography frames an entropic portrayal of relations with the otherworld, a slide toward chaotic admixture that is only provisionally averted by a strong ruler's legal and martial remedies. Yet intermingling has already occurred, and seems to resume after Awshhanj's death (if this is indeed the implication behind the resurgent devils' entry into human homes). As he synthesizes Islamic and Zoroastrian concepts and figures, al-Tabari must reckon with both the inevitability of commingling and the fissures that result. Like Awshhanj's proclamation "upon white paper," the *Ta'rikh* demonstrates how otherworld narratives challenge the authority of the hegemonic text even as they spur its production.

By translating and adapting al-Tabari's opus into the emergent literary idiom of New Persian, Abu Ali Mohammad Bal'ami further enmeshed Islamic world history in a dense network of sociocultural influences. A. C. S. Peacock is careful to note that "to see the *Tarikhnameh* as a product of state-sponsored Persian nationalism is erroneous"[16]—rather, it aimed to establish the Samanids' credentials as custodians of Islamic culture generally and Sunnism more particularly.[17] Both through the widespread importance of Persian as a literary language and later translations into Arabic and Turkish, however, Bal'ami's text achieved a distribution and popularity that eclipsed al-Tabari's original.[18]

---

[13] Shaul Shaked, "First Man, First King," *Gilgul: Essays on Transformation, Revolution, and Permanence in the History of Religions*, ed. S. Shaked, D. Shulman, and G. G. Stroumsa (Leiden: Brill, 1987), 247.

[14] al-Tabari, *Ta'rikh*, 167.

[15] Sarah Bowen Savant, *The New Muslims of Post-Conquest Iran: Tradition, Memory, and Conversion* (New York: Cambridge University Press, 2013), 237.

[16] Peacock, *Historiography*, 107.

[17] Ibid., 168–70.

[18] Ibid., 141.

Bal'ami's work has a fraught textual history. Much of the material analyzed below is from an early fourteenth-century CE manuscript (RAS, Persian 22), which Peacock considers idiosyncratic.[19] Yet, whether the "Bal'ami" discussed here belongs to the tenth century or several hundred years later, relative chronology is less important to my argument than the creative ways in which medieval Iranian Muslims reimagined their world's past.

Early in the *Tarikhnameh*, Bal'ami inserts an unusual *hadith* into his discussion of the world's origin:

> There is another narration from the sayings of Wahb ebn-e Monabbeh, which says thus: I heard from our Prophet, peace upon him, that God Almighty said: The first things he created among the creatures were the demons [*div*], and for seven thousand years the world was theirs. Then he deposed them and gave this world to the fairies [*pariyan*], and for five thousand years the fairies had it. Then he deposed them also, and gave this world to the angels [*fereshtegan*], and they had it for two thousand years; and their nobility were the genies [*jinn*]. Then he sent Iblis, and made him master over them, and he curbed the genies, not allowing them to act depravedly and deterring them. When Iblis curbed the genies, he was so amazed with himself, that he said: then who am I? For if I wish, I can go up into the heavens, and if I wish, upon the earth, and this creation is within my command. God Almighty knew Iblis's heart, and created Adam, peace upon him, and gave this world to Adam and to his children, and cursed Iblis.[20]

Bal'ami's sources for this alternate cosmic history are unclear. Al-Tabari offers only a few vaguely similar accounts, such as those attributed to ibn Abbas and al-Rabi' bin Anas.[21] But the first of these mentions only a single race of primordial *jinn* defeated by Iblis, the second only a successive creation of angels, *jinn*, and Adam on the final three days of creation. Neither gives anything like the extensive taxonomy or expansive chronology of the above *hadith*.[22]

The historian here asks his readers to imagine—if not necessarily believe in—a vast and largely unrecorded prehuman history, significantly exceeding orthodox calculations for the age of creation. These lost ages are populated with an array of beings from both Persian and Islamic legend, resulting in a cross-cultural menagerie of otherworld entities. Indeed, it is difficult to imagine what such an account might look like in the ostensibly original Arabic, given that the Persian categories of *div* and *pari* are often equated to *jinn*, which in turn are hardly distinguishable from *jann*.

---

[19] Ibid., 54.
[20] Abu Ali Mohammad Bal'ami. *Tarikh-e Bal'ami*. ed. Mohammad-Taqi Bahar Malek al-Sho'ara with Mohammad Parvin Gonabadi, Tehran: Edareh-ye Koll-e Negaresh-e Vezarat-e Farhang, 1341/1962, 16–17.
[21] al-Tabari, *Ta'rikh*, 84.
[22] Closer parallels do exist in later sources, such as the *Rawzat al-Safa'* of Mir-Khwand (d. 1498 CE), which provides an even more extensive pre-Adamic chronology.

Furthermore, by situating this narrative early in his text, Bal'ami invites readers to view the *div* and *pari* that appear later as the former masters of the world, dispossessed but not vanished.

Their lingering antihegemonic resentment surfaces powerfully in the *Tarikhnameh*'s account of Gayumars (al-Tabari's Jayumart). Very little of this is taken from the Arabic source. Bal'ami provides a much more accurate summary of Zoroastrian doctrine regarding the first mortal, evocatively referring to a tradition that in those early times, "the world was waste and [Gayumars] was in mountain ravines and not a single human was with him."[23] Taking up the story in detail sometime later, he tells how after a dispute with his Mesopotamian kindred, Gayumars flees to Mount Damavand along with his children and establishes "cities and refuges" there. However, the region is not unpopulated—"at that border [*hadd*], the demons [*divan*] had refuges." The *div* here are autochthons, inhabiting spaces just beyond the pale of human settlement. Yet the ambiguity of *hadd* makes it unclear if this "border" is purely spatial and geographical, or more fundamentally ontological. These *div* occupy an unsettling position between the physical and metaphysical—to defeat them, Gayumars employs both literal and spiritual weaponry, brandishing his "divine aura" (*farr-e izadi*) along with a "big club and sling, and the name of God Almighty was written upon them."[24]

Now Bal'ami introduces Gayumars' son, Bashang or Pashang[25] (other manuscripts call this figure Mishang, Hishang, or Hushang). Bashang is a prototypic ascetic, wandering the mountains and worshiping God apart from his fellow men. Eventually, however, "a group of those demons who had suffered defeat at the hands of his father Gayumars" see Bashang alone in the mountains and "schemed to slay him, they said, so that his father's heart will be broken and he will not be able to contend with us." Seeing an opportunity while the pious youth is at prayer, the demons tear off a fragment of the mountain and hurl it down upon his head. No one knows of the murder, but thanks to his divine *farr*, Gayumars has a premonition of ill—he becomes sad "without knowing the cause." A screeching owl alerts him to the location of his son's body.[26] Evidently some time has passed, since the corpse is described as "rotten."[27] This graphic emphasis on human mortality may recall the parallel event in Zoroastrian myth, in which Gayumart's murder at the hands of Ahriman is the first death experienced within creation. Though Bashang has taken his father's place and the context is no longer officially primordial, the suggestion of unnatural and unprecedented tragedy lingers.

Bal'ami tells how Gayumars prays for God to identify his son's killers and is eventually rewarded with a dream vision in which the culprits are revealed: "a group of rebels [*maradeh*] did it, who are in such-and-such a place."[28] The identification of the *div* as *maradeh*, "rebels, upstarts," may be an echo of al-Tabari's use of the same word

[23] Bal'ami, *Tarikh*, 12.
[24] Bal'ami, *Tarikh*, 114.
[25] This voweling is conjectural—Bahar's edition gives only *b.š.n.k/g*.
[26] Bal'ami, *Tarikh*, 115.
[27] Ibid., 116.
[28] Bal'ami, *Tarikh*, 116.

to identify the shifty enemies of Awshhanj; the term also recalls the apostates who rose against Abu Bakr following Muhammad's death. It further contributes to the image of these *div* as a force of indigenous and antihegemonic resistance, occupying a liminal position amongst human, spirit, natural, and supernatural identities.

Eventually Gayumars comes upon those who have murdered his son (*marrada*, once again) where they have their lair on a riverbank near the future site of Balkh, in modern Afghanistan. He kills some, puts others to flight, and captures three. As retribution for their actions, he orders these to build a city for him on that spot, making Balkh "the oldest city of the world's cities." Intriguingly, as Gayumars plans the city, the narration begins referring to his otherworldly captives as *pari*. This term, often translated into English by its unrelated near-homophone "fairy," derives from *pairika-*, "a class of female demonic beings … often translated 'sorceress, witch, or enchantress.'"[29] With the exception of a handful of equivocal references, the word has overwhelmingly negative valence in pre-Islamic sources. Yet, in New Persian, it shifts dramatically to connote beautiful, benevolent spirits, grouped with the *div* as otherworldly beings but contrasted to them in both appearance and demeanor. Already in the poetry of Rudaki, two generations older than Bal'ami and living in the same region, *pari-ruy*, "fairy-faced," indicates superlative beauty.[30] By the early modern period, the visual vocabulary of manuscript illumination clearly distinguishes *pari* (winged, feminine, dainty) and *div* (hideous, hulking, often zoomorphic); and the rollicking *Qesseh-ye Amir al-Mo'menin Hamzeh* could portray its hero intervening on behalf of the virtuous kingdom of the *pari* against their oppressive enemies, the *div*.[31]

Against this cultural background, Bal'ami's equation of *div* and *pari* results in an unusually negative portrayal of the latter. It also seems to contradict his *hadith* of successive pre-Adamic epochs, which bases its periodization on a distinction between the two (though does not indicate any differing ethical evaluation of them). It is possible that the naming pattern in Bal'ami's account of Gayumars, which moves from *div* to *maradeh* to *pari*, is significant. According to this scheme, the natives of Damavand are seen first as starkly othered monsters; then, as recalcitrant opponents; and finally, enslaved to Gayumars' urbanization project, they become beings whose strangeness can be reconfigured as a positive attribute. However, this neat progression is undermined immediately afterwards, when Gayumars fights another bloody battle against enemies identified successively as *jinnian*, *divan*, and *maradeh*, and loses his brother in the combat.

Instead, it may be more productive to read Bal'ami's attempts at both categorizing and homogenizing these beings as fundamentally indicative of the relation between world systems and their otherworld counterparts. As Jeffrey Jerome Cohen puts it,

---

[29] Adhami, "Pairika."

[30] E.g., in his famous *qasideh*, "Madar-e Mey." Poetic references to *pari* ghoulishly munching on bones (e.g., in the works of Khaqani) merely derive from an equation of the *pari* with the *jinn*, who according to a *hadith* (Sahih, *Muslim*, 450a) take the bones left over from Muslims' meals as their provision.

[31] *Qesseh-ye Amir al-Mo'menin Hamzeh*, ed. Ja'far She'ar, 2nd rev. ed. Tehran: Farzan, 1362/1983.

"the monster always escapes," specifically because "it refuses easy categorization."[32] In its shifting signifiers, the otherworld resists colonial taxonomies even as it forces a recognition of its own multiplicity. At the same time as the text outlines a political, ecological, and geographic shift from the trackless highland wastes in which Gayumars wages his frontier campaigns to the legible landscape of cities and named locations in which he establishes his dynasty, it also notes the contingency of this project. City-building (civilization, literalized) here rests on a narrative archaeology of ghostly violence—the slavery that Gayumars imposes upon unclassifiable beings who have killed his son because he has encroached on their territory because he himself has been consigned to exile and alterity. This is true for the character both within the text, through his feud with his Mesopotamian family, and in a broader sense, as a Zoroastrian mythological concept searching for meaning within a Muslim universe. Otherworldly narrations allow Gayumars to reclaim the relevance and prestige lost through his incorporation into an altered cultural-ideological context. But this incurs a price: the unruly presence of the *div*, a Derridean *supplément* that both defines and critiques the histories to which it accretes.

Following his account of Balkh's founding, Bal'ami offers a brief overview of parahuman history that is both frustratingly oblique and tantalizingly beautiful:

> Many scholars say thus in the histories, that demons [*div*] and fairies [*pari*] were manifest from the beginning, and manifestly they saw one another, and love and enmity and war and reconciliation were out in the open, until the time of the prophets, peace upon them, after the Flood; then they became hidden.[33]

This acts as a warrant, explaining why the historian is devoting time to these beings in this early section of his tome but will not refer to them in his description of later eras. His insistence that the *div* and *pari* were "manifest" or "visible" (*ashkar*) and their actions were likewise "evident" (*zaher*) in the antediluvian period allows him to present accounts of them as historical evidence, before they disappeared (*penhan shodand*) and so became removed from the record. Other editions of the text clarify that "one another" (*yekdigar*) here refers not to internal otherworld politics but rather to interactions between parahumans and *bani-adam*, the Children of Adam.[34] And while Bal'ami's narration has focused more on enmity (*doshmani*) and war (*harb*), the invocation here of love (*dusti*) and reconciliation (*ashti*) suggests untold versions of this history that emphasize mutuality and generative possibility. If Bal'ami is here drawing on al-Tabari's reference to *ikhtilat* between Awshhanj's subjects and the armies of Iblis, he is offering a much more positive view of such mixing. By using the unreservedly positive term *dusti* and removing the designs of a satanic overlord from the equation,

---

[32] Jeffrey Jerome Cohen, "Monster Culture: Seven Theses," in *Monster Theory: Reading Culture*, ed. Jeffrey Jerome Cohen (Minneapolis: University of Minnesota Press, 1996), 6.

[33] Bal'ami, *Tarikh*, 121.

[34] See, for example, Abu Ali Mohammad Bal'ami, *Tarjomeh-ye Tarikh-e Tabari: Qesmat-e Marbut beh Iran*, ed. Mohammad Javad Mashkur (Tehran: Ketabforushi-ye Khayyam, 1337/1958-9), 14.

Bal'ami gestures toward a pluralistic, borderless vision of the past whose traces—in human lineages, urban archaeology, and historical understanding—persist even as the possibility of direct encounter recedes into purely literary space.

In his *Shahnameh* (completed c. 1010 CE), Abolqasem Ferdowsi presents a vision of history in which hostile interactions with supernatural powers define the earliest strata of history but gradually and unevenly cede place to conflicts amongst human polities. Ferdowsi's vast work contains far more material about otherworldly beings and spaces than either al-Tabari or Bal'ami. Rather than attempting to tackle all of it, my analysis here will focus on Ferdowsi's version of the Gayumart legend at the epic's beginning, and on his re-introduction of daevic political power during the later reign of Kaykavus.

Ferdowsi's account of Gayumart directly follows his exordia and dedications, avoiding the links to Semitic material that situate the al-Tabari and Bal'ami versions. Ferdowsi simply states that Gayumart was the first crowned king, who had "lordship over the world" from his base in the mountains. "Wild beasts and tame and every creature [*janevar*, 'soul-bearer'] that might be seen / in the world bowed down before him." His son, Siyamak, is described as "handsome, / wise, and eager for glory like his father," and "Gayumart's heart lived for him." Gayumart's love for his son, and sadness when they part, sets up the inaugural tragedy. When Siyamak comes of age, "in the world no one was his enemy / except, secretly, the villainous Ahriman." This spirit, who may or may not be distinct from the Islamic Iblis, feels an unexplained "envy" for the young man, and so sends his own son, a warrior like a "raging wolf," with a large army against Siyamak.[35] Ahriman's son is later referred to as the "Black Demon" (*Div-e Siyah*), his epithet demonically inverting the first element of his opponent's name.

Warned by the angel Sorush, Siyamak raises an army and faces the Black Demon in single combat. But his unarmored body is torn apart by the demon's "contrary claws" (*chang-e varuneh*, invoking an adjective of inversion and perversion frequently applied to *div*). In an epic overwhelmingly concerned with battle, this is the first conflict and so sets the terms for all that follow. The defeat of an Iranian royal army at the hands of invaders mirrors the triumph of Islam at the poem's conclusion. When he learns of his loss, Gayumart falls into despair. He abandons his throne to lament, and not only his retinue but all of creation, "wild animals and birds and prey creatures," cry out unto the mountains, mourning for an entire year.[36]

Then Sorush again appears, telling Gayumart to leave off weeping and seek revenge. Siyamak, it transpires, has a valiant son named Hushang. This youth raises a wildly heterogenous army—"fairies [*pari*] and leopards he gathered, and lions / and from the predators, wolves and brave tigers." This alliance engages the Black Demon's hordes. Hushang's creatures are victorious, and Hushang himself violently dismembers the Black Demon, flaying its skin as a trophy.[37]

---

[35] Abolqasem Ferdowsi, *Shahnameh*, vol. 1, ed. Jalal Khaleqi-Motlaq (New York: Persian Text Series, 1377–96/1988–2007), 22.

[36] Ferdowsi, *Shahnameh* I, 23.

[37] Ferdowsi, *Shahnameh* I, 23–5.

In contrast to Balʿami's account of localized colonial wars between humans and parahumans, Ferdowsi depicts a cosmic battle between the *div* and the rest of creation. While Balʿami casts not only the *pari* but also predatory animals as Gayumars' enemies[38] (mirroring orthodox Zoroastrian views, in both cases), Hushang's army represents an Edenic solidarity that fractures over the course of the epic. Lions especially will feature throughout the poem as monstrous foes that challenge heroes; wolves likewise make later villainous appearances. But in this battle, they are aligned with humanity against Ahriman's forces. Furthermore, Ferdowsi's decision to represent the *pari* as Pishdadi partisans constitutes another intervention in the question of mixing between humans and otherworldly beings. The "mixing" that al-Tabari portrays as a symptom of primordial chaos becomes, in the *Shahnameh*, a united front that the "soul-bearing" present against the demonic. And in taking the skin of his father's killer, Hushang performs a sort of oedipal pantomime. Outsourcing the parricide to a demon and then carrying off its leathery husk, he both defers and foreshadows the battles between human fathers and sons that define many of the *Shahnameh*'s pivotal episodes.[39]

Yet even the *div*, who seem uncomplicatedly wicked in this first war, acquire considerable complexity in their last major appearance in the poem, during the campaign waged by the hubristic Kaykavus against the otherworld refugium of Mazandaran. The conflict begins, Ferdowsi narrates, when a *div* "in the guise of a minstrel" comes to the Iranian court and performs a song about his homeland. There, he sings, "Nightingales fill the gardens with singing / And deer fill the mountain meadows, prancing, / Never resting from seeking a mate. / All year everywhere scent and tint await."[40]

For a story of demonic deception, there is curiously little duplicity at work here. By performing his song, the *div* seems to transcend his "guise" and become, in fact, simply a musician. Likewise, his song describes the beauty and wonders of Mazandaran— beauty and wonders that, according to the *Shahnameh,* it indeed possesses. While both the invading Kaykavus and his eventual rescuer Rostam experience dangerous and foreboding regions of the land, they likewise encounter areas every bit as enchanting as those described by the demon bard. In the end, this nameless singer is no more deceptive than a curated tourist brochure. If the *div* mean to lure Kaykavus into their country, they do simply by telling him about what is truly there.

Yet this visit also seems to function as an invitation, a reminder of parahumanity's lingering presence in the poem's increasingly anthropocentric world. Mazandaran has maintained its autonomy thus far partly as a result of its impenetrable geography, the same "deserts and mountains and valleys" that delay human subjugation of otherworld zones in al-Tabari and Balʿami. But it also stubbornly and fundamentally resists mapping. For some commentators, it is roughly the same as modern Mazandaran, the

---

[38] In between his battles against the *div*, Balʿami's Gayumars drives off noxious leopards and wolves (Balʿami, *Tarikh*, 117).

[39] Dick Davis, *Epic and Sedition: The Case of Ferdowsi's Shahnameh* (Washington: Mage Publishers, 2006).

[40] Ferdowsi, *Shahnameh* II, 4.

Iranian province on the southern shore of the Caspian Sea. Like neighboring Gilan, Mazandaran is green and forested, a marked contrast to the desert on the other side of the Alborz Mountains. The people of these provinces have historically differed culturally and linguistically from other Iranians. At least as far back as the Hellenistic Era, outsiders have commented on the relationship between the region's rugged terrain and the rebelliousness of its inhabitants. After the Arab invasions, the Caspian littoral was one of the last regions to convert to Islam—its final Zoroastrian ruler, Mardavij, was killed in 935 CE. Steadfast insurgent resistance helped feed a perception that the fastnesses of Gilan and Mazandaran have preserved facets of authentic "Iranian-ness" that have eroded away out on the heavily trafficked plateau.[41]

Strange, wild, and enchantingly antique, the modern Mazandaran seems an appealing fit for its ancient namesake. But there are problems with the identification. No historical sources explicitly link the name Mazandaran to the Caspian coast until long after Ferdowsi finished his epic. Previously, the littoral was referred to as Tabarestan or Padishxwargar, names which appear nowhere in the *Shahnameh*.

Beyond this, though, lurks a sense that the legendary Mazandaran is too alien to be an Iranian locale. Its etymology, suggesting something like "Gates of the Monsters,"[42] certainly contributes to this impression. Modern scholars have thus placed the "real" Mazandaran in a dizzying variety of places—Egypt, the Maghrib, Central Asia, India, and Yemen. Many of these are not new guesses. In his *Zayn al-Akhbar*, the eleventh-century historian Abu Sa'id 'Abd al-Hayy Gardizi records the story of Kaykavus's ill-fated attack on Mazandaran and his rescue by Rostam. Gardizi's retelling, however, includes details that in the *Shahnameh* belong to a subsequent adventure, Kaykavus's expedition to Hamavaran—most prominently, the king's meeting his future wife, the princess Sudabeh, while imprisoned by her father. Hamavaran is generally situated in southern Arabia, and Gardizi attempts to reconcile his sources here. When Rostam leaves his home in Sistan (southeastern Iran) to rescue the king, he sets sail (something he clearly wouldn't do were he headed to the Caspian coast) and comes "to Mazandaran, which they call Yemen."[43]

Al-Tabari had himself struggled with the question of Queen Sudabeh's origins. Though he has nothing to say about a war with Mazandaran, he does describe Kaykavus's marriage to Sudabeh. But al-Tabari is uncertain whether she is the daughter of a Yemeni king or of the Central Asian ruler Afrasiyab. Either way, she is a *sahira*, a practitioner of witchcraft.[44] The Persian equivalent, *jadu*, is often diagnostic of daevic associations. Gardizi, in fact, replaces the *div* who guard Kaykavus in the *Shahnameh* with *jadu*, down to the squeezing of their livers onto the eyes of the Iranian captives

[41] Christian Bromberger, "Gilān xv: Popular and Literary Perceptions of Identity," *Encyclopaedia Iranica*, accessed June 7, 2019.

[42] Ehsan Yarshater, "Iranian National History," *The Cambridge History of Iran*, vol. 3: *The Seleucid, Parthian, and Sasanian Periods*, ed. Ehsan Yarshater (Cambridge: Cambridge University Press, 1983), 446.

[43] Abu Sa'id Abd al-Hayy Gardizi, *Zayn al-Akhbar*, ed. Rahim Rezazadeh Malek (Tehran: Anjoman-e Asar va Mafakher-e Farhangi, 1384/2005), 73.

[44] al-Tabari, *Tarikh*, 505.

to cure their magically induced blindness.[45] This ghoulish physicality, much like Hushang's skinning of the Black Demon or Bal'ami's emphasis on visual presence, insists on a past tangible referent for forces now etherealized, hidden, or extinct.

This interplay of accessibility and impenetrability likewise animates the geographical question outlined above. The uncertainties over Mazandaran's location and Sudabeh's homeland are overlapping uncertainties. Linked most explicitly by Gardizi, they can be taken together to suggest that Mazandaran is not synonymous with any modern, mappable location. It is an otherworld fundamentally opposed to cartography, just over the Alborz Mountains and also far across the Indian Ocean, and Sudabeh, sweetly sympathetic to the imprisoned king and later brutally wicked to his saintly son Siyavakhsh, is neither Yemeni nor Turkish, but rather parahuman. Her coupling with the human realm, like so many similar pairings across global medieval literature, produces abundant narrative and terrible catastrophe.

Gardizi's Sudabeh is not the only inhabitant of Mazandaran to possess an ambiguous humanity. Awlad, a Mazandarani lord whom Rostam first captures to serve as his guide and later, in gratitude, enthrones as king of the newly subjugated country, is described only as a "fame-seeker, brave and young."[46] Torn between these positive adjectives and his demonic context, later manuscript illuminators depicted Awlad sometimes as a human, sometimes as a *div*.[47] In the *Shabrangnameh*, a short epic sometimes appended to the Mazandaran section of the *Shahnameh*, the Iranian hero Bahram falls in love with and marries Mahyar, former concubine of the *Div-e Sepid* ("White Demon") slain by Rostam at the culmination of his odyssey into Mazandaran.[48]

Epic literature thus reengages the *ikhtilat* between humans and otherworldly beings allegedly forbidden by Awshhanj. Patricia McCormack writes that "all encounters with alterity will create a choice—to turn away by knowing the other as abnormal and therefore affirming the self as normal, or to enter into a bordering or pack with the monstrous, creating a revolutionary hybridity of two who were already hybrids."[49] This interest in bordering and hybridity between humans and parahumans constitutes a persistent thread in the historical imagination of medieval Iran, as writers sought to craft a contested past into meaningful narratives for new, cosmopolitan kingdoms. Unlike the kings and heroes they lionize, these authors don't seek to remove uncanny beings and enchantments from the foundational events of the world they depict. The cultural memories that the *div* inscribe on places and bodies become inseparable from the narration of the past.

If world literature imagines a polyphonic human community of letters, interlinked through translation and globalization, otherworld literature insists on a parahuman

---

[45] Gardizi, *Zayn*, 74.

[46] Ferdowsi, *Shahnameh* II, 32.

[47] Gabrielle van den Berg, "Demons in the Persian Epic Cycle: The *Div /Shabrang* in the Leiden *Shabrangnama* and in *Shahnama* Manuscripts," in *Shahnama Studies II: The Reception of Firdausi's Shahnama*, ed. Charles Melville and Gabrielle van den Berg (Leiden: Brill, 2011), 42.

[48] Ibid., 43.

[49] Patricia MacCormack, *Posthuman Ethics* (London: Routledge, 2012), 91.

alterity that cannot be co-opted into any project of unification. It reveals the ways in which universalizing claims depend upon hegemonies and the violence that produces them, and worlds emerge out of the otherworldly spaces that precede and interpenetrate them. In the classical Persianate case, issues of translation and intercultural adaptation highlight rather than smooth these disjunctures. At the same time, a productive interplay between seemingly irreconcilable ontologies is made possible through the literary space of the otherworld. Viewed this way, premodern Persian literature functions not only as world literature but also as world-building literature, assembling a cosmopolitan array of traditions to depict otherworlds that themselves shape, influence, and blend with the world of direct, quotidian human experience.

While otherworlds are fundamentally literary creations, medieval Persianate writers imbue their denizens with historical agency. These beings insert themselves irreducibly at the origins of cities and lineages; become figures whose dangerous otherness stamps them with a deep authenticity. As they battle, craft, and mate, they work themselves imperceptibly and irreversibly into the lineage of the present, reminding us of the contingency and insufficiency of the human as category. Times may change, invaders may come, but a fundamental alterity is already mixed into whoever, and whatever, we are.

Bibliography

Adhami, Siamak. "Pairika." *Encyclopaedia Iranica*, 2010. Web. Available at www.iranicaonline.org/articles/pairika (accessed June 3, 2020).

al-Tabari, Abu Ja'far Muhammad bin Jarir. *Ta'rikh al-Rusul wa-l-Muluk*, vol. 1, ed. Muhammad Abu-l-Fadl Ibrahim. Cairo: Dar al-Ma'arif, 1960.

Bal'ami, Abu 'Ali Mohammad. *Tarikh-e Bal'ami*. Ed. Mohammad-Taqi Bahar Malek al-Sho'ara with Mohammad Parvin Gonabadi. Tehran: Edareh-ye Koll-e Negaresh-e Vezarat-e Farhang, 1341/1962.

Bal'ami, Abu 'Ali Mohammad. *Tarjomeh-ye Tarikh-e Tabari: Qesmat-e Marbut beh Iran*. Ed. Mohammad Javad Mashkur. Tehran: Ketabforushi-ye Khayyam, 1337/1958-9.

Bromberger, Christian. "Gilān xv: Popular and Literary Perceptions of Identity." *Encyclopaedia Iranica*, 2011. Web. Available at www.iranicaonline.org/articles/gilan-xv-identity (accessed June 7, 2019).

Byrne, Aisling. *Otherworlds: Fantasy and History in Medieval Literature*. Oxford: Oxford University Press, 2016.

Cohen, Jeffrey Jerome. "Monster Culture: Seven These." In *Monster Theory: Reading Culture*. Ed. Jeffrey Jerome Cohen. Minneapolis: University of Minnesota Press, 1996.

Davis, Dick. *Epic and Sedition: The Case of Ferdowsi's Shahnameh*. Washington: Mage Publishers, 2006.

Ferdowsi, Abolqasem. *Shahnameh*, vol. 1. Ed. Jalal Khaleqi-Motlaq. New York: Persian Text Series, 1396/1988.

Gardizi, Abu Sa'id 'Abd al-Hayy. *Zayn al-Akhbar*. Ed. Rahim Rezazadeh Malek. Tehran: Anjoman-e Asar va Mafakher-e Farhangi, 1384/2005.

Halberstam, Jack. *Skin Shows: Gothic Horror and the Technology of Monsters*. Durham: Duke University Press, 1995.

Herrenschmidt, Clarisse and Jean Kellens. "Daiva." *Encyclopaedia Iranica*. 2011. Web. Available at www.iranicaonline.org/articles/daiva-old-iranian-noun (accessed June 3, 2020).

ibn al-Athir al-Jazari, ʿAli ʿIzz al-Din. *Al-Kamil fi al-Taʾrikh*, vol. 9. Ed. C. Tornberg. Beirut: Dar Sadir, 1966.

MacCormack, Patricia. *Posthuman Ethics*. London: Routledge, 2012.

MacDonald, D. B., H. Massé, P. N. Boratav, et al. "Djinn." In *Encyclopaedia of Islam*, 2nd ed. Ed. P. Bearman, Th. Bianquis, C. E. Bosworth, et al. Web. Available at http://dx.doi.org/10.1163/1573-3912_islam_COM_0191 (accessed June 4, 2019).

Omidsalar, Mahmoud. "Dīv." *Encyclopaedia Iranica*. 2011. Web. Available at www.iranicaonline.org/articles/div (accessed June 3, 2020).

Peacock, A. C. S. *Medieval Islamic Historiography and Political Legitimacy: Balʿamiʾs Tarikhnamah*. London: Routledge, 2007.

Rosenthal, Franz. "General Introduction." In *The History of al-Tabari, Volume I: General Introduction and from the Creation to the Flood*. Trans. and ann. Franz Rosenthal. Albany: State University of New York Press, 1989.

Savant, Sarah Bowen. *The New Muslims of Post-Conquest Iran: Tradition, Memory, and Conversion*. New York: Cambridge University Press, 2013.

Shaked, Shaul. "First Man, First King." In *Gilgul: Essays on Transformation, Revolution, and Permanence in the History of Religions*. Ed. S. Shaked, D. Shulman, and G. G. Stroumsa. Leiden: Brill, 1987.

Sheʿar, Jaʿfar. *Qesseh-ye Amir al-Moʾmenin Hamzeh*. 2nd rev. ed. Tehran: Farzan, 1362/1983.

van den Berg, Gabrielle. "Demons in the Persian Epic Cycle: The *Div*/Shabrang in the Leiden *Shabrangnama* and in *Shahnama* Manuscripts." In *Shahnama Studies II: The Reception of Firdausiʾs Shahnama*. Ed. Charles Melville and Gabrielle van den Berg. 35–48. Leiden: Brill, 2011.

Williams, A. V. "Dēw." *Encyclopaedia Iranica*. 2011. Web. Available at www.iranicaonline.org/articles/dew (accessed on 7 June 2019).

Yarshater, Ehsan. "Iranian National History." In *The Cambridge History of Iran*, vol. 3. *The Seleucid, Parthian, and Sasanian Periods*. Ed. Ehsan Yarshater. Cambridge: Cambridge University Press, 1983, 359–480.

3

Globalization in Pre- and Postrevolutionary Iranian Literature: A Comparative Study of Authors inside and outside Iran

Naghmeh Esmaeilpour

> *Who was he in truth? At Tehran airport, during the inspection, he had pointed to his books and said, "I am an author. These few things—they're my own books."*
> *The officer had looked him with surprise: "An author?"*
> *He had looked at his passport to double-check and compare his first and last names with those written at the bottom of one of his books. Now what?*
> Golshiri, *Ayeneh-ha-ye Dar-dar* (5–6)

Now what? Facing this question for an author seeking to introduce Persian literature raises an internal doubt about the task of being an author. Hushang Golshiri writes the story of an author (implicitly, himself) who travels from Tehran to London to Berlin as well as other European cities in order to read his books, present the new wave of authors from the East (predominantly from Iran), and challenge the place of Persian literature within the globalized context of World Literature. Literature, for Golshiri, serves as a medium that transfers "an important moral, ethical, and cultural purpose through its sociological and psychological insight into cultures and human life."[1]

Following the same outlook toward literature, I endeavor to discuss a transformational perspective toward globalization by examining Simin Daneshvar's *Seh-ganeh-ye Sargardani* (*The Wandering Trilogy*),[2] Shahrnush Parsipur's *Asiyeh dar Miyan-e Do Donya* (*Asiyeh between Two Worlds*, hereafter *ABTW*), Shariar Mandanipour's *Censoring an Iranian Love Story* (*CILS*), and Hushang Golshiri's *Ayeneh-ha-ye Dar-dar* (*Mirrors in Doors*). The rationale for this selection is that each author helped create a new wave in Persian literature, and provides a cultural atmosphere through which we can view different groups and various parties negotiating the use of literature. I begin this chapter by first pointing to the major

---

[1] Daniel Grassian, *Iranian and Diasporic Literature in the 21st Century: A Critical Study* (Jefferson: McFarland, 2013), 2.

[2] With the manuscript allegedly lost, as claimed by its publisher, the third volume of the trilogy is yet to be published.

definitions and issues currently being debated in the sphere of globalization and then take a step forward by initiating my own approach to globalization through reading the texts. I will then assess and decipher the globalization of Persian literature through analyses of the mentioned texts. As such, I attempt to investigate how (Persian) literature, through intertextuality or at some point transfictionality,[3] transmediality,[4] and interconnectivity of textual interactions, act as a medium in the representation of a globalized world. Finally, I delve into how Persian literature has become a medium to represent and position globalization.

Viewing Globalization from Eastern and Western Perspectives

I open this discussion with definitions of globalization in Western studies, which are brought forth with respect to postmodernism, neo-capitalism, digitalization, Americanization, and consumerism. Since its popularity in the 1970s, globalization as a term and phenomenon has oscillated between two perspectives: one from above that ends in a hegemonic world and one from below, which results in a heterogeneous world (McLuhan; Robertson; Giddens; Ritzer; Kellner). Harking back to the polar definition of globalization, Richard W. Mansbach and Edward Rhodes introduced three groups or waves within globalization: Skeptics, Hyperglobalizers, and Transformationalists. Transformationalists—whose perspective most closely resembles my own—view globalization as an "unprecedented and multidimensional" process that "produces profound changes in politics and economics," and which involves "technological, cultural, security, migration, human rights, and environmental" developments and alterations. From this perspective, globalization "enable[s] people to interact with one another regardless of where they reside, and this means that global interconnectedness is among people rather than among states."[5] Glocalization is therefore an important term in this perspective,[6] as it refers to the "simultaneous presence of globalizing and

---

3   According to Thomas Bronwen, Barthes introduces a new way of looking at narratives and texts by presenting intertextuality and interpreting a text "as something that is always in process" (Thomas Bronwen, *Narrative: The Basics* [New York: Routledge, 2016], 79). Transfictionality should also be introduced as a supplement to Barthes's notion of intertextuality. For Marie-Laure Ryan, transfictionality is defined as a relation among texts or as "the migration of fictional entities across different texts" (Marie-Laure Ryan, "Transmedial Storytelling and Transfictionality," *Poetics Today* 34, no. 3 (2013): 366).

4   Transmediality, as Ryan defines it, refers to "the creation of a storyworld through multiple documents belonging to various media," such as by alluding to films, songs, newspapers and the like, in a story (Ryan, "Transmedial Storytelling," 361).

5   Richard Mansbach and Edward Rhodes, eds., *Introducing Globalization: Analysis and Readings* (London: Sage, 2013), 5, 6.

6   Ritzer and Dean define glocalization "as the interpenetration of the global and the local resulting in unique outcomes in different geographic areas." Its theory "sees individuals and local groups as important and creative agents." It emphasizes that "the world is growing more pluralistic" and "individuals and local groups have great power to adapt, innovate, and maneuver within a glocalized world" (George Ritzer and Paul Dean, *Globalization: A Basic Text* [Chichester: Wiley-Blackwell, 2015], 255).

localizing dynamics where precise boundaries between the two do not exist and where neither dominate the other."[7] Accordingly, Jack Lule considered globalization to be a set of multiple historical processes consisting "oral, script, print, electronic, and digital" media in which print media such as books, "provide more permanent media" by relating people "over distances." Globalization, for Lule, refers to "the commingling of global and local," which "is a process in which global facts take the local form."[8]

In comparison, Iranian thinker Ali Farhadi describes globalization as a process through which "the free flow of ideas, people, goods and products, services, and capital" becomes both accessible and possible. Farhadi considers globalization to have five dimensions and general categories: "economic, social and political, cultural, technological, and finally population."[9] In another instance, Masoud Ghaffari and Masoud Shahramnia define globalization "as a procedure of pressure of time and place which imposes on human beings, because of their mutual needs, to consciously become one unique global society and consequently brings along more political and geographical limitations in relation to cultural and social orders of societies." Referring to Huntington's thesis of various waves of democracy as major elements toward becoming a globalized country, they identify four periods in Iranian history for this process: The Constitutional Revolution (1905–11), the dethroning of Reza Shah in August 1941 and the nationalization of oil industry in 1959, the Islamic Revolution of 1979, and finally the presidential election of May 1997.[10] In another study, Mehdi Semati highlights the strategic importance of Iran's role in a globalized world because of its function as a vital actor in "the world energy sector."[11] For this reason, Iran's economy, its foreign policy toward regional and global states, as well as its "alleged interest in developing nuclear weapons" become crucial global issues. In Semati's analysis, "Iranian society has engaged modernity and the current wave of globalization" and has successfully "managed contradictory forces and tendencies," even though such achievements may not be apparent due to the Islamic Republic's status as a "theocratic state."[12]

My argument, springing from transformationalist perspectives, is that we inhabit a world that ought to be approached in a transnational, multicultural, and globally interdependent way. In my view, globalization can be described with the emphasis on the common structural elements that connect the countries rather than the different positions taken by states within the global structure in terms of culture, society, media,

---

[7] Richard Mansbach and Edward Rhodes, eds., *Introducing Globalization: Analysis and Readings* (London: Sage, 2013), 7.

[8] Jack Lule, *Globalization and Media: Global Village of Babel* (Plymouth: Rowman & Littlefield, 2012), 31–8, 133.

[9] Ali Farhadi, "Barrasi-ye Thahlili-ye Padideh-ye Jahani Shodan ba Tamarkoz bar Howzeh-ye Farhang [An Analytical Study of Globalization with a Focus on Culture]," *Motale>'at-e Rahbordi-ye Siyasat-gozari-ye Omumi* 2, no. 5 (1390/2009): 64.

[10] Masoud Ghaffari and Amir-Masoud Sharamnia, "Globalization and the Democratic Turn in Iran," *Journal of Humanities* 12, no. 1 (2005): 84, 89.

[11] Mehdi Semati, "Living with Globalization and the Islamic State: An Introduction to Media, Culture, and Society in Iran," in *Media, Culture and Society in Iran: Living with Globalization and the Islamic State*. Ed. Mehdi Semati (London: Routledge, 2008), 2.

[12] Ibid., 2, 3.

and governance. Thus, glocalization, transfictionality, and transmediality are key terms in the following pages. More specifically, globalization connects countries by means of cultural interactions and literature, as an example of old media, plays a vital role in this corelation. Literature allows various cultures, from disparate backgrounds and countries, to contact and relate with one another. In this sense, the globalization of literature refers to the way in which literary texts' interactions, in the manner of intertextuality or transfictionality or even transmediality, remove the boundaries between states, nations, and their cultures. Persian literature has been negotiating its place within World Literature not only through its translation and reception in other countries, but by presenting globalization in its content, and concerning both local and global cultures in glocalized fashion. In this interpretation, reading and analyzing globalization in Persian literature is equal to how stories from other parts of the world are represented in Persian works in order to broadcast general themes about humanity, religion, civilization, war, and specifically the Iranian revolution and its effect on the world order.

Persian Literature and Globalization

Omid Azadibougar raises this question in *The Persian Novel*. He asks, "what delays the globalization of Persian novels: is the problem textual and in the quality of works, is it extra-textual and in the networks that contribute to the globalization of a novelistic tradition, or is it a combination of these two factors?"[13] To answer this question, I must first present a brief sketch of the Iranian novel from its inception to the present time.

Iranian novel writing began its existence under the influence of French Romanticism. After the Second World War, and with the increasing presence of Europeans and Americans in Iranian society, Iranian novel writing was more heavily influenced by American literature.[14] Abdolali Dastgheib believes that Iranian literature (especially novels) passed through the same developmental process as Western literature.[15] Dastgheib argues that Iranian novels were at first historical, but then shifted toward more social, cultural, and political subjects, and more recently have tended to deal with stylistic and linguistic concerns.[16] In comparison, Homa Katouzian identifies modern Persian novels by their interest in, and imitation of, Western styles, thematically categorizing them into historical novels, social-critical novels, sociopolitical or sociocultural novels, as well as some religious pieces. The techniques most often used

[13] Omid Azadibougar, *The Persian Novel: Ideology, Fiction and Form in the Periphery* (Leiden: Rodopi | Brill, 2014), 1.
[14] Hassan Mirabedini, *Seyr-e Tahavvol-e Adabiyat-e Dastani va Namayeshi, 1320 ta 1332 (A Survey of the Development of Persian Fiction and Play, 1941–1953)*, vol. 2. (Tehran: Farhangestan-e Zaban va Adab-e Farsi, 1391/2012), 145.
[15] Abdolali Dastgheib, *Kalbod-shekafi-ye Roman-e Farsi (Dissecting the Persian Novel)* (Tehran: Sureh, 1393/2014), 36.
[16] Ibid., 437.

have been "critical realism" and "surrealism."[17] In another categorization, Hassan Mirabedini points to two pillars for Iranian novel writing: the influence of French, Russian, and American movements and styles on one hand, and oral and written national literature of any kind on the other, which point to the presence of glocalization in the literary field. In his view, the Persian novel is specified as a "globalized genre" that "narrates the cultural shifts and movements of Iranian society towards a modern period."[18]

To answer Azadibougar's questions from my perspective, Iranian literature becomes globalized when the style moves from expressionism to international surrealism and its content shifts from national themes and topics to more general humanistic subjects. In other words, while characters in Persian novels present traditional beliefs and customs as well as national changes—social, cultural, economic, and political—they tend to be individuals struggling to find their identity or individuality in a national context that has itself been globalized. Simply put, characters in the Persian novels under my scrutiny are not static in one place and time, but are instead in a constant state of movement from one place or time to another, thereby causing the mobility of their traditions, values, and experiences—which can be taken as a feature of globalization. In my interpretation, a novel can be termed globalized when it makes its connection with other cultures and nations by means of intertextuality, transfictionality and depicting images of a globalized world by traveling to other places and meeting new nations and traditions, rather than simply depicting a local nation. In the following sections, I attempt to present how globalization is represented and positioned within Persian literature and how literature itself acts as a medium in making globalization apparent.

Authors inside Iran

Simin Daneshvar is regarded as the first Iranian female novelist who established a new tradition of writing through the use of historical, social, cultural, and at some point critical sur/realism. She is typically known for her 1966 debut novel, *Savushun* (translated under *A Persian Requiem*). Her major work published after the Revolution is *The Wandering Trilogy* (1992 and 2001). Hushang Gloshiri is widely recognized as the leader of the so-called "modern novel," which is famous for its innovative stories and streams of consciousness by presenting irony, metaphorical language, surrealism, and an off-target style of storytelling. Golshiri's first collection of short stories was *Mesl-e Hamisheh* (*As Always*) (1968), though his first novel *Shazdeh Ehtejab* (*Prince Ehtejab*) (1968/69) propelled him to fame.

My argument is that Daneshvar endeavors to represent the Iranian intelligentsia and bourgeoisie through their concerns and crises of identity under the influence of

---

[17] Homa Katouzian, *Iran, Politics, History, and Literature* (London: Routledge, 2013), 195–6.
[18] Hassan Mirabedini, "Raf'-e Etteham az Jahan-e Dastani-ye Iraniyan dar Goftegu ba Hassan Mirabedini [Exonerating Iranians' World of Fiction: An Interview with Hassan Mirabedini]," *Iran Newspaper*, accessed 13 Esfand 1392 (March 4, 2014).

the dominant global ideologies of the time, Marxism versus capitalism, along with American neo-colonization and British imperialism, which had a deep impact on Iran and the rest of the developing world. Comparatively, Golshiri tries to address the author's identity as to why and for whom they write in order to address key questions about the role of (Persian) literature in the world, how it affects the perception of other nationalities, and how literature helps build a bridge between various cultures. In this sense, whereas Daneshvar demonstrates globalization by foregrounding predominantly global political and economic issues and their impacts on Iranian society (glocalization), Golshiri illustrates globalization by referring to the crux of immigration, authorship, and inter/national identity in the life of intellectuals who emigrate in comparison to those who remain in their country of origin by describing these matters through world as well as Persian literature (transfictionality). Equally important is the recurrence of "wandering" as a theme to highlight the confrontation, and rapid changes, experienced by Iranians and non-Iranians in the twenty-first century.

Simin Daneshvar

Daneshvar's *The Wandering Trilogy* is about the life of Hasti, a woman who works in the Ministry of Culture and Art, and her love story with two men, Morad and Salim. Hasti's family is representative of the Iranian bourgeoisie, whose concerns are money, profits, home, marriage, and so on. *Jazireh-ye Sargardani (The Wandering Island,* hereafter *TWI)* depicts the major incidents of the 1970s, while *Sareban-e Sargardan (The Wandering Cameleer,* hereafter *TWC)* does the same not only in Iran but around the globe. In both volumes, three major concerns are tackled from transcultural perspectives and through the narratives of various characters: global experiences regarding post/colonialism, democracy and revolution, the dilemma of Iranians (especially intellectuals and laypersons) in face of the confrontation between Western/Eastern ideologies, and commentary on general worldly concepts and beliefs surrounding history, society, and culture.

For example, two contradictory ideas concerning changes both within and outside of Iran are narrated by Salim and Morad in *TWI*. On the one hand, Salim believes in "yes to humanity but no to humanism. Humans, regardless of whether they support the left, the right or the centre, first of all, must be Human and have humanity. The origin of colonizing and being oppressed in third world countries [*jahan-e sevvom*] is Western humanism. Colonized countries imitate and follow the West."[19] Furthermore, his solution for developing countries (implicitly Iran) is to begin anew by focusing on "revolutionary Islam" because "we have to turn to our Islamic thought and beliefs." He mentions Tito, Nehru, Sohrevardi, and Shariati to support his argument (transfictionality and intertextuality). On the other hand, Morad believes

---

[19] Simin Daneshvar, *Jazireh-ye Sargardani* [*The Wandering Island*] (Tehran: Khvarazmi, 1372/1993), 31.

in the restoration of the people through eschewing the bourgeois lifestyle ("changing the consumption pattern"), noting that the sorrow and sadness of Iranian literature stems from "authoritarian culture, and in the current era comes out of authoritarian-colonized culture. It is for this reason that there is an illusion in reality that sometimes becomes nightmarish and sometimes seems symbolic."[20] Salim also refers to Karl Marx, Friedrich Nietzsche, Jean-Paul Sartre, Khalil Maleki, Fidel Castro, Che Guevara, among others, to make his argument more appealing (transfictionality). Since the victory of either Salim or Morad means the triumph of the group of people each represent, in my view, Daneshvar wants to inform us that Hasti (symbolizing Iranians) makes a big mistake by selecting Salim (*TWI*), while the correct choice would have been Morad (*TWC*). In this respect, Hossein Payandeh declares that Hasti's "oscillation and hesitation between Morad and Salim is a metaphor of the doubt and hesitation of a generation that has found Marxism and Islamic theosophy as two alternative ideologies for their salvation."[21]

Hasti, in comparison, states her perspectives either through her conversation with Morad and Salim or by her asides or monologues. For example, in her conversation with Salim in *TWI*, Hasti describes the current state of the world as if "a human being is passing the last stage of industrialism and informatics. Human beings move toward nihilism … this is the end of human civilization … our epoch is the era of Kafkaism. It is the representation of the depressed unconscious and impatient character of Kafka." She concludes that our age will end, as predicted by Nietzsche, "a chaotic world full of ruckus."[22] In another aside, or stream of unconsciousness, Hasti remembers her dialogue with Salim about the comparison between "Western feminism"—which "takes the man's right and gives it to the woman" and thus disturb the balance between the oppressor and the oppressed—and Eastern or Islamic feminism, using the Qur'an as a source that "upgrades women's right to become equal with the men" by giving "The right to divorce. The right of inheritance. And the right of custody." She recalls how she was deceived by these words into marrying Salim.[23] Setting aside the deceit, the very notion of Islamic feminism itself, as Daneshvar implies, is a somewhat contradictory concept that was brought into existence by the combination of rigid, traditional/Islamic thoughts with the concept of feminism as a result of cultural globalization. In both of the above examples, there are references to such global themes as humanity in informational age and feminism, which are themselves elements that represent globalization in literature.

Therefore, in countries like Iran, people are uncertain which direction to take. They can be drawn to public protest by a simple motivational slogan, only to later sneak to their homes with another: "in the morning they shout, 'Death or Mosaddeq', in the

---

[20] Ibid., 17, 24, 32, 64.
[21] Hossein Payandeh, *Gofteman-e Naqd: Maqalati dar Naqd-e Adabi* [*The Discourse of Criticism: Essays in Literary Criticism*] (Tehran, Nilufar, 1382/2003), 46.
[22] Daneshvar, *Island*, 32–4.
[23] Simin Daneshvar, *Sareban-e Sargardan* [*The Wandering Cameleer*] (Tehran: Kharazmi, 1380/2001), 82.

evening they shout 'Death to Mosaddeq.'" This can be seen as a direct consequence of "Wandering ... wandering in historical thought ... our country is a great wandering island."[24] This wandering, as Payandeh points out, is "ideological and ontological wandering of a generation who were in search of their independent identity in the 1970s."[25] Payandeh continues that Daneshvar employs "different voices for narration and Wandering in time sequences" in the novel "to spill over this Wandering to readers."[26] Consequently, Daneshvar refers not only to major historical events and their roots throughout Iranian history, but she also mentions more general problems that exist in developing countries.

Regarding literary techniques, it is also noteworthy to mention that Daneshvar employs authorial presence (postmodern features) as she and Mani are present as the real figures who cast their real-life roles as author and artist, both commenting on the actions of Hasti, Morad, and Salim. Furthermore, Daneshvar uses cinematic techniques such as cut-scenes for flashforwards or flashbacks, or montages in an Eisensteinian manner as well as dramatic tools like monologues and asides, which make her work stand as a postmodern text. Reading classic Persian poets such as Hafez and Attar, as well as new wave poets like Akhavan Sales and Nima Yushij (along with some pieces from Hasti), are examples of transfictionality that are used to describe the story world. Metaphorical meanings are also present both within the names of the characters as well as their roles. For example, "Hasti" as a name has two meanings in Persian: "existence" and "universe." Daneshvar selects this name to address two major issues that are vital in making her piece globalized. This is the reason behind the appearance of Totak, a fictional persona, to Hasti. Daneshvar, in an interview, introduces Totak as Daneshvar's own voice to "state her beliefs toward the current global issues" by making "it global and universal rather than national and spiritual."[27] I end my analysis with Daneshvar's message to all humans:

Who are you?
Totak ...
I am a messenger from your country to your conscious.
What is your message?
Love, that is the common denominator and the whole agent among all humans.
What is life?
Life is a lyric; sing it with passion. Life is a game; play it with joy. But be careful
  that the origin of life is a circulation of life and death ... Death is not the end.
Spirit is immortal.
  [...]

---

[24] Ibid., 242, 243.
[25] Payandeh, *Gofteman*, 46.
[26] Ibid., 57.
[27] Cited in Mohammad-Reza Sarshar, *Jelveh-ha-yi az Adabiyat-e Siyasi-e Emruz-e Iran* [*Aspects of Contemporary Political Literature in Iran*] (Tehran, Markaz-e Asnad-e Enqelab-e Islami, 1391/2012), 27.

Humans are equal. The whole world is the home and shelter of the human family. Do not destroy this home.[28]

Hushang Golshiri

Mirrors in Doors narrates the story of an Iranian author, Ibrahim (implicitly standing for Golshiri), who travels to Europe both to present and read his works, and to discuss major aspects of Iranian literature. This extensive journey acts as a quest for him to realize the reality of his life as an author as well as the lives of his émigré friends. Ibrahim is on a search to find an answer to his internal and external doubts regarding the position of the author in society. There are three parallel stories in this concise novel: firstly, Ibrahim's story as an author as he visits Europe and encounters Iranian exilic intellectuals (a matter of immigration and migration), engaging in conversation about the 1979 Revolution, specifically its background and consequences; secondly, Ibrahim's meeting and conversations with an old school friend, Sanam, and their discussion about the role of literature and the author in general, Persian authorship and literature in particular. In the course of their conversation, there are references to both current and classical Persian literature (intertextuality) as well as to world literature (transfictionality), along with the culture and society of the places that Ibrahim has visited; thirdly, Ibrahim's readings of his story in the form of a metafiction in which both previous concerns—Persian literature and Iran's political transformations—are revisited and narrated.

The story opens with Ibrahim's meeting with some Iranian friends who have immigrated to Europe. They arrange a gathering to relive old memories, which in turn becomes a recollection of the Iranian Revolution, the fight for democracy, and the changes that followed.[29] This remembrance of Iranian events is a historical narration of a specific period, "in order to recognize oneself and reach a better understanding of national identity."[30] It is for this reason that Ibrahim asks himself what the importance of publishing books is either here or there, and ends by asking, "Where am I from?"[31] He wandered both as an observer and traveler to where he belongs as "he had seen the long queue of East Germans and Polish in front of West Berlin's shops. These have also been wandering."

Ibrahim's wandering, much like Hasti in *The Wandering Trilogy*, continues when he arrives in Paris to present his works and meanwhile meet Sanam. Here, he appears mesmerized by famous names and places: drinks in a café once frequented by Hemingway, visits to the Louvre, Balzac's statues, the Orsay Museum, Voltaire's Statues, and Saʿedi's tombstone. Then, to demonstrate the variety of topics included

---

[28] Daneshvar, *Cameleer*, 131–2.
[29] Hushang Golshiri, *Ayeneh-ha-ye Dar-dar* [*Mirrors in Doors*] (Tehran: Nilufar, 1371/1392), 18–23.
[30] Hassan Mirabedini, *Sad Sal Dastan-Nevisi dar Iran* [*One Hundred Years of Fiction-Writing in Iran*], rev. ed., 3 vols. (Tehran: Nashr-e Cheshmeh, 1380/2001), 471.
[31] Golshiri, *Mirrors*, 6.

in his stories, he compares his work to the paintings of van Gogh. Further, he again describes his sorrow by referring to "the sketch of van Gogh's grief in black pen." Later, Ibrahim and Sanam, in a series of different conversations in various Parisian locations, discuss issues of living as an immigrant, especially an émigré author: "you should learn their language, or even think in their language, otherwise you stay out of the circle, a stranger or an offender." Elsewhere: "Human is in a place because of necessity," and "the roots that we desperately fight for should be inside ourselves, not in water and dust and customs that we have gotten used to."[32] Through these observations and comparisons, Ibrahim attempts to demonstrate "the real and internal description of social life in a specific period" by focusing on immigrants who wander so as to follow Western norms and traditions or those who stick to their own national indigenous values and customs.[33]

The second layer of *Mirrors in Doors* begins when Ibrahim reads his own works throughout his journey to both his audience and the readers. In doing so, he narrates the Iranian social, political, and cultural shifts occurring since the 1960s. He reads *Arusi* (*Wedding*)[34] and *Maryam* about a love triangle, and the traditional southern culture in wedding ceremonies. This is followed by an unpublished, and terribly dark satire. Finally, he reads *Mina*, the story of a renowned author and his relationship with an eponymous woman, detailing his struggles with writing and publication under the censorship of Savak, reflecting also on the fate of the Tudih Party of Iran.[35] The use of metafiction for narrating major issues concerning Ibrahim (or Golshiri) stands as one of the major elements that enable the text to demonstrate current methods in global novel writings. Another postmodern feature is transmediality, manifest in the reoccurrence of listening or reading the "Willow" song.[36] In various circumstances, this song is repeated as if to remind us and Ibrahim that things are headed for change. The choice of this song is noteworthy, as it contains various references to Shakespeare (*Othello*, Act IV Scene 3), William Carlos Williams ("Willow Poem"), and Hubert Parry ("Willow Song")—which can be taken as the presence of globalization.

Mirrors in Doors is a critique of those Iranian writers who have emigrated to the West but still write only about "Savak's interrogators, dusty alleys ... Café Salman in Shahabad ... the Amrabad Home." Ibrahim answers this question more fully by saying that it is unimportant "to sit on the table of Pissarro or go to Saint-Michel palace and find the same Café where Hemingway went and wrote his stories." Iranian authors—even those who have migrated and live outside Iran—are not able to write globally or win global recognition in world literature because "they have left half of their feelings and thoughts in Iran, they still feel homesick and have a nostalgia and write an elegy for Isfahan." The solution Ibrahim gives is that authors should broaden

---

[32] Ibid., 33–4, 49, 87, 102, 109, 123.

[33] Mirabedini, *One Hundred Years*, 698.

[34] Golshiri, *Mirrors in Doors*, 9–11.

[35] Ibid., 12–13, 51–86. Savak was the secret police, domestic security and intelligence service in Iran during the reign of the Pahlavi dynasty. It was established by Mohammad Reza Shah with the help of the US Central Intelligence Agency and the Israeli Mossad.

[36] Ibid., 7, 8, 24, 98, 109, 127, 148, 152.

their perspectives and see people as belonging to the world—using national themes to address global issues.[37] The task of the author, Ibrahim argues, is "writing a story to put into form the nightmare of a person, it is an attempt to remember or even document the dream that we have forgotten, and sometimes with this doing, we can present the collective nightmares,"[38] because "humanity's spirit has a thousand layers."[39] In other words, the way to globalize Persian literature is "instead of fighting with the world, reaching a peace." And "to make peace with the whole world means to awaken all details in the world from what is a part of the world and what is not."[40] To support the notion that Persian literature conveys global themes, Ibrahim mentions the Persian classics, such as Rudaki, Farokhi Sistani, Hafez, Manuchehri Damqani, and then refers to such modern authors as Nima and Hedayat,[41] much like in Daneshvar's *The Wandering Trilogy*. As Mirabedini argues, Golshiri is among those intellectuals who concern themselves with "their role as a social activist as well as the influential power of literature on the alteration in the society."[42]

Authors outside Iran

Shahriar Mandanipour, as an author of the *nouveau roman* movement, is among those contemporary Iranian authors who are pioneers in making the most effective use of existing literary techniques to develop their own method of narration and writing.[43] Mandanipour has had the chance to use Gloshiri's comments and instructions to benefit his stories and build his career as an author. He achieved global popularity by publishing *Censoring an Iranian Love Story* (2009) and *Moon Brow* (2018) in English. Shahrnush Parsipur is a fiction writer and essayist, whose works are regarded as the first instances of magical realism in Iranian novel writing. She won international acclaim for her second novel *Tuba va Ma'na-ye Shab* (*Touba and the Meaning of Night*, 1989). She is a prolific author who has thus far published eight novels including *The Blue Reason* (1994) *Shiva* (1999), and *Asiyeh between Two Worlds* (2009).

Both authors were forced to leave Iran due to their commitment to freedom of speech and rejection of censorship—issues they address extensively in their works. However, while Parsipur attempts to address the lives of the ordinary people, intellectuals, emerging authors, and the Iranian middle classes as well as the issue of immigration and the problems it can pose, Mandanipour strives to indicate how an émigré author still struggles with censorship when writing a story about the changes

---

[37] Ibid., 89, 94.
[38] Ibid., 14.
[39] Hushang Golshiri, *Barreh-ye Gomshodeh-ye Ra'i* [*The Lost Lamb of Raei*] (Tehran: Zaman, 1356/1977), 74.
[40] Golshiri, *Mirrors*, 136–7.
[41] Ibid., 103, 104, 112, 125, 130.
[42] Mirabedini, *One Hundred Years*, 418.
[43] Ibid., 1060.

occurring in Iran. To demonstrate globalization, Parsipur concentrates on retelling general facts relating to global politics and economics, and their influences on Iran (glocalization), as well as proposing a new perspective with which to view world mythologies and the new wave of Persian literature (poems and novels) along with their cautionary effects on people and the changes within Iran (transfictionality). In contrast, Mandanipour grapples with the actual act of censorship in literary texts and writing in Iran by alluding to both world and Persian literature in his description of emotions, circumstances, and events (transfictionality).

Shahrnush Parsipur

ABTW narrates the story of Asiyeh, who moves from the village to the city due to the displacement and disintegration of her family that changes her fate from being the daughter of a landowner to a maidservant who must work hard to support herself. As the title of the story shows, Asiyeh, as a representative of the working classes, struggles to choose which path is best for her: to follow her traditional religious beliefs, or accept the changes and begin a new life. The choice is thrust upon her by her employers: Maryam, Fereshteh, Victoria, Timsar Javidan (Stephan's father), and Mrs. Mozayeni, all of whom belong to various groups and hold opposing ideologies. Generally, the novel is divided into three major parts: first, historicizing Iran's condition on the verge of transformation from the Pahlavi era until the early years of the Islamic Revolution, as well as addressing the historical alterations in the world and their influences on Iran (1926–89); second, picturing the influences of the Western lifestyle on Iranians both inside the country and across the diaspora; and finally, discussing the role of literature in society. In this sense, Mirabedini designates elements that are dominant in Parsipur's works: "spiritual crisis, surrealistic perspective, mental conflicts, bourgeois lifestyle, social trends, and the consumerism environment."[44]

Historicizing the event begins with addressing the influence of the Second World War on the lives of the international community and Iran's role within it. As an example of glocalization, Asiyeh hears from Mr. Ardashes that "the Allies named Iran the Victory Bridge because it was through Iran that America sent guns and equipment to the Soviet Union."[45] This is followed by the narration of some facts about the World War, such as "draught, high costs of living, and unemployment." The Vietnam War is another international issue that Asiyeh has heard about on the Radio, and knows that her son-in-law's daughter wants to go to Vietnam as a voluntary nurse.[46] These are some general historical facts, and their influences on Iran, that Parsipur retells through conversations between Asiyeh and other characters.

---

[44] Mirabedini, *One Hundred Years*, 719.
[45] Shahrnush Parsipur, *Asiyeh dar Miyan-e Do Donya* [*Asiyeh between Two Worlds*] (Los Angeles: Sayeh, 2009), 62.
[46] Ibid., 26, 75–7.

It is worth mentioning that, in *ABTW*, the influence of the Western lifestyle among Iranians develops in two stages. The first occurs because of the presence of Americans and British people in both government and society—a kind of Westernization or as Jalal Al-e Ahmad calls it *Gharbzadegi* (*Occidentosis* or *Westoxication*). Examples of this include Sarhang Javidan's marriage to a French woman along with the Balmaske Party in his villa in northern Iran where Iranians adopt Western customs and styles, and Victoria's gambling house where the rich gather to play cards. Another example is Fereshteh, who studies English Language and Literature, adores Western culture, and is married to a man who invites British and Americans to take opium for pleasure. Moreover, after the Revolution, Fereshteh, Stephan, Maryam, and Victoria—along with the religious minorities—emigrate to Europe or the USA to live freely. For example, Fereshteh participates in various cultural, artistic, and political meetings in Paris where she enjoys her newly earned freedom. Conversely, Maryam migrates to Paris and constantly thinks about her love for Iran, questioning the real reason for her migration but ending up in the United States. Parsipur implicitly criticizes the reasons behind immigration by declaring that "Iranian immigration has happened aimlessly and everyone immigrated to wherever they could go"—while Europe is good for political and cultural activity (in this respect, similar to Iran), the USA is suitable for those who want to "improve their financial position."[47]

Above all, transfictionality in *ABTW* is based on three sources: first, Persian fables as well as the Qur'an, Chubak's *Sang-e Sabur* (*The Patient Stone*), the tales of Jamshid and Zahhak, and Yusef and Zoleykha—which Asiyeh uses to compare different stages of her life. The second refers to Western films and music such as *Tarzan*, *the Sweet Life* by Federico Fellini, and Elvis Presley, with whom "the whole Tehran" and "the whole women and girls in the world are in love."[48] Finally, there are extensive references to the *Epic of Gilgamesh*, its relation to the story of Noah, Zoroastrianism and Buddhism, and its connection to Iranian and Sumerian mythology[49]—these are used by Maryam, Fereshteh, and Stephan to describe their thoughts about life and shifts in Iran. The variety of sources and references in *ABTW* is representative of people's (both laypersons and intellectuals) search for an identity, whether national or international, to give meaning to their lives and help find their place in the world—again a sense of wandering emerges.

Equally important is the presence of metafiction in *ABTW* through which Parsipur endeavors to express her views on how literary texts become globalized, and form a part of world literature. For example, in a discussion about the new wave of poetry, it is said that a good poem must transfer "a good feeling or emotion to its readers," even though "the words have been changed" due to censorship and "ironical or metaphorical language is used" instead. Further on, "what is the purpose of writing a story?" emerges as a question, and here Parsipur reveals two answers by alluding to the socialist-realist

---

[47] Ibid., 18–19, 33–5, 70, 131, 151.
[48] Ibid., 14, 18, 38, 59, 64–5, 87, 89, 114.
[49] Ibid., 88, 90, 94, 98–101, 102–4, 114.

literature versus pure literature. For her, "pure literature deals with the hidden and unknown layer of humans' unconscious of which you cannot have a recognition if you do not know them," which makes the language "unclear and unknown for the society." Conversely, the opposing view asks, "what is the aim and benefit of writing a story if the ordinary people (commoners) cannot understand your story? For who[m] do you write?"[50] The latter group (to which Parsipur implicitly belongs) believes that, just as Charlie Chaplin movies can be understood by everyone, a story (either a novel or short story) should be written in such a way so that everyone everywhere can comprehend it—much like Golshiri's suggestions for Persian literature.

Shahriar Mandanipour

In countries like Iran writers and authors face a constant change of methods and techniques in order to be able to publish their novels. Mandanipour is "an experienced writer" who is "tired of writing dark and bitter stories," and "with all my being," he declares, "[I] want to write a love story" and publish it in his "beloved Iran." Yet he must first face "Porfiry Petrovich" to get the license of publication.[51] This is the beginning of Shahriar Mandanipour's most internationally acclaimed novel. He began his writing in Iran but, due to governmental restrictions and censorships, moved to the United States where he published *CILS* in English in 2008. Although, as James Wood states, *Censoring* "depends on translation for its being," the novel is "thoroughly Iranian, lovingly and allusively so, dense with the local reference."[52]

Mandanipour's *CILS* narrates three parallel stories by employing transfictionality, and, in structuralist terms, intertextuality. The central plot revolves around Mandanipour, a writer and character within the story, who begins his own tale of writing a love story in Iran and his confrontation with Mr. Petrovich (the detective in Dostoevsky's *Crime and Punishment*)[53] whose job it is to censor whatever is against or in opposition to Islamic rules and norms. Mandanipour's regular confrontation with Mr. Petrovich, as the chief censor who can grant certificates for publication from the Ministry of Culture and Islamic Guidance, is an example of the intertextuality or transfictionality within the novel. Through referring to the roots of censorship and the Islamic Revolution, Mandanipour reveals how difficult it is to write based on cultural norms on the one hand and governmental censorships on the other.

To portray these hardships, Mandanipour presents his attempt at writing a love story as *CILS*'s secondary plot. The love story commences with Sara's search of Sadeq Hedayat's *The Blind Owl* in a public library where Dara is a member. He hears her request and decides to play the role of the street bookseller to give her a copy of book

[50] Ibid., 76, 110.
[51] Shahriar Mandanipour, *Censoring an Iranian Love Story*, trans. Sara Khalili (London: Abacus, 2011), 9, 5, 6, 7.
[52] James Wood, "Love, Iranian Style," *The New Yorker*, June 22, 2009.
[53] Mandanipour, *CILS*, 33.

(which itself is among the books banned in Iran). When Sara begins reading *The Blind Owl* after buying it from the street bookseller (Dara), she notices some purple dots in specific pages and under particular words and sentences. She decodes them and finds a letter from Dara telling her how he fell in love with her. From this time on, as Sara and Dara embark on a virtual relationship by means of literary books, the transfictionality and transmediality reach their pitch. For instance, Sara becomes familiar with such works as *Anna Karenina*, *The Great Gatsby*, *Invisible Cities*, and the poetry of Federico García Lorca, Pablo Neruda, and Forough Farrokhzad.[54] These are the books that Dara sold as a street peddler in order to sell *The Blind Owl* to Sara.

As their love story grows in seriousness and meaning, so do the books with which they communicate. Dara asks Sara to borrow *The Little Prince*, Bram Stoker's *Dracula* (with a subsequent reference to Coppola's film *Dracula*), *Khosrow and Shirin* (which is described at length by Mandanipour through including some original poems from the book, referring not only to the art of literature but also to the significance of love for Iranians, and the attitudes of dynasties and kings towards their rule), Milan Kundra's *The Unbearable Lightness of Being* (referring to the first presence of censorship in Iranian translation, through the use of ellipses), and Henrik Ibsen's *An Enemy of the People*. An interesting example of transfictionality and transmediality is when Dara is arrested for illegally disseminating films (from both Hollywood and Europe) by the Campaign against Social Corruption. His interrogation is compared to Franz Kafka's *The Trial* and its film adaptation by Orson Wells.[55]

Another instance of the dominant transfictionality is how Mandanipour describes the time he spent "reading novels from the farthest reaches of the world—*The Soul Enchanted, David Copperfield, Moulin Rouge, Resurrection*, and … and … and had not stopped the exercise of writing … with *Great Expectations* of my future as a writer"[56] in the threshold of the 1979 Revolution following the establishment of the Islamic Republic of Iran (transfictionality). Through repeated references to George Orwell's *Animal Farm*,[57] as an example of how a democratic revolution can end, Mandanipour attempts to compare the Iranian Revolution to this novel as both cases appear to have followed the same path. The presence and repetition of *The Thousand and One Nights*, with references to its stories, also serves Mandanipour as he seeks to prolong his story—and his life as an author—by alluding to the tales.[58]

The third story (or sub-sub-plot) begins when Mandanipour repeatedly appears within Sara and Dara's love story, reporting the conditions faced by the Iranian youth in their relationships: problems of being arrested by a patrol from the Campaign against Social Corruption, or being seen by a relative.[59] Meanwhile, Sara has a suitor, Sinbad, who is rich and (like Mr. Petrovich) works for the Ministry of Culture and Islamic

---

[54] Ibid., 17.
[55] Ibid., 18–19, 20–7, 29, 70–8.
[56] Ibid., 31.
[57] Ibid., 13 and 46.
[58] Ibid., 1, 49, 101, 145, 199, 248, 266, and 277.
[59] Ibid., 41.

Guidance. Sinbad's presence, as Grassian mentions, serves to illustrate "not only the economic disparity in Iran, but also how Iran is not all that economically dissimilar to the West" because "despite its self-preservation as anti-Western, Iran is still largely a capitalistic country."[60] Such a capitalist mentality can be seen with Sara's mother, who tells her daughter that "she will never forgive" her if she falls "in love with a penniless man."[61] One snowy night, Dara decides to visit Sara's house but is arrested by the police for acting suspiciously like a robber (in this case, for hugging the wall). To release Dara from jail, Sara asks the help of Sinbad, whom she promises to marry afterwards. Finally, while Mandanipour becomes disappointed by his confrontation with Mr. Petrovich and the censors of his story, he ends the love story with Dara inviting Sara to his home. With lots of fear and brevity, Sara comes to Dara's home and for the first time they are alone in a private place. Through this, Mandanipour presents the rebellion of the young generation against the norms.[62]

Therefore, as Grassian points out, "Mandanipour concludes that these restrictions themselves encourage seemingly contradictory tendencies between romance and pornography, realism (in the text) and postmodernism (implied) and politicization and apoliticization."[63] Similar to Golishiri's comments, Grassian argues that Mandanipour attempts to demonstrate that "there is nearly always more to language than its actual meaning"—as "a hallmark of contemporary Iran."[64]

Conclusion

In this chapter, I have attempted to introduce a new approach toward reading globalization in Iranian literature by focusing on cultural globalization and following a transformationalist perspective. I argue that literature, specifically Persian literature, is globalized by employing transfictionality, transmediality, and intertextuality in connecting to other texts from various cultures and nations. Moreover, Persian literature becomes globalized by addressing such global themes as immigration, war, revolution, and identity (wandering and hesitation) with a distinctly local perspective. To search for traces of this globalization, I analyzed Daneshvar's *The Wandering Trilogy*, Parsipur's *Asiyeh between Two Worlds*, Mandanipour's *Censoring an Iranian Love Story*, and Golishiri's *Mirrors in Doors* by considering transversal and eclectic approaches.

Consequently, in my view, all of the authors in question illustrate globalization by placing the emphasis firmly on either glocalization or transfictionality. Although Daneshvar stayed and wrote in Iran until her death and Parsipur immigrated to the United States and continued her career there, they similarly address the role of women as intellectuals, artists, or authors in raising their respective societies' awareness of

---

[60] Grassian, *Iranian and Diasporic Literature*, 185.
[61] Mandanipour, *CILS* 193.
[62] Ibid., 281–93.
[63] Grassian, *Iranian and Diasporic Literature*, 176.
[64] Ibid.

upcoming transformations. Both primarily concentrate on glocalization rather than transfictionality in their works for presenting globalization. While Daneshvar's major concern is the role of global forces in shaping such developments as the universality of love, the beauty of life and equality for all in Iran, Parsipur addresses the lives of immigrants and questions the (neo)capitalist view toward life in her discussion of the difference between classical and modern literature.

In comparison, both Golshiri and Mandanipour tackle with authorship issues inside and outside of Iran along with Persian literature's place in a globalized world. As such, they tend to focus more on transfictionality than glocalization. Whereas Golshiri seeks to question identity crises for people inside and outside of their countries of origin, together with describing the role of literature in connecting people from various backgrounds, Mandanipour's main interests lie in how to present the forces and causes of his immigration as an author along with employing World Literature to serve as a medium for this purpose. In brief, from my perspective, the representation of the globalized world and the use of Persian literature as a medium to highlight these features are apparent in all of the above works. However, it should be noted that this matter is more tangible in the works of Golshiri and Mandanipour rather than in Daneshvar and Parsipur.

Bibliography

Azadibougar, Omid. *The Persian Novel: Ideology, Fiction and Form in the Periphery.* Leiden: Rodopi | Brill, 2014.

Daneshvar, Simin. *Jazireh-ye Sargardani (The Wandering Island).* Tehran: Kharazmi, 1372/1993.

Daneshvar, Simin. *Sareban-e Sargardan (The Wandering Cameleer).* Tehran: Kharazmi, 1380/2001.

Dastgheib, Abdolali. *Kalbodshekafi-ye Roman-e Farsi (Dissecting the Persian Novel).* Tehran: Sureh, 1393/2014.

Farhadi, Ali. "Barrasi-ye Thahlili-ye Padideh-ye Jahani Shodan ba Tamarkoz bar Howzeh-ye Farhang [An Analytical Study of Globalization with a Focus on Culture]." *Motale'at-e Rahbordi-ye Siasat-gozari-ye Omumi* 2, no. 5 (1390/2009): 63–96.

Ghaffari, Masoud, and Amir-Masoud Sharamnia. "Globalization and the Democratic Turn in Iran." *Journal of Humanities* 12, no. 1 (2005): 83–95.

Giddens, Anthony. *The Consequences of Modernity.* Cambridge: Polity Press, 1990.

Giddens, Anthony. *Modernity & Self-Identity.* Cambridge: Polity Press, 1991.

Giddens, Anthony. *Runaway World: How Globalization Is Reshaping Our Lives.* 2nd ed. London: Routledge, 2002.

Golshiri, Hushang. *Ayeneh-ha-ye Dar-dar (Mirrors in Doors).* Tehran: Nilufar, 1371/1992.

Golshiri, Hushang. *Barreh-ye Gomshodeh-ye Ra'i (The Lost Lamb of Raei).* Tehran: Zaman, 1356/1977.

Grassian, Daniel. *Iranian and Diasporic Literature in the 21st Century: A Critical Study.* Jefferson: McFarland, 2013.

Katouzian, Homa. *Iran, Politics, History, and Literature.* London: Routledge, 2013.

Kellner, Douglas. *Media Culture: Cultural Studies, Identity, and Politics between the Modern and the Postmodern.* London: Routledge, 2003.

Kellner, Douglas, and Meenakshi Gigi Durham. Rev. ed. *Media and Cultural Studies*. London: Blackwell, 2006.

Lule, Jack. *Globalization and Media: Global Village of Babel*. Plymouth: Rowman & Littlefield, 2012.

Mandanipour, Shahriar. *Censoring an Iranian Love Story*. Trans. Sara Khalili. London: Abacus, 2011.

Mandanipour, Shahriar. *Sharq-e Banafsheh* (*East of Violet*). Tehran: Nashr-e Markaz, 1386/2007.

Mansbach, Richard W., and Edward Rhodes, eds. *Introducing Globalization: Analysis and Readings*. London: Sage, 2013.

Mirabedini, Hassan. *Seyr-e Tahavvol-e Adabiyat-e Dastani va Namayeshi, 1320 ta 1332* (*A Survey of the Development of Persian Fiction and Play, 1941–1953*). Vol. 2. Tehran: Farhangestan-e Zaban va Adab-e Farsi, 1391/2012.

Mirabedini, Hassan. *Sad Sal Dastan-Nevisi dar Iran* (*One Hundred Years of Fiction-Writing in Iran*). Rev. ed., 3 vols. Tehran: Cheshmeh, 1380/2001.

Mirabedini, Hassan. "Raf'e Etteham az Jahan-e Dastani-ye Iraniyan dar Goftegu ba Hassan Mirabidini" [Exonerating Iranians' World of Fiction: An Interview with Hassan Mirabedini]. *Iran Newspaper*, Esfand 13, 1392 [March 4, 2014], https://cgie.org.ir/fa/news/10117.

Parsipur, Shahrnush. *Asiyeh dar Miyan-e Do Donya* (*Asiyeh between Two Worlds*). Los Angeles: Sayeh, 2009.

Parsipur, Shahrnush. *Majara-ha-ye Sadeh va Kuchak-e Ruh-e Derakht* (*The Simple and Small Adventures of the Spirit of the Tree*). Stockholm: Baran, 1999.

Payandeh, Hossein. *Gofteman-e Naqd, Maqalati dar Naqd-e Adabi* (*The Discourse of Criticism: Essays in Literary Criticism*). Rev. ed. Tehran: Nilufar, 1390/2011.

Payandeh, Hossein. *Goshudan-e Roman: Roman-e Iran dar Partow-e Nazariyeh va Naqd-e Adabi* (*Opening the Novel: Iranian Novel in Light of Literary Theory and Criticism*). Tehran: Morvarid, 1393/2014.

Ritzer, George, and Zeynep Atalay, eds. *Readings in Globalization: Key Concepts and Major Debates*. Chichester: Wiley-Blackwell, 2010.

Ritzer, George, and Paul Dean. *Globalization: A Basic Text*. Chichester: Wiley-Blackwell, 2015.

Ritzer, George, and Paul Dean. *Globalization: The Essentials*. Chichester: Wiley-Blackwell, 2011.

Robertson, Roland, ed. *Global Modernities*. London: Sage, 1995.

Robertson, Roland. *Globalization: Social Theory and Global Culture*. London: Sage, 1992.

Robertson, Roland. "Globalization: Social Theory." In *Literature and Globalization: A Reader*, ed. Liam Connell and Nicky Marsh. 23–9. London: Routledge, 2011.

Ryan, Marie-Laure. "Transmedial Storytelling and Transfictionality." *Poetics Today* 34, no. 3 (2013): 361–88.

Sarshar, Mohammad-Reza. *Jelveh-ha-yi az Adabiyat-e Siyasi-e Emruz-e Iran* (*Aspects of Contemporary Political Literature in Iran*). Tehran: Markaz-e Asnad-e Enqelab-e Islami, 1391/2012.

Semati, Mehdi. "Living with Globalization and the Islamic State: An Introduction to Media, Culture, and Society in Iran." In *Media, Culture and Society in Iran: Living with Globalization and the Islamic State*, ed. Mehdi Semati, 1–13. London: Routledge, 2008.

Thomas, Bronwen. *Narrative: The Basics*. London: Routledge, 2016.

Wood, James. "Love, Iranian Style." *The New Yorker*, June 22, 2009. Web. Available at www.newyorker.com/magazine/2009/06/29/love-iranian-style (accessed June 2, 2020).

4

Contemporary Persian Literature and Digital Humanities

Laetitia Nanquette

In this chapter, I use the data of *Khaneh-ye Ketab* ("Iran Book House") to analyze the production of books within Iran after the 1979 Revolution and its ties to politics. This analysis is an example of how the methods of digital humanities can be used to understand aspects of a literature that has not often been its object of study. While several projects have been successful in classical Persian literature in this field, contemporary literature has mostly been left out of digital humanities, partly because of the difficulty to access reliable data since the 1979 Revolution. The use of digital humanities firmly anchors this chapter in reflections on world literature. By reading contemporary Persian literature with numbers and on a large scale, it contributes to the branch of World Literature debates that uses "distant reading" to bring about new ways to think about the literary.

I do a quantitative study of book production to give precise figures to phenomena that are often only sketched. Contrary to Western markets, where sales are easily traceable, there are no reliable statistics on sales in Iran and no centralized database. In addition, the government is an important buyer of certain categories of books, which disrupts the sales number. The most reliable data we have on the Iranian market is thus the publication of books, before the sales. The study will confront practice to discourse on these publications, the one I have been exposed to when doing fieldwork in the literary field in Iran. To preserve the anonymity and safety of my interviewees, I do not quote them as such. This chapter will thus confirm some ideas, for example the ebb and flow of publications according to politics, and will contradict some, for example that governmental publishers publish a higher quantity of texts than independent ones.

I use Iran Book House (IBH) as the primary source for understanding the production of books within Iran. One must bear in mind that because IBH is a semi-governmental institute, it does not take into consideration some books that are produced outside of the official networks and that do not get an ISBN, that is, all books published underground forming the black and gray book markets. I will explain later that underground publications are scarce. I use three sets of data, all related to IBH, and compare them to determine how the production of literature works in postrevolutionary Iran.

In this chapter, my findings insist on the link between books' production and who is in government; the decline of the number of books published over the years since 1979; the decreasing number of translations versus original texts; the increased centralization of book production in Tehran; and the relative minority of governmental publishers compared to independent publishers.

Method and Resources

In many Western countries, the most reliable data on the production of books over a certain period would come from national libraries. In Iran, although the National Library is also a valid resource, the most reliable data on contemporary books are provided by IBH, which is a semigovernmental institute, officially established in 1996.[1] Why is it so? Before getting a permission for distribution, each publisher must hand out two copies of the book, one to the Ministry of Culture and Islamic Guidance, and one to Iran Book House. IBH is the institute that receives physically all the books that have been published, checks them, and logs them. It also copies a few pages of each book and archives them. IBH is thus the primary source for understanding the production of books within Iran. While the National Library mainly serves book professionals and researchers, IBH aims to inform a wider audience. It thus also publishes journals, in addition to their daily updated website, and runs cultural events including Iran's Book of the Year Awards, the Parvin Etesami Literary Award, and the Jalal Al-e Ahmad Literary Award. IBH has also been the Iranian representative for the International Standard Book Number (ISBN) since 1994. An ISBN is assigned to each edition and variation (except reprints) of a book. IBH gives ISBNs to publishers depending on their activity; for example, to a big publisher, it might give a package of a hundred ISBNs. In this way, publishers do not have to be in touch with IBH for each book they publish.

In this chapter, I use three resources: the first one is a report that IBH published in 2016 on statistics of book publishing in all categories between 1980 and 2016, on the occasion of the publication of one million books since the 1979 Revolution.[2] They updated the report and published an English version of it in 2017.[3] I am using both the English and the Persian versions. The second are data that I have obtained directly from the IBH for literature books. They are in the form of Excel files, containing all information on books in the category of literature only, for this period. The third is the report *Writer's Block: The Story of Censorship in Iran*, written by the independent Small Media,[4] a UK-based institute that defines itself as an "action lab, providing

---

[1] Faramarz Masoudi, "Interview with Hamidreza Nowrouzpour," *Ketab-e Mah-e Kolliyat*, vol. 11, October 1998.
[2] Majid Gholami Jaliseh, "Amar-e Nashr-e Ketab dar Iran: 1358–1393 [Statistics of Book Publications in Iran: 1980–2015]" (Tehran: Khaneh-ye Ketab, 1394/2016).
[3] Majid Gholami Jaliseh, Mojtaba Tabriznia, and Esmaeil Afghahi, *The Statistics of Books in Iran: Statistical Data of Book Publishing in Iran from 1979 to 2016* (Tehran: Khaneh-ye Ketabe, 1395/2017).
[4] James Marchant, *Writer's Block: The Story of Censorship in Iran* (London: Small Media Publication, 2015).

digital research, training and advocacy solutions to support the work of civil society actors that provides assistance to at-risk communities globally." Small Media have also worked on the database of IBH, but because they do not have direct access to Iran, their method was to scrap the data from the IBH website. Small Media's report, like the IBH one, is also focused on books in all categories, not only literature. I thus have two resources that have data on the whole of book production, and one that is only on literature book production. I contend that the production in literature does not differ enough from the whole of the production for this difference in the resources to be an issue when comparing them. However, this variety needs to be remembered when analyzing the particularities of my sources.

I compare these three resources, concentrating on the link between the production of books and who is in government; the decline of the number of books published over the years since 1979; the decreasing number of translations versus original texts; the increased centralization of book production in Tehran; and the relative minority of governmental publishers compared to independent publishers.

Digital Humanities and Contemporary Persian Literature

Before I get into the analysis of book production, I need to reflect first on the construction of the data, and second on the place of this kind of analysis in Iranian Studies. The Small Media report is accessible online, and the published report *Statistics of Book Publications in Iran* is not accessible outside of Iran and difficult to access within Iran. However, it is possible to get it in IBH or at the yearly Tehran Bookfair where they have a stand. The co-author of *Statistics of Book Publications in Iran*, Esmaeil Afghahi, helped me get access to the data in the form of Excel files of IBH.[5] It contains between ten and thirteen variables depending on the years: title of the book, writer, publisher, translator, subcategory, original versus translation, Dewey classification, number of pages, number of reprints, number of copies, price, province of publisher, and details about the publisher. In digital humanities, it is important not to "deny the critical and interpretive activities that construct that data and digital record and make them available for analysis."[6] In this case, one can see some variables are not included every year. There is also the issue of selecting "literature" as a category in a large database, with a potential for error, although they follow the Dewey classification, which is standard. As for the construction of the large database itself, I do not know about the processes in place, nor the criteria for selecting books under certain categories, for example. It is also important to remember that we are dealing with contemporary resources and data, which are constantly evolving. It is not an archive, fixed in library

[5] I would like to thank PhD candidate Elham Naeej for introducing him to me, and Esmaeil Afghahi for his help. This research was supported under the Australian Research Council's Discovery Projects funding scheme (project number DE150100329).
[6] Katherine Bode, *A World of Fiction: Digital Collections and the Future of Literary History* (Ann Arbor: University of Michigan Press, 2018), 20.

bookshelves. This evolution should be remembered, especially when we are studying the most recent years.

A part of my argument in this chapter is that because the three resources largely overlap and confirm each other, the minor inconsistencies between them are negligible. It is particularly important to note that Small Media and the two resources from IBH come from opposite political sides. The fact that their readings of the data overlap nonetheless is testimony to its validity, as well as to the relative accuracy of the construction of the data.

Studying within a framework of digital humanities, defined here for my purpose as the use of computational methods for humanities disciplines, is relatively recent in Iranian Studies. Persian digital humanities focus on educational and research resources to make available texts of Persian literature, usually classical texts, including manuscripts or visual texts. An important part of this work relates to collecting and digitizing. This is the case of the Roshan Initiative in Persian Digital Humanities at the University of Maryland, as well as other initiatives around the world, including major libraries like the Library of Congress. There are also interesting publications on text mining, comparing for example lines of classical poems. Concerning contemporary Iran, most resources are within Iran, for example the University of Tehran's *Hamshahri* collection, which collects the data of the newspaper *Hamshahri*. As far as contemporary Persian literature goes, the only project that I know of is "Persian, Translated" by Alireza Taheri Araghi, who started collecting titles of Persian books translated into English and published.[7] Just like the rest of digital humanities, which started with archiving of texts, digitization programs, and the creation of textual corpora for large-scale analysis, digital Persian literature has primarily achieved results in these areas. This chapter uses a method that has thus not been used in the field of contemporary Persian literature to offer new perspectives. To this aim, it is combined with methods of book history, which studies the creation, circulation, and reception of printed texts. I show that using these methods allows us to tell different stories from the ones told by traditional literary methods. The method used here gives us access to information critical if we want to understand the Iranian literary field, which would otherwise be inaccessible.

A major reason for this lack of information is the difficulty of accessing resources in Iran. Whereas libraries are easily accessible, I accessed the report of the IBH by chance, after having looked for their CDs, which they used to produce in the 2000s, but did not anymore in the 2010s. Access to the Excel spreadsheet was also dependent upon chance and a kind student who helped me to find the right person, himself willing to help a researcher. Such reliance on encounters and fieldwork chance, although at the basis of my work on contemporary Persian literature, is not applicable to all topics and periods, and is dependent upon the possibility to travel to Iran. I have slowly constructed this possibility and the networks in the literary field in Iran over the past 15 years, and rely on them for such work.

7　Alireza Taheri Araghi, "Persian, Translated," www.persiantranslated.wordpress.com, accessed June 20, 2020.

Literary Production and Its Ties to Governments

Literary practitioners in Iran often mention the years of president Mohammad Khatami's term of office as a golden age for publishing, and criticize the periods preceding and following it. How does this compare with the data on the topic? The IBH report states that literary production increases and decreases according to governments.[8] According to the report, in the early years of the Islamic Republic and during the war with Iraq, book production was low. It reached a peak during President Khatami's government, while during President Ahmadinejad's presidencies, there was a decrease. Data for Rouhani's presidencies show a small increase but are too few to be interpretable.[9] This evolution is also what Small Media reports in its analysis.[10]

Figure 4.1 shows the evolution of the total market volume – that is, the total number of books published (book titles from Figures 4.2 and 4.3 multiplied by the number of copies from Figure 4.4) – according to both Small Media and the IBH. One can see that the Ali Khamenei presidency, which also coincided with the war against Iraq, was a period of stagnation for book production. Ali-Akbar Hashemi Rafsanjani's presidency, a conservative presidency, saw an increase. It can be noted that whereas the liberal Khatami was his Minister of Culture and Islamic Guidance for a time, Rafsanjani also had two other conservative Ministers during his presidency. It is only with Khatami's presidencies that production boomed. The reformist period had "a policy known as 'open doors,' when the books received a permanent publishing license, some large publishers were allowed to be responsible for their own books and some permanent publishing licenses were issued to certain publishers."[11] There was a decrease with Ahmadinejad's first presidency, which banned altogether some writers, without allowing their books to go through the process,[12] and then another decrease at the beginning of his second term in 2009, which saw massive upheavals in the country with an important impact on literary life. Actors in the sector mention *ketabsazi* (literally, "building books," that is, making up books) as a factor to take into consideration when counting books during Ahmadinejad's presidencies.[13] This would allow the IBH to count as books some texts that should usually not be included, for example academic theses or a collection of academic articles. Such books would scarcely make a contribution to the book market but the strategy has been used so as to keep face and counterargue to those who said book publication decreased dramatically during Ahmadinejad.[14] Figure 4.1 includes data according to the IBH report, which adds a couple more years of data from Rouhani's presidency (up to 2016), indicating

---

[8] Gholami Jaliseh, Tabriznia, and Afghahi, *The Statistics of Books*, 18.
[9] Ibid., 18.
[10] Marchant, "Writer's Block," 9.
[11] Gholami Jaliseh, Tabriznia, and Afghahi, *The Statistics of Books*, 19.
[12] Marchant, "Writer's Block," 17.
[13] Ibid., 42; Afshin Shahneh Tabar, email interview with author, May 27, 2014.
[14] Marchant, "Writer's Block," 17.

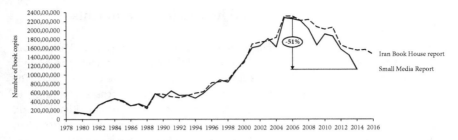

Figure 4.1 Market volume.

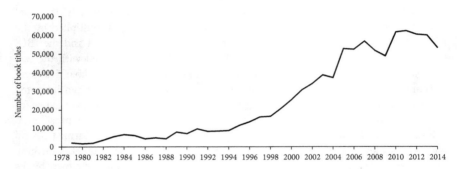

Figure 4.2 Number of book titles produced per year according to Small Media.

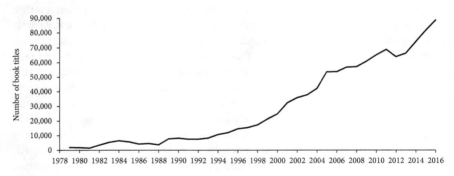

Figure 4.3 Number of book titles produced per year according to Iran Book House.

a small increase in publications since. One can see the curves from the two reports are very similar, apart from a few discrepancies in the last years, maybe due to errors in data extraction. The fact that they are identical, although they could have different agendas in producing the figures due to their different political belongings, is a sign that the data is solid.

Number of Books Published versus Number of Copies per Book

Literary practitioners in Iran say that the number of copies per book published is now at a ridiculously low number, but that this was not always the case. What do the numbers tell us? Figures 4.2 and 4.3 show the numbers of books published per year. An important aspect to remember is that the number of copies is a different matter altogether. There has indeed been a huge decline in the number of copies published per book in the last decades. Whereas it used to be an average of 8,000 copies in the early years of the Islamic Republic, a standard number in the late 2010s is around 1,500 copies. Figure 4.4 gives the average number of copies per book and confirms this drastic decline.[15]

Although this decline does not explain everything, the fact that the price for books has increased drastically, in a shrinking economic space, might be one reason. For example, between 2011 and 2014, the price of a book doubled in a period of four years.[16] It is difficult to assess price augmentation, nonetheless, because inflation has been high in the last forty years for all consumer goods and services. The Central Bank of Iran notes there has been a rise in products of 100 percent during the same period.[17] The rise of e-books and the absence of copyright laws are other factors explaining this decrease, which I will not detail here.

Categories of Books Published

Opinions vary on which categories of books are most published among literary practitioners, although many mention that Religion is very high, a lot higher than Literature. The IBH mentions Religion coming first with 17 percent of publications,

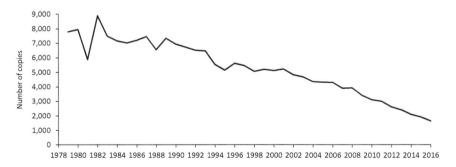

Figure 4.4 Average number of copies produced per book title per year.

---

15 Gholami Jaliseh, Tabriznia, and Afghahi, *The Statistics of Books*, 34.
16 Gholami Jaliseh, "Statistics," 14.
17 "Nerkh-e Tavarrom va Shakhes-e Baha-ye Kala-ha va Khadamat-e Masrafi [Inflation Rate and Consumer Price Index for Goods and Services]," Bank-e Markazi-ye Jomhuri-ye Islami-ye Iran, accessed June 20, 2020.

then Children and Young Adult literature as well as Applied Sciences both at 14 percent, and literature 13 percent.[18] Literature is thus relatively important compared to the other categories.

Gender of Literary Practitioners

While I have not done a comparison with the gender of writers from the spreadsheets I have, since this would require assigning a gender to hundreds of thousands of names, it is interesting to use Small Media's report on how the categories of books compare to the gender of writers, which seems to be a general appreciation, as they do not seem to have organized their data according to gender either. According to Small Media's report:

> Women are most prolific in the sphere of literature; it is in this field that they comprise the greatest proportion of active authors. The proportion of women that have published works in the fields of technology and natural sciences is fairly similar to that of men … The least women-friendly genre is religion. Women face numerous obstacles in climbing the ranks of the clergy, and make up just a small contingent of the seminaries in Qom and Mashhad. As a result, male writers are responsible for much of Iran's religious output.[19]

This is interesting to compare to a general sense that women are active as literary writers, as argued by journalists like Nazila Fathi: "Over the past decade, Iran's best-selling fiction lists have become dominated by women, an unprecedented development abetted by recent upheavals in Iranian society."[20] She adds that women publish as much as men in today's Iran, "but the women's books are outselling the men's by far." Although Fathi does not confirm this with data, this is the perception in the field, maybe because suddenly women becoming active in the field makes them hyper-visible. Iranian Student's News Agency, a governmental institution, reports that in the best-selling books over a fourteen-year period, the top three are by women. In the forty-seven books ranked, twenty are by women and twenty-seven by men.[21]

Whereas women writers thus seem to be important in terms of numbers and reputation, this is not the case for other literary practitioners like publishers. IBH's revised report in English does not have statistics about the gender of the writers but about the gender of the publishers: "The female directors have published 13% of the books."[22] It is indeed a very small number.

---

[18] Gholami Jaliseh, Tabriznia, and Afghahi, *The Statistics of Books*, 21.
[19] Marchant, "Writer's Block," 29.
[20] Nazila Fathi, "Women Writing Novels Emerge as Stars in Iran," *The New York Times* (June 29, 2005).
[21] Iranian Student's News Agency, "Guzaresh az Roman-ha-ye Por-forush-e Iran dar 14 Sal-e Gozashteh [Report on Bestselling Novels in Iran during the Past 14 Years]," *ISNA* (August 25, 2006), accessed June 20, 2020.
[22] Gholami Jaliseh, Tabriznia, and Afghahi, *The Statistics of Books*, 85.

Translation versus Original

The issue of translated texts versus texts in Persian is a fraught one, as it relates to issues of dependency on foreign markets and foreign languages, and on the quality of the local production compared to the foreign one. Therefore, it is crucial to get the numbers right. There is no doubt that Iran publishes many translations. But so do a lot of non-English-speaking Western countries. Gisèle Sapiro says that in the late 1990s, the percentage of translated texts was "15–18% in France and Germany, 25% in Italy and Spain, 40% in Greece."[23] In literature, France publishes as much as 35 percent of translations: "English is far and away the most translated language: it represents two-thirds of the books translated into French."[24]

I have shown elsewhere, based on the UNESCO database *Index Translationum*, that English is the most translated language in Iran, with some 7,981 translations between 1979 and 2011, significantly more than French and Arabic, which account for only around 700 translations each. Despite the official rhetoric of the Islamic government against its American counterpart and against imperialism, including cultural imperialism (*tahajom-e farhangi*), Iranian market trends are in accordance with American and English-speaking cultural dominance across the globe, as most of the translations into Persian of foreign-language texts are from English. In the same 30-year period, however, there have been only 350 translations from Persian in the US.[25]

Because of the dominance of the book market in English, it is now a global fact that all literatures translate a lot of English books. The fact that Iran, which is isolated somewhat from the global book market, follows similar trends, is interesting in itself. Its isolation is not to the point where it would only publish local literature.

What is maybe more important is to look at the evolution of the field of translation. Have there been significant changes in the proportion of translations versus originals? Figure 4.5 from IBH shows the increase in the number of publications of original books compared to translations over the years.[26] Whereas in 1994, there were around one third of translations versus two thirds of originals, in 2015, there are around 19 percent of translations versus 81 percent of originals. The production of books in Persian has increased four times more rapidly than that of the translations in a thirty-year period. Is it due to policies that aimed to minimize cultural imperialism? Is it a consequence of the *ketabsazi* of the two Ahmadinejad governments (2005–13) and the fact that most of the books of concern to *ketabsazi*, like academic theses, except for those in language studies, are in Persian? The IBH report warns against the possibility that this data might be difficult to analyze as originals include "all the compilations, collections, poetry and etc."[27]

---

[23] Gisèle Sapiro, "Translation and Symbolic Capital in the Era of Globalization: French Literature in the United States," *Cultural Sociology* 9, no. 3 (2015): 6.

[24] Sapiro, "Translation," 6.

[25] Laetitia Nanquette, "The Translations of Modern Persian Literature in the United States: 1979–2011," *The Translator* 23, no. 1 (2017): 3–4.

[26] Gholami Jaliseh, Tabriznia, and Afghahi, *The Statistics of Books*, 26.

[27] Ibid., 27.

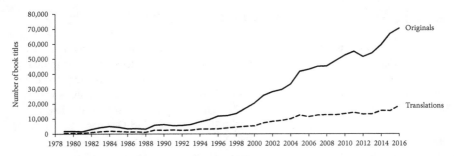

Figure 4.5 Number of book titles produced per year per type, originals versus translations.

This data seems contradictory with the discourse in the field about the increase of the role of translations in literature. Indeed, when one works on fiction and browses bookshops, one is always struck by the fact that foreign fiction titles seem more numerous than Persian ones.

I compare this graph to the data for the category of literature I have gathered from IBH, bearing in mind that the comparison does not look at the same data, since IBH's report is for the whole of book publications, not literature only. In my data for literature, I look at two years: In 1983 (1361), there were 276 translations versus 490 originals, which means 37 percent of translation. In 2003 (1381), there were 5,556 originals versus 1,741 translations, that is, 24 percent of translation. This comparison confirms the data for the whole of publications: there are more originals than translations in recent years than there were forty years ago. This increase of originals contradicts parts of the discourse of literary practitioners, who insist that translations are an increasing part of the market.

Centralization of the Production

Iran is very centralized. During my fieldwork, I myself have mostly spent time in Tehran, and a bit in Shiraz. This is because all the literary events and all the main publishers are in the capital. I have chosen to analyze the centralization of the books' production on a given year to give an idea of the number of books published per year. IBH reports that although Tehran has always been the central point of publication, it has become increasingly so. The following graph confirms this argument.[28] "The publication of books in Tehran increases compared to all the other cities, and this gap has widened in the recent years."[29]

---

[28] Gholami Jaliseh, Tabriznia, and Afghahi, *The Statistics of Books*, 28.
[29] Ibid., 29.

The curve in the regular line shows the production in Tehran and the one in dotted line in the provinces. Without the productions from Qom and Mashad, which are religious centers and thus account for a lot of religious texts, the production in provincial cities would be insignificant.

I compare these data to the spreadsheet for the year 2012 (1391). For a total of 13,245 books published, 9,957 were published in Tehran, that is, 75 percent. Although my data only contain books categorized as literature, the cities coming just after Tehran are cities where religious books are dominant, Qom and Mashad. The category of literature is large enough to include literary texts with religious elements, but it excludes the vast production of Qur'anic exegesis, biographies of Islamic figures, or Islamic commentaries. Therefore, it might look different with the whole of book

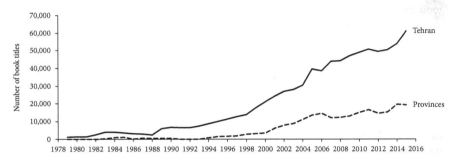

Figure 4.6 Number of book titles produced per year per production location.

Table 4.1 Number of Books Published per City for the Year 2012

Tehran	9,957
Qom	991
Mashad	518
Tabriz	197
Esfahan	164
Rasht	144
Shiraz	138
Karaj	125
Qazvin	80
Kashan	56
Kerman	49
Sari	47
Semnan	45
Sanandaj	43
Zanjan	41

production. The next major cities, Tabriz, Isfahan, Rasht, Shiraz, and Karaj, only publish fewer than 200 books per year. I have not included the cities publishing less than 40 books per year.

Small Media, which considers all categories of books, says that 76 percent of titles printed since the 1979 Revolution have been produced in Tehran,[30] thus its number is very close to mine, although it looks at the whole of the period, while I look at one year only.

Why is centralization important to consider? Small Media rightfully notes that the "massive centralisation of production wouldn't be such a big deal if Iran had an effective distribution network to carry regionally-published books to the rest of the country, but the necessary infrastructure is concentrated almost exclusively in the capital."[31] The centralization of the production is indeed a concern, since it is not compensated by good distribution networks. De facto, it means that the provinces of Iran get scant access to new publications.

Are the Publishers Independent or Governmental?

Small Media notes that the most prolific publishers are not, maybe contrary to expectations, religious and governmental publishers, but academic publishers. The field of textbooks and universities publications is huge.[32] The *konkur*, the entry examination to university, is crucial to the higher education system and represents a whole industry in itself, with specialist publishers like Mobtakeran and Gaj competing for the market. The data I have include the category of literature only, so they do not take into account academic textbooks; however, one of the five most prolific publishers that Small Media underlines, Mobtakeran, is also a top ten in publishing literary books in the spreadsheets from IBH, so it overlaps with my data. Mobtakeran was established in 1986, and its stated aim is to increase scientific awareness. It is also heavily involved in educational activities pre- and post-university, with a math Olympiad and scientific workshops.

The IBH report clearly shows that most of the books published are published by independent publishers. Today, this is in a relation of one to seven.[33]

It is important to bear in mind that independent publishers are not always entirely independent from the government. For example, during some periods, most publishers got paper supplies from the government, which was an important financial contribution. It is also common for independent publishers to receive some direct funding from the government occasionally; however, this issue is difficult to investigate, because an independent publisher, who builds its credentials on its independence

---

[30] Marchant, "Writer's Block," 43.
[31] Ibid., 44.
[32] Ibid., 41.
[33] Gholami Jaliseh, Tabriznia, and Afghahi, *The Statistics of Books*, 78.

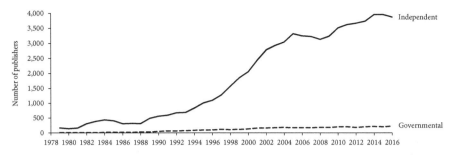

Figure 4.7 Number of publishers per type.

from the government, would not want such help to be known about. Therefore, it is important not to draw a strict line between the two categories.

These data clearly show that independent publishers are in a very large majority compared to governmental publishers. It is true that some governmental publishers are enormous in size thanks to the support they get, like Sureh-ye Mehr, the publishing press of the Howzeh-ye Honari, but most of the production in terms of numbers is done by independents. IBH says, "even though the state-run publishers benefit from state budgets and generally do not rely on the income of their book sales, overall they cover for 12 percent of the book market."[34] This somehow contradicts a recurrent discourse among scholars and literary practitioners working on contemporary Iranian literature, which insists that independent publishers are in a minority and always struggling. The data prove, on the contrary, that although they do not really struggle because they do not need to abide by the law of the market since they are given money from the government, governmental publishers are a minority in terms of numbers and that most book production comes from independent publishers. The independent publishers, on the other side, lack political support and can thus be considered as marginalized.

Underground Publications and Self-Publishing

One could argue that underground publications come to disrupt this analysis and that not taking them into account does not give a complete view of the field. It is true that underground publications are there, sometimes quite visibly, especially in the publishing area around the University of Tehran in the center of the capital. However, my fieldwork led me to the conclusion that it is quite a small proportion of publications. It is not prestigious, and it is expensive since writers have to pay for publication themselves. It is important to clarify that I am discussing here new underground

[34] Ibid., 83.

publications only. The reprints in cheap paper for a lower price of previously published texts compose an important part of the book market, but it is outside of my analysis in this chapter. Mohamad Zenderu, a member of the Tehran Publishers and Bookshops Union, states that the practice of *khod-nasheri* ("self-publishing") or *nasher-mo'allef* can be divided into three types:[35]

- A writer gets a publishing permit from the Ministry of Culture and Islamic Guidance and publishes the book without having a publisher involved. There is no publisher's name for this type of books. Such books are often published by organizations and institutions that do not specialize in publishing.
- Writers pay fully or partly the expenses to a publisher.
- The writers publishes their book online, which does not require permission from the Ministry of Culture and Islamic Guidance but follows the rules of the censorship of the internet. I have detailed this aspect of publications somewhere else.[36]

While I expected more books to be published underground given the restrictions to publication, underground publishing is a marginal segment. There are significant numbers of self-publishing houses, but they do not publish large quantities of books and often come and go. Their very number contributes to the issues faced in the whole field by publishers who criticize its lack of professionalism. The Persian version of the IBH report states that in the ten years between 1993 and 2014, 3,584 self-publishers have published one book, while only 10 have published more than 50 books.[37]

Conclusion

Where is book production going? The data I have for literary publishing only go to 2015, meaning the first two years after Rouhani's first presidency, which is too scarce to give definitive answers; but there seems to be an increase of publications. However, what actors in the field have told me and what I have noticed during several fieldwork trips since 2013 is that publications have not increased as much as anticipated despite the reformist presidency of Rouhani. This might be due to the fact that *ketabsazi* has gone down but expectations of a booming of the cultural field after Rouhani were certainly not met. In general, only the Khatami years were overly positive for literary production.

This chapter is an example of the possibility to use methods and ideas from digital humanities and book history in the analysis of contemporary Persian literature. It also situates contemporary Persian literature in debates that use "distant reading" and

---

[35] Mohammad Zendehru, "Khod-Nasheri, Asib ya Tahavvol?" *Ketab-e Hafteh* (Dec 23, 2014).
[36] Laetitia Nanquette, "Iranian Literary Blogs: Towards a Globalization of Contemporary Iranian Literature?" in *The Edinburgh Companion to the Postcolonial Middle East*, ed. Anna Ball and Karim Mattar (Edinburgh: Edinburgh University Press, 2019), 383–406.
[37] Gholami Jaliseh, "Statistics," 102.

numbers to think about the literary—and world literature. Studying different resources all devoted to books' production has allowed to give verifiable and cross-checkable answers. These resources, all coming from Iran Book House, have been selected and treated in different ways, and by two different institutions that have very different aims and agendas in publicizing them. The fact that they nonetheless overlap makes us confident in their validity in helping us to understand several elements in the field: the link between book production and who is in government in the postrevolutionary era; the decline of the number of books published over the years since 1979; the decreasing number of translations versus original texts; the increased centralization of book production in Tehran; and the relative minority of governmental publishers compared to independent publishers.

I hope that the conclusions in this chapter encourage other scholars to undertake work that uses resources more varied than literary texts to understand the contemporary Iranian literary field. I believe that having a broad view of the field and using a variety of sources is key to understanding it in all its complexities.

Bibliography

Bank-e Markazi-ye Jomhuri-ye Islami-ye Iran. "Nerkh-e Tavarrom va Shakhes-e Baha-ye Kala-ha va Khadamat-e Masrafi [Inflation Rate and Consumer Price Index for Goods and Services]." Web. Available at www.cbi.ir/Inflation/Inflation_FA.aspx (accessed June 20, 2020).

Bode, Katherine. *A World of Fictions: Digital Collections and the Future of Literary History*. Ann Arbor: University of Michigan Press, 2018.

Fathi, Nazila. "Women Writing Novels Emerge as Stars in Iran." *New York Times*, June 29, 2005. Web. Available at www.nytimes.com/2005/06/29/books/29wome. html?pagewanted=all&_r=2& (accessed June 20, 2020).

Gholami Jaliseh, Majid. "Amar-e Nashr-e Ketab dar Iran: 1393–1358 [Statistics of Book Publications in Iran: 1980–2015]." Tehran: Khaneh-ye Ketab, 1394/2016.

Gholami Jaliseh, Majid, Mojtaba Tabriznia, and Esmaeil Afghahi. *The Statistics of Books in Iran. Statistical Data of Book Publishing in Iran from 1979 to 2016*. Tehran: Khaneh-ye Ketab, 1395/2017.

ISNA. "Gozaresh az Roman-ha-ye Por-forush-e Iran dar 14 Sal-e Gozashteh [Report on Bestselling Novels in Iran during the Past 14 Years]," August 25, 2006. Web. Available at https://bit.ly/3e7eiZz (accessed June 20, 2020).

Marchant, James. "Writer's Block: The Story of Censorship in Iran." Small Media Publication, 2015.

Masoudi, Faramarz. "Interview with Hamidreza Nowrouzpour." *Ketab-e Mah-e Kolliyat*, vol. 11, October 1998.

Nanquette, Laetitia. "Iranian Literary Blogs: Towards a Globalization of Contemporary Iranian Literature?" In *The Edinburgh Companion to the Postcolonial Middle East*, ed. Anna Ball and Karim Mattar, 383–406. Edinburgh: Edinburgh University Press, 2019.

Nanquette, Laetitia. "The Translations of Modern Persian Literature in the United States: 1979–2011." *The Translator* 23, no. 1 (2017): 49–66.

Sapiro, Gisèle. "Translation and Symbolic Capital in the Era of Globalization: French Literature in the United States." *Cultural Sociology* 9, no. 3 (2015): 1–27.

Shahneh Tabar, Afshin, email interview with Laetitia Nanquette, May 27, 2014.

Taheri Araghi, Alireza. "Persian, Translated," https://persiantranslated.wordpress.com/.

Zendehru, Mohammad. "Khod-Nasheri: Asib ya Tahavvol? [Self-Publishing: Damage or Transformation?]" *Ketab-e Hafteh*, Nov. 23, 2014.

Part Two

Traveling Texts

5

Genres without Borders: Reading Modern Iranian Literature beyond "Center" and "Periphery"

Marie Ostby

In the first stanza of the Iranian poet Simin Behbahani's 1995 *ghazal* "Zamin Koravi Shekl Ast" ("The World is Shaped Like a Sphere"), the speaker casts immediate doubt on the division of the world, and perhaps literature, into Western and Eastern spheres by pondering the visual relativism of a globe.[1] She writes: "You can't take your bearings from a globe, / if with the flick of a finger you can make it turn this way and that":

جهت نتوانی جُست ز اطلس جغرافی

به زخم سرانگشتش جهت چو بگردانی

"Mocking the artificiality and arbitrariness of dividing humanity into East and West," as the poem's co-translator Kaveh Safa writes, "this globally oriented poem suggests how porous and flexible national and cultural borders are."[2]

In a recent article, Jahan Ramazani evaluates whether this poem should be considered "an example of world literature" through the prism of its translatability. The larger framework of Ramazani's analysis is the question of whether Persian poetry as a whole is considered part of the canon of "world literature": "Is Persian poetry a kind of world poetry? Maybe not, if we are to judge by the current state of 'world literature.' Poetry written and recited in Persian for centuries across a vast swath of West, Central, and South Asia is barely visible in the developing field."[3] The dearth of translation from Persian to English in the world literary market—largely predetermined by geopolitical tensions and their consequent economic limitations—has been a key factor in this exclusion of Persian literature as a major player on the "world" literary stage.

---

[1] Simin Behbahani, "Zamin Koravi Shekl Ast" ["The World Is Shaped like a Sphere" in *Majmueh Ash'ar* [*Collected Poems*], Simin Behbahani (Tehran: Negah, 1388/2009), 863.

[2] Kaveh Safa, "Afterword: Translating Simin Behbahani," in *A Cup of Sin: Selected Poems*, Simin Behbahani, trans. Farzaneh Milani and Kaveh Safa (Syracuse: Syracuse University Press, 1999), 137. All lines from this poem quoted in English are taken from Milani and Safa's translation.

[3] Jahan Ramazani, "Persian Poetry, World Poetry, and Translatability," *University of Toronto Quarterly* 88, no. 2 (2019): 210.

So, I will argue below, has the liminal position of Iran within the category of "postcolonial literature," which often overlaps with "world literature" categorization in curricular contexts. Iran was heavily influenced by multiple colonial powers on cultural and political planes, but never officially colonized under a single foreign banner. Ramazani asks us to consider: is the seeming exclusion of Persian from the world literary canon merely an oversight, or is it related to the translatability of Persian as a language, particularly in its multidimensional sonority, diction, and the meter and rhyme of the *ghazal* form? He closely reads the Behbahani poem cited above and determines that certain elements of Ezra Pound's *melopoeia*, "in which words are charged in meaningful ways with music, can be appreciated in an unknown, foreign language." He acknowledges that some of these musical resonances are inevitably missed: "with small exceptions, 'it is practically impossible to transfer or translate it from one language to another.'"[4] Still, in his final judgment, more is gained than lost when the poem is rendered in English. Considering Behbahani's poem as a "world poem" and contextualizing it within Goethe's fascination with Hafez and Behbahani's own insistence that she, in Safa's words, "always resisted binary modes of thinking," Ramazani makes a forceful argument for the poem as an example of "world literature."[5] Does this classification, however, make sense because of its translation and circulation in the literary markets of two languages, or because of its thematic exploration of the globe as image and paradigm, or both?

Paradoxically, the process of world-making through representation can be either unifying or divisive. As Eric Hayot reminds us in an interrogation of the category of "world literature," "world" can indicate both the *whole* world in question (planet, humanity, cultural world, city, community) and individual worlds within that world (continents, regions, nations, subcultures, neighborhoods, subgroups).[6] Literary studies cannot hope to catch up with the speed and direction of the global flows of world-construction in the literary culture in which we have always lived. The profession's areas of specialization are most often defined in terms of period, geographical region, and genre, which can prevent crucial insights about cross-cultural literary histories that transcend these categories and often engender new ones. Franco Moretti's terminological frustration at the outset of "Conjectures on world literature" (2000) comes to mind: "What does it mean, studying world literature? How do we do it? I work on west European narrative between 1790 and 1930, and already feel like a charlatan outside of Britain or France. World literature?"[7] In addition—to state the obvious—some regions often receive more focus than others. In the past several decades of growing research and pedagogy about world literature, the Middle East—and in particular, the Persian literary sphere—has often remained severely underrepresented on US syllabi.

---

[4]   Ibid., 217.
[5]   Ibid., 222.
[6]   Eric Hayot, "On Literary Worlds," *Modern Language Quarterly* 72, no. 2 (2011): 135–6.
[7]   Franco Moretti, "Conjectures on World Literature," in *Distant Reading* (London: Verso, 2013), 45.

As Ramazani points out, in the field of world literature, the importance of modern Persian texts has been generally downplayed compared to postimperial literature from other regions such as South Asia and West Africa, where long-term, formalized colonization produced generations of Anglophone authors who often wrote with Euro-American audiences in mind. This oversight is ironic, given that Edward Said's *Orientalism*, the cornerstone text of postcolonial studies, locates the source of many cross-cultural stereotypes in literary culture precisely at the nexus between Europe/the United States and the Middle East—and specifically within Iran, colonially known as Persia. Said writes about the inclusion of Persia alongside longtime British and French colonial possessions in distinguishing between the role of "Far East" and "Near East" in Orientalist imaginaries: Whereas "one could discuss Europe's experience of the Near Orient, or of Islam, apart from its experience of the Far Orient ... particular parts of the Orient like Egypt, Syria, and Arabia cannot be discussed without also studying Europe's involvement in the more distant parts, of which Persia and India are the most important."[8] While "Arabia" of course remains a vague archaism, it is striking that Said's umbrella that otherwise covers only British or French mandates or protectorates— Egypt, Syria, and India—extends to cover Persia as well. Iran has never undergone a Fanonian progression from anti- to postcolonial state. In the region, it stands apart from the Sunni majority, pan-Arabist history, and Bedouin origins of the Arab countries to its west; never explicitly colonized, it has not gone through the radical imperial border redefinition of India, Pakistan, and Afghanistan to its east. Recent work by Farah Ghaderi, Hamid Dabashi, and others[9] has begun to more squarely address the long-standing exclusion of Iran from the field of postcolonial studies, prefigured in this oblique way by Said, exploring ways in which Iran's twentieth-century history and culture was deeply shaped by colonial and imperial influence.

To what extent Iran's literature, classical and modern, is inflected by colonialism is a related, but separate question from the extent to which it may be regarded as "world literature." Meanwhile, Iran and the United States constantly constitute the headlines of each other's news media, and Iran's geopolitical isolation from the West has only grown more entrenched with the 2018 nuclear deal cancelation, the travel ban, and renewed sanctions under the "maximum pressure" campaign. As I began work on this piece, Donald Trump and Ali Khamenei were reaching yet another peak of escalated rhetoric following possible Iranian involvement in the September 2019 attacks on Saudi oil fields. Iran is almost always a major player in "world" geopolitical escalations in the MENA region, whether supporting Houthi rebels in Yemen or benefiting from

---

[8]   Edward W. Said, *Orientalism* (New York: Knopf Doubleday, 1979), 17. One of Said's earliest examples in *Orientalism* is Aeschylus's play *The Persians*, in which ancient Persia is chosen to represent the most extreme version of "a very far distant and often threatening Otherness" and is, in turn, "made into a symbol for the whole Orient" (ibid., 21, 18).

[9]   See Farah Ghaderi, "Iran and Postcolonial Studies: Its Development and Current Status," *Interventions* 20, no. 4 (2018): 455–9; Hamid Dabashi, *Iran without Borders: Towards a Critique of the Postcolonial Nation* (London: Verso, 2016). Elena Andreeva's *Russia and Iran in the Great Game: Travelogues and Orientalism* (London: Routledge, 2007) provides a comprehensive geopolitical overview of nineteenth-century imperial players in Persia through the intriguing lens of the travelogue genre.

Turkish attacks on Kurdish forces in Northern Syria. The simultaneous rise of far-right nationalism and interventionism in the global North, coupled with the defensive stance of Iran's hardline regime, affects culture and literature in almost entirely punitive ways: sanctions and embargoes, curtailed or canceled visas for artists and writers, and so forth.[10]

Despite the impact of this political entrenchment and escalation on the creative arts, however, there is a deep and wide network of connections between Persian and Euro-American literary cultures that has only grown richer since the early twentieth century. This network is sustained and expanded, I argue, by experimentation with genre and creation of new literary forms. Many genres and forms (in literature, art, and film) that have been sites of both xenophobia and cultural purity discourse have, through their expansion and adaptation, come to serve as vehicles for cross-cultural understanding in a long-standing circuit between Persophone, Anglophone, Francophone, and other traditions. In tracing the path of these formal vessels, I work from the critical premise of world literature, well established by Said, Fredric Jameson, Homi Bhabha, and others, that genre (like all cultural constructs) is inherently hybrid—the result of a millennia-long history of global cultural flows. A frequently overlooked long twentieth-century story of transnational genre-creation thus unfolds within modern Iranian literature. In our increasingly complex field of world literature, David Palumbo-Liu writes, "form is the meeting-place of a number of aesthetic and psychic investments, both the common ground and vehicle for planetary thinking."[11]

World literature syllabi in North American and European curricula may include brief examples of Persian authors from the classical period working in classical forms, such as Ferdowsi, Hafez, Rumi, or Khayyam, but deep, contextualized knowledge of the cosmopolitan nature of Iranian literature in the twentieth and twenty-first centuries is often lacking. From the crackdown on civil liberties during the Pahlavi era to the diplomatic isolation, sanctions, censorship, and human rights violations of the Islamic Republic, Iran's modern geopolitics have made it more difficult and more urgent for modern Iranian literature to cross borders. In defying and expanding genre categorization, modern Iranian writers have not only resisted a global hegemony in which forms are too often seen to move only from a Euro-American "center" to a series of "peripheral" literary communities and markets. Keeping in mind the shared root of *genre* and *genus*, they also resist reductive and potentially racist typology and

---

[10] Iranian artists Tarlan Rafiee and Sahand Hesamiyan and curators Hormoz Hematian and Ali Bakhtiari detail limited access to materials in Iran, the difficulty of managing foreign bank accounts and cashing checks abroad with Iranian passports, and many other obstacles that amount to a "superhuman determination required to present Iranian art to the world today" (Proctor, *artnet news*). Authors and musicians in diaspora are also rallying around the sanctions issue: in one January 2019 example, poets Sepideh Jodeyri, Charles Bernstein, and Pierre Joris and the musician Roya Bahrami performed at a Washington, DC event with a title drawn from a Forugh Farrokhzad poem: "No One Wants to Believe the Garden is Dying: American Poets against US sanctions on Iran" (Busboys and Poets).

[11] David Palumbo-Liu, "Atlantic to Pacific: James, Todorov, Blackmur, and Intercontinental Form," in *Shades of the Planet: American Literature as World Literature*, ed. Wai Chee Dimock and Lawrence Buell (Princeton: Princeton University Press, 2007), 196.

classification altogether. We might think of modern Iranian genre evolution as a constant flight or fugitivity—an escape from a relentless series of pejorative colonial representation tropes that have especially clustered around Islamophobia in the post-1979 period.

Debates surrounding the tension between modernization and Westernization in Iranian literature have been ongoing for over a century. In many ways, nation has remained a rigid category in the dominant discourses of modern Iranian intellectual life, as in Jalal Al-e Ahmad and Ali Shariati's notion of *gharbzadegi* ["Westoxification"].[12] On the other hand, the transnationalism of Iranian cultural identity has been evident at all ends of the political spectrum. This ranges from the performative multiculturalism of Mohammad Reza Shah's revamped Persepolis at his (heavily criticized) 2,500-year celebration of the Persian Empire, to the multifaceted uprisings against the Shah just a few years later, which eventually came to center on Ayatollah Khomeini's leadership but was originally sparked by a wide range of dissidents including constitutionalists, Marxists, feminists, atheists, and a range of Islamists. The most influential early twentieth-century Iranian writers, such as Nima Yushij, Sadeq Hedayat, and Mohammad Ali Jamalzadeh, who were early adapters of what many perceived as "Western" forms—a departure from classical metrical versification, the modernist novel, and the short story respectively—were uninterested in Iranian nationalism, and many of them even permanently left Iran for Europe. (Reinforcing the association of the European with the modern, Yushij is often seen as the founder of the *she'r-e now*, or "new poetry," movement.) Their work, however, must also be understood in the context of "Persianism," a cultural movement to which Kamran Talattof ascribes "several immediate purposes":

> to reduce the use of Arabic terminology; to work toward the purification of the Persian language; to promote a language closer to the common parlance instead of the formulaic style; to link ancient Iran to the present time through diverse linguistic structures; and finally, to promote modernity by presenting new literary genres.[13]

Modernist brevity and newfound independence from classical forms associated with Arabic were alternatively seen as indications of an insidious Westernization, and as empowering gestures that reclaimed a national Persian heritage. Iranian literary

---

[12] The title of Jalal Al-e Ahmad's influential 1963 treatise, also translated as "Occidentosis." From the dawn of Islamic civilization, Al-e Ahmad states, "ma hamisheh beh gharb nazar dashteh-im [we have always looked Westward]" (Jalal Al-e Ahmad, *Gharbzadegi* [*Weststruckness/Westtoxication*], 18). He argues that the "contagion" of Western influence has reached its apex in modern industrial society, and attacks Westernized Iranians for having no affiliation with their national culture. Al-e Ahmad's vocabulary of contamination, corruption, and disease suggests a vulnerability that complements the classic Orientalist tropes founded on the West's own notions of power, superiority, and rights to conquest.

[13] Kamran Talattof, "Ideology and Self-Portrayal in the Poetry of Nima Yushij," in *Essays on Nima Yushij: Animating Modernism in Persian Poetry*, ed. Ahmad Karimi-Hakkak and Kamran Talattof (Leiden: Brill, 2004), 71.

culture thus presents a unique point along the imaginative spectrum of Orientalism. Following the Islamic Revolution, its writers do not simply "write back" after the ebb of Pahlavi-era UK and US interventionism, engaging in—to borrow Said's term—a "rhetoric of blame,"[14] but instead continue a long-standing project of writing through, around, and beyond postcolonial affect in a complex dialectic with not only English but many other modern literatures. Some of the most progressive and iconic literary Persophone intellectuals of the past hundred years have been deeply engaged with the work of writers in French, Russian, Turkish, and many other world languages through their mutual and synchronous experimentation with genre and form.

Simin Behbahani, Adrienne Rich, and the Global *Ghazal*

Let me return to Behbahani's poem in a more expansive formal-historical context. The full text of the poem reads:[15]

زمین کروی شکل است

شنیدی و میدانی	زمین کروی شکل است
چنین که تو میخوانی	یمین و یسارش نیست
ز اطلس جغرافی	جهت نتوانی جست
جهت جو بگردانی	به زخم سرانگشتش
که شرق بخوانیمش	قرار تو شد با من
به غرب، به آسانی	اگر چه توان راندش
غروب نخواهی دید	مگو سخن از مغرب!
همیشه به تک رانی	اگر ز پی خورشید
دو پاره ی مردار است	جهان به خط تقسیم
نشسته به مهمانی	که کرکس و کفتارش
نشسته بر این مردار	تو با مگسان بسیار
که منعم این خوانی	به شادی ی این پندار
به خورنسئ از کفتار	به جنبسئ از کرکس
به کار پرافشانی	گروه مگس خیزد
که شکر چنین خوان را	تو را چو مگس این بس
دعای شکم خوانی	دو دست به سر گیری

"The World Is Shaped Like a Sphere"[16]

You have heard it.
You know about it.

---

[14] Edward W. Said, *Culture and Imperialism* (New York: Vintage, 1994), 18.

[15] Behbahani, *Majmu'eh Ash'ar*, 863.

[16] Simin Behbahani. "The World Is Shaped like a Sphere," in *A Cup of Sin: Selected Poems*, trans. Farzaneh Milani and Kaveh Safa (Syracuse: Syracuse University Press, 1999), 57.

The world is shaped like a sphere.
It has no left or right, the way you see it.
You can't take your bearings from a globe,
if with the flick of a finger you can make it turn this way and that.
It was our agreement to call this the East,
though we could push it westward, with ease.
Don't speak to me of the West, where the sun sets,
if you always run after the sun,
you will never see a sunset.
The world divided by a line is a dead body cut in two
on which the vulture and the hyena are feasting.
You sit on the corpse with a crowd of flies
in self-contentment imagining
you are the host and patron.
A hyena snarl, the vulture flapping its wings
set the flies dancing in the air.
All that remains for you to do,
is to raise your hands to your head like a fly
and pray the prayer of stomachs.

The first half of the *ghazal* insists on resistance to cultural hegemony. The speaker embraces neither imperialist importation of Western thought—"run[ning] after the sun" (*az pey-e khorshid*)—nor the bitter schism of "the world divided by a line" (*jahan beh khatt-e taqsim*). Behbahani's poem relies on two extended metaphors: the hopeful image of the world as spinning globe, and the sinister figure of the world as stinking corpse. These exist side by side to suggest that the same object, in two different sets of hands, can be a source of creativity or of destruction. That object is in this case the whole world, whose fate is left in the hands of those who wield representative power, whether through politics (which can cause a "divide" [*taqsim*] in the world with military, religious, and other types of lines) or through language (those who "agree to call this the East" [*qarar shod keh sharq bekhanimash*]).

To convey the dual notion cited above (that the imagining of worlds can be either constructive or destructive) through the rhythm of variations on a theme, Behbahani relies on the formal restrictions of the *ghazal*—namely, the internal end-rhyme and refrain of each couplet known as its *qafiyeh* and *radif*—to render the language of the poem more participatory, more communal, and thus more global. Although the *radif* is fixed, Behbahani's chosen consistent rhyme scheme ends simply on the syllable "*i*", which is the suffix of Persian verbs in the second person singular. This means that the refrain continually circles back to an initial emphasis on placing action and responsibility upon the poem's addressee. The rhyme of the *matla'* (opening couplet) establishes the close connection between "you know" (*midani*) and "you read" (*mikhani*), centering the poem's focus on epistemology and cartography further through the symbolism of the "globe" (*atlas-e joghrafi*) before quickly destabilizing it. Behbahani's flexible *radif* is one of the ways in which that destabilization occurs, as the suffix "*i*" can also form a noun, as in "ease" (*asani*).

The *ghazal* form is traditionally so autographic that it is signed in the final couplet, or *makhta*, with the poet's name, a convention called *takhallos*—but this poem, like so many of Behbahani's other *ghazals*, instead reaches outward in both content and form to ask its readers what their responsibilities might be in the project of defining our globalized reality.

The addressee of Behbahani's poem is disoriented throughout the text, but that position of spatial confusion goes from being a source of power at the beginning, embodied in the casual flick of a finger, to one of disempowerment. Polarizing the world and erecting barriers to cultural exchange wreaks damage tantamount to murder—"a dead body cut in two" (*do pareh-ye mordar ast*). Whereas the roundness and dynamism of the world are theoretical in the first half, after the volta the addressee becomes viscerally attuned to the violent damage that cross-cultural judgment has wrought. There is an initial feeding frenzy as the addressee feasts on the scraps of the decaying, divided world alongside fellow "flies" (*magas*). But the outcome that the *makhta* provides for its hypothetical xenophobic addressee is an inevitable state of hunger and exasperation: "All that remains for you to do, / is to raise your hands to your head like a fly and pray the prayer of stomachs."

تو را چو مگس این بس   که شکر چنین خوان را
دو دست به سر گیری   دعای شکم خوانی

The phrase "prayer of stomachs" (*do'a-ye shekam*) sets up an association between the soul and the gut, of faith rooted in instinct, rather than the poem's opening link between the head and the ears, or knowledge based on hearsay. Ultimately, the poem moves from a panoptic position of learned superiority at the beginning, to an immersive, despairing surrender once the violence of that position becomes clear. What makes this revelation possible is the geographic relativism that Behbahani establishes between West and East.

From its Middle Eastern roots to its influential echoes through contemporary American poetry, the *ghazal* form that Behbahani modernized to grapple with global themes in Persian literature has always existed in a multinational poetic playing field. Two of several anthologies that illustrate the form's propensity toward cross-cultural experimentation in English are Aijaz Ahmad's *Ghazals of Ghalib* (1971), which carried the nineteenth-century *ghazal* master Ghalib's Persian sentiments across the centuries into multiple interpretations for an Anglophone audience, and Agha Shahid Ali's *Ravishing DisUnities* (2000), which insists more strictly on neo-formalism but whose contributions are nonetheless stylistically diverse, from John Hollander's playful, contemporary "*Ghazal* on *Ghazals*" to Andrew McCord's non–end-rhyming translation of Faiz Ahmed Faiz's somber, nostalgic "A Southern *Ghazal*." Sara Suleri Goodyear, in her afterword to Ali's volume, explains the *ghazal*'s paradox of cultural interconnection despite inevitable disconnection as follows:

> The cultural moment that surrounds the moment of poetry … may always remain
> untranslatable. There are poems in this collection that touch upon precisely that

point of translation that converts a simple imitation of form into an opening, one that even Ghalib could admire. Cultural transitions take place.[17]

The Persophone *ghazal* has undergone this kind of "cultural transition" in the hands of Behbahani, whose removal of the *takhallos* and radical simplification of the *qafiyeh-radif* renders her poetry more translatable and removes a necessarily national or cultural positioning. Her thoughtful experimentation with form in fact makes the poem even more globally oriented than its content already suggests.

In the *Ghazals of Ghalib* volume, Ahmad provides the Persian originals for some of Ghalib's most famous *ghazals*, along with his own literal translations and free-form "adaptations" of the poems by a wide range of contemporary American poets including Adrienne Rich, W. S. Merwin, William Stafford, and Mark Strand. This collaborative volume is a hybrid of homage, technical translation studies, and original poetry. For Rich, the cross-cultural collaboration was instrumental in her own turn to the *ghazal* form, which persisted throughout her poetic oeuvre, often interwoven with other variants of adaptation, translation, and derivation from different languages and cultural or historical contexts. She found a new spectrum of possibilities in the *ghazal*, a form that was "foreign" to her but became an integral part of her dissident self-positioning as she protested against the Vietnam War in the late 1960s. David Caplan argues that to Rich, immersed in this cross-cultural collage of resistance and inspired by Ghalib and his anticolonial and multilingual verse, the *ghazal* form acted "as a gesture of affinity, likening Ghalib's desperation to the turmoil Rich experienced in 1968, amid the year's riots, assassinations, and war."[18] She composed two *ghazal* sequences: "*Ghazals* (Homage to Ghalib)" (published in *Leaflets*, 1969) and "The Blue *Ghazals*" (published in *The Will to Change*, 1971) that combined formal modernizations not unlike Behbahani's with a similarly transnational perspective.

In the growing violence of colonial rule, Ahmad writes, Ghalib foresaw "much suffering" ahead, which precipitated "an intense moral loneliness, a longing for relations which were no longer possible, and a sense of utter waste" (xxii). In their more despairing lines, such as "For the work undoes itself over and over: / the grass grows back, the dust collects, the scar breaks open" ("7/14/68: I"),[19] Rich's *ghazals* echo this sense of futility and circularity and what should be, and could be, an eye-opening "moment of change." The circularity of violence present in such lines is reminiscent of a similar pattern in Behbahani's spinning globe that becomes a decaying, fragmented world. The *ghazal* is, at its core, an oscillation between fragmentation and unification, mapped onto a constant process of identifying cross-cultural similarities and differences in Rich's American adaptations of the form. The main thrust of Ahmad's collection—and the role of contemporary American poets like Rich within it—is

---

[17] Sara Suleri Goodyear, "Ideas of Order in an Afterword," in *Ravishing DisUnities: Real Ghazals in English*, ed. Agha Shahid Ali (Middletown: Wesleyan University Press, 2000), 180.
[18] David Caplan, *Questions of Possibility: Contemporary Poetry and Poetic Form* (New York: Oxford University Press, 2005), 44.
[19] Adrienne Rich, *Collected Early Poems: 1950–1970* (New York: W. W. Norton & Co., 1992), 342.

less the formal preservation of a tradition with a single cultural origin, and more the globalization of Persophone literature and culture through formal evolution and transnational content.

As more and more poets cease to think of themselves within singular national or cultural categories, forms diversify alongside them, if not before them. By being critical of their particular political contexts, innovating in meter and rhyme, and tempering the autographic component of the *ghazal*, transnational poets like Behbahani, who "revivified" the *ghazal* in the 1960s and 1970s in Iran,[20] along with early American *ghazal* poets like Rich, set the stage for poets like Roger Sedarat, whose *Ghazal Games* (2011) is one example of how an archaic form has been thoroughly integrated with twenty-first-century experimental modes.

"Conjectures" on Persian Genres as World Genres

The question of what defines a literary genre or form—whether genre is singular or multiple, fixed or dynamic—has been debated by some of the most influential scholars in the past several decades of literary criticism. Jacques Derrida, in "The Law of Genre" (1980), explains how intrinsic the notion of sociocultural genre categorization is to the study of literary texts: "A text cannot belong to no genre, it cannot be without or less a genre. Every text participates in one or several genres, there is no genreless text."[21] Genres, as Jameson points out in *The Political Unconscious* (1981), can function as established social agreements that provide us with formulas for how to read a text within a foreign cultural context: "Genres are essentially literary *institutions*, or social contracts between a writer and a specific public, whose function is to specify the proper use of a particular cultural artifact."[22] Literature itself, of course, does not adhere to such social and critical norms of what a novel, poem, or play "should" look like anywhere in the world.

As Derrida goes on, however, he draws an important distinction between passive and active categorization:

> There is always a genre and genres, *yet such participation never amounts to belonging.* And not because of an abundant overflowing or a free, anarchic and unclassifiable productivity, but because of the *trait* of participation itself, because of the effect of the code and of the generic mark. *Making genre its mark, a text demarcates itself.*[23]

---

[20] Dominic Parviz Brookshaw, "Revivification of an Ossified Genre? Simin Behbahani and the Persian *Ghazal*," *Iranian Studies* 48, no. 1 (2008), 75.

[21] Jacques Derrida, "The Law of Genre," trans. Avital Ronell, *Critical Inquiry* 7, no. 1 (1980), 65.

[22] Fredric Jameson, *The Political Unconscious: Narrative as a Socially Symbolic Act* (Ithaca: Cornell University Press, 1981), 87.

[23] Derrida, "The Law of Genre," 65 (emphasis mine).

In other words, a text can actively situate itself within a genre, self-reflexively commenting on its place within that genre and its tensions with other works in that category—and in so doing, can redefine the boundaries of the genre as a whole.

My observations about the globalizing impact of open forms and intergenres in modern Iranian literature proceeds from this early indication in Derrida that, by playing in the spaces between genres and by hybridizing genres to create new, constantly evolving forms, texts create new literary and sociocultural places of exchange. Starting with Ralph Cohen, who argued in 1986 that the openness of genre is based in "the human need for distinction and interrelation,"[24] and building on the Saidian premise above that all cultural constructs are inherently hybrid, many contemporary genre theorists (Perloff, Beebee, Devitt) agree that all literary genres contain a degree of multiplicity and that new genres are formed recursively, from the evolution and interaction of existing genres. The constant nature of this evolution and hybridization means that there is no such thing as a fixed genre with set qualities. Like Behbahani's globe, a genre or form is a concept without fixed definitions—its shapes and orderings depend on how the given reader of the literary landscape decides to look at it and move it around. But second, and more importantly, one must consider what the flexibility and dynamism of literary genre can do, and has in fact done, for the members of literary communities reaching across particularly fraught political and cultural borders in today's world. Shape-shifting formal containers, I argue, can and do help authors, artists, and audiences who live in climates of xenophobia, demonization, and cross-cultural stereotypes simply talk to each other in ways that resonate in global parallels across borders—yet they sensitively adapt to cultural specificities of local places, and do not flatten unique historical particulars.[25]

What are the political implications of centering modern Iran in these repeated acts of genre-creation, rather than categorizing its literature as either traditionalist or "borrowing" from European forms? I believe it challenges Moretti's much-discussed claims about form and genre as indicators of the uneven distribution of world-literary production. "Yes, forms *can* move in several directions," he allows in "More Conjectures" (2003). "But *do* they?" His proffered answers include that "movement from one periphery to another (without passing through the centre) is almost unheard of; movement from the periphery to the centre is less rare, but still quite unusual, while that from the centre to the periphery is by far the most frequent."[26] Why might this be? Referring to his 2000 essay "Conjectures on World Literature," he continues: "Cultures from the centre have more resources to pour into innovation (literary and otherwise), and are thus more likely to produce it … the model proposed in 'Conjectures' does not

---

[24] Ralph Cohen, "History and Genre," *New Literary History* 17, no. 2 (1986), 204.

[25] Contemporary examples of genre-busting Iranian works abound; I will mention two such remarkable ones here: Kaveh Akbar's long free-verse multimedia poem "The Palace" (*The New Yorker*, 2019) and Négar Djavadi's mix-tape and cinema-inspired novel *Disoriental* (trans. Tina Kover [New York: Europa Editions, 2018]). Both illustrate in dazzling ways that Iran's history is inescapably global, its creative expression inescapably intergeneric.

[26] Franco Moretti, "More Conjectures," in *Distant Reading* (London: Verso, 2013), 112.

reserve invention to a few cultures and deny it to the others: it specifies *the conditions under which it is more likely to occur*, and the forms it may take."[27] In the case of Iran—a relatively wealthy nation suffering from twenty-first-century economic isolation, unemployment, and sanctions that nonetheless funds the arts and fosters vibrant cultural life, but censors, imprisons, and even tortures its artists using the rationale of fundamentalist theocracy—should we consider such a literary site "central" or "peripheral"? What "resources" should we consider to make such an assessment, and what should we consider them against?

In the 2000 piece, Moretti concludes "that the encounter of Western forms and local reality did indeed produce everywhere a structural compromise."[28] The implications of his terms and syntax here are vexing: "form" is a possession of the West, while non-Western cultures grapple with "realities." What must result in the case of, say, modern Iranian literature in this view is a series of derivations or "compromises" rather than original and cross-culturally influential works. Aamir Mufti reframes such positions in a postcolonial spirit:

> Humanistic culture is saturated with [an] informal developmentalism, a 'first in the West, and then elsewhere' structure of global time, as Dipesh Chakrabarty puts it (*PE*, p. 6)—in which cultural objects from non-Western societies can be grasped only with reference to the categories of European cultural history, as pale or partial reflections of the latter, to be seen ultimately as coming late, lagging behind, and lacking in originality.[29]

What is the suggestion that only "peripheral" cultures must "compromise" and adapt to forms from the "center," if not an example of this developmentalist stance? I find valuable insights on this question in Efraín Kristal, who writes in a 2002 response to "Conjectures" that "Moretti's schema of world literature needs to be corrected":

> The assumption that literary and economic relationships run parallel may work in some cases, but not in others. Moretti's model is designed to show how the periphery comes to terms with Western forms, but it falls short on the other side of the equation, where what we have seen is, firstly, an emancipation of the periphery from Western forms, even in situations where Western political or economic hegemony is still operational; and secondly, the interplay of forms and genres across literatures in ways that have little to do with the centre.[30]

Kristal critiques Moretti's focus on the novel, arguing that it is "not necessarily the privileged genre for understanding literary developments of social importance in

---

[27] Ibid., 113.
[28] Moretti, "Conjectures on World Literature," 54.
[29] Aamir Mufti, "Global Comparativism," *Critical Inquiry* 31, no. 2 (2005): 474.
[30] Efraín Kristal, "Considering Coldly … : A Response to Franco Moretti," *New Left Review* 15 (2002): 73.

the periphery."[31] He ultimately provides an alternative vision of a multi-sited "world literature," identifiable by the multi-sited creation of new genres and forms:

> I am arguing, however, in favour of a view of world literature in which the West does not have a monopoly over the creation of forms that count; in which themes and forms can move in several directions—from the centre to the periphery, from the periphery to the centre, from one periphery to another, while some original forms of consequence may not move much at all.[32]

Kristal's analysis is also more relativist than Moretti's, suggesting that which genres will wield undue influence as "hegemonic" varies across cultures, periods, and literary traditions. His destabilization of world literary hierarchies depends on this genre-relativism. For instance, he writes, "any discussion of Spanish American literature that neglects poetry, the hegemonic genre, must go astray."[33] He invokes Rubén Darío, the Nicaraguan poet, as the writer who most propelled the globalization of Latin American literature through *modernismo* ("the first literary expression to transcend national boundaries, making it possible for histories of Spanish American literature to be envisaged by Spanish Americans themselves; and which set the tone for future developments in several genres, including the novel") to challenge Moretti's terms of "compromise": "The forms of Latin American fiction cannot be understood merely as compromises with metropolitan norms."[34] He cites Gerald Martin's *Journeys through the Labyrinth* (1989) as a precedent for this claim, which observed at the high moment of global postmodernist magical realism: "Whereas most important Latin American fiction between the 1940s and the 1960s is recognizably 'Joycean' or 'Faulknerian,' it is equally arguable that since the 1960s many of the most important writers—Italo Calvino, Milan Kundera, Salman Rushdie, Umberto Eco—have had to become 'Latin American' novelists."[35]

The way in which Kristal's analysis dismantles notions of "center" and "periphery" brings us back to the bifurcation in world literary studies to which I alluded in pondering Ramazani's conclusion above; that is, a split between the emphasis on circulation (as in Moretti and Pascale Casanova) and one on world-making by literary works themselves. Instead of a market-based analysis, or one in which marketing and publicity machines or major international prize committees determine the extent to which a work is "worldly," Hayot suggests that whether or not a work is "world literature" should be determined by a number of diegetic factors such as "amplitude, completeness, metadiegetic structure, connectedness, and character-system."[36] Pheng

---

[31] Ibid., 73.
[32] Ibid., 74.
[33] Ibid., 64.
[34] Ibid., 64, 70.
[35] Ibid., 71.
[36] Eric Hayot, "On Literary Worlds," *Modern Language Quarterly* 72, no. 2 (June 2011): 157.

Cheah also challenges the market-based definition of "world literature" that inevitably follows the inequitable hierarchies of global capitalism:

> It is assumed that the spatial diffusion and extensiveness achieved through global media and markets give rise to a sense of belonging to a shared world, when one might argue that such developments lead instead to greater polarization and division of nations and regions. The globe is not a world. This is a necessary premise if the cosmopolitan vocation of world literature can be meaningful today.[37]

What is the connection to Iranian literature here, keeping in mind the contrapuntal transnational echoes of a formal expansion such as Behbahani's revivification of the *ghazal*? We might think of Kristal's multidirectional genre-based cartography of power flows in world literary circuits and Hayot's and Cheah's rejection of a market-based "world literature" alongside Wai Chee Dimock's conceptualization of genre "less as a law, a rigid taxonomic landscape, and more as a self-obsoleting system, a provisional set that will always be bent and pulled and stretched by its many subsets."[38] In the end, globally oriented writers will harness and transport forms with national and transnational origins, adapting and transforming them along the way so that it can ultimately be difficult to separate the "worldliness" of content from that of its form. Instead of conceiving of Iran as a "peripheral" or "semi-peripheral" culture "compromising" within a Western form, I believe scholars of Iranian literature, following Kristal, should seek alternate spatial metaphors for understanding its generative and, yes, central role in world literary cross-pollination. Perhaps we should discard the tired terms "center" and "periphery" altogether, and instead consider spatial metaphors for forms and genres themselves as they move within places and across borders.

In *Forms*, her 2015 book exploring the relation between artistic forms and sociopolitical institutions, Caroline Levine invokes the notion of *affordance*—the suitability of a given material or design (such as glass) for its intended purpose (such as the transparency of a window)—to assert that "each shape or pattern, social or literary, lays claim to a limited range of potentialities." But just as materials and objects can exceed their intended purpose in the hands of a creative user (who might use a water glass as a bug-trap or a stencil), Levine continues: "shapes and patterns are iterable—portable. They can be picked up and moved to new contexts."[39] Rich in the 1960s, for instance, found in the nineteenth-century *ghazals* of Ghalib a "way of dealing with very complex and scattered material which [demanded] a different kind of unity from that imposed on it by the isolated, single poem"[40]—but for her Anglophone audience

[37] Pheng Cheah, *What Is a World? On Postcolonial Literature as World Literature* (Durham: Duke University Press, 2016), 42.

[38] Wai Chee Dimock, *Through Other Continents* (Princeton: Princeton University Press, 2006), 73–4.

[39] Caroline Levine, *Forms: Whole, Rhythm, Hierarchy, Network* (Princeton: Princeton University Press, 2015), 6, 7.

[40] Aijaz Ahmad, ed., *Ghazals of Ghalib: Versions from the Urdu by Aijaz Ahmad, W. S. Merwin, Adrienne Rich, William Stafford, David Ray, Thomas Fitzsimmons, Mark Strand, and William Hunt* (New York: Columbia University Press, 1971), xxv.

and her literary-political climate of American free verse, realized that the effect of returning to the same end-rhyme would not carry the same weight as it does in Persian. Her *ghazals* thus preserve the spirit of the *qafiyeh-radif* without being constrained by the technicalities of the form in its strictest definition. The capaciousness of such open forms results not in a homogenizing network of literary exchange, but in a constantly evolving and diversifying cross-cultural polysemy of genres.

In addition to the malleability of forms, it is important to remember their *multiplicity*. Levine insists, "in any given circumstance, no form operates in isolation ... Literary form does not operate outside of the social but works among many organizing principles, all circulating in a world jam-packed with other arrangements."[41] When Shirin Neshat's film *Zanan Bedun-e Mardan* (adapted from Shahnush Parsipur's iconic 1989 novella by the same name) was released in 2009, the rising Green Movement in Iran was a historical context as important as the story's setting in 1953. Neshat's aesthetics of interwoven poetry, painting, and montage makes space for viewers to hear the historical echoes between both moments of political crisis, and more.[42] Similarly, the visual monument and anti-monument that is Amir and Khalil's Omid Project appendix at the end of their graphic novel *Zahra's Paradise* (2009) urges readers to remember the simultaneous interconnectivity and incommensurability of the stories of the victims of human rights abuses in the Islamic Republic.[43] For the *ghazals*, the film, and the graphic novel alike, the distinct affordances of separate forms and genres are as important as their ability to open up to influence and hybridization with others.

As a final illustration of affordance, I offer Marjane Satrapi's tongue-in-cheek use of the flying carpet in *Persepolis*, in the full-page panel that depicts Marji's family vacation through Europe shortly after the 1979 Revolution, when political ties between Iran and the West were quickly approaching total severance. In the image, Marji is seated at the top-center with her parents on a flying carpet that slips between icons of Western tourism such as the Coliseum, the leaning tower of Pisa, and a flamenco dancer, all framed under a night sky.[44] Satrapi's surprising assemblage of a few key symbols in this panel seems to encapsulate something of what the continuous and productive interaction of authors and texts, across politically and culturally erected barriers of fear and stereotype, has shown to be true. First, the affordance of forms can be imaginatively stretched—a carpet, the communal centerpiece of a home or an individual prayer rug, can be creatively repurposed as a means of travel. Second, the symbolic and historical associations of certain forms with certain notions and expectations, as in Jameson's claim that forms are both literary and social institutions, can be reversed and undone— as Satrapi cleverly does in her panel, turning a potentially Orientalist trope on its head as the family uses the carpet to fly as tourists among flattened caricatures of Occidental

[41] Levine, *Forms*, 7.
[42] *Zanan Bedun-e Mardan* [*Women without Men*], dir. Shirin Neshat in collaboration with Shoja Azari (IndiePix, 2009).
[43] Amir and Khalil, *Zahra's Paradise* (New York: First Second, 2011), 240.
[44] Marjane Satrapi, *Persepolis: The Story of a Childhood*, trans. L'Association (New York: Pantheon Books, 2003), vol. 1, 77.

sights and sounds. Like the magical flying carpet, the literary form is also mobile—not a container meant to impose conventional boundaries upon stories and reinforce ideological lines, but a *vehicle* that can allow those stories to travel into new contexts, new audiences, and new homes in the world.

Throughout the modern and contemporary period, genre-bending is one way that Iranian literature has resisted the cultural impositions of colonialism. Simultaneously resisting both a Eurocentric hegemony of genre and the nativist politics of *she'r-e now*, Behbahani could see the close link between nationalism and inevitable colonial domination—given the rule of the Pahlavi dynasty, which was installed and always at least partially controlled by American and British petroleum interests. As I have discussed elsewhere, Satrapi's *Persepolis* similarly resists a West/East division of graphic narrative by thoroughly hybridizing the genre through many formal elements.[45] Similar trends are observable across many liminal genres, from the travelogue to the documentary film to the social media post. Ultimately, the dynamism of open-ended literary and cultural genres—simultaneously formal and fluid—has consistently made possible a process of "worlding" of both content and perspective in the stories told from and about Iran. Locating Iran's impact on world literature and culture and vice versa in this way might help us, ultimately, to reconceive the global circulation of texts in terms of genre and form, turning the malleable containers that literary forms inhabit into live translators who enable active and evolving forms of cross-cultural dialogue.

Acknowledgments

I gratefully acknowledge Farzaneh Milani for introducing me to Behbahani's poem and years of helping me think through her work; Jahan Ramazani, for always encouraging me to center the study of Persian literature as world literature, for introducing me to Levine's book, and for providing a new prism through which to think about Behbahani's poem; and Nirvana Tanoukhi and David Damrosch, whose IWL seminars in 2013 and 2018 helped me better understand and critically reflect on Moretti's work.

Bibliography

"A Night with American Poets against US Sanctions on Iran." *Busboys and Poets*, January 22, 2019. Web. Available at www.busboysandpoets.com/events/th-evt-7436610/(accessed October 16, 2019).

Ahmad, Aijaz, ed. *Ghazals of Ghalib: Versions from the Urdu by Aijaz Ahmad, W. S. Merwin, Adrienne Rich, William Stafford, David Ray, Thomas Fitzsimmons, Mark Strand, and William Hunt.* New York: Columbia University Press, 1971.

---

[45] Marie Ostby, "Graphics and Global Dissent: Marjane Satrapi's *Persepolis*, Persian Miniatures, and the Multifaceted Power of Comic Protest," *PMLA* 132, no. 3 (2017); 558–79.

Akbar, Kaveh. "The Palace." Illustrations by Maria Medem. *The New Yorker*, April 18, 2019. Web. www.newyorker.com/magazine/poems/kaveh-akbar-the-palace (accessed October 16, 2019).

Al-e Ahmad, Jalal. *Gharbzadegi [Weststruckness/Westtoxication]*. Web. http://mohsen.1.banan.byname.net/content/republished/doc.public/politics/iran/gharbzadegi/restoration/main.pdf (accessed March 25, 2013).

Ali, Agha Shahid, ed. *Ravishing DisUnities: Real Ghazals in English*. Middletown: Wesleyan University Press, 2000.

Amir and Khalil. *Zahra's Paradise*. New York: First Second, 2011.

Andreeva, Elena. *Russia and Iran in the Great Game: Travelogues and Orientalism*. London: Routledge, 2007.

Beebee, Thomas O. *The Ideology of Genre: A Comparative Study of Generic Instability*. University Park: Penn State University Press, 1994.

Behbahani, Simin. *A Cup of Sin: Selected Poems*. Trans. and ed. Farzaneh Milani and Kaveh Safa. Syracuse: Syracuse University Press, 1999.

Behbahani, Simin. *Majmueh Ash'ar [Collected Poems]*. Tehran: Negah, 1388/2009.

Bhabha, Homi. *The Location of Culture*. London: Routledge, 1994.

Brookshaw, Dominic Parviz. "Revivification of an Ossified Genre? Simin Behbahani and the Persian *Ghazal*." *Iranian Studies* 48, no. 1 (2008): 75–90.

Caplan, David. *Questions of Possibility: Contemporary Poetry and Poetic Form*. New York: Oxford University Press, 2005.

Casanova, Pascale. *The World Republic of Letters*. Trans. M. B. DeBevoise. Cambridge, MA: Harvard University Press, 2004.

Cheah, Pheng. *What Is a World? On Postcolonial Literature as World Literature*. Durham: Duke University Press, 2016.

Cohen, Ralph. "History and Genre." *New Literary History* 17, no. 2 (1986): 203–18.

Dabashi, Hamid. *Iran without Borders: Towards a Critique of the Postcolonial Nation*. London: Verso, 2016.

Derrida, Jacques. "The Law of Genre." Trans. Avital Ronell. *Critical Inquiry* 7, no. 1 (1980): 55–81.

Devitt, Amy J. *Writing Genres*. Carbondale: Southern Illinois University Press, 2004.

Dimock, Wai Chee. *Through Other Continents*. Princeton: Princeton University Press, 2006.

Djavadi, Négar. *Disoriental*. Trans. Tina Kover. New York: Europa Editions, 2018.

Ghaderi, Farah. "Iran and Postcolonial Studies: Its Development and Current Status." *Interventions* 20, no. 4 (2018): 455–9.

Hayot, Eric. "On Literary Worlds." *Modern Language Quarterly* 72, no. 2 (2011): 129–61.

Jameson, Fredric. *The Political Unconscious: Narrative as a Socially Symbolic Act*. Ithaca: Cornell University Press, 1981.

Jay, Paul. *Global Matters: The Transnational Turn in Literary Studies*. Ithaca: Cornell University Press, 2010.

Kristal, Efraín. "Considering Coldly … : A Response to Franco Moretti." *New Left Review* 15 (2002): 61–74.

Levine, Caroline. *Forms: Whole, Rhythm, Hierarchy, Network*. Princeton: Princeton University Press, 2015.

Milani, Farzaneh. *Words, Not Swords: Iranian Women Writers and the Freedom of Movement*. Syracuse: Syracuse University Press, 2011.

Moretti, Franco. "Conjectures on World Literature" and "More Conjectures." In *Distant Reading*. 43–62 and 107–20. London: Verso, 2013.

Mufti, Aamir. *Forget English!: Orientalisms and World Literatures*. Cambridge, MA: Harvard University Press, 2016.

Mufti, Aamir. "Global Comparativism," *Critical Inquiry* 31, no. 2 (2005): 472–89.

Ostby, Marie. "Graphics and Global Dissent: Marjane Satrapi's *Persepolis*, Persian Miniatures, and the Multifaceted Power of Comic Protest." *PMLA* 132, no. 3 (2017): 558–79.

Palumbo-Liu, David. "Atlantic to Pacific: James, Todorov, Blackmur, and Intercontinental Form." In *Shades of the Planet: American Literature as World Literature*, ed. Wai Chee Dimock and Lawrence Buell, 196–226. Princeton: Princeton University Press, 2007.

Parsipur, Shahrnush. *Women without Men: A Novel of Modern Iran*. Trans. Faridoun Farrokh. New York: Feminist Press, 2012.

Perloff, Marjorie, ed. *Postmodern Genres*. Norman: University of Oklahoma Press, 1989.

Proctor, Rebecca Anne. "For Years, Iran's Art Scene Has Been a Pioneer in the Middle East. Now US Sanctions Are Knocking Its Artists Back to the 18th Century." *artnet news*, June 17, 2019. Web. Available at https://news.artnet.com/art-world/iran-art-scene-sanctions-1575094 (accessed October 16, 2019).

Ramazani, Jahan. "Persian Poetry, World Poetry, and Translatability." *University of Toronto Quarterly* 88, no. 2 (2019): 210–28.

Rich, Adrienne. *Collected Early Poems: 1950–1970*. New York: W. W. Norton & Co., 1992.

Said, Edward W. *Culture and Imperialism*. New York: Vintage Books, 1994.

Said, Edward W. *Orientalism*. New York: Knopf Doubleday, 1979.

Satrapi, Marjane. *Persepolis: The Story of a Childhood*. Trans. L'Association. New York: Pantheon Books, 2003.

Talattof, Kamran. "Ideology and Self-Portrayal in the Poetry of Nima Yushij." In *Essays on Nima Yushij: Animating Modernism in Persian Poetry*, ed. Ahmad Karimi-Hakkak and Kamran Talattof, 69–98. Leiden: Brill, 2004.

Zanan Bedun-e Mardan [*Women without Men*]. Dir. Shirin Neshat in collaboration with Shoja Azari. Perf. Shabnam Toloui, Pegah Ferydoni, Arita Shahrzad. IndiePix, 2009. Film.

6

Persian Epistemes in Naim Frashëri's Albanian Poetry

Abdulla Rexhepi

Persian language was made for poetry, whereas poetry was made for the Persian language.

Shemsedin Sami Frashëri[1]

From the fourteenth century onwards, three different cultural and linguistic spheres dominated the lands inhabited by Albanians: the Orthodox Greeks, the Catholic Latins, and the Muslim Turks. All three of these cultures tried to extend their influence and in their rivalry with each other, they sought to convert and assimilate the Albanians.[2] In order to expand and maintain their cultural and political impact, they needed religious texts. Theological developments in Western Europe, especially the emergence of the Protestant movement, influenced the Catholic Church to encourage its Albanian priests to translate and write religious texts in the Albanian language. Thus, the first written text in the Albanian language was of a religious-ecclesiastical character, and early Albanian literature, especially of the sixteenth and seventeenth centuries, was also religious. As Robert Elsie, scholar and translator of Albanian literature notes,

> Early Albanian literature of the late sixteenth and seventeenth centuries was an essentially religious literature. It consisted initially of translations of Latin and Italian devotional texts in the service of the Counter-Reformation and later of original works composed in a new vernacular not yet entirely adapted to theological and philosophical abstractions.[3]

The Ottomans' arrival and settlement in Albanian lands led to the expansion and establishment of Islamic culture, which later extended its influence over other cultures, too.

---

[1] Şemseddin Sami, *Hurdeçin* (Istanbul: Mihran Matbaası, 1885), 2.
[2] Shefik Osmani, *Panteoni iranian dhe iranologët shqiptarë* (Tiranë: Fondacioni Saadi Shirazi, 1998), 65.
[3] Robert Elsie, *History of Albanian Literature* (New York: Colombia University Press, 1995), 44.

From the fourteenth century onwards, after the Ottoman conquest and settlement of the Balkans, a new social system was gradually installed, consisting of the army, administration, schools, mosques, and Muslim tekkes. The epistemology of Islamic culture that the Turks brought with them to the Balkans relied upon the use of Arabic in science and theology, Turkish in the field of administration, and Persian in literature and culture:

> With the Ottoman Empire at the zenith of its power, Turkish forces occupying Albania brought with them a new Moslem culture which was to survive there up to the twentieth century. The languages of culture and learning in Moslem Albania during this period were Turkish, Persian and Arabic ... Albania remained a handicap to intellectual fulfilment in this ever-expanding empire with its rich Turkish and Persian cultural traditions and was not discovered as a vehicle of Islamic literary creativity until the mid-eighteenth century.[4]

Therefore, after the conquest of Albanian lands by the Ottoman Empire, those who adopted the Islamic religion and integrated into the political and social life of the Empire, also began to cultivate an oriental culture. This included oriental literature and art, but this Albanian class also adopted the Arabic-Ottoman script, which they used to write in Albanian. Consequently, an Albanian literature with oriental poetics emerged among the Albanian people, and this was the beginning of secular literature in the Albanian language. In addition to writing in Albanian, the Albanian poets of the Oriental school also wrote in Arabic, Turkish, and especially in Persian. We have today a considerable number of works of this literature in manuscript form, stored in state archives and libraries in Albania, Kosovo, and Macedonia, while some texts are also held in the buildings of tekkes and private houses.[5]

Although the Ottoman Empire consisted of diverse ethnicities and cultures, scholars agree that the dominant culture was Persian, from the beginning of the Empire until the seventeenth/eighteenth centuries. The sultans of the Ottoman Empire made significant investments to bring Persian artists and poets to Istanbul, in order to establish the city as a great center of knowledge and art.

According to Halil İnalcık, Ferdowsi's *Shahnameh* is one of the most translated literary works, in the East and the West. He notes, "it was translated and read in the entire cultural geosphere of the Ottoman Empire, though not as much as Sa'di, Hafez and Jami's works."[6] To further demonstrate the influence of Persian culture on the Ottoman court, İnalcık notes a very interesting historical event:

> Lali, one of the calligraphers of the time, stayed in Iran for a long time and when he returned, he presented himself as an Iranian. He became a *musahib* (close

4 Ibid., 43.
5 Nehat Krasqniqi, *Zhvillimi i kulturës shqiptare me ndikime orientale prej shekullit XVIII deri në fillimet e rilindjes kombëtare* (Prishtinë: Instituti Albanologjik, 2017), 62.
6 Halil İnalcık, *Has-Bağçede Ayş u Tarab* (Istanbul: İş Bankası Kültür Yayınlar, 2015), 23.

friend) of Mehmet II, but when the truth was revealed, he was removed from the leadership of the tekke and his salary was cut off. Many Ottoman poets like Halimi, Rumi and Jami were sent to Iran for further education and on their return were received as masters.[7]

Accordingly, knowing the Persian language and poetics in this language was extremely important to the poets and writers of the Sultan's court. It was also essential to the literary and theological creativity of the tekkes, which were also dominated by literary-mystical Persian works. Thus, the influence of the Persian language had extended so far that, in the lands ruled by the Ottoman Empire, knowing Persian and writing in this language was considered a cultural privilege, and "those who spoke this language were considered intellectual and civilized."[8] We encounter this in the Albanian Muslim poets of that time.[9]

The Albanian poets who wrote under the influence of Persian poetry, aesthetics, and literature were following the example set by the Persian poets, thus Nezim Frakulla, an eighteenth-century Albanian poet, wrote this about his approach and the role model for his poetry:

Unë Urfi-i i zemanit
unë Firdusi hakani
unë sahibi maani (meani)
ti më je ihsani enam
Ti më je oll shahi pyrnaz
ti më je sirr, ti më je raz
unë jam Hafëzi Shiraz unë jam Saadi-i ejam.[10]

I'm the ʿOrfi of all time
I'm strong like Ferdowsi
I'm the possessor of meaning
You are my provider of goodness
You are my king of compliments
You are my secret, you are my mystery
I'm the Hafez of Shiraz
I'm the Saʿdi of this time.

In this verse, Nezimi compares himself to ʿOrfi Shirazi (1555–91) and Abolqasem Ferdowsi (940–ca. 1020), claiming that he understands the meaning of things as told to him by God. Also, addressing his lover, he says you are full of compliments, you are

---

[7] Halil İnalcık, "Qytetërimi Osman dhe Patronazhi i Sarajit," in *Qytetërimi Osman*, ed. Halil İnalcık and Gunsel Renda (Tiranë: Alsar, 2018), 23.

[8] Hayati Develi, *XVIII. Yüzyıl İstanbul Hayatına Dair "Risâle-i Garîbe"* (İstanbul: Kitabevi, 2014), 26.

[9] Hakan Karateke, *İşkodra şairleri ve Ali Emirî'nin diğer eserleri* (İstanbul: Enderun Kitabevi, 1995), 15.

[10] Nezim Frakulla, *Divani shqip*, ed. Genciana Abazi-Egro (Tiranë: Toena, 2006), 56.

my secret and my mystery, but I am the Hafez of Shiraz and the Saʿdi of this time. It is clear that he wants to be identified with Persian poets and his poetry associated with their work.

Thus, historical-cultural relations between Albanians and Persians must be seen within the context of the Ottoman Empire, which for more than five centuries ruled in the Balkans and during this period, created a new cultural identity among the Albanians. Influential Albanian cultural personalities (such as Naim Frashëri) emerged in the epistemes of this culture, and they later created the modern Albanian ethnic identity.

Naim Frashëri and Persian Language and Literature

Naim Frashëri (1846–1900) read and studied the works of the Iranian and Turkish poets and philosophers,[11] and thereby constructed his concepts of life and the world on Persian epistemology, as well as Bektashi theosophy teachings. This conceptual approach shaped Naim's first period of poetic creativity,[12] during which a considerable part of his poetry was inspired by Oriental-Islamic culture, especially Persian. It was as a result of his education in oriental language and knowledge that Naim Frashëri wrote and created, and even translated into Turkish and Persian.

The various writings of Naim and Lumo Skendo indicate that after Naim settled in Istanbul, he taught Persian for some time. Skendo writes, "On Fridays and Sundays, Naim never came to the office. Those days were when I had my Persian lessons: we recited all of *Golestan*, and then some extracts of *Bustan* and *Hafez*."[13] As a result, Naim wrote a Persian grammar called *Qavaʿed-e Farsi beh Tarz-e Novin* (*Rules of Persian: A New Method*), which he published in Istanbul in 1871. In the introduction to the second part of the book, Naim criticizes the way in which the Persian language was taught in the schools of the Ottoman Empire; apparently, his purpose in producing the grammar was to establish a new Persian teaching methodology. Naim's Persian grammar was also written using the new grammar methodology for European languages, so it may be considered the first modern Persian grammar.[14]

Naim also expressed his first poetic experiences and inspiration in Persian and as a result, in 1885, in Istanbul, he published the poetry collection *Takhayyolat* (*Dreams*). The collection is written in the *masnavi* poetic form, constituting a total of twenty-

---

[11] Lumo Skendo, *Naim Frashëri* (Tirana: "Kristo Luarasi" Publishing House, 1941), 9–10.

[12] As Krist Maloki has noted, although Naim taught and studied modern European knowledge, his early life apparently did not impress Naim, and it was only after settling in Istanbul and his presence in his brother Sami bey Frashëri's National Activist Society that Naim began to write about the nation, as well as translate Homer's *Iliad* and French literature (Krist Maloki, *Oriental apo Okcidental* [Tiranë: Plejad], 84–5).

[13] Lumo Skendo, "Naim be Frashëri – Studim dhe Kujtime," *Kalendari Kombiar Journal* 21 (1926), 45.

[14] The allegedly first Persian grammar, *Dastur-e Sokhan*, by Mirza Habib Isfahani was written in 1872, whereas Naim published his grammar a year earlier, in 1871.

four poems, each of which is given a title and year of creation. The work contains 501 couplets. Naim's modern Persian editor writes:

> Perhaps at the age of twenty-five, Naim Frashëri came to the conclusion that the Persian language was the most appropriate means of expressing his poetic imagination. Thus, his poetic musings are overflowing with the richness of Persian literature. The concepts and poetics of this literature, as well as the poetic tradition of the Persian language, helped the Albanian poet to express his deep poetic experiences and insights, which resulted in the creation of the *Takhayyolat* collection. In other words, the *Takhayyolat* collection is a manifestation of Frashëri's intellectual and spiritual thought, expressed in coordination with the ideas of the great Iranian poets.[15]

The *Takhayyolat* is a lush collection of spiritual poems in Persian, while each poem is a spiritual and philosophical miniature. Its symbolism derives from the Qur'anic source, that is, from the same source that inspired much of Persian poetry. Naim's Persian verses are less significant when assessed with regard to rhetoric, as there are few comparisons and metaphors, and most are emotional and basic, although occasionally we observe rich figurative language. In general, when Naim describes nature, his poetry is rhetorically rich, but when he expresses his experiences, spiritual state, and subjective moods, such as love, hope, and so on, we observe the narrowing and dimming of the literary and artistic language, and this results in poorer philosophical contemplation. Rumi's influence is evident because Naim wrote all his poetry in the *masnavi* form and metric. As Abdolkarim Golshani remarks,

> The sweetness of Naim's poetry lies not only in listening to Persian poetry written by a European, but also in the knowledge and acquisition the poet has gained of the secrets, precision and syntagma of Persian poetry, which he has achieved to this degree of professionalism and mastery. In Naim's poetry, we see no boasting, self-exaltation, drifting, hyperbole and bigotry. In short, Naim's poetry has everything a good poem requires.[16]

Frashëri also published a collection of poems in Persian, called *Sokhanan-e Bargozideh* (*Selected Words*), about which L. Skendo says,

> I remember one day, while organizing some books on a shelf, Naim passed me a small volume, about 200 pages long; it contained handwritten poems in Persian, and he told me that he wrote it when he was still a student, an exercise of language and talent.

[15] Mehmet Naim Frashëri, *Divan-e Takhayyolat*, ed. Naser Nikoubakht (Tehran: The Center for International Cultural Studies, 1396/2017), 28.
[16] Abdolkarim Golshani, *Farhang-e Iran dar Qalamrov-e Torkan: Ashar-e Farsi-ye Naim Frashëri, Sha'er va Nevisandeh-ye Qarn-e Nuzdahom-e Albani* (Shiraz: Golshani, 1354/1975), 48.

Skendo adds, in a footnote, "this does not refer to the *Takhayyulat* collection of poems."[17] This collection of Naim's poetry has not yet been found and it is not known whether it was indeed poetry or proverbs.

Naim also collected extracts from the thirteenth-century Persian poet Saʿdi Shirazi's work, *Golestan*, in a book called *Tartib-e Jadid-e Montakhabat-e Golestan* (*A New Classification of Selections from Golestan*), published in Istanbul in 1903 (1321 AH), after his death. Given Naim's concerns about the unconstructive method of teaching Persian in Ottoman schools, it is likely that he edited this selection from *Golestan* in order to facilitate the teaching of this language. The introduction states that the book is designed to be a textbook for schools in the Ottoman Empire.

The discussion above regarding the published works of Naim Frashëri indicates that he had a broad background and very deep connection with the Persian language, through which he expressed his first poetic experiences and expressions. Poetic creation may perhaps be regarded as an individual's most original, ontological expression, and it seems that in the early days of his creative work, Naim was more comfortable expressing himself in Persian. He also integrated into his work in the Albanian language, the mystical spirit, archetypes, poetics, topics, and many figurative styles of Persian literature.

Traces of Persian Literature in Frashëri's Albanian Poetry

The first Albanian poem published by Frashëri was *Fjalët e Qiririt* (*Words of the Candle*). Through this poem, Naim unfolds his poetic mission using the symbol of the "candle," borrowed from Persian mystical poetry, to mark the spiritual sacrifice of the author in the service of humankind. However, he uses the candle archetype "in an original way and gives it a new sound, departing in some points from the essential Persian mystical essence and spirit contained in its genesis, to emphasize the civic, humanistic, and enlightenment mission of the poet to show Albanians the path to freedom."[18] The candle, a well-known archetype in Persian literature, especially for the Hindi-style poets (*sabk-e Hendi*), such as Saʾeb Tabrizi, one of Naim's favorite poets,[19] symbolizes among other things the poet, who, like the candle, sacrifices itself for others' good. Various examples from the Persian poets demonstrate the similarity between Naim's poems and their concept of the candle:

> Both of us burn ourselves out to help friends
> Because of us, our friends are in comfort, whilst we suffer.[20]

[17] Skendo, Naim Frashëri, 52.

[18] Jorgo Bulo, *Naim Frashëri midis iluminizmit dhe misticizmit sufi* [*Naim Frashëri between Enlightenment and Sufi Mysticism*], in *Perla Journal* 65, no. 2 (Tiranë: Iranian Cultural Foundation of Saʿdi Shirazi, 1392/2013), 11.

[19] Mehmet Naim Frashëri, *Qavaʿed-e Farsi beh Tarz-e Novin* (Istanbul: Şirket-i Mürettebiye Matbaası, 1303/1885), 121.

[20] Manuchehri Damghani, *Divan-e Manuchehri*, ed. Mohammad Dabirseyaqi (Tehran: Zovvar, 1363/1984), 71.

If you don't burn and shine like a candle - Don't tell others about your devotion.[21]
I burned while others' hearts warmed.
As a candle, I gave my all to the world, and nothing to myself.[22]

Thus Naim, inspired by Persian poets, identified as they did with the candle, and thus denied himself, in order to enlighten others:

Here among you have I risen,
And aflame am I now blazing,
Just a bit of light to give you,
That I change your night to daytime,
I'll combust and I will wither,
Be consumed and be extinguished,
Just to give you brightness, vision,
That you notice one another.[23]

If we consider the two approaches to the Oneness of Being ("wahdat al-wujud") in the Islamic mystical tradition,[24] that of the theoretical mysticism represented by Ibn Arabi and his followers, and the practical or love approach, whose most worthy representative is Rumi, then we can conclude that Naim is part of the latter: he belongs to the school of love. Mowlana Rumi was a love poet and he saw everything in this world through this prism. Naim Frashëri, like Rumi, does not discuss the Oneness of Being on the theoretical plane in any of his works, although in his poems we may come across many verses that reflect this same approach to God and other creatures. Naim did not have such an outlook only because he belonged to the Bektashi sect of Islam, since he was well aware of the works and authors of other Eastern and Western schools and doctrines, and was not influenced solely by the beliefs inherited from his Bektashi ancestors. In his poetic work, Naim creates a very wide space for God, and many verses involve turning to Him and relying on Him, but always loving and respecting nature and human beings—whose mind and soul is enlightened by God. In his work, we have many verses expressing the pantheistic Islamic worldview:

What you see is true God,
What you hear is his voice,

---

[21] Farideddin Attar, *Divan-e Attar*, ed. Taqi Tafazzoli (Tehran: Bongah-e Tarjomah va Nashr-e Ketab, 1345/1966), 143.

[22] Mirza Mohammadali Saèb, *Kolliyat-e Divan-e Saèb*, ed. Mohammad Abbasi (Tehran: Entesharat-e Javaheri, 1373/1994), 639.

[23] Naim Frashëri, *Vepra 2* (Prishtinë: Rilindja, 1986), 9. "The Words of the Candle," translated by Robert Elsie.

[24] See William Chittick, "Rumi and Wahdat al-Wujud," in *Poetry and Mysticism in Islam: The Heritage of Rumi*, ed. Amin Benani, Richard Hovannisian, and George Sabagh (Cambridge, MA: Harvard University Press, 1994).

All there is and is not in life,
Is God himself.[25]

For Rumi, only through love of creatures which belong to God can we reach True Love,
that is, also love for God—because they both burn and become ashes for man. In many
verses of his poems, Rumi says that God is in every direction you turn, God is in man,
but in order to reach Him you have to immerse yourself in Him, that is, to be cleansed
of human vices and desires. According to him, the way that leads you to God is love of
man and nature. Rumi wrote,

Who are we, O soul of our soul?
Who can we be if there is distance between us?
We are nothing and do not exist,
You are the absolute, eternal being.[26]

For Naim, like Rumi, everything we see and hear in this world is divine, and in this life,
there is nothing but God. He writes,

And the man and the cattle,
And all that is in life,
I love as God,
From whence their eyes turn.
I see the true God there,
He is one and indivisible.[27]

Naim Frashëri shared Rumi's ideas about the search for God in what surrounds us.
Thus, he writes,

After this, comrades, never
Never seek God
Among the walls and stones,
You will easily find man![28]

This mystical concept of God as an absolute Being in Albanian literature entered
through Naim's work, and thus love for man, animal, and nature is understood as
love for the Creator. Naim's pantheistic perspective, the mystical convictions of love
for the Other, and many other mystical beliefs were valuable contributions toward
the development of an open mindset that recognizes and respects the existence and
thought of the other. Thus, he left deep traces in the cultivation of a society dominated

---

[25] Naim Frashëri, *Vepra 1* (Prishtinë: Rilindja, 1986), 78.
[26] Mowlana Jalaleddin Rumi, *Masnavi*, ed. Reynold A. Nicholson (Tehran: Qatreh, 1392), 356.
[27] Naim Frashëri, *Vepra 1*, 76.
[28] Ibid., 136.

by a spirit of brotherly cohabitation. His humanist teachings reflected the esoteric philosophy (*batiniyyah*) of the mystical school of Khorasan and evoked love and respect for other religions, thus, in his view, all religions are the same and equal. This approach prompted him to sing to Jesus Christ, the prophet of Christian believers.

Naim, whether in Turkish or Persian, or in Albanian, does not mention the name of Mowlana Jalaleddin Rumi. Although he mentions dozens of names of Iranian scholars, poets, historians, and philosophers, especially in the second part of his *Persian Grammar*, he does not say a single word about Rumi. Yet he translated, borrowed, and recreated some fables from Rumi's *Masnavi*, entitled "Weight," "Dragons with Friends," and "Two Bulls and a Wolf." However, Naim, unlike Rumi—who uses fables for expressing his philosophical, mystical ideas—greatly simplifies them and reduces them, taking them from the high, mystical-philosophical level to a didactic, moralizing level.

The direct influence of Rumi's *masnavi* form on Naim Frashëri is found in his own poem "The Flute," over half of which is a literal translation of Rumi's "Ney-nameh."[29] Naim's borrowing from Rumi has also been noted by Albanian literature scholars.[30] Naim's "The Flute" differs from Rumi's "Ney-nameh," which is in *masnavi* form. "The Flute" is a poem in four strophes, with eight-stringed syllables and the alternating rhyme *abab*, containing a total of fourteen strophes. Up to the ninth strophe, Naim remains faithful, even directly translating the verses of Rumi, but from the tenth verse onward, he creates his own original verses, though still under the influence of the earlier verses. The similarities and differences outlined are illustrated by the following strophes of "The Flute," translated into English by Robert Elsie:

> Listen to the flute a-speaking,
> Tell the tale of wretched exile,
> Weeping for this world of sorrow
> Using words of truth to spin it.
> Since the day they seized and took me
> From my friends and my companions,
> Men and women have been weeping
> At the echo of my sobbing.
> I have rent my breast from beating,
> Gaping holes have made within it,
> How I've wept and have lamented,
> Thousand sighs my heart has rendered.
> I'm a friend and blithe companion

---

[29] See Rumi, *Masnavi*, 15–17.
[30] For example, Eqrem Çabej calls Naim's poem "The Flute" "Naim's inspiration from Rumi" (see Eqrem Çabej, *Elemente të gjuhësisë e të literaturës shqipe* [Tiranë: Çabej, 1936], 48). Shuteriqi considers the poem "a recreation that cannot be separated from Naim's original poems" (Dhimitër Shuteriqi, *Naim Frashëri - Jeta dhe Vepra* [Tiranë: Naimi, 1982], 85), while Jorgo Bulo, comparing Naim's and Rumi's poems, argues for considerable similarity of Naim's poem to Rumi's "Ney-nameh," stating that the Albanian author, while being inspired by Rumi, also recreated the latter's poetry (Jorgo Bulo, *Magjia dhe Magjistarët e fjalës* [Tiranë: Dituria, 1998], 47).

Both of this world's happy people
And of all folk sad, embittered,
With them do I make alliance.
Whate'er be the situation,
I can weep and mourn in longing,
At any time and any place will
My heart sigh and be a-moaning.
All the world does listen to me,
Sees though only my appearance,
Of my wishes they know nothing,
Nor the fire that burns within me.
People come and gather 'round me
When I weep and tell of longing,
Yet they do not know my secret,
Thus I find no consolation.[31]

The text of the poem clearly corresponds to the text of Rumi, and if we compare the two, we note that nine strophes of this poem are a word-for-word translation of "Ney-nameh," while from the tenth verse onward, Naim is released from the text of Rumi and writes freely, though he is still operating within the mystic concept of love-as-fire.

In his original verses, Naim also touches on the main subject of mystic discourse: love. According to Muslim mystics, God created everything out of love, and love gives cause to every movement and creation, so it gives sense to everything in this life. Even in the last verses of the "The Flute," Naim wants to say that it is the fire of love that gives the phenomenon or thing its true meaning. Thus, the fire of love gave the rose its scent and the song to nightingale, while love caused the creation of man himself. According to Naim, without love, nothing would be meaningful, not even our existence in this world. So, the immersion in love for the Creator is the highest mystic level, where all racial, religious, sectarian, and ethnic differences are eliminated. The deeds of a mystic who has achieved this level reflect nothing but love and goodness for every creature of God.

Naim and the Persian Epic

During this period, Naim became more interested in the Persian epic than in mysticism because he and his brothers established a movement for the independence of Albania from the Ottoman Empire, thus laying the foundations of modern Albanian identity.

For Naim, humankind first appeared in this world somewhere in the mountains of Persia; hence, in his Turkish language book, *Ekhtera'at va Kashfiyyat* (*Inventions*

---

[31] Frashëri, *Vepra 1*, 172–3. Taken from "The Flute," translated by Robert Elsie.

and Discoveries), the first references to human knowledge in this world are borrowed from the Persian mythology in the *Shahnameh* epic by Ferdowsi. Thus, Naim's epistemological starting point is Persia, and to be more precise, the most famous Iranian epic, many traces of which can be found in his works. In the *Shahnameh*, there is a discussion of the creation of the world, the first man, the first king, and the origins of the many elements and mechanisms that ensure the continuation of human life in this world. In his *Ekhtera'at va Kashfiyyat*, Naim writes, "In the beginnings of the Ferdowsi's *Shahnameh*, based on antiquity, the initial state of man is described this way," and then he goes on to tell the story of Hushang.[32]

It is no accident that Naim and Sami Frashëri[33] were both devoted to this epic-literary masterpiece. Like Sami, Naim knew Ferdowsi's work very well, and the latter influenced the structure of his ethnic and national ideas. Indeed, Eqrem Çabej, a pioneering scholar of Albanian studies among Albanians, claims that Naim's desire to write a long epic poem, in the style of the great Persian epic,[34] meant that his resulting work, "The History of Skanderbeg," did not become the Albanian national epic; instead, this place was taken by the epic "The Highland Lute," by the author Gjergj Fishta (1871–1940).

As noted earlier, Ferdowsi's *Shahnameh* was widely translated and read in the Ottoman Empire. But the worldview and motives in *Shahnameh* also stimulated Muslim peoples ruled by the Sultanate/Caliphate, the highest religious-political authority, to consider their own ethnicities and nations, and they used this text to legitimize and justify nationalist and liberationist ideas, which could be considered "seditious" toward Empire or Caliphate.

This is why many Albanian intellectuals read and attempted to copy the *Shahnameh*:[35] by adopting it as a model, they were apparently trying to arouse nationalism in their people.[36]

In addition to the poetic dimensions of the *Shahnameh*, there were also aspects of nationality and patriotism that led Naim to the conclusion that "the best poets are the Persians and the best and greatest among them is Ferdowsi, who wrote *Shahnameh*, and who recounts the events of the kingdoms of Persia so beautifully and is said to

---

[32] Mehmed Naim Frashëri, *Ekhtera'at va Kashfiyyat* (Istanbul: Mehran, 1298/1880), 3–5.

[33] In addition to translating from the Persian into Turkish a selection of *Shahnameh*, which is preserved in the manuscript, Sami also wrote the play *Kaveh, the Blacksmith*, as well as *Sohrab*, the latter still missing. As Kemal Erol observes, Sami wrote these works to express political criticism of the oppression of his own time (see Kemal Erol, "Şemsettin Sami'nin Besa ve Gâve Adliyeslerinde Sömürüye Karşi Politik Eleştiri," *Uluslararası Sosyal Araştırmalar Dergisi* [*The Journal of International Social Research*] 9, no. 44 (2016): 117–28.

[34] Eqrem Çabej, *Shqiptarët midis Perëndimit dhe Lindjes* (Tiranë: Çabej, 2006), 111.

[35] Hafez Ali Korça, in his book *The Holy History and the Four Caliphs*, also intends to imitate Ferdowsi and as if he created a *Shahnameh* for Albanians (34): I'm like Ferdowsi I'm not saying it / But I have done as much work—As the poor Ferdowsi / If he was alive today—He would tell me and you / You have suffered with history—Like me with *Shahnameh* / That I tired myself We are both Aryan / Languages have a harmony—I came from Persia / You came out of Albania.

[36] Zahra Rajabi and Abdulla Rexhepi, "Survey of the Place of Ferdowsi's *Shahnameh* in the Albanian Language and Literature," *Modern Journal of Language Teaching Methods* 8, no. 4 (2018): 114–20.

have been the wisest poet."[37] Thus, Naim would follow the path of Ferdowsi and like him, would use all his talents and abilities in the creation of the modern Albanian nation. For Naim, as with Ferdowsi, language was primary because it would then create the possibilities of creation, culture, and literature, and as a result would keep alive the spirit and ethnic identity of the people. The impact of *Shahnameh* can be found throughout Naim's work, but most significantly, in *The History of Scanderbeg*.

The meta-narration of Ferdowsi's *Shahnameh* and Naim's *The History of Scanderbeg* is the conflict, confrontation and dualism between good and evil, which also has its source in ancient Iranian teachings. The *Shahnameh*, from the beginning to the end, is full of stories of confrontation between Good (as manifested through the Iranians, Jamshid, Rostam, Zal, etc.) and Evil (as represented by Turan, Sohrab, Dahaq, Satan, etc.). Thus the confrontation begins between the stone and the fire from which iron results, between nature and animals, and man, between Rostam and Sohrab, between the dark spiritual powers and the enlightening power of humans.[38] In *The History of Scanderbeg*, too, stories are structured around the topic of conflict between the Albanian hero, Scanderbeg, who fought for liberation of Albania and Albanians on one side, and the Sultan and his army that had occupied Albanian lands. In the *Shahnameh*, Iran is a symbol of the good; as Ferdowsi states:

> Iran is like a garden in springtime,
> where scented flowers always blossom,
> Surrounded by soldiers and walls,
> At the tip of the spear lies the blow,
> Beware, lest you cross that wall,
> And anger the Iranians.[39]

As for Naim,

> Albania always
> has been highly praised,
> there were men, now deceased,
> famous, wise and brave.[40]
> O desolate Adrianople!
> the throne of wickedness,
> an evil name for life
> against humankind.[41]

---

[37] Frashëri, *Vepra 6*, 286.

[38] Mohammad Biranvandi and Hosseinali Qobadi, *Ayin-e Ayeneh: Seyr-e Tahavvol-e Namad-pardazi dar Farhang-e Irani va Adabiyat-e Farsi* (Tehran: Daneshgah-e Tarbiyat-e Modarres, 1386/2007), 86.

[39] Abolqasem Ferdowsi, *Shahnameh* (Tehran: Ketab-Sara-ye Nik, 1378/1999), 539.

[40] Frashëri, *Vepra 3*, 8.

[41] Ibid., 56.

The above verses clearly represent Albania as a symbol of goodness, and of glory, with wise and learned people, whereas Adrianople, then capital of the Ottoman Empire, is portrayed as a deserted place and a symbol of evil and wickedness. However, it should be noted that Naim's patriotism is very different from the epics and legends of the Middle Ages, which saw their ethnicities as a divine mission to establish "Justice" on earth. European nationalism, resulting from European Romanticism, which also inspired Naim, was more universal and rational, and Naim's ideas are closer to the European national and ethnic idea.

Naim and Bektashi Religious Poetry

Naim Frashëri intended to stimulate a sense of Albanian national identity through the Bektashi sect of Islam,[42] a popular idea and movement in Iran, where it had succeeded in making twelve Sh'ia imams an integral part of the modern Iranian nation.[43] As a result of this endeavor, Naim wrote the epic poem "Qerbelaja" ("Karbala"), which he created based on the work *Rowzat-ol Shohada* (*The Garden of the Martyrs*) by the author Mulla Hussain Vaez Kashefi, under whose influence the Turkish poet Fozuli also wrote the work *Hadiqat-ol Sa'adah* (*The Garden of the Blessed*).[44] In his heroic religious epic, Naim wanted to present part of the history of Islam and Bektashism,[45] while also showing how good and truth would triumph over evil. Knowing well the Bektashi philosophy, which was characterized by tolerance of religions and other religious sects, having humanity, tolerance, human and divine love at the forefront, Naim drew upon this knowledge to address his subject. The narrative and historical context of Naim's poem are almost identical to those in the works of Kashefi and Fuzuli, yet unlike either of these two works, Naim's story is often shaped by national sentiment. In this epic poem and in many other poems, he invites the Albanians to follow the family of Ali, the first Shi'a Imam and the fourth Sunni caliph, so that like those who did not submit to the rule of the Umayyad Caliphate, the Albanians would not surrender, but would rebel against Ottoman rule:

> Brave Albanian with wings,
> How it was, let it be,

---

[42] Albert Doja, "The Politics of Religious Dualism: Naim Frashëri and His Elective Affinity to Religion in the Course of 19th-century Albanian Activism," *Social Compass* 60, no. 1 (2013): 115–33.

[43] Ali Mirsepassi, *Political Islam, Iran, and the Enlightenment: Philosophies of Hope and Despair* (New York: Cambridge University Press, 2011).

[44] This work by Fuzûlî was translated in an extended manner by Dalip Frashëri; based on this work, Shahin Frashëri (Naim's uncle) wrote his *Myhtarnameja*. His poem *Myhtarnameja* (Mokhtarnameh: Book of Mukhtar) is one of the longest and earliest epics in Albanian literature. It describes the events post Battle of Karbala of 680 AD, when Hossein ebn-e Ali was killed, an important event in the chronology of Islam.

[45] Qazim Qazimi, *Ndikime orientale në veprën letrare të Naim Frashërit* (Prishtinë: Këshilli i Bashkësisë Islame të Gjilanit, 1996), 134.

To have all wisdom,
And to love Albania,
To die for the Motherland,
Like Mukhtar for Hussain,
The same as Ibrahim,
And with Eba Muslim.[46]

The Bektashi tropes in Naim's work are so intertwined with his own national narrative that in one of his poems, Abbas Ali, the brother of Imam Hussein, killed in the battle of Karbala, comes down to Mount Tomorr in Albania in the form of divine intervention, so as not to leave Albania in a bad state of affairs:

Abbas Ali came to Tomorr
Came close to us
Albania is not abandoned
Because God loves her.[47]

In many places in "Karbala," but also in other poems about the family of the prophet Muhammad (i.e., the Ahl-e Beyt), Naim Frashëri aims to combine the history and "suffering" of this family with the history and "suffering" of the Albanian people and thus, to awaken nationalist sentiments in his audiences, inciting them to break free from Ottoman rule and establish the Albanian state and nation. "Karbala" had a deep impact on the thought and spiritual world of the Albanian dervishes, who still read this work during the days of the month of Moharram. Through this work, they engage in the mystical imagination, and thus, they weep and mourn for an event that happened many centuries ago. As such, Naim's work, though not his alone, creates another ontological environment for them, and accordingly, the bitter events of Karbala are experienced as freshly as if they have just happened. Therefore, Naim's "Karbala" is perhaps one of the most influential works in Albanian popular culture.

Most Albanian scholars[48] agree that Naim Frashëri is one of the most influential poets in Albanian literature, and that he "can be called the initiator of a new faith in the history of literature and culture of the Albanian people."[49] He introduced to later Albanian literature a series of figurative concepts, topics, and elements that he borrowed from Persian literature. As Ernest Koliqi states, "I dare to argue that five centuries of Ottoman rule did not affect Albanian literature, or the Albanian spirit, as much as the work of a single writer, Naim Frashëri. He was a representative of the

[46] Frashëri, *Vepra* 4, 49.
[47] Frashëri, *Vepra* 1, 170.
[48] See, for example, Bulo, *Magjia dhe Magjistarët e fjalës*, 134; Rexhep Qosja, *Historia e letërsisë shqipe, Romantizmi III* (Prishtinë: Rilindja, 1985), 134.
[49] Rexhep Qosja, *Porosia e madhe – Monografi mbi krijimtarinë e Naim Frashërit* (Tirana: Sh. b. Naim Frashëri, 1989), 474.

oriental culture, an enlightened, inspired and skilled representative of this culture. Through his work, the Orient left the liveliest and deepest traces on us."[50]

Naim's poetic works in Persian, and in the Albanian language under the influence of Persian poetry, have established literary connections between Albanian and Persian, in world literature. In this manner, Naim has brought Albanian literature into contact with the concept of World Literature. Embracing many archetypes and motifs of Persian literature, which later became part of Albanian literature and culture, he built bridges of communication between Albanian and Persian languages and literatures. Furthermore, as Rexhep Qosja concludes,

> The historical-literary and cultural significance of Naim Frashëri's work, also lies in its broad and lasting impact on the lives of the Albanian people. It played a major literary, educational, cultural, moral and national role at the time of its publication, and it continues to play such a role to this day.[51]

Naim's mystical ideas and beliefs about love for the Other, the mystical conception of God, as well as many of his mystical teachings, have profoundly influenced the formation of the contemporary Albanian mentality. As a result, a cultural reality was created among the Albanians, enabling them to transcend the form of religion, and thus maintain a spirit of interreligious and intercultural tolerance and coexistence in the region.

Conclusion

This chapter argues that Naim Frashëri, educated in Persian knowledge and culture, wrote his first linguistic text and poetic expression in the Persian language, and thus he connects the Albanian with the Persian, and with world culture and literature. Naim's Persian grammar, his Persian poetry compilation *Takhayyolat* and the selection of Saadi's *Golestan*, are a valuable contribution to Persian language and literature. Furthermore, Naim's poetry in the Albanian language was also influenced by the figurative concepts, devices, and topics of Persian literature, such as the candle, butterfly, nightingale, the mystical concept of God, and many others. Through Naim's works, many elements of Persian literature succeeded in infusing and integrating into Albanian literature and culture.

Naim Frashëri combined the spirit of patriotism, that of Ferdowsi's *Shahnameh*, with European Romantic ideas about the nation, and thus he created poems that inspired Albanians to seek liberation from the Ottoman Empire. Inspired also by the ideas of the Bektashi sect and of the authors, Kashefi and Fuzuli, in his poem "*Karbala,*" in which he combined the historical Bektashi being with the Albanian, he succeeded

---

[50] Ernest Koliqi, *Ese të letërsisë shqipe*, trans. Dhurata Shehri (Tirana: IDK, 2009), 186.
[51] Qosja, *Porosia e madhe*, 461.

in constructing a consciousness of resistance that would outlast the Ottoman Empire. Through the immense influence he left on Albanian literature and culture, Naim Frashëri brought to Albanian literature a version of the mystic concept of love and God, as all things are god (pantheism), and the idea that the poet/intellectual, just like the candle, should burn for the enlightenment and emancipation of his/her people. Frashëri beautified an Albanian being, identified with pragmatic, practical, and physical values, with a particular conception of mystical love and an idea of God as an absolute Being.

Naim also introduced an Eastern mystical imagination into Albanian literature, through which the reader could make connections to very deep and distant spiritual realms. Above all, in Albanian literature and culture, he instilled universal love for everything, starting from humans, animals, nature, and every other living organism because to him, they all constitute God, the Supreme Creator. These mystical ideas and teachings of Naim have left a deep imprint on Albanian intellectuals and readers.

Bibliography

Attar, Farideddin. *Divan-e Attar*. Ed. Taqi Tafazzoli. Tehran: Bongah-e Tarjomeh va Nashr-e Ketab, 1345/1966.

Biranvandi, Mohammad, and Hosseinali Qobadi. *Ayin-e Ayeneh: Seyr-e Tahavvol-e Namad-pardazi dar Farhang-e Irani va Adabiyat-e Farsi*. Tehran: Daneshgah-e Tarbiyat-e Modarres, 1386/2007.

Bulo, Jorgo. *Magjia dhe Magjistarët e fjalës*. Tiranë: Dituria, 1998.

Bulo, Jorgo. "Naim Frashëri Midis Iluminizmit dhe Misticizmit Sufi." *Perla Journal* 65, no. 1 (2013): 15–22.

Çabej, Eqrem. *Elemente të gjuhësisë e të literaturës shqipe*. Tiranë: Çabej, 1936.

Çabej, Eqrem. *Shqiptarët midis Perëndimit dhe Lindjes*. Tiranë: Çabej. 2006.

Chittick, William. "Rumi and Wahdat al-Wujud." In *The Poetry and Mysticism in Islam: The Heritage of Rumi*. Ed. Amin Benani, Richard Hovannisian, and George Sabagh. Cambridge, MA: Harvard University Press, 1994.

Develi, Hayati. *XVIII. Yüzyıl İstanbul Hayatına Dair "Risâle-i Garîbe."* Istanbul: Kitabevi, 1998.

Doja, Albert. "The Politics of Religious Dualism: Naim Frashëri and His Elective Affinity to Religion in the Course of 19th-Century Albanian Activism." *Social Compass* 60, no. 1 (2013): 115–33.

Elsie, Robert. *History of Albanian Literature*. Vol. I. New York: Columbia University Press, 1995.

Ferdowsi, Abolqasem. *Shahnameh*. Ed. Saeid Hamidian. Tehran: Ketab-Sara-ye Nik, 1378/1999.

Frashëri, Mehmed Naim. *Ekhtera'at va Kashfiyyat*. Istanbul: Mehran, 1298/1880.

Frashëri, Mehmed Naim. *Qava'ed-e Farsi Beh Tarz-e Novin [Rules of Persian: A New Method]*. Istanbul: Şirket-i Mürettebiye Matbaası, 1303/1885.

Frashëri, Mehmed Naim. *Divan-e Takhayyolat*. Ed. Naser Nikoubakht. Tehran: The Center for International Cultural Studies, 1396/2017.

Frashëri, Mehmed Naim. *Vepra 1*. Prishtinë: Rilindja, 1986.

Frashëri, Mehmed Naim. *Vepra 2*. Prishtinë: Rilindja, 1986.
Frashëri, Mehmed Naim. *Vepra 3*. Prishtinë: Rilindja, 1986.
Frashëri, Mehmed Naim. *Vepra 4*. Prishtinë: Rilindja, 1986.
Golshani, Abdolkarim. *Farhang-e Iran dar Qalamrov-e Torkan: Ash'ar-e Farsi-ye Naim Frashëri, Sha'er va Nevisandeh-ye Qarn-e Nuzdahom-e Albani*. Shiraz, 1354/1953.
İnalcık, Halil. *Has-Bağçede Ayş u Tarab*. Istanbul: İş Bankası Kültür Yayınlar, 2015.
Karateke, Hakan. *İşkodra şairleri ve Ali Emirî'nin diğer eserleri*. Istanbul: Enderun Kitabevi, 1995.
Koliqi, Ernest. *Ese të letërsisë shqipe*. Trans. Dhurata Shehri. Tirana: IDK, 2009.
Korça, Hafez Ali. *Historia e Shenjtë dhe Katër Halifetë*. Shkup, North Macedonia: Logos A, 2006.
Krasniqi, Nehat. *Zhvillimi i kulturës shqiptare me ndikime orientale prej shekullit XVIII deri në fillimet e rilindjes kombëtare*. Prishtinë: Instituti Albanologjik, 2017.
Manuchehri Damghani. *Divan-e Manuchehri*. Ed. Muhammad Dabirseyaqi. Tehran: Zovvar, 1363/1984.
Mirsepassi, Ali. *Political Islam, Iran, and the Enlightenment: Philosophies of Hope and Despair*. New York: Cambridge University Press, 2011.
Mowlana Rumi, Jalaleddin. *The Mathnawi of Jalaluddin Rumi*. Trans. Reynold A. Nicholson. London: Messrs. Luzac, & Co., 1926.
Osmani, Shefik. *Panteoni iranian dhe iranologët shqiptarë*. Tiranë: Fondacioni Saadi Shirazi, 1998.
Qazimi, Qazim. *Ndikime orientale në veprën letrare të Naim Frashërit*. Prishtinë: Këshilli i Bashkësisë Islame të Gjilanit, 1996.
Qosja, Rexhep. *Historia e letërsisë shqipe, Romantizmi III*. Prishtinë: Rilindja, 1986.
Qosja, Rexhep. *Porosia e madhe: Monografi mbi krijimtarinë e Naim Frashërit*. Tirana: Sh. b. Naim Frashëri, 1989.
Rajabi, Zahra, and Abdulla Rexhepi. "Survey of the Place of Ferdowsi's *Shahnameh* in the Albanian Language and Literature." *Modern Journal of Language Teaching Methods* 8, no. 4 (2018): 114–20.
Sa'eb, Mirza Mohammad Ali. *Kolliyat-e Divan-e Sa'eb*. Ed. Mohammad Abbasi. Tehran: Javaheri, 1373/1994.
Sami, Şemseddin. *Hurdeçin*. Istanbul: Mihran Matbaası, 1885.
Shuteriqi, Dhimitër. *Naim Frashëri: Jeta dhe Vepra*. Tiranë: Naimi, 1982.
Skendo, Lumo. "Naim be Frashëri: Studim dhe Kujtime." *Kalendari Kombiar Journal* 21 (1926): 12–16.
Skendo, Lumo. *Naim Frashëri*. Tirana: "Kristo Luarasi" Publishing House, 1941.

7

Ecumenism and Globalism in the Reception of Ferdowsi and His *Shahnameh*: Evidence from the "Baysonqori Preface"

Olga M. Davidson

Preliminaries

The focus here is on two Persianate texts. The first is the *Shahnameh* or *Book of Kings*, the monumental poem of a poet retrospectively named Ferdowsi, or "man of paradise," who lived in the late tenth and early eleventh century CE. The second text is in prose: it is a comparably monumental preface to a lavish new edition of the *Shahnameh* that was commissioned in 1426 CE and published in 1430 under the aegis of a Timurid prince named Baysonqor. The preface, which was likewise commissioned by the prince, tells the story of the poet and of his poetry. Such a story can be mined by literary historians as a source for reconstructing the *reception* of the *Shahnameh*—not only in the era of Ferdowsi but also in later times, culminating in the era of Baysonqor. From the standpoint of the preface, as I will argue, the reception of the *Shahnameh* can be described in modern literary critical terms as a model of *ecumenism* and *globalism*.

Such a modernistic description, of course, would at first seem alien to ancient readers of an edition stemming from the fifteenth century of our era, distanced as they are from our own century by well over half a millennium. On the other hand, these same ancient readers would also be distanced, by almost as long a stretch of time— over 400 years—from the era of the poet Ferdowsi himself, who first put together the *Shahnameh* as we know it.

In view of this relative equidistance, I find it justifiable to reexamine the two terms *ecumenism* and *globalism*, testing the value they bring to my project, which is to reconstruct historically the ancient reception of the *Shahnameh*. Such a reexamination, as we will see, will show that these terms are perfectly applicable to the ancient reception of the *Shahnameh* in the era of the preface commissioned by the Prince Baysonqor.

The two terms that I just highlighted, *ecumenism* and *globalism*, are ordinarily used in the context of studying *world literature* as it is understood today, and all three of these terms, including now *world literature*, are relevant to an assertion that we will see being made in the text of the "Baysonqori Preface" about the newly edited version of the *Shahnameh*, which as I already noted was composed over 400 years earlier. Basically, the preface asserts that the poem is universal in its appeal. In terms of such an assertion, then, this monumental poem could be described as world literature.

But there is an impediment here, in that the world in which the literature represented by the *Shahnameh* came to life was different from the world today. To put it in a slightly different way, the world literature of the *Shahnameh* was different from the world literature of today.

If this statement holds, then the terms I have highlighted so far will need to be adjusted in the context of my analyzing the historical background that shaped the two texts under study here, that is, both the poetic *Shahnameh* composed by Ferdowsi and its prosaic preface commissioned by the Prince Baysonqor. For such an analysis, I find it useful to stress the importance of another term I am using, *reception*—precisely in the context of analyzing the relevant historical background.

An Adjusted Application of the Terms *Ecumenism* and *Globalism*

The terms *ecumenism* and *globalism* are suited to the study of world literature as viewed in the world of today, where the word *world* ideally includes all of humanity, that is, everyone who inhabits planet earth. Such idealism admittedly tends to be "Westernized," as in the work of William H. McNeill, *The Rise of the West: A History of the Human Community*, for whom the "ecumene" of the world today arose from European interactions in the realms of science and technology combined with political and economic know-how.[1] By contrast, the world of Ferdowsi as mediated in the edition and preface commissioned by the Prince Baysonqor in 1426 CE was an *empire* that included all of humanity inhabiting whatever realms were controlled—either for real or at least notionally—by the dynasty of the Timurids as represented in this case by Baysonqor. In other words, this world of Ferdowsi was an imperial project.

Ironically, the history of the word "ecumene" as used by McNeill actually reveals, in its earlier history, a comparably imperial project. This word, which had been *oikouménē* in the original Greek and which had once meant simply "inhabited [earth]" to ancient Greek geographers, was eventually appropriated by the Roman Empire as a designation of all the realms populated by all humans under Roman control. One of many examples is the picturing of Oikoumene as a goddess in the act of crowning the Roman emperor Augustus, as carved into the Gemma Augustea, dating from the early first century CE.[2]

Similarly, in the case of geographically globalistic expressions like "Planet Earth," ancient contexts point to projects of empire. A most striking example in this case is the use of the Latin word *orbis*, meaning "globe" or "sphere," with reference to the

---

[1] William H. McNeill, *The Rise of the West: A History of the Human Community* (Chicago: The University of Chicago Press, 1991 [1963]).

[2] Nancy H. and Andrew Ramage, *Roman Art: Romulus to Constantine* (New York: Abrams, 1991), 106–7.

shield of Aeneas in Virgil's *Aeneid* (8.449): this hero, as the poeticized originator of the Roman Empire, is pictured as carrying the weight of his enormous new shield upon his shoulder, and, as the description proceeds, this enormity is pictured as the *orbis* or "globe," analogous to the entire world weighing on the shoulder of Atlas, mainstay of the universe. That is to say, the mythical originator of the Roman Empire is carrying on his shoulder the weighty burden of his imperial project.[3]

Having shown the rootedness of the terms *ecumenism* and *globalism* in the historical context of what I have so far been describing as imperial projects, I am now ready to adjust these terms before I apply them further to the historical realities surrounding the *Shahnameh* in the era of the Timurid Prince Baysonqor. Basically, my adjustment amounts to this: the ecumenism and globalism of the poem, asserted in the preface to the poem, is limited in reality, if not in ideology. Although the preface to the poem asserts an idealized universal acceptance of the poem, such universalism is in reality limited to the historical confines of the Empire ruled by the Timurid dynasty at the time.

The idea of universal acceptance, asserted in the "Baysonqori Preface" to the *Shahnameh*, is relevant to the term *reception* as used by literary critics. This term is nowadays generally applied to rereadings, in the present, of literature once read in the distant past. In terms of such a general understanding, the rereadings in the present are neutral about valuing or devaluing the readings in the past. In the case of the "Baysonqori Preface," however, the attitude is not neutral but one-sidedly positive in evaluating the *Shahnameh* as read in the present, by contrast with negative as well as positive evaluations in the past. In the "present time" of the "Baysonqori Preface," the text of the monumental poem that it introduces is supposedly perfect and thus worthy of universally positive evaluation. So, I adjust the use of the term *reception* with reference to the *Shahnameh* as introduced by the "Baysonqori Preface."

An additional adjustment must be noted here: as we will see in the stories told in the "Baysonqori Preface," the reception of the *Shahnameh* can be viewed not only as the act of reading the poetry composed by Ferdowsi but also as the act of listening to the performance of his compositions.

Modern Receptions of the *Shahnameh*

Aside from the traditional reception of the *Shahnameh* as viewed from the standpoint of the "Baysonqori Preface," I would argue that various kinds of modern reception can be just as favorable. I would also argue that the poetry of Ferdowsi can have a universal appeal even outside its historical contexts. So long as this poetry is translated effectively, as for example in the English-language renditions by Dick Davis, the *Shahnameh* can become "user-friendly" for non-Iranians as well as Iranians.[4]

---

[3] Gregory Nagy, *Homer the Preclassic* (Berkeley: University of California Press, 2010), 357.
[4] Dick Davis, trans., *Shahnameh: The Persian Book of Kings* (New York: Viking, 2006).

If the *Shahnameh* were to be "owned" exclusively by Iranians, there would always linger an assumption, implicit or even explicit, that this masterpiece of poetry cannot really be appreciated properly by non-Iranians. In translation, however, this poetry can be recognized by non-Iranians together with Iranians as a jewel of world literature amongst such "Western" classics as Virgil's *Aeneid* or the Homeric *Iliad* and *Odyssey*—to cite perhaps the most formidable points of comparison.

The argument that I just presented about the value of reading the *Shahnameh* of Ferdowsi in translation can be extended, I argue here, to a parallel reading, again in translation, of four surviving biographies of Ferdowsi. I will hereafter refer to these four narratives as Lives of Ferdowsi, the fourth one of which, as we are about to see in the Excursus that follows, is found in the Baysonqori Preface to the *Shahnameh*.

Excursus on the Lives of Ferdowsi

The four Lives of Ferdowsi are found in the prefaces to various manuscripts of the *Shahnameh*. These have been edited, with commentary, by Mohammad-Amin Riyahi, in *Sar-Cheshmeh-ha-ye Ferdowsi-shenasi*—a work that I will hereafter abbreviate as MAR.[5] I list here, in chronological order, these prefaces (and I indicate the page numbers in MAR):

> Preface 1. The so-called Older Preface, dated 346 AH/958 CE (MAR 170–80);
> Preface 2. The preface to the so-called Florence manuscript of the *Shahnameh*, dated 614 AH/1217 CE (supplemented by the preface of the Topkapı manuscript, dated 731 AH/1330 CE) (MAR 264–87);
> Preface 3. The third or "intermediate" preface (MAR 326–38);
> Preface 4. The preface to the so-called *Baysonqori Shahnameh*, commissioned 829 AH/1426 CE and completed 833 AH/1430 CE (MAR 349–418).

I also list here three other biographical sources:

> Source A. The "autobiographical" references to Ferdowsi in the *Shahnameh* itself;
> Source B. A short episode about Ferdowsi in *Tarikh-e Sistan*, the "core text" of which is dated to 448 AH/1062 CE;[6]
> Source C. An abbreviated Life of Ferdowsi, Episode 20 in the *Chahar Maqaleh* of Nezami Aruzi, composed somewhere around 550–2 AH/1155–7 CE.[7]

Of special significance is the fact that all of the four Lives that I listed as Prefaces 1, 2, 3, and 4 are linked directly to the textual transmission of the *Shahnameh*, in

---

5   Mohammad-Amin Riyahi, ed., *Sar-Cheshmeh-ha-ye Ferdowsi-shenasi* (Tehran: Mo'asseseh-ye Motale'at va Tahqiqat-e Farhangi [Pazhuheshgah], 1993).
6   Mohammad-Taqi Bahar, ed. *Tarikh-e Sistan* (Tehran: Zovvar, 1314/1935).
7   Mohammad Mo'in, ed., *Chahar Maqaleh-ye Nezami-ye Aruzi* (rev. ed., 3rd printing, Tehran: Zovvar, 1333/1954; earlier ed. 1327/1948 by Mohammad Qazvini), 75–83.

contrast to the three Sources A, B, and C, listed immediately after Prefaces 1, 2, 3, and 4. Also, to be contrasted, if we go farther afield, there are eleven Lives of Homer that have survived from the ancient Greek world: in the case of these Homeric Lives, not one of them is linked directly to the textual transmission of the Homeric *Iliad* and *Odyssey*. The absence of evidence for such linking is a disadvantage for Hellenists who study Homeric poetry, and this disadvantage is noted somewhat sardonically in a conversation that I once had with Gregory Nagy wearing his hat as a Hellenist, while I was wearing mine as an Iranist.[8]

Focusing on the "Baysonqori Preface"

Of the four Lives of Ferdowsi, I focus on the grandest one. It is found embedded in Preface 4, the "Baysonqori Preface." This preface is in its own right a grand introduction to a truly monumental book known as the *Baysonqori Shahnameh*. The production of this book, containing the *Shahnameh* of Ferdowsi in its most expansive form, around 58,000 verses in length, was commissioned by a Timurid prince, introduced earlier. His full name was Ghiath-al-Din Baysonqor b. Shahrokh, and he died in 837 AH/1433 CE. The date for the commissioning, as I already mentioned, is recorded as 829 AH/1426 CE, and the laborious process of producing the book was finally completed in 833 AH/1430 CE by Mowlana Ja'far Baysonqori, a calligrapher from Tabriz who was apparently a librarian to the prince.

For almost two decades now, I have been working on a long-term project of translating Preface 4 into English. The results to date of this work in progress are scheduled to be published online, and there will be regular updates thereafter. While working on this translation for all these years, I have published a series of six essays about the Life of Ferdowsi as contained in the Baysonqori Preface, citing earlier versions of the translation in progress to which I have just referred. In the bibliography for my present work here, under the name "Davidson," I list these six essays in chronological order, giving only the dates of publication: 2001, 2008, 2013c, 2013d, 2014, and 2015.12.17. The last of these essays, Davidson 2015.12.17, has already been mentioned

---

[8] This conversation happened in the context of our introducing twin papers on the "Lives of Homer" and the "Lives of Ferdowsi" that we presented for an international conference held at Baku, November 27–28, 2015, and organized by Rahilya Geybullayeva and Sevinj Bakhyshova (Müqayisəli ədəbiyyat və mədəniyyət: Ədəbiyyatın və mədəniyyətin başlanğıc meyarları). The conversation is found in the video linked to the URL https://classical-inquiries.chs.harvard.edu/the-rhetoric-of-national-literature-in-the-shaping-of-two-different-biographies-of-poets-one-greek-and-one-persian/. The point that I was making there is recorded in what I say starting at minute 7:40 in a conversation that lasts from minute 0:00 to minute 8:48. Later on in the presentation that I am offering here, I will elaborate on what I said in my "twin paper" about the advantage of studying Prefaces 1, 2, 3, and 4 in the context of the overall textual transmission of the *Shahnameh*. For now, however, it will suffice to note that this "twin paper" about the Lives of Ferdowsi is the same text as the essay that is listed in my bibliography below, under the entry Davidson (December 17, 2015). Similarly, the "twin paper" of Nagy about the Lives of Homer is the same text that is listed in my bibliography under the entry Nagy (December 18, 2015).

earlier. It appeared as an online publication and represents the beginnings of an online monograph that I am planning. The monograph will develop further the arguments already presented not only in the sixth essay but also in the other five. And the title will be *Lives of Ferdowsi as Evidence for the Reception of the Shahnameh*—which is based on the title of the sixth essay. For such an online monograph to take shape, however, I first needed to produce a seventh essay that would supplement and augment what I had already presented in the sixth essay, that is, in Davidson 2017.13.17. What I present here, then, is the seventh essay.

A Story about the Poet's Disappointment: Genesis of the "Satire"

In studying the narratives preserved in the Lives of Ferdowsi, especially in the "Baysonqori Preface," I will focus here on one particular story that tells about the feelings of disappointment experienced by the poet Ferdowsi in reaction to the indifference or even hostility of the Sultan Mahmud of Ghazna, king of kings, whom the poet hoped to have as his primary patron—and who, as patron, would have been expected to reward Ferdowsi for producing poetry that glorified him. The poet's reaction to the negativity of the Sultan, according to this story, was to change course and compose verses that now turned around and blamed Mahmud instead of praising him. These negative verses of blame are conventionally known as the "Satire." In the version of the Life of Ferdowsi as transmitted in the "Baysonqori Preface," that is, in Preface 4, we read a retelling of the story of the Satire. Even more, the verses of the Satire are extensively quoted in Preface 4.

Many experts who study the *Shahnameh* have a big problem with the retelling, in Preface 4, of the story about the Satire—and even more so with the actual quoting, as it were, of verses from the Satire. The problem can be restated by way of asking three questions:

> One, how could Ferdowsi in the *Shahnameh* praise the Sultan for his greatness and then go ahead and undo that praise?
> Two, if he did try to undo such praise, how in fact could it possibly get undone?
> And, three, if the poet really intended to undo the praise that he had already lavished on the Sultan in various passages of the *Shahnameh* by then turning around and blaming him in the Satire, why would the text of Preface 4, which introduces the *Shahnameh* that contains all those praises of the Sultan by the poet, include in this same introduction the blame that is intended to undo the praise—together with a framing story that justifies the blame?

All three of these questions are reactions to a basic fact: the acts of praise for Mahmud by Ferdowsi were organically embedded inside the text of the *Shahnameh* and could therefore not be readily extricated from that text. Secondly, the embedding of the praise was chronologically layered. That is to say, Ferdowsi praises Mahmud at several different points within the length of the *Shahnameh*—and these points in time are regularly contextualized, as when the praise happens at a point where the poet is referring to a particular phase of his own life. It is like saying: I the poet praise you the Sultan because you are great, and I praise you at a point in time when I am X years old and when Y things have been happening to me. For an appreciation of these two facts, namely, the embedding of the praise and the chronological layering of that praise, I recommend a thorough reading of a book by Shapur Shahbazi, who conscientiously tracks all the self-references of Ferdowsi throughout the vast corpus of verses contained in the transmission of the *Shahnameh* through the ages.[9]

Although I disagree, as we are about to see, with the solution proposed by Shahbazi in confronting the problem that I have just outlined, I must put on record my deep respect for his systematic approach in collecting all the details to be gleaned from the text of the *Shahnameh* itself about the life and times of Ferdowsi. For Shahbazi, the one and only reliable source we have for learning any details about the life of Ferdowsi is the actual text of the *Shahnameh*, which I have labeled as Source A in my earlier listing of three sources, A, B, and C.

Before we consider the solution proposed by Shahbazi, however, I ask this hypothetical question: what if Ferdowsi, in "real life," simply changed his mind about the Sultan Mahmud? "I thought you were a great man, but you are not, and so I will now blame you instead of praising you." Such a question, simplistic as it is, runs the risk of viewing the poet himself in a bad light. How could Ferdowsi praise Mahmud so lavishly and for so long in the course of his lengthy poetic career? Was the poet all that naïve? Or was he perhaps insincere? "I did not really mean it when I said, wherever I was praising you in my poetry, that you were oh so generous, but now, finally, after all these years, I can say for sure that you were in fact always mean-spirited."

The very idea of entertaining such hypothetical questions about naïveté or insincerity is understandably unappealing to experts who insist on defending the character of Ferdowsi, since, to their own way of thinking, such questions undermine the moral integrity of the poet and even of his poetry.

I have reached the point where I am ready to consider the solution proposed by Shahbazi. Defending the poetic integrity of Ferdowsi, he argues that the story about the Satire is an invention, and that the Satire itself is a "forgery," in the sense that Ferdowsi himself could never have composed it.[10] Shahbazi goes even further, arguing that Ferdowsi himself never even went to the court of Mahmud, and that he merely sent copies of his poetry to the Sultan.[11]

But then the question remains: why would such a story about the Satire get to be retold—and why would the verses of the Satire get to be requoted—in the prestigious Preface 4, the "Baysonqori Preface," which at the same time introduces the text of the very same *Shahnameh* that proclaims as its patron the same king of kings who is defamed by the Satire?

---

[9] Shapur Shahbazi, *Ferdowsi: A Critical Biography* (Costa Mesa: Mazda Publishers, 1991).
[10] Ibid., 8, 97–103.
[11] Shahbazi, *Ferdowsi*, 18, 83–103.

A New Way of Analyzing Inclusions of the "Satire" in the Poetry of Ferdowsi

I propose a different solution. Let me start, however, by making three concessions. First, I accept the idea that the Ferdowsi of the Satire is a Ferdowsi who is different from the Ferdowsi of the *Shahnameh* as we know it. Second, I also accept the idea that this different Ferdowsi would seem to be a false poet, not a true one, to *some* Iranians. And, third, I would even accept the idea that the verses of the Satire would seem to be a "forgery." But I should quickly add that the Satire would seem to be a forgery only to some Iranians in the era of Prince Baysonqor, especially to those who embrace a Sunni worldview, but not to other Iranians, especially to those whose world view is Shi'ite and not Sunni. In terms of my proposed solution to the problem confronting us today as we read in Preface 4 both the Satire and the story that contextualizes the Satire, what we see in this part of the preface is a life of Ferdowsi that contradicts other lives of the poet. I use here the word "life" not in the everyday sense of "a real life" but in the literary sense of a vita, that is, of a story of a life—a story that is a *myth*. And I use the word "myth" here not in the everyday sense of "a story that is not true"—which is what Shahbazi means when he says that the story about the Satire is "merely a myth."[12] Rather, I use the word *myth* in the anthropological sense of a narrative that conveys, by way of storytelling, the truth-values of the society in which the given narrative had evolved in the first place. Such an anthropological understanding of myth is in fact far closer to the original meaning of the ancient Greek word *mūthos*, from which the modern word *myth* has been borrowed. In the "twin paper" of Nagy 2015.12.18 about the Lives of Homer, which I cited earlier, the term *Lives* in his title actually refers to different myths about the life of Homer. Correspondingly in the title of my "twin paper," Davidson 2015.12.17, about the Lives of Ferdowsi, the same term, *Lives*, refers to different myths—in the anthropological sense of the word—about the life of Ferdowsi.

In the sixth paragraph of his "twin paper" on the Lives of Homer, Nagy says that his aim is "to show that the narratives of these Lives are myths, not historical facts, about Homer." In this context, he adds an important qualification:

> To say that we are dealing with myths, however, is not at all to say that there is no history to be learned from the Lives. Even though the various Homers of the various Lives are evidently mythical constructs, the actual constructing of myths about Homer can be seen as historical fact. The claims made about Homer in the Lives can be analyzed as evidence for the various different ways in which Homeric poetry was appropriated by various different cultural and political centers throughout the ancient Greek-speaking world.

The same can be said, as I argued in my "twin paper," about the Lives of Ferdowsi. Here too, the different claims that we read in different sources about the life of the

---

[12] Ibid., 91.

poet can be analyzed as evidence for different historical contexts that shaped the transmission of poetry attributed to the poet.

A New Way of Analyzing the Reception of the *Shahnameh*

In both the "twin papers" I just cited, a theoretical term that Nagy and I both used in addressing the question of finding historical contexts for the transmission of poetry is *reception*. And, in both papers, it is argued that there had existed two parallel media for the reception of both ancient Greek poetry and medieval Persian poetry: one medium was of course the *text*, which had to do with whatever was *written to be read*, but there was also the parallel medium of *oral tradition*, which had to do with whatever was composed to be performed for listeners.

Since I am focusing on Preface 4, which as we saw was an introduction to a vastly expanded version of the *Shahnameh*, produced in 1430 CE, I need to focus also on the kind of *reception* that was in store for the poetry of Ferdowsi in that era. For the moment, then, I must concentrate not on the life and times of the poet Ferdowsi, who flourished in the late tenth and early eleventh century CE, but on the status of the poetry attributed to him in the era of the text of the *Shahnameh* as published by the Prince Baysonqor over four hundred years later, in 1430 CE. How this poetry was received in 1430 and thereafter is what I need to highlight here.

I have already elaborated on the ecumenism, as it were, of Prince Baysonqor in producing an augmented form of the *Shahnameh* that spoke to the widest possible range of reception—as would befit the Timurid dynasty, which demonstrated its claim to imperial greatness by trying to outdo even the cultural as well as political ambitions of the Sultan Mahmud, who had once been, so many years earlier, the ultimate patron of the *Shahnameh*.

What I see, then, is a rivalry between Baysonqor and Mahmud as patrons of the *Shahnameh* of Ferdowsi. I say it this way because, even though the two of them are separated by hundreds of years, Baysonqor is competing with Mahmud in promoting the *Shahnameh*. That is why, I think, Preface 4 can give some credit to Mahmud as a potential supporter of Ferdowsi, but the ultimate credit must go to Baysonqor for his full support. Moreover, Preface 4 makes Mahmud look bad occasionally, especially in the Satire, but even this negativity about Mahmud is primarily motivated, I think, by a correlative positiveness: Mahmud must be demeaned as a foil for the sake of elevating someone else who is supposedly a far better patron of poetry, and that ultimate patron must be the princely figure of Baysonqor himself.

Details about the Reception of the *Shahnameh* before the Era of Baysonqor

I will be concluding this chapter with a translation of a striking passage taken from the Satire embedded in Preface 4, that is, in the introduction to the *Baysonqori*

Shahnameh. But before I show this passage, I propose to provide here some details about the reception of the *Shahnameh* before the era of Baysonqor. These details come from sources A, B, and C as I have listed them earlier. I will proceed here in chronological order:

In Source A, which is the actual text of the *Shahnameh* as we know it, we can already see signs of potential disapproval, on the part of Ferdowsi, in situations where he is praising Mahmud. Even Shapur Shahbazi, who does not even accept the idea that Ferdowsi ever tried to demean Mahmud, takes note of passages in the *Shahnameh* where the poet offers "advice and warnings" to the Sultan in contexts where he is primarily praising him.[13]

In Source B, which is a short episode found in the *Tarikh-e Sistan*, dated at around 1062 CE, it is reported that the Sultan Mahmud commissions Ferdowsi to turn stories about the hero Rostam into verse, and that Ferdowsi recites his composition to Mahmud; it is added that the performance lasted for seven days. But Mahmud is not satisfied with the content of the stories, and he expresses his dissatisfaction to Ferdowsi: 'I have a thousand warriors like Rostam in my army.' Ferdowsi is ready with a retort: 'I don't know about your army, but Rostam is unique, and God has never again created anyone else like Rostam.' Upon saying this, Ferdowsi takes his leave, politely. After he leaves, Mahmud says to his minister: 'I think this man has just now insulted me.' And the minister says back to the Sultan: 'Ferdowsi must be killed.' But Ferdowsi cannot be found. The upshot of the story is that Ferdowsi has left the court of Mahmud without any reward and that he ultimately died in exile.[14]

In Source C, which is Episode 20 in the *Chahar Maqaleh* of Nezami Aruzi, composed somewhere around 1155–7 CE,[15] we read that Ferdowsi, who is a *dehqan* or landowner in Tus, spends twenty-five years composing the *Shahnameh*, hoping that the reward for his labors will provide a dowry for his daughter, who is his only child. The governor of the city, whose name is Hoyayy son of Qotayba, treats fairly the landowner poet, not oppressing him with taxes. When the poet completes the *Shahnameh*, then and only then (so it seems, in terms of the narrative) the composition is transcribed, by a scribe named Ali Deylam, in seven volumes. Then and only then (so it seems, in terms of the narrative) the composition is performed by a "reciter" named Abu Dolaf. After that, together with Abu Dolaf the reciter, Ferdowsi sets out for Ghazna, capital of Sultan Mahmud. There he finds as patron a *kateb* ("scribe") of the Sultan. This scribe, named Ahmad-e Hassan [Maymandi], "presents" the *Shahnameh* to Mahmud. The Sultan "accepts" it and is grateful to Ahmad-e Hassan. But Ahmad-e Hassan has enemies, and, when the Sultan asks these other men how much he should pay to Ferdowsi (I note here that payment is somehow assumed), these detractors suggest 50,000 *derham*s [= silver coins], and even this sum would be too much, they say, given that Ferdowsi is a *rafezi* ("rejecter" [of Sunni values]). So, Mahmud, Sunni that he is, follows the advice of the detractors, and the poet "receives" only 20,000 *dirham*s. Insulted, Ferdowsi spends

[13] Shahbazi, *Ferdowsi*, 102–3.
[14] Ibid., 4.
[15] Ibid., 2 n. 4.

the sum on a "bath-man" and a "drink-seller." Then, "fearing the wrath" of the Sultan, he flees to Harat, where he spends six months hiding in the house of Esmaʿil Warraq, father of the poet Azraqi Heravi. Then, when it is safe for him to travel, he takes "his" *Shahnameh* to Tabarestan, to the court there of the king Spahbad Shahriyar. This king treats Ferdowsi kindly, and the poet composes a "satire" in 100 verses against Mahmud, "offering to dedicate" his *Shahnameh* to Spahbad Shahriyar, since the poet's *Shahnameh* "glorifies" the ancestors of this king. (I note a contrast here with the king Mahmud as patron, whose ancestry is questioned in the Satire.) But Sepahbad Shahriyar "was one of the vassals of Mahmud," and, "appealing" to the Shiʿite orientation of Ferdowsi, he "advised" him to "follow the path of the House of the Prophet" and to seek no "worldly gains." The king offered a gift of 60,000 *derham*s to the poet and persuaded him to destroy the Satire; Ferdowsi went ahead and destroyed the hundred verses, so that now "only six verses are extant." Now, an added detail (almost as an afterthought): Ferdowsi was also persuaded to retain the "original" dedication to Mahmud. That was the additional advice of the vassal-king. (Further below, I describe this maneuver as *catch and kill*.) After that, Ferdowsi eventually goes back to Tus, where "he spent the rest of his life in poverty and in fear of the Sultan." But, meanwhile, Ahmad-e Hassan is working on Mahmud to forgive Ferdowsi "and to reward him properly." One day, as Mahmud is dictating a letter threatening an adversary, he asks Ahmad-e Hassan for the right wording, who then quotes for the king a memorable passage from Ferdowsi. Now Ahmad-e Hassan guilt-trips Mahmud, how this "poor poet" had labored for twenty-five years and "was left unrewarded." Finally, Mahmud repents and sends to Ferdowsi 60,000 *dinar*s [gold coins] plus an apology. But, too late. The caravan that is bringing all the gold enters Tabaran via Gate Rudbar while the corpse of Ferdowsi exits via Gate Razan. A cleric in Tabaran forbids burial in the cemetery, and so Ferdowsi is buried in his own orchard, inside the Gate. His tomb is still there, and "I [Nezami Aruzi] made a pilgrimage" to it [*ziyarat kardam*] in the year 510 AH/1116 CE. "They say" that Ferdowsi left a daughter, who refused the gift. The amount was spent on a *rebat* ("hostelry") on the road between Marv and Neshapur.[16]

In Source C, the lengthy narrative of Nezami Aruzi that I have just now finished epitomizing here, I find a stunningly interesting point of comparison with a kind of event that is still with us today. I indulge myself here by making the comparison. As we see in the version of the story as told by Nezami Aruzi, Ferdowsi reacts to being rejected by Mahmud, king of kings, by seeking the patronage of another king. This alternative patron is well disposed toward Ferdowsi but fears retaliation from Mahmud, since this particular king is a mere vassal of the king of kings. I should quickly note here, in passing, that Mahmud and this "vassal-king" were not really contemporaries, in terms of history. In any case, in terms of the story, this alternative patron persuades Ferdowsi to destroy most of his verses that blamed Mahmud. In return for destroying these verses, Ferdowsi now receives a reward from this alternative patron. Such a reward, I find, is comparable to a ploy known today in the world of tabloid journalism

---

[16] In my paraphrase here, wordings formulated by Shahbazi, *Ferdowsi*, 2–3 are embedded in double quotation marks.

as *catch and kill*. The owner of a given tabloid, pretending that he wants to publish an incriminating story about a Very Important Person, proceeds to buy the story from the seller of the story, but the real purpose of the publisher is not to publish the incriminating story but, rather, to keep that story from ever getting published, thus protecting the Very Important Person.[17]

I have drawn attention to this point of comparison because it brings home to us the sheer liveliness of Lives of Poets stories. For me, at least, these stories are at times just as engaging as the poetry they elucidate. And, for those who are newcomers to, say, the poetry of Ferdowsi, I think that the experience of reading in translation the Lives of Ferdowsi—especially the Life that we find in Preface 4—would enhance the experience of reading the *Shahnameh* itself, which I had described from the start as a jewel of world literature.

Coda

With these thoughts in mind, I close this chapter by showing here a sample taken from the Satire as quoted in Preface 4 (MAR 403–4). This sample gives an idea of the poetic power that drives the Satire, which is a poem that one observer—to the dismay, however, of Shahbazi[18]—has described as "perhaps the most terrific denunciation of an individual in the history of literature."[19] Here is the text, with my translation:

مرا برسرگه بودی نشست	جهاندار اگر نیسیئ تنگدست
بد آن بد که بختش جوانه نبود	چو فردوسی اندر زمانه نبود
شاهان گیئ درخشنده ای	چنان پادشاهی و بخشنده ای
زگفتار بدگویش آمد گناه	نکرد اندراین نامه از بن نگاه
عجم زنده کردم بدین پارسی	بسی رنج بردم دراین سال سی

If the king, who possesses the world, had not been so tightfisted,
my place would have been on a seat of dignity.
There has never been anyone like Ferdowsi—
what is cruel is that his fate is to be no longer youthful.
Such a king and such a potential benefactor,
a most splendid one among the kings of the world,
did not delve all that deeply into this book;
his iniquity was galvanized by the calumny of the backstabbers.
I labored hard in these past thirty years,
bringing to life what was incomprehensible, through the Persian language so pure.

---

17 For a relevant article about *catch and kill*, see Erik Hayden, "Ronan Farrow Gets New Book Deal for Investigative Title 'Catch and Kill,'" *Hollywood Reporter*, May 11, 2018.
18 Shahbazi, *Ferdowsi*, 89 n. 56.
19 Phirozeshah Benjani Vaccha, *Ferdousi and the Shahnama: A Study of the Great Persian Epic of the Homer of the East* (Bombay: New Book Company, 1950), 72.

Bibliography

Bahar, Mohammad-Taqi, ed. *Tarikh-e Sistan*. Tehran: Zovvar, 1314/1935.

Davidson, Olga M. *Comparative Literature and Classical Persian Poetics*. 2nd ed. Ilex Foundation Series 12. Cambridge, MA: Harvard University Press, 2013 [2000].

Davidson, Olga M. "Interweavings of Book and Performance in the Making of the *Shahnama* of Ferdowsi: Extrapolations from the Narrative of the Preface to the Baysonqor Manuscript." In *Ferdowsi's Shahnama: Millennial Perspectives*, ed. Olga M. Davidson and Marianna Shreve Simpson, 1–11. Ilex Foundation Series 13. Cambridge, MA: Harvard University Press, 2013.

Davidson, Olga M. "'Life of Ferdowsi' Myths as Evidence for the Reception of Ferdowsi: A Multiform Reception of the *Shahnama* as Reflected in the Baysonghori Preface." *Classical Inquiries*, December 17, 2015. Web. Available at https://classical-inquiries.chs.harvard.edu/life-of-ferdowsi-myths-as-evidence-for-the-reception-of-ferdowsi/ (accessed May 15, 2020).

Davidson, Olga M. "Parallel Heroic Themes in the Medieval Irish *Cattle Raid of Cooley* and the Medieval Persian *Book of Kings*." In *Erin and Iran: Cultural Encounters between the Irish and the Iranians*, ed. H. E. Chehabi and Grace Neville, 36–44. Ilex Foundation Series 16. Cambridge, MA: Harvard University Press, 2015.

Davidson, Olga M. "Persian/Iranian Epic." In *A Companion to Ancient Epic*, ed. John M. Foley, 264–76. Malden: Blackwell, 2005.

Davidson, Olga M. "A Pictorial Aetiology of Ferdowsi as a Transcendent Poet." In *Ferdowsi, the Mongols and the History of Iran: Art, Literature and Culture from Early Islam to Qajar Persia*, ed. Robert Hillenbrand, A. C. S. Peacock, and Firuza Abdullaeva, 245–8, plates 9–10. London: I.B.Tauris, 2013.

Davidson, Olga M. *Poet and Hero in the Persian Book of Kings*. 3rd ed., Ilex Foundation Series 11. Cambridge, MA: Harvard University Press, 2013 [1994].

Davidson, Olga M. "Some Iranian Poetic Tropes as Reflected in the 'Life of Ferdowsi' Traditions." In *Philologica et Linguistica: Festschrift für Helmut Humbach*, ed. Maria Gabriela Schmidt and Walter Bisang, supplement, 1–12. Trier: Wissenschaftlicher Verlag, 2001.

Davidson, Olga M. "The Testing of the Shahnama in the 'Life of Ferdowsi' Narratives." In *The Rhetoric of Biography: Narrating Lives in Persianate Societies*, ed. Louise Marlow, 11–20. Ilex Foundation Series 4. Cambridge, MA: Harvard University Press, 2008.

Davidson, Olga M. "Why the Baysonghori Recension Is a Recension." In *No Tapping around Philology: A Festschrift in Honor of Wheeler McIntosh Thackston Jr.'s 70th Birthday*, ed. Alireza Korangy and Daniel J. Sheffield, 127–30. Wiesbaden: Harrassowitz Verlag, 2014.

Davidson, Olga M. "The Written Text as a Metaphor for the Integrity of Oral Composition in Classical Persian Traditions and Beyond." In *Singers and Tales in the 21st Century: The Legacies of Milman Parry and Albert Lord*, ed. David Elmer and Peter McMurray. Cambridge, MA: Harvard University Center for Hellenic Studies, 2016.

Davis, Dick, trans. *Shahnameh: The Persian Book of Kings*. New York: Viking, 2006.

Hayden, Erik. "Ronan Farrow Gets New Book Deal for Investigative Title 'Catch and Kill,'" *Hollywood Reporter*, May 11, 2018. Web. Available at www.hollywoodreporter.com/news/ronan-farrow-gets-new-book-deal-investigative-title-catch-kill-1111126 (accessed May 15, 2020).

McNeill, William H. *The Rise of the West: A History of the Human Community*. Chicago: University of Chicago Press, 1992 [1963].

Mo'in, Mohammad, ed. *Chahar Maqaleh-ye Nezami Aruzi*. Rev. ed., 3rd printing. Tehran: Zovvar, 1954. Earlier ed. 1948 by Mohammad Qazvini.

Nagy, Gregory. *Homer the Preclassic*. Berkeley: University of California Press, 2010.

Nagy, Gregory. "'Life of Homer' Myths as Evidence for the Reception of Homer: The Lives of Homer as Aetiologies for Homeric Poetry." *Classical Inquiries*, December 18, 2015. Web. Available at https://classical-inquiries.chs.harvard.edu/life-of-homer-myths-as-evidence-for-the-reception-of-homer/ (accessed May 15, 2020).

Ramage, Nancy H., and Andrew Ramage. *Roman Art: Romulus to Constantine*. New York: Abrams, 1991.

Riyahi, Mohammad-Amin, ed. *Sar-Cheshmeh-ha-ye Ferdowsi-shenasi*. Tehran: Mo'asseseh-ye Motale'at va Tahqiqat-e Farhangi (Pazhuheshgah), 1993.

Shahbazi, Shapur. *Ferdowsi: A Critical Biography*. Costa Mesa: Mazda Publishers, 1991.

Vaccha, Phirozeshah Benjani. *Ferdousi and the Shahnama: A Study of the Great Persian Epic of the Homer of the East*. Bombay: New Book Company, 1950.

8

Cats and Dogs, Manliness, and Misogyny: On the *Sindbad-nameh* as World Literature

Alexandra Hoffmann

Introduction

As a form of circulation and translation of literary texts, World Literature is hardly a modern phenomenon. The premodern world saw a large amount of translation (or adaptation) of all kinds of texts—particularly tales that traveled vast distances, crossing both linguistic and cultural boundaries. One such collection of tales is the subject of the present chapter. Although it has various names and a varying number of embedded tales, its frame tale shows remarkable consistency over centuries. It goes like this: A king sends his only son away from court to be educated. Upon his return to court, the prince is falsely accused of attempted rape by the king's favorite concubine. Since the prince cannot defend himself due to a seven-day vow of silence imposed by his teacher Sindbad, seven of the king's viziers try to avoid his execution by each narrating tales. Each day, the concubine tells a story and one of the seven viziers responds with two, in a battle of narration that means life or death for the prince. After seven days, the prince's vow of silence is over, the truth is discovered, and the concubine is punished.

This collection of tales, known as the *Sindbad-nameh* (*The Book of Sindbad*) in Persian, the *Seven Viziers* in Arabic, or as the *Seven Sages (of Rome)* in medieval European adaptations, emerged as a literary trend around the twelfth century CE and spanned a geographical distance from Southern India to Iceland within a few centuries.[1] The frame tale of the collection is likely of Persian origin,[2] and although a Persian text from 950 CE is mentioned, the earliest extant Persian version we have is the *Sindbad-nameh*

---

[1] Scholarship has separated the literary tradition, based on textual differences, into an "Eastern" and a "Western" branch. See Hans R. Runte, J. Keith Wikeley, and Anthony J. Farrell, *The Seven Sages of Rome and the Book of Sindbad: An Analytical Bibliography* (New York: Garland Publishing, 1984); Hans R. Runte, "Portal, Society of the Seven Sages" (2014), retrieved from http://dalspace.library.dal.ca/handle/10222/49107, accessed June 2, 2020.

[2] B. E. Perry has argued that the frame tale does not, as had been assumed before, have Indian, but Persian origins ("The Origin of the Book of Sindbad," *Fabula* 3, no. 1 [1960]: 1–94). Stephen Belcher has further argued that it could have parallels to the narrative Persian tradition of Siyavash in the *Shahnameh* (Stephen Belcher, "The Diffusion of the Book of Sindbād," *Fabula* 28, no. 1 [1987]: 48).

by Zahiri Samarqandi (written between 1160 and 1164 CE).[3] Various versions of the collection circulated in the Islamicate world, and through channels of transmission that are unknown, the frame tale and a varying number of embedded tales appeared in the medieval European literary milieu first in Old French (between 1155 and 1190 CE) and Latin (ca. end of the twelfth century CE). In the following centuries, the collection was translated into almost every European language. This collection of tales was thus immensely widespread in Islamicate and European textual and oral storytelling, much like *Kalila wa Dimna* and the *Arabian Nights*.

Given its geographic scope, there is good reason to consider the *Sindbad-nameh* as World Literature, not because of its connection to medieval Europe, but because of its participation in a shared "mode of circulation and reading" which transgresses specific cultural and linguistic boundaries.[4] This is evident from the sheer number of manuscripts, languages, and locations of production associated with the *Sindbad-nameh*. At the same time, however, it seems that the concept of World Literature—with a modern, Western, readership in mind[5]—does not do justice to the premodern literary entanglement of the Middle Ages. Hence, we may have a skewed sense of what was historically important to, and read by, large numbers of people—as is the case with the different versions of the *Sindbad-nameh*—simply because we tend to disregard works that are not currently treated as part of a modern canon of World Literature. In short, we also need to imagine past conceptions of World Literature as they were practiced in the premodern era. I therefore follow Geraldine Heng and Lynn Ramey's proposal to use the terms "early globalities" and "global literature," since they allow for a de-Eurocentralization of the term "World Literature" while also accounting for the interconnectedness of the premodern world and its network of texts.[6] This chapter thus examines the *Sindbad-nameh* as early global literature and aims to foreground the importance of Persian literature by highlighting premodern literary connections between Islamicate and medieval European reading cultures.

The *Seven Sages* tradition, a vast corpus of texts that form the Islamicate and medieval European worlds, has been categorized under the uniting theme of medieval misogyny.[7] Even though the European Middle Ages produced literature rife with misogyny, scholarship of the nineteenth and early twentieth centuries tended to

---

[3] I use the following edition: Mohammad b. Ali Zahiri Samarqandi, *Sindbad-nameh*, ed. Mohammad Baqer Kamaloddini (Tehran: Miras-e Maktub, 1381/2002). Samarqandi's *Sindbad-nameh* was translated into French by Dejan Bogdanovic as *Le Livre des sept vizirs: Zahiri de Samarkand* (Paris: Sindbad, 1975).

[4] David Damrosch, *What Is World Literature?* (Princeton: Princeton University Press, 2003), 4–5.

[5] Franklin Lewis addresses Persian Literature as it relates to Goethe's concept of World Literature in "The *Shahnameh* of Ferdowsi as World Literature," *Iranian Studies* 48, no. 3 (2015): 313–36.

[6] Geraldine Heng and Lynn Ramey, "Early Globalities, Global Literatures: Introducing a Special Issue on the Global Middle Ages," *Literature Compass* 11, no. 7 (2014): 1–6.

[7] See Bea Lundt, *Weiser und Weib: Weisheit und Geschlecht am Beispiel der Erzähltradition von den «Sieben Weisen Meistern» (12.–15. Jahrhundert)* (Munich: Wilhelm Fink Verlag, 2002), 37ff. She rightly points out that such a categorization has long hindered a more in-depth study of themes hidden under a misogynist layer.

attribute the misogynist content of the European versions to its "oriental provenance."[8] When considered as a whole, the Islamicate versions of the *Sindbad-nameh* or the *Seven Viziers* certainly contain misogynist elements,[9] both in the form of tales on "wiles of women" (known as *kayd al-nisaʾ* in Arabic or *makr-e zanan* in Persian) as well as in the commentaries of the viziers as they frame these tales. However, as many Islamicate texts are still not fully studied and understood, such Orientalist prejudice, with its simplistic notions of cultural transmission of misogyny between the Islamicate world and medieval Europe, needs to be reevaluated.

More precisely, we should study Islamicate and non-Islamicate versions comparatively and examine whether the "Western" branch of the *Seven Sages* does not enhance the structural misogyny present in the tradition. In the "Eastern" versions, for example, the viziers each tell two tales, with the first one oftentimes exemplifying the consequences of haste, and the second recounting the "wiles of women." In the "Western" versions, on the other hand, the viziers tell only half as many tales. As Marcus Landau observed more than a hundred years ago, "the tales that narrate the wiles of women enjoyed such popularity that they were included in almost all adaptations, while others only appear in one or two."[10] The reduction of tales in medieval Europe thus tended to result in a loss of tales that did not contain a misogynist moral, and an increase of stories that did. As Yasmina Foehr-Janssens argues for the Old French *Roman des sept sages*, the choices made in the "Western" versions produce a particularly strong misogyny, leading, for example, to an emphasis on the queen's (or concubine's) culpability.[11] Hence, these scholars suggest that through such adaptations in the process of transmission to medieval Europe, the presence of misogyny was heightened in the European tradition of the *Seven Sages*.

While it is difficult to convincingly show an overall increase in misogyny in European versions due to the sheer number of texts, I can demonstrate a misogynist shift in a single tale passing from the Islamicate tradition to a selection of medieval European texts. As a point of comparison, I use a tale from the text known in

---

[8] Bea Lundt, for example, points to a 1928 publication: "The main motif of the narration, the evilness and wickedness of women, is a true characteristic of India, where women have always been regarded as more inferior than in the West" (Michael Schmidt, "Neue Beiträge zur Geschichte der *Sieben weisen Meister*" [PhD diss., Cologne: Studentenburse, 1928], 8, cit. in Lundt, *Weiser und Weib*, 38).

[9] I use "misogyny" not in the narrow sense of "hatred of women," but rather in the sense of various modes of anti-feminine discourse. Such a broad definition of misogyny has the disadvantage of terminological imprecision (see, e.g., Paula M. Rieder, "The Uses and Misuses of Misogyny: A Critical Historiography of the Language of Medieval Women's Oppression," *Historical Reflections* 38, no. 1 [2012]: 1–18), but until new definitions of misogynist subcategories are established within *Seven Sages* scholarship, I find it useful to use "misogyny" as an umbrella term, enabling me to trace anti-feminine speech throughout this comparative study while acknowledging the wide range of functions which expressions of misogyny can fulfill.

[10] Marcus Landau, *Die Quellen des Dekameron* (Stuttgart: J. Scheible, 1884), 60. See also Schmidt, "Neue Beiträge zur Geschichte der *Sieben weisen Meister*," 62.

[11] Yasmina Foehr-Janssens, "Misogyny and the Trends of a European Success: The French Prose *Roman des sept sages de Rome*," *Narrative Culture* 7, no. 2 (2020): 171.

Seven Sages scholarship as "Canis" (dog).[12] In many of the medieval European versions of the *Seven Sages*, the blame for the hasty killing of a faithful animal is placed on a woman instead of the actual perpetrator, a man. I argue that "Canis" only acquired this misogynist tendency once it was incorporated into European literary culture. A close reading of "Canis" in Samarqandi's *Sindbad-nameh* suggests that the hasty act is based on fear and is associated with a lack of manliness. I further argue that the tale does not employ misogynist speech in any of the relevant "Eastern" versions of the *Seven Sages*. With this chapter, I thus provide a more in-depth analysis of the Persian version of one of the most widespread tales in the global Middle Ages and complicate the picture of a simplistic "misogynist import" of the *Seven Sages* tradition to medieval Europe.

"Canis" in Zahiri Samarqandi's *Sindbad-nameh*

Zahiri Samarqandi's *Sindbad-nameh*, written around 1160–4 CE, is the earliest extant text of a total of seven Persian versions.[13] As Samarqandi was a chancellery scribe at the Qarakhanid court in Samarqand, his *Sindbad-nameh* was anything but a work of popular literature. Stylistically, the *Sindbad-nameh* is written in ornate prose full of poetic and Qur'anic citations, true to the literary conventions of the adorned prose of the twelfth century CE. Dedicated to the local ruler, Rokn al-Donya va l-Din Abu l-Muzaffar Qilij Tamghaj Khaqan b. Mas'ud b. al-Hasan (r. 1160/1–1170/1 CE),[14] the *Sindbad-nameh* illustrates a code of ethics by virtue of its embedded tales. As I have argued elsewhere, these tales address the management of emotions through themes like the balancing of emotion and reason, as well as the consequences of rash behavior

---

[12] In narratology or folklore studies, this tale is categorized as tale type ATU 178 A "The Innocent Dog." See Hans-Jörg Uther, *The Types of International Folktales: A Classification and Bibliography, Based on the System of Antti Aarne and Stith Thompson*, vol. 1 (Helsinki: Suomalainen Tiedeakatemia, 2004), 122; Jean-Claude Schmitt, "Hundes Unschuld," in *Enzyklopädie des Märchens: Handwörterbuch zur historischen und vergleichenden Erzählforschung*, vol. 6, ed. Doris Boden, Rolf Wilhelm Brednich, and Kurt Ranke (Berlin: De Gruyter, 2011), cols. 1361–8. The tale is known elsewhere as the Welsh legend of Prince Llewelyn and his dog Gelert or as the cult of St. Guinefort the faithful greyhound (Jean-Claude Schmitt, *The Holy Greyhound: Guinefort, Healer of Children since the Thirteenth Century* [Cambridge: Cambridge University Press, 1983]). The tale itself is first attested in the Sanskrit Pañcatantra (see Stuart Blackburn, "The Brahmin and the Mongoose: The Narrative Context of a Well-Traveled Tale," *Bulletin of the School of Oriental and African Studies*, 59, no. 3 [1996]: 494–507), and is also included in the *Kalila wa Dimna* tradition. For an overview of the Islamicate versions, see François de Blois, *Burzoy's Voyage to India and the Origin of the Book of Kalilah wa Dimnah* (London: Royal Asiatic Society, 1990).

[13] Three lost *Sindbad-nameh*s precede Samarqandi's text: a version that Fanaruzi translated from Pahlavi in 950 CE; another tenth-century version by Rudaki (d. 940/941 CE); and a version by Azraqi (d. 1132 CE). Three further Persian versions were written in the thirteenth and fourteenth centuries: a version by Daqayeqi (d. around the turn of the thirteenth century), believed to be lost; a verse version by Azod Yazdi (1374/5 CE); and an abridged version in Ziya' al-Din Nakhshabi's *Tuti-nameh* (1330 CE). For an overview, see Ali-Mohammad Honar, *Yaddasht-ha-ye Sindbad-nameh* (Tehran: Bonyad-e Mowqufat-e Doktor Mahmud-e Afshar-e Yazdi, 1386/2007); or Ulrich Marzolph, "Sendbad-name," *Marvels & Tales* 25, no. 2 (2011): 376–9.

[14] Samarqandi gives different versions of the ruler's title (*Sindbad-nameh*, 6, 11, 18, 238).

motivated by "vices of the soul," such as anger, fear, desire, or appetite.[15] The embedded tales fall into two categories—either illustrating the consequences of hasty actions or warning, at least superficially, against the "wiles of women." However, as a text on the management of (male) emotions, the *Sindbad-nameh* connects the themes of haste and misogyny to contrast the ideal manly behavior—characterized by rational restraint— with female behavior, which is negatively stereotyped as emotional.

In the *Sindbad-nameh*, the tale "Canis" does not feature a dog (as the Latin name would suggest), but a cat. It is a tale that exemplifies the dangers of hasty action based on fear. Its result, the killing of a faithful cat, is condemned as unchivalric and unmanly. When the third vizier steps before the king to persuade him not to kill his son, he frames "the story of the soldier, the child, the cat, and the snake" as an example of the dangers of haste. Before he begins his tale, he admonishes the king that it is not suitable to use haste in punishment lest the king regret it afterwards like the soldier who killed the cat in haste.[16]

The tale itself begins with a soldier and his beautiful wife, whom he loves dearly. However, his wife dies in childbirth and the soldier expresses the pain of her loss by alluding to lovers well known in the Arabo-Persian world, such as Leyli and Majnun. He finds his only comfort in his young son, for whom he engages a kind and skilled wet-nurse.[17] He also has a cat [*gorbeh*] that sits beside the cradle, watching over the child. One day, when both father and nurse are not at home, a black snake creeps out of a hole and takes aim at the sleeping child. While the cat fights and kills the snake, much blood is shed. When the soldier comes home, the cat goes to meet him in hope of receiving a reward. However, the soldier sees only the cat's blood-stained mouth and thinks that it killed his child. Fear and terror overcome his heart [*khowfi va ro'bi bar delash ghaleb shod*] and this idea [*khayal*] becomes so powerful due to his hasty disposition, the whispering of suspicion, and the weakness of his nature [*az sar-e 'ajaleh-ye tab' va vasvaseh-ye zann va za'f-e bonyat*] that he kills the cat. Once the soldier sees the dead snake, however, he realizes his mistake. He cries and regrets the haste [*ta'jil*] that was a result of devilish delusions [*tasvil-e sheytan*] and blames himself for acting on it: "This excessive behavior is the result of my hasty nature [*tab'-e 'ajul*] and my weary, unjust soul [*nafs-e malul-e bi-ensaf-e man*]! What a lack of manliness [*na-javanmardi*] and mercy ... ! According to the laws of chivalry [*shari'at-e morovvat*] and the path of brotherhood [*tariqat-e fotovvat*], this shameful act that sprang from haste will never be remediated!"[18]

Let us note here that the tale of the soldier and the cat is not a tale about the unreliability of women at all. Rather, it is a tale that associates fear with a lack of manliness. The soldier of the tale, having killed the cat, blames himself for his "unmanliness" [*na-javanmardi*] and deviation from the path of *morovvat* and *fotovvat*,

---

[15] Alexandra Hoffmann, "Angry Men: On Emotions and Masculinities in Samarqandi's *Sindbad-nameh*," *Narrative Culture* 7, no. 2 (2020): 145–64.

[16] Samarqandi, *Sindbad-nameh*, 108–9.

[17] Ibid., 110.

[18] Ibid., 112.

terms that can be summarized as "chivalry."[19] Such unmanly, unchivalric behavior is the result of a state of emotions that is not ideal. In near-contemporary ethical thought, for example in the treatise *Tahdhib al-Akhlaq* (*The Refinement of Character*) by the eleventh-century philosopher Abu Ali Miskawayh, fear is treated as one of the illnesses of the soul [*amrad al-nafs*].[20] Like other philosophers such as al-Ghazali (d. 1111 CE), Miskawayh maintains that reason should govern the irascible part of the soul as well as the lustful faculty. Having an under-irascible faculty, according to Miskawayh, can lead to fear [*khowf*], sluggishness, cowardice, and weakness.[21] As for possible causes of fear, Miskawayh states that it can occur in anticipation of evil or the expectation of danger in the future, and that "the rational man should not fear them [*laysa yanbaghi li-l-ʿaqil an yakhafa minha*]."[22] Like many Islamicate authors, Samarqandi (at least overtly) construes men as more rational creatures than women. The rational man [*ʿaqel*], especially as contrasted with the "dim-witted woman" [*naqes-eʿaql*, literally: "of deficient intellect"],[23] should thus exhibit a kind of "mental manliness." The author portrays the soldier's impulsive act as a weakness, given that the implicit criticism of the tale shows that he should have ignored his fears and exhibited the "mental manliness" required of his gender. While it is certainly not the case that misogyny is not part of the cultural background that produced this version of the tale, it is important to note that the tale brings across its point—a critique of unmanly behavior—without overt misogynist speech. It is a tale about a man's weakness, not about wicked women.

Misogynist speech does occur in the vizier's framing of the story, however—or rather, in his transition between two stories. This vizier, like all others, tells two tales and uses a short misogynist pivot to transition from one story to another. At the end of the first tale, the vizier explains the reason he has told the king this story: "so that he does not allow haste, which is the result of the devil's enticement ... to have its way over his laudable nature."[24] The vizier concludes his admonition with the Arabic proverb "haste is from the devil [*al-ʿajala min al-shaytan*]; especially," he adds immediately afterwards, "since women are in a nest of treachery and excuses ... and their tricks are more numerous than the sand in the desert."[25] With this sudden misogynist pivot, the vizier asks permission to tell a story on the "wiles of women." Thus, this second part of the vizier's speech is not a comment on the previous tale, but acts as an introductory frame to his second tale. The vizier's second tale, "the story of the merchant's wife and her husband" (called "The Libertine Husband" by Domenico Comparetti),[26] is

19 Both terms are somewhat fuzzy and have intertwined semantic fields denoting manliness, courtesy, civility, and generosity—and for *javanmardi*, also youthfulness.
20 Abu Ali Miskawayh, *Tahdhib al-Akhlaq* [*The Refinement of Character*], ed. Constantine K. Zurayk (Beirut: AUB Press, 1967), 206.
21 Miskawayh, *Tahdhib al-Akhlaq*, 205–6.
22 Ibid., 206–7.
23 See, e.g., Samarqandi, *Sindbad-nameh*, 82.
24 Ibid., 113.
25 Ibid.
26 See Domenico Comparetti, *Researches Respecting the Book of Sindibâd* (London: E. Stock, 1882), 31; it is the second part of ATU 1515 "The Weeping Bitch" ("Canicula"). The first part of the tale is told as a separate tale by the fourth vizier.

about a woman who, left alone by her traveling husband, enjoys herself with a beloved every night. When her husband returns to the city and asks an old woman for an amorous arrangement with a beautiful lady, the old woman unknowingly leads him to his wife. Thinking quickly on her feet, his wife takes the opportunity to chastise him for intending to cheat on her. Hence, the vizier's second tale is a story about the "wiles of women," and his framing acts both as a moralization of the first tale as well as an introduction to the second. We will see that the same pattern emerges in other Islamicate versions of the story.

"Canis" in Other Versions of the *Sindbad-nameh* and the *Seven Viziers*

"Canis" does not appear as a misogynist tale in other versions of the *Sindbad-nameh* or the *Seven Viziers* in Persian, Ottoman Turkish, or Arabic. There are variations across these versions—the Arabic texts, for example, feature a dog, and the emotion leading to the killing is sometimes anger rather than fear. What remains consistent throughout, however, is that no woman is blamed for the killing of the animal in any of these versions.

In the Persian *Sindbad-nameh* of Azod Yazdi (written *c.* 1375 CE),[27] a verse adaptation of Samarqandi's text, the wife of the young man is described in very positive terms: she is devout, God-fearing, and chaste.[28] Here too, she dies in childbirth and leaves the man devastated; and similarly, the man's cat is a very well-behaved, clean, and sociable companion.[29] One day, when both the man and his nurse are absent, the cat, as we have seen before, defeats the black snake and runs to greet the returning man with a blood-stained mouth. When the man sees the blood, "his blood boils over for his son, and out of fear smoke clouds his mind [*bejushid khunash baray-e pesar / ze andisheh dudash bar-amad be sar*]."[30] Thinking that the cat killed his son, he swings a mallet onto the cat's head and kills it. As before, when he finds out the truth, he regrets killing his old friend, cries, and slaps his chest. Hence, in this version, the man's emotional state (*andisheh*, or fear) troubles his rational mind, and he only blames himself for his action.

The Ottoman Turkish version, *Tuhfetü'l-Ahyar* (*A Present for the Virtuous*; early 1540s CE), is an adaptation of Samarqandi's *Sindbad-nameh*.[31] Here, the tale is referred to as "the unjust soldier, the malicious snake, and the good-natured cat." The story

---

[27] Azod Yazdi, *Sindbad-nameh-ye Manzum*, ed. Mohammad Jaʿfar Mahjub (Tehran: Tus, 2002), 161–3. "Canis" is not included in Nakhshabi's *Tuti-nameh* (1330 CE), which incorporates only an abridged version of the *Sindbad* collection.

[28] Yazdi, *Sindbad-nameh-ye Manzum*, 161.

[29] Ibid., 162.

[30] Ibid., 163.

[31] Abdülkerim b. Muhammed, *Tuhfetü'l-Ahyar* [c. 1540 CE], Walters Art Gallery, Baltimore, MD, no. W.662. The manuscript is available at: https://art.thewalters.org/detail/35391, accessed June 2, 2020.

unfolds as we have seen before, but the characterization of the soldier differs, as does the description of the nurse: When the man and nurse return to the house, the "stupid, ignorant man and the imbecile, heedless woman [*merd-ı ahmaq-ı cahil ve zen-ı ebleh-ı gafil*]" see the blood-stained cat and think that it has killed the child. Without reflection, they become angry [*gazabnak*] and kill the cat.[32] When "the despicable [literally: unmanly] man and the stupid woman [*merd-ı namerd ve zen-ı ahmaq*]" considered the cat's chivalrous deeds [*ef al-ı fütüvvet*], while they, as humans, were ignoble [literally: without manliness; *ahval-ı bi-mürüvvet*], they were bewildered by their bad comportment and cruelty.[33] Apart from the fact that their hasty action was influenced by anger and not fear, there is another important difference between this Ottoman version and the Persian ones: namely that the man and the nurse kill the cat together and are therefore both to blame. However, the recurring theme of unmanliness may imply that the soldier would be expected to act reasonably and with restraint, or at least more so than the nurse. Hence, it is not a tale that singles out the unreliability of women in particular, but also criticizes a man's lack of mental manliness.

The distinguishing characteristic of the Arabic versions[34] is that the animal of the tale is a dog and the man's wife is still alive. In *Mi'at Layla wa Layla* (*101 Nights*; dating unclear),[35] the tale unfolds in much the same way as in the Persian versions: The man thinks that the dog has harmed his son, so he beats and kills it. After finding out what had actually happened, he slaps his face in regret. In the other Arabic version, *al-Wuzara' al-Sab'a* (*Seven Viziers*; 1533/34 CE)[36] the man also believes that the dog has killed his son and beats it severely. Due to his "violent temperament [*shiddat khulqihi*]," he draws his sword and kills the dog. Once he discovers the dead snake, however, he slaps his face, tears his shirt, and regrets his haste [*isti'jal*].

Common to all these versions of the tale is the fact that the woman is not blamed for the unfortunate death of the beloved animal in question. This is also true for the Syriac, Greek, Hebrew, and Old Spanish versions, which are included in the same group of "Eastern" texts of the *Seven Sages* tradition.[37] In all of these texts, the vizier tells "Canis" as his first tale, followed by a second tale. As we have seen, the second tale

---

[32] Ibid., fol. 57b.

[33] Ibid., fol. 58a.

[34] Even though the frame tale and a number of tales are incorporated in versions of *Alf Layla wa Layla* (1001 Nights), "Canis" is not.

[35] Bruce Fudge, *A Hundred and One Nights* (New York: New York University Press, 2016), 255–7. Fudge does not specify a date but assumes that the previous dating to the thirteenth century is too early (xxxiif).

[36] This version (ms. Şehid Ali Paşa 2743) is published in Ahmed Ateş, ed., *Sindbad-name yazan Muhammed b. Ali az-Zahiri as-Samarqandi: Arapça Sinbad-name ile birlikte* (Istanbul: Milli eğitim basımevi, 1948), 347–88, here at 371–2.

[37] The woman is not blamed for the killing of the animal in the Syriac version (Friedrich Baethgen, *Sindban oder die sieben weisen Meister* [Leipzig: J. C. Hinrichs'sche Buchhandlung, 1879], 25–6), nor in the Hebrew version (see Morris Epstein, *Tales of Sendebar: Mishle Sendabar* [Philadelphia: Jewish Publication Society of America, 1967], 167), the Greek version (see Redondo i Sánchez, "The Faithful Dog: The Place of the Book of Syntipas in Its Transmission," *Revue des études byzantines* 71 [2013]: 43), or the Old Spanish version (Comparetti, *Book of Sindibad*, 141). The second tale the vizier tells in all of these versions is ATU 1378 "The Marked Coat in the Wife's Room."

is "The Libertine Husband" in the case of the Persian texts and the Ottoman Turkish adaptation. The Arabic texts, along with the rest of the versions mentioned, feature a story called "Pallium" (ATU 1378 "The Marked Coat in the Wife's Room") as the second tale. In this story, a cunning old woman places a cloth under a merchant's cushion to help a young man attain his object of desire—the merchant's wife. Hence, in all of these versions, the tale "Canis" does not have a misogynist moral, but the vizier's framing pivots to misogynist speech when he introduces his second tale. As I will demonstrate below, this pattern changes once the tale moves to the "Western" tradition and markedly misogynist characteristics begin to appear in "Canis" itself.

Medieval European Adaptations

It is fair to say that the European versions of the *Seven Sages* are much more studied than the Islamicate ones. The same is true for "Canis." Notable studies on the tale have been conducted by Mary Speer,[38] Yasmina Foehr-Janssens,[39] and Bea Lundt,[40] on whose scholarship I rely for this section. Since the number of versions of the tale in European languages is immense, however, a few examples must suffice here to show that the blaming of women for the death of the faithful greyhound is not an isolated incidence.

In an Old French version of the *Seven Sages of Rome* from the first quarter of the thirteenth century (version A),[41] the plot of the tale unfolds as follows: a knight has a greyhound and a newborn son. He and his wife engage three nurses to look after the baby. One day, there is a tournament that the knight and his wife attend, leaving their child with the nurses. However, the three nurses sneak out of the house in order to see the tournament as well, leaving the knight's wise greyhound alone with the child. As in other versions, the greyhound fends off a snake in order to protect the infant. When the nurses come back, they find a bloody scene, and frightened of possible punishment, decide to run away. During the course of their escape they meet the mother of the child and tell her that the dog has killed the baby. The mother screams and tells her husband that his greyhound has killed the child. The knight then kills the greyhound but finds the baby alive.

As Mary Speer notes, women clearly play a negative role in this version. The three nurses who abandon the child in order to watch the tournament misread the situation and cowardly flee to evade punishment. The mother, falsely informed by them, then

---

[38] Mary Speer, "Specularity in a Formulaic Frame Romance: 'The Faithful Greyhound' and the Roman des Sept Sages," in *Literary Aspects of Courtly Culture*, ed. Donald Maddox and Sara Sturm-Maddox (Woodbridge and Rochester: D. S. Brewer, 1994), 231. See also Mary Speer, "The Prodigal Knight, the Hungry Mother and the Triple Murderer: Mirrors and Marvels in the Dolopathos Dog Story," in *The Court and Cultural Diversity*, ed. Evelyn Mullally and John Thompson (Cambridge: D. S. Brewer, 1997), 375–84.

[39] Yasmina Foehr-Janssens, "Le chien, la femme, et le petit enfant: Apologie de la fable dans le Roman des Sept Sages de Rome," *Vox Romanica* 52 (1993): 147–63.

[40] Bea Lundt, *Weiser und Weib*, 163–6, 379–82.

[41] See Yasmina Foehr-Janssens, "Misogyny," 167.

passes on the information to her husband, thereby "prejudicing his own interpretation of what he sees."[42] It is thus no longer just the man's own thinking and misreading that leads to the killing of the dog. Consequently, the knight blames his wife for the death of his greyhound. He says to her:

> "Madam, you made me kill my greyhound over our child that he had saved from death. I believed you, which [means that] I did not act wisely. But know this much: for what I did upon your advice, nobody will give me penance, rather I will give it to me myself." He sat down, removed his shoes, cut off the front part of his shoes, left without looking at his wife or child, and fled into exile because of the affliction [*courrouz*] his greyhound [had caused him].[43]

In *Li Ystoire de la Male Marastre* (*The Story of the Wicked Stepmother*), another Old French text (version M) from the late thirteenth century CE, the story begins very similarly. But here, the knight even threatens his wife with a sword once he discovers that he killed the greyhound unjustly:

> He was so angry that he drew his sword and went toward his wife. And when she saw him come, she did not dare to wait but turned around, fleeing. And he was so sorrowful because of his greyhound that had been slain in such a way, because of his wife's lie [*mençoigne*], and for the good deed he [the hound] had done, that he swore to God that he would only stay there one more night.[44]

As in the previous version, the knight announces that he is leaving his wife in order to do penitence. However, this version further emphasizes the wife's culpability both through the knight's threatening move and by calling the woman's false interpretation of the situation a "lie."

In many versions in other medieval European languages, the story of the faithful greyhound develops along similar lines. For example, in Hans von Bühel's fifteenth-century German version *Dyocletianus' Leben* (*The Life of Diocletian*), the knight exclaims after having killed the greyhound: "How could I kill my dear greyhound so cruelly? I believed the words of my wife!"[45] He then tears out his hair, breaks his sword, and for his misdeed he decides to go to Jerusalem and never returns. Another German text, the *Die Sieben Weisen Meister* (*The Seven Wise Masters*, version H; 1473 CE) by Johannes Bämler, has the knight similarly bewail the fact that "he listened to his evil wife."[46]

[42] Speer, "The Prodigal Knight," 382.
[43] Section de Traitement Automatique des Textes Littéraires Médiévaux, ed., *Les sept sages de Rome: Roman en prose du XIIIe siecle* (Nancy: CRAL de l'Univ. de Nancy II, 1981), 12–14. Translation adapted from Runte, "Portal, Society of the Seven Sages," 264–5.
[44] Hans R. Runte, ed., *Li Ystoire De La Male Marastre: Version M of the Roman Des Sept Sages De Rome* (Tübingen: Max Niemeyer, 1974), 16. I thank Sam Lasman for assistance with the Old French text.
[45] Hans von Bühel, *Dyocletianus' Leben*, ed. Adelbert Keller (Quedlinburg and Leipzig: G. Basse, 1841), 32.
[46] See Katherine Kent Skow, "The Whole is the Sum of its Parts: A Structural and Thematic Analysis of 'Die sieben weisen Meister'" (PhD diss. Urbana: University of Illinois, 1992), 76.

Of course, it is not the case that women are blamed for the death of the dog in all European versions, as Mary Speer has shown for the Old French text (version K).[47] Speer notes that "[o]ne surprising element in [version] K's handling of the events leading to the slaying of the greyhound is that the threefold discovery motif is presented without the explicit antifeminism found in some other *Seven Sages* versions."[48] The earliest Latin text, John of Alta Silva's *Dolopathos* (end of the twelfth century CE), similarly does not blame the wife.[49] Thus, the two earliest medieval European versions do not incorporate a misogynist moral into the tale, which further points to the conclusion that whatever Islamicate text—oral or written—on which they are based, did not include one either.

Conclusion

It would be too easy to brand the "Western" versions of "Canis" simply as misogynist tales—of course, they carry other connotations, too. Scholars have rightly argued that certain versions express a critique of knightly masculinity and worldly values, a point illustrated, for instance, by the protagonist going to Jerusalem and leading a life devoted to religion. Hence, misogyny is also a vehicle to express or critique masculinities. As I have shown, however, in the Persian, Ottoman Turkish, and Arabic versions of "Canis," misogynist speech is not employed to convey similar concerns about masculinities. In fact, Samarqandi's version of the tale is an intricate story of a man who is overcome by fear and is motivated by this emotion to trust the anxious, devilish thoughts that take hold of his heart. Furthermore, this same man then realizes that his fearful behavior was unmanly and blames only himself for his deed. In the absence of blameworthy women, it is thus a tale that warns against hasty action and addresses the management of emotions as a necessary trait of a rational man. In all Islamicate versions of the *Seven Sages*, this tale operates without overt misogyny.[50]

---

47 The archetype of the Old French version (dated between 1155 and 1190 CE) is lost, but the oldest redaction (version K) is thought to stem from the first half of the thirteenth century. See Mary Speer, ed., *Le Roman des Sept Sages de Rome: A Critical Edition of the Two Verse Redactions of a Twelfth-Century Romance* (Lexington: French Forum Publishers, 1989), 71.

48 Speer, "Specularity," 238.

49 See Speer, "The Prodigal Knight," 382; Lundt, *Weiser und Weib*, 163ff.

50 I thank Ulrich Marzolph for bringing two early Arabic versions of the tale to my attention: Ibn al-Marzuban (d. 921/2 CE), *The Book of the Superiority of Dogs over Many of Those Who Wear Clothes*, ed. M. A. Abdel Haleem and G. Rex Smith (Warminster: Aris & Phillips, 1978), 33–4, 57; as well as al-Tanukhi (d. 994 CE), *Nishwar al-Muhadara wa Akhbar al-Mudhakara* [*The Table-Talk of a Mesopotamian Judge*], ed. 'Abbud al-Shalji, vol. 6 [Beirut: Dar Sadir, 1971], 150). In both of these tales, the man's wife has passed away, and there is no nurse. I should further note again that the tale also circulated as part of the *Kalila wa Dimna* tradition, a vast corpus of texts which cannot be treated in the present chapter and deserves its own study. Based on a preliminary assessment, however, it seems that the misogynist moral of "Canis" in some of the medieval European versions of the *Seven Sages* cannot be attributed to Islamicate versions of *Kalila wa Dimna*. A quick overview will have to suffice here: In various versions of *Kalila wa Dimna*, the husband kills a weasel and is admonished by his wife that this is the result of haste. This is the case for various editions of Ibn

It is thus time to reevaluate cultural transmissions between the Islamicate and the non-Islamicate worlds, especially since "Canis" is not an isolated incidence. Two further examples are discussed by Ulrich Marzolph, the first of which is known as "The Old Woman as Trouble Maker" (ATU 1353). It is first attested in Arabic literature where the titular "trouble maker" is a slave who is acquired although he is known to be a slanderer. He makes a woman believe that she can secure her husband's love by cutting three hairs from his beard at night, while telling the husband that his wife is secretly plotting to kill him—leading to the death of one or both of them. The Arabic versions can thus be understood as a warning against the heedless purchase of slaves. This tale found its way into the European literary tradition through Joseph ibn Zabara's *Sefer Sha'shu'im* (*The Book of Delight*) in the second half of the twelfth century. In this version, the "trouble maker" is a scheming old woman who is challenged by the devil to sow discord between a married couple. When she succeeds, even the devil dares not approach her again. Ibn Zabara thus records the tale as a warning against women who are more scheming than the devil himself. In subsequent European collections, the tale thus appears as a more misogynist, religiously tinged exemplum.[51]

The second example Marzolph discusses is the tale type "An Ox for Five Pennies" (ATU 1553), which in Arabic and Hebrew traditions features a trickster who circumvents an oath that he made in a precarious situation. Instead of selling his camel cheaply, as sworn, he offers to sell it only together with a very expensive cat. It is thus an anecdote about legal trickery. In the European literary tradition on the other hand, it is often a widowed woman who aims to avoid fulfilling her late husband's wish to donate the profits of the sale to the church. By having the widow act for her own profit, some versions thus exhibit a misogynist touch.[52] Marzolph therefore argues that

---

al-Muqaffa''s text (d. *c.* 757 CE), for example in Louis Cheikho, ed., *La Version arabe de Kalîlah et Dimnah, ou: Les fables de Bidpai* (Beirut: Imprimerie catholique, 1905), 177. In Ibn al-Habbariya's (d. *c.* 1115 CE) *Kitab Nata 'ij al-Fitna fi Nazm Kalila wa-Dimna*, ed. Ni'mat Allah al-Asmar (Ba'abda: al-Matba'ah al-Lubnaniyah, 1900), 190–1, both the wife and the man exhibit haste. The Persian adaptation by Nasrollah Monshi (*c.* 1146 CE) in Mojtaba Minovi, ed., *Tarjomeh-ye Kalileh va Demneh* (Tehran: Daneshgah-e Tehran, 1964), 264–5 follows Ibn al-Muqaffa''s version. The version by Mohammad al-Bokhari (late 1140s CE) in Parviz Natel Khanlari and Mohammad Rowshan, eds., *Dastanha-ye Bidpay* (Tehran: Sherkat-e Sahami-ye Entesharat-e Kharazmi, 1361/1982), 214, differs in that it is the husband who informs his wife that this is what happens when people act in haste and not the other way around. This is also the case in the Syriac version (Friedrich Schulthess, ed. and trans., *Kalila und Dimna* [Berlin: G. Reimer, 1911], 84). The Hebrew version attributed to Rabbi Joël (twelfth century CE) in Joseph Derenbourg, ed. and trans., *Deux versions hébraïques du livre Kalîlâh et Dimnâh: la première accompagnée d'une traduction française* (Paris: F. Vieweg, 1881), 149, has the wife admonish the husband of the fruits of haste again. In *Kalila wa Dimna*, the tale "The Innocent Dog" operates under a different frame tale and is usually preceded by a combination of ATU 1430A "Foolish Plans for the Unborn Child" and ATU 1430 "The Man and His Wife Build Air Castles," and hence may lend itself less to a misogynist twist as it occurs in the *Seven Sages* tradition.

51 See Ulrich Marzolph, *101 Middle Eastern Tales and Their Impact on Western Oral Tradition* (Detroit: Wayne State University Press, 2020), 314–19; and Ulrich Marzolph, "Böses Weib schlimmer als der Teufel," in *Enzyklopädie des Märchens*, vol. 14 (2012), 551–5.

52 Marzolph, *101 Middle Eastern Tales*, 411. See also Ulrich Marzolph, "Ochse für fünf Pfennig," in *Enzyklopädie des Märchens*, vol. 10 (2002), 193–6.

the misogyny of both of these tales was increased through the reception in Jewish-Christian works of the European Middle Ages.

As we have seen above, a similar mechanism is at work with "Canis." When the tale of the "faithful cat" became the tale of the "faithful greyhound" as it crossed linguistic boundaries, it also changed and adapted to new cultural and religious milieux. The tale must have acquired its misogynist moral in Jewish-Christian adaptation somewhere in medieval Europe, through oral or textual intermediary steps that remain unknown. One may speculate, however, about one such step: When the vizier's tale that followed "Canis" was abandoned or rearranged in the processes of transmission, a part of the vizier's framing—including the misogynist pivot—may have stuck to the first tale. And authors who reworked a tale with a "mismatched" moral may have chosen to integrate misogyny into the tale itself. Such a shift from misogynist speech to misogynist moral most likely happened at some point in the medieval European context, since none of the extant Islamicate versions show any indication of such a shift.[53]

In any case, the *Seven Sages* tradition, like perhaps no other networks of texts, demonstrates the interconnected mode of circulation and translation of literature that characterized early globality. The study of cats and dogs, and of manliness and misogyny has provided new insights into the mechanisms of cultural transmission between the Islamicate and the non-Islamicate worlds, as well as processes of Christianization of Islamicate narrative material. Given the extent to which this multilinguistic and comparative analysis of the *Sindbad-nameh* has allowed me to shed light on the cross-cultural life of one of its tales, I hope that future studies of early global literature will attend to this text as well as other Persian works of the premodern era.

Acknowledgments

I am grateful to Helga Anetshofer, Sam Lasman, Franklin Lewis, Ulrich Marzolph, Austin O'Malley, and Arlen Wiesenthal for their comments on previous versions of this chapter.

Bibliography

Abdülkerim b. Muhammed. *Tuhfetü'l-Ahyar* [c. 1540 CE], Walters Art Gallery, Baltimore, no. W.662. Manuscript available at: *https://art.thewalters.org/detail/35391* (accessed June 2, 2020).

---

[53] The Old Spanish *Libro de assayamientos et engaños de las mugeres* (1253 CE), a direct translation from an Arabic version, for example, includes the vizier's framing at the end of "Canis," alluding to the stepmother of the frame tale: "Do not kill thy son, for the deceits of women have no end" (Comparetti, *Book of Sindibad*, 141). The heading of the next tale is then visually set apart with red ink (Don Juan Manuel, *El Conde Lucanor*, Real Academia Española, Ms. 15, fol. 72r). Manuscript available at: https://bibliotecavirtualmadrid.comunidad.madrid/bvmadrid_publicacion/es/consulta/registro.do?id=13725 (accessed June 2, 2020).

al-Bokhari, Mohammad. *Dastanha-ye Bidpay*. Ed. Parviz Natel Khanlari and Mohammad Rowshan. Tehran: Sherkat-e Sahami-ye Entesharat-e Kharazmi, 1361/1982.

al-Tanukhi, Muhassin b. Ali. *Nishwar al-Muhadara wa Akhbar al-Mudhakara [The Table-talk of a Mesopotamian Judge]*. Ed. Abbud al-Shalji. Vol. 6. Beirut: Dar Sadir, 1971.

Ateş, Ahmed. *Sindbad-name yazan Muhammed b. Ali az-Zahiri as-Samarqandi: Arapça Sinbad-name ile birlikte*. Istanbul: Milli eğitim basımevi, 1948.

Baethgen, Friedrich. *Sindban oder die sieben weisen Meister*. Leipzig: J. C. Hinrichs'sche Buchhandlung, 1879.

Belcher, Stephen. "The Diffusion of the Book of Sindbād." *Fabula* 28, no. 1 (1987): 34–57.

Blackburn, Stuart. "The Brahmin and the Mongoose: The Narrative Context of a Well-Traveled Tale." *Bulletin of the School of Oriental and African Studies* 59, no. 3 (1996): 494–507.

Bogdanovic, Dejan, trans. *Le Livre des sept vizirs. Zahiri de Samarkand*. Paris: Sindbad, 1975.

Bühel, Hans von. *Dyocletianus Leben*. Ed. Adelbert Keller. Quedlinburg and Leipzig: G. Basse, 1841.

Comparetti, Domenico. *Researches Respecting the Book of Sindibâd*. London: E. Stock (published for The Folklore Society), 1882.

Damrosch, David. *What Is World Literature?* Princeton: Princeton University Press, 2003.

de Blois, François. *Burzoy's Voyage to India and the Origin of the Book of Kalilah wa Dimnah*. London: Royal Asiatic Society, 1990.

Derenbourg, Joseph, ed. and trans. *Deux versions hébraïques du livre Kalîlâh et Dimnâh: la première accompagnée d'une traduction française*. Paris: F. Vieweg, 1881.

Don Juan Manuel. *El Conde Lucanor*. Real Academia Española, Ms. 15. Web. Available at https://bibliotecavirtualmadrid.comunidad.madrid/bvmadrid_publicacion/es/consulta/registro.do?id=13725 (accessed June 2, 2020).

Epstein, Morris. *Tales of Sendebar: Mishle Sendabar*. Philadelphia: Jewish Publication Society of America, 1967.

Foehr-Janssens, Yasmina. "Le chien, la femme, et le petit enfant: Apologie de la fable dans le Roman des Sept Sages de Rome." *Vox Romanica* 52 (1993): 147–63.

Foehr-Janssens, Yasmina. "Misogyny and the Trends of a European Success. The French Prose Roman des sept sages de Rome." *Narrative Culture* 7, no. 2 (2020): 165–80.

Fudge, Bruce. *A Hundred and One Nights*. New York: New York University Press, 2016.

Heng, Geraldine, and Lynn Ramey. "Early Globalities, Global Literatures: Introducing a Special Issue on the Global Middle Ages." *Literature Compass* 11, no. 7 (2014): 1–6.

Hoffmann, Alexandra. "Angry Men: On Emotions and Masculinities in Samarqandī's *Sindbād-nāmeh*." *Narrative Culture* 7, no. 2 (2020): 145–64.

Honar, Ali-Mohammad. *Yaddasht-ha-ye Sindbad-nameh*. Tehran: Bonyad-e Mowqufat-e Doktor Mahmud-e Afshar-e Yazdi, 1386/2007.

Ibn al-Habbariya. *Kitab Nata'ij al-Fitna fi Nazm Kalila wa-Dimna*. Edited by Ni'mat Allah al-Asmar. Ba'abda: al-Matba'ah al-Lubnaniyah, 1900.

Ibn al-Marzuban. *The Book of the Superiority of Dogs over Many of Those Who Wear Clothes*. Ed. M. A. Abdel Haleem and G. Rex Smith. Warminster: Aris & Phillips, 1978.

Ibn al-Muqaffaʿ. *La Version arabe de Kalîlah et Dimnah, ou: Les fables de Bidpai*. Edited by Louis Cheikho. Beirut: Imprimerie catholique, 1905.

Kent Skow, Katherine. "The Whole Is the Sum of Its Parts: A Structural and Thematic Analysis of 'Die sieben weisen Meister.'" PhD diss., Urbana: University of Illinois, 1992.

Landau, Marcus. *Die Quellen des Dekameron*. Stuttgart: J. Scheible, 1884.

Lewis, Franklin. "The *Shahnameh* of Ferdowsi as World Literature." *Iranian Studies* 48, no. 3 (2015), 313–36.

Lundt, Bea. *Weiser und Weib. Weisheit und Geschlecht am Beispiel der Erzähltradition von den "Sieben Weisen Meistern" (12.–15. Jahrhundert).* Munich: Wilhelm Fink Verlag, 2002.

Marzolph, Ulrich. "Böses Weib schlimmer als der Teufel." In *Enzyklopädie des Märchens. Handwörterbuch zur historischen und vergleichenden Erzählforschung.* Ed. Doris Boden, Rolf Wilhelm Brednich, and Kurt Ranke. Vol. 12, cols. 551–5. Berlin: De Gruyter, 2015.

Marzolph, Ulrich. "Ochse für fünf Pfennig." In *Enzyklopädie des Märchens. Handwörterbuch zur historischen und vergleichenden Erzählforschung.* Ed. Doris Boden, Rolf Wilhelm Brednich, and Kurt Ranke. Vol. 10, cols. 193–6. Berlin: De Gruyter, 2011 [2002].

Marzolph, Ulrich. *101 Middle Eastern Tales and Their Impact on Western Oral Tradition.* Detroit: Wayne State University Press, 2020.

Marzolph, Ulrich. "Sendbad-name." *Marvels & Tales* 25, no. 2 (2011): 376–9.

Miskawayh, Abu Ali. *Tahdhib al-Akhlaq. The Refinement of Character.* Ed. Constantine K. Zurayk. Beirut: AUB Press, 1967.

Monshi, Nasrollah, *Tarjomeh-ye Kalileh va Demneh.* Ed. Mojtaba Minovi. Tehran: Daneshgah-e Tehran, 1343/1964.

Perry, Ben Edwin. "The Origin of the Book of Sindbad." *Fabula* 3, no. 1 (1960): 1–94.

Redondo i Sánchez, Jordi. "The Faithful Dog: The Place of the Book of Syntipas in Its Transmission." *Revue des études byzantines* 71 (2013): 39–65.

Rieder, Paula M. "The Uses and Misuses of Misogyny. A Critical Historiography of the Language of Medieval Women's Oppression." *Historical Reflections* 38, no. 1 (2012): 1–18.

Runte, Hans R. *Li Ystoire De La Male Marastre: Version M of the Roman Des Sept Sages De Rome; a Critical Edition with an Introduction, Notes, a Glossary, Five Appendices, and a Bibliography.* Tübingen: Max Niemeyer, 1974.

Runte, Hans R. "Portal, Society of the Seven Sages." 2014. Web. Available at http://dalspace.library.dal.ca/handle/10222/49107 (accessed June 2, 2020).

Runte, Hans R., J. Keith Wikeley, and Anthony J. Farrell. *The Seven Sages of Rome and the Book of Sindbad: An Analytical Bibliography.* New York: Garland Pub., 1984.

Samarqandi, Mohammad b. Ali Zahiri. *Sindbad-nameh.* Ed. Mohammad Baqer Kamaloddini. Tehran: Miras-e Maktub, 1386/2007.

Schmidt, Michael. "Neue Beiträge zur Geschichte der Sieben weisen Meister." PhD diss., Cologne: Studentenburse, 1928.

Schmitt, Jean-Claude. "Hundes Unschuld." In *Enzyklopädie des Märchens. Handwörterbuch zur historischen und vergleichenden Erzählforschung.* Ed. Doris Boden, Rolf Wilhelm Brednich, and Kurt Ranke. Vol. 6, cols. 1361–8. Berlin: De Gruyter, 2011.

Schmitt, Jean-Claude. *The Holy Greyhound. Guinefort, Healer of Children since the Thirteenth Century.* Trans. Martin Thom. Cambridge: Cambridge University Press, 1983.

Schulthess, Friedrich, ed. and trans. *Kalila und Dimna.* Berlin: G. Reimer, 1911.

Section de Traitement Automatique des Textes Littéraires Médiévaux, ed. *Les Sept Sages de Rome: Roman en prose du XIIIe siècle.* Nancy: CRAL de l'Univ. de Nancy II, 1981.

Speer, Mary, ed. *Le Roman des Sept Sages de Rome: A Critical Edition of the Two Verse Redactions of a Twelfth-Century Romance.* Lexington: French Forum Publishers, 1989.

Speer, Mary. "Specularity in a Formulaic Frame Romance: 'The Faithful Greyhound' and the Roman des Sept Sages." In *Literary Aspects of Courtly Culture: Selected Papers from the Seventh Triennial Congress of the International Courtly Literature Society, University of Massachusetts, Amherst, USA, 27 July–1 August 1992.* Ed. Donald Maddox and Sara Sturm-Maddox, 231–40. Woodbridge and Rochester: D. S. Brewer, 1994.

Speer, Mary. "The Prodigal Knight, the Hungry Mother and the Triple Murderer: Mirrors and Marvels in the Dolopathos Dog Story." In *The Court and Cultural Diversity. Selected Papers from the Eighth Triennial Congress of the International Courtly Literature Society. The Queen's University of Belfast, 26 July – 1 August 1995.* Ed. Evelyn Mullally and John Thompson, 375–84. Cambridge: D. S. Brewer, 1997.

Uther, Hans-Jörg. *The Types of International Folktales: A Classification and Bibliography, Based on the System of Antti Aarne and Stith Thompson.* Vol. 1. Helsinki: Suomalainen Tiedeakatemia, 2004.

Yazdi, Azod. *Sindbad-nameh-ye Manzum.* Ed. Mohammad Ja'far Mahjub. Tehran: Tus, 2002.

9

Cinema Joins Forces with Literature to Form Canon: The Cinematic Afterlife of Saʿedi's "The Cow" as World Literature

Adineh Khojastehpour

Introduction

Much has changed since Goethe welcomed the era of *Weltliteratur*, a term that "crystallized both a literary perspective and a new cultural awareness."[1] During the last few decades the concept of World Literature has gone through considerable theoretical shifts. Casanova points to a world literary republic with its own economy, history, and geography.[2] Moretti refers to a "world literary system" that is "profoundly unequal,"[3] whereas Damrosch defines world literature as "all literary works that circulate beyond their culture of origin," contending that "in its most expansive sense, world literature could include any work that has ever reached beyond its home base."[4] Bassnett notes the significance of translation "in the movement of texts across linguistic and cultural boundaries."[5] Elsewhere she asks why translation has been "relegated to a secondary position in the literary hierarchy for so long, given its fundamental importance in the transmission of texts across cultures."[6] She notes that there had for a long time been "an abyss between the study of world literature and the study of translation."[7]

Extending Bassnett's question to apply to the interconnectedness of literature and media, one can ask, why is there a schism between the studies of world literature and world cinema? As Robert Stam observes, "World Literature theory has existed in a state of denial about the intimate connection between World Literature and World

---

[1] David Damrosch, *What Is World Literature?* (Princeton: Princeton University Press, 2003), 1.
[2] Pascale Casanova, *The World Republic of Letters*, trans. M. B. DeBovois (Cambridge, MA: Harvard University Press, 2005), 11–12.
[3] Franco Moretti, "Conjectures on World Literature," *New Left Review* 1 (2000): 56.
[4] Damrosch, *What Is World Literature?*, 4.
[5] Susan Bassnett, "Introduction: The Rocky Relationship between Translation Studies and World Literature," in *Translation and World Literature*, ed. Susan Bassnett (London: Routledge, 2018), 11.
[6] Susan Bassnett, "The Figure of the Translator," *Journal of World Literature* 1, no. 3 (2016): 311.
[7] Bassnett, "Introduction," 11.

Cinema."[8] Scholarly works in edited volumes and journals in the field of World Literature continue to be published with general ignorance toward world cinema, or toward adaptations of literary works. For example, The *Routledge Companion to World Literature* "ignores cinema generally and cinematic adaptations specifically, with the exception of one welcome essay by Jan Baetens which stresses the role of remediations in rescuing literature from oblivion."[9] Despite being related in practice, literature and film have often been considered apart. Be it the normative assumptions in the fidelity studies that in one way or another attested to the cultural superiority of literature over film, or the essentialist arguments of the defenders of medium-specificity who rejected the possibility of transforming the "true essence" of the work of art to a form other than its own, critical discourses have for the most part widened the breach between literature and film.

Literature has always been in close contact with other media. Literary forms have developed as a result of such exchanges. Since the emergence of cinema, literature and cinema entered a relationship that has gradually become "a two-way dynamic,"[10] where not only do novelistic techniques influence films, but certain cinematic techniques have been adopted by writers. As Murphet and Rainford contend, "the very terms in which we have come to think of literature and the literary have been ineluctably shaped by the fact, the experience and the language of film and film criticism."[11]

My aim in this chapter is to enrich understanding on the relationship between two neighboring fields of World Literature and World Cinema, that, as Stam puts it, "share their objects of study and their methods of interpretation, yet rarely speak to or learn from one another."[12] Informed by the intertextual turn of adaptation studies, I draw particularly on theorists such as Stam who argues that all formed media, including literature and cinema, "have been endlessly enriched by their dialogue with all the other arts."[13] Both adaptation and translation have been evaluated based on fidelity to the so-called original, and both are striving to be set free from such arguments. In this regard, Benjamin's argument in "The Task of the Translator" forms the main theoretical framework of this chapter. Benjamin points to the "afterlife" of the literary work, which involves "a transformation and a renewal" of the literary work and in which "the original undergoes a change."[14] He further argues that the idea of fidelity seems to be "no longer serviceable to a theory that looks for other things in a translation than

[8] Robert Stam, *World Literature, Transnational Cinema, and Global Media: Towards a Transartistic Commons* (London: Routledge, 2019), 64–5.
[9] Ibid., 65.
[10] Simone Murray, "Materializing Adaptation Theory: The Adaptation Industry," *Literature/Film Quarterly* 36, no. 1 (2008): 6.
[11] Julian Murphet and Lydia Rainford, "Introduction," in *Literature and Visual Technologies: Writing after Cinema*, ed. Julian Murphet and Lydia Rainford (New York: Palgrave Macmillan, 2003), 7.
[12] Stam, *World Literature*, 1.
[13] Ibid.
[14] Walter Benjamin, "The Task of the Translator," in *Illuminations*, ed. Hannah Arendt (New York: Schocken, 1968), 73.

reproduction of meaning."[15] Drawing on Benjamin's theory, I investigate the "afterlife" of Gholamhossein Sa'edi's short story published originally in a collection entitled *Azadaran-e Bayal (The Mourners of Bayal)* (1964).

To advance my argument, I also draw upon Bakhtin's theory of re-accentuation and intergeneric transposition. Toward the end of his 1935 essay, "Discourse in the Novel," Bakhtin discusses re-accentuation as what helps literary images "become more understood" by being embedded into new contexts. Bakhtin asserts that through re-accentuation, literary works can uncover "in each era and against ever new dialogizing backgrounds ever new aspects of meaning."[16] This process, he argues, "is enormously significant in the history of literature."[17] Old works are re-accentuated into new works. New literary images "are very often created through a re-accentuation of old images, by translating them from one accentual register to another."[18] Bakhtin also aptly underscores the intergeneric transposition: "Of Great importance as well is the re-accentuation of images during their translation out of literature and into other art forms—into drama, opera, painting."[19] To illustrate, he gives the example of "Tchaikovsky's rather considerable re-accentuation of Evgenij Onegin,"[20] a classic example of moving beyond generic boundaries, or intersemiotic transposition. Bakhtin's idea of re-accentuation is particularly significant in studying Gholamhossein Sa'edi's literary career. As I will demonstrate in this chapter, Sa'edi's concern for the longevity of his literary images prompted him to re-accentuate as well as re-mediate his work via the medium of cinema. The significance of Sa'edi and Dariush Mehrjui's collaboration in adapting Sa'edi's short story, "Gav" ("The Cow," 1964) into Mehrjui's *Gav (The Cow*, 1969) has already received considerable scholarly attention.[21] Yet no work so far has attended to the importance of this collaboration in the formation of modern Persian literary canon, the emergence of Iranian cinema as world cinema, as well as in the development of Persian literature as world literature. As I will argue in this chapter, the collaboration between Sa'edi and Mehrjui in adapting Sa'edi's short story for screen is of great importance not only in bringing international recognition for Iranian cinema and, on a domestic level, securing the place of cinema in the Islamic Republic, but also in developing the canon of modern Persian literature and creating, as Benjamin would put it, cinematic "afterlives" that have contributed to the globalization of modern Persian literature.

---

[15] Ibid., 78.
[16] Mikhail Bakhtin, "Discourse in the Novel," in *The Dialogic Imagination: Four Essays*, ed. Michail Holquist, trans. Caryl Emerson and Michael Holquist (Austin: University of Texas Press, 1980), 421.
[17] Ibid., 420–1.
[18] Ibid., 421.
[19] Ibid.
[20] Ibid.
[21] The short story was published in a collection titled *Azadaran-e Bayal (The Bayal Mourners)*. For a recent translation of the collection, see Gholamhossein Saedi, *The Mourners of Bayal: Short Stories by Gholam-Hossein Sa'edi*, trans. Edris Ranji (Bethesda: Ibex Publishers, 2018).

Cinema in Literature

Gholamhossein Saʿedi was born in 1936 in Tabriz. He graduated in medicine at Tabriz University and specialized in psychiatry at the University of Tehran. After graduation, he started medical practice in a working-class neighborhood in Tehran. Soon he "came to critical notice by publishing a series of short fiction and dramatic sketches highlighted by a collection of twelve interconnected short stories titled *Shabneshini-ye ba-shokuh* (*The Grand Soirée*, 1960).["22"] The 1960s saw Saʿedi's most prolific period in his literary career: "In this period Saʿedi astonishingly produced a good quantity of works that were also brilliantly high in quality."[23] His plays, short stories, screenplays as well as essays brought him recognition among the intellectuals of the time. This intellectual recognition reached its culmination after his collaboration with Dariush Mehrjui in adapting into a film the short story "The Cow" from his collection *The Mourners of Bayal* (1964).[24] Although Saʿedi was already popular among the intellectuals, "it was not until the release of *The Cow* in 1969 that he achieved something of a celebrity status in the Persian society of the time."[25] Saʿedi was "involved with the period's politics of dissent, and much of his work displays the hallmarks of left-leaning liberal thought."[26] He was also a founding member and active participant of *Kanun-e Nevisandegan-e Iran* (The Writers Association of Iran). Like many other politically committed writers who supported the regime change, he soon "found himself at odds with the rules" of the new government.[27] He went in 1981 to France, an exile that was unbearable for a writer with such deep emotional and intellectual attachments to his homeland. After a period of desperate drinking, smoking, and sleeplessness, he died of a heart attack and was buried in Père Lachaise near another Iranian literary icon, Sadeq Hedayat (1903–51).

 The fact that Saʿedi wrote adeptly in various genres including the short story, the novel, and the play, indicates his interest in crossing generic boundaries. Yet, to put it in Bakhtin's terms, it was Saʿedi's concern for the longevity of his literary images that prompted him to re-accentuate his works and to avoid being restrained within the framework of one particular genre. The publication of his seminal short story collection *The Mourners of Bayal* almost coincides with the publication of *Chub be Dast-ha-ye Varazil* (*The Club-Wielders of Varazil*, 1965), a play that was admired by his renowned contemporary writer and social critic Jalal Al-e Ahmad as "the best

---

[22] Faridoun Farrokh and Houra Yavari, "Saʿedi, Gholam-Hosayn," *Encyclopaedia Iranica*, online edition (2016).

[23] Javad Mojabi, *Shenakhtnameh-ye Gholamhossein Saʿedi* [*A Reader's Guide to Gholamhossein Saʿedi*] (Tehran: Atiyeh, 2000), 34.

[24] None of the eight stories in Saʿedi's collection have specific names. Instead, they are titled by an ordinal number: First Story, Second Story, etc. The "Fourth Story," referred to here as "The Cow," formed the basis of Mehrjui's film adaptation.

[25] Mojabi, *Shenakhtnameh*, 34.

[26] Ibid.

[27] Ibid.

Persian play ever."[28] Sa'edi's dramatic works can be divided into four main categories: Social realist plays, political allegories, historical plays transplanted into the present, and *lalbazi-ha* ("pantomimes").[29] As Hassan Javadi points out, prior to Sa'edi, the pantomime dramatic form "was little used in Persian folk theater, and he revived it by harnessing its rich sense of symbolism … creating masterful vignettes that are as forceful as his plays."[30] This tendency toward re-accentuation and intersemiotic transposition was regarded by Sa'edi's contemporaries as an obsession of some sort, "a lifelong doubt" on which genre and medium could best express what he had in mind.

Even within the framework of specific genres, Sa'edi's propensity to cross the borders and re-accentuate his literary images is plainly evident. It is known today that modern fiction writers in Iran and the world are influenced by cinema. As Ghanoonparvar contends, cinema started to influence "aspects of fiction writing including narrative structure, experiments with point of view, fragmented narrative, and the narrative strategies employed in fiction."[31] Modern fiction writers "make use of such cinematic practices as shots, cutting, lighting, depth of field, and so forth in their descriptive narratives of scenes."[32] Naficy asserts that the stories and styles of modern writers such as Sa'edi and Hushang Golshiri (1938–2000) were cinematic in that "their characters had psychological interiority and their narratives involved temporal, spatial, and point-of-view shifts."[33] This influence is also evident in Sa'edi's works. Naficy cites the literary critic Reza Baraheni who contends that "cinema, in particular Charlie Chaplin's silent movies, had influenced both the characters in Saedi's stories and the style of his one-act plays, which he collectively called *lalbazi* (literally, playing with muteness, or pantomime)."[34] Cinema, as Naficy argues, "had formed the author [Sa'edi] as well as his texts."[35]

Sa'edi's cinematic style of writing is particularly evident in his fiction. In *The Mourners of Bayal*, for instance, each story can simultaneously be regarded as a short film script. The opening paragraph of the first story is significant in this regard:

> When the village alderman came out of his house, the Landlord's dog, Papakh, which was at the garden wall started barking and jumped into the alley. The other dogs, which were sleeping on the low roofs, raised their heads and saw the village alderman's long stature, walking in the moonlight; they put their heads on their forelegs and slept again.[36]

---

[28] Ibid., 484.

[29] Hassan Javadi, "Gholamhosseyn Sa'edi," *The Literary Encyclopedia*, April 10, 2017.

[30] Ibid.

[31] Mohammadreza Ghanoonparvar, *Iranian Film and Persian Fiction* (Costa Meza: Mazda Publishers, 2016), 115.

[32] Ibid.

[33] Hamid Naficy, *A Social History of Iranian Cinema, Volume 2: The Industrializing Years 1941–1978* (Durham: Duke University Press, 2011), 345.

[34] Ibid.

[35] Ibid.

[36] Gholamhossein Sa'edi, *Azadaran-e Bayal* [*The Mourners of Bayal*] (Tehran: Negah, 1349/1970), 1.

This opening paragraph uses what seems to be a cinematic syntax, which defines a dexterous *montage*. The paragraph is a *scene* divided into five *shots*, connected to each other by simple *cuts*. The first shot, which is somewhat a *full shot*, shows Kadkhoda (the alderman) coming out of his house. A cut connects this shot to a second one. Here, another camera is shooting Papakh, the landlord's dog, who starts barking from where it is standing and then jumps into the alley. The third shot shows other dogs that wake up and raise their heads at the sound of Papakh barking. A fourth shot, a point-of-view shot, shows again the alderman, this time from the dogs' point of view. This point-of-view shot is cut back to the fifth one, showing the dogs again, that put their heads in their forelegs and go back to sleep.

Sa'edi's cinematic style is not merely evident in descriptive paragraphs. In sections with dialogues, the author's mise-en-scène as well as editing techniques can also be deciphered. A case in point is an excerpt from the fourth story of *The Mourners of Bayal*, the one that actually forms the basis of Mehrjui's *The Cow*:

> The people surrounded Mashdi Hassan's wife while women stayed closer to her and men stayed farther, all waiting.
> Mashdi Islam, Mashdi Islam, what's the matter?
> Mashdi Baba shouted through the hole over the door.
> Islam signaled with his hand to keep him silent. Everyone bent down. Mashdi Hassan's wife wiped her tears with the corner of her chador and said: "The cow, Mashdi Hassan's cow has died last night."
> The men turned with surprise and looked at each other. Naneh khanoom stood up suddenly and said: "What? What did you say?"
> "When I went to water her in the morning, I saw that she'd stretched out on the ground and her legs were stretched too, and her mouth was full of blood," Mashdi Hassan's wife said.
> The men turned and looked at Mashdi Hassan's house.
> The women whispered, and Naneh Fatemeh said, "O Imam of the time."[37]

The opening statement, seen in cinematic language as a full or *wide shot*, can function as an *establishing shot* that also carries a part of the story, depicting the men in the back and the women in the front coming closer to Mashdi Hassan's wife and circling around her. This shot is cut to a full shot of the house door with a hole on it, and Mashdi Baba, who is probably looking through this hole, calls Mashdi Islam, asking if something has happened. This shot is cut to a *medium close-up* of Mashdi Islam who uses his hand to signal silence. A second *long shot* shows that everyone around Mashdi Hassan's wife has bent down. Now the conversation between Mashdi Hassan's wife and Mashdi Islam is shown in three close-up shots. A full shot shows the men who look at each other with surprise. This is cut to another shot, this time a full shot of women, one of whom, Granny Khanoom, stands up in surprise and asks Mashdi Hassan's wife

---

[37] Ibid., 109–10.

what she has said. The full shot of women's whispering and the close-up of old Granny Fatemeh invoking "Imam of the time!" bring a touch of supernatural horror to the whole scene. Besides the pictorial development of the narrative in this section, Mashdi Hassan's wife's account of the cow's death is also pictorial, functioning as the literary equivalent of a *flashback scene* with her *voice-over* describing what we see. As the next section will illustrate, Saʿedi's re-accentuating tendency and yearning for intersemiotic transposition, as seen above in his cinematic style of writing, became actualized in his collaboration with the young, ambitious filmmaker Dariush Mehrjui (1939–). The director indeed provided a cinematic "afterlife" for the writer's short story, with a film that "became by far the most significant achievement of Iranian cinema after the pioneering works of Farrokhzad and Golestan,"[38] and which eventually started the new wave of cinema in Iran.

Literature in Cinema

Dariush Mehrjui was born in 1939 in Tehran. After his high school education, Mehrjui left for the United States to study cinema. He switched his academic field at the University of California, Los Angeles, from film to philosophy, mainly due to dissatisfaction with the Hollywoodian ideals imposed on students at the film college. Upon returning to Iran in 1965, he started his filmmaking career with an unsuccessful debut. A parody of James Bond films, *Almas 33* (*Diamond 33*, 1965) was an expensive production (about twenty million Rials were spent on the film, a very large amount for its time), and, although not a total failure, it did not recoup its production costs at the box office. Despite being far from Mehrjui's ideals, the humorous and absurd mood of the film was admired, especially by today's critics.[39] After *Diamond 33*'s failure at the box office, Mehrjui considered changing course. After contemplating different options for his next project, it was at last his chats with his writer friend Gholamhossein Saedi that made a tremendous change in Mehrjui's filmmaking career in particular, and Iranian cinema and culture in general.

Mehrjui had become interested in Saedi's works when he was studying in Los Angeles. He translated Saedi's plays and stories into English and published them in a student journal on Iranian literature and culture. He then sent the published journal containing translations of Saedi's works to Saedi himself and received positive feedback from him. They kept corresponding and when Mehrjui returned to Iran, they often visited each other.[40] Mehrjui's second film, *Gaav* (*The Cow*), was an outcome of this friendship. Mehrjui has frequently narrated the story behind their first coming up with the idea of their collaboration:

---

[38] Hamid Dabashi, *Masters and Masterpieces of Iranian Cinema* (Washington, DC: Mage, 2007), 109.
[39] Ibid., 107–32.
[40] Haghighi, Mani, and Dariush Mehrjui, *Mehrjui, Karnameh-ye Chehel-Saleh* [*Mehrjui: Forty Years of Filmmaking Career*] (Tehran: Nashr-e Markaz, 1392/2013), 26.

One day, as Sa'edi and I were riding in Tehran, we ran out of petroleum. We got off the car, and holding buckets, walked to the gas station. On the way, we chatted about Sa'edi's short story collection, *Azadaran-e Bayal* [The Mourners of Bayal, 1964]. Sa'edi mentioned one of the stories of this collection entitled "The Cow" and suggested that the story was suitable for cinema. He narrated the plot, and it all began.[41]

The collaboration between a writer and a filmmaker in Iran was not unprecedented. A few years before Sa'edi and Mehrjui came up with the idea of adapting Sa'edi's short story for screen, the acclaimed poet Forough Farrokhzad (1934–67) and the short story writer and film producer Ebrahim Golestan (1922–) collaborated in making *Khaneh Siah Ast* (*The House Is Black*, 1963), a short documentary that now stands as a seminal work in the history of Iranian cinema. Yet, it was the *type* of partnership that developed between a literary figure and a filmmaker that was unique at that time, hailed by Hamid Dabashi as the "best example of this kind of partnership."[42] Dabashi compares this particular collaboration between a writer and filmmaker with Stanley Kubrick's adaptation of Howard Fast's historical novel *Spartacus* (1951), arguing that "Kubrick's accidental work on Howard Fast's fiction momentarily diminished him as a filmmaker. But Mehrjui's prolonged relationship with Sa'edi generated and sustained his significance as a director."[43] Thus, it was not the collaboration itself; rather, as Ghanoonparvar puts it, it was "the type of collaboration that was formed between Mehrjui and Sa'edi" that "was unprecedented in Iran."[44]

"The Cow" is originally called the "Fourth Story" in Sa'edi's short story collection. The story begins when Mashdi Hassan's wife rushes out of their house weeping. She informs the rest of the villagers that Mashdi Hassan's cow died last night. The elders of the village, aware of Mashdi Hassan's deep obsession with the cow, try to hide the dead cow and when he returns to the village, tell him that his cow has run away. Unable to believe what he has heard, Mashdi Hassan, in a devastated psychological breakdown as a result of the death of his cow, acts in the manner of a cow, telling everybody that he is Mashdi Hassan's cow. His wife and the village elders try to help him come to his senses. They do everything, but nothing works. At last, they decide to tie him up and take him to a doctor in the city. However, as becomes clear at the end of the story from the conversation among villagers, Mashdi Hassan dies on the way to the city. In the film, however, characters and scenes from some other stories of Sa'edi's collection are also added to the main plotline. The film preserves the basic plot of Mashdi Hassan and the death of his beloved cow, with minor changes; for instance, it opens the story not with the cow's death, but with intimate moments that highlight the affectionate relationship between the villager and his cow.

---

41 Dariush Mehrjui, "Az *Almas-e 33* ta *Dayereh-ye Mina* [From *Diamond 33* to *The Cycle*]," in *Dariush Mehrjui: Naqd-e Asar az Almas 33 ta Hamoun*, ed. Nasser Zera'ati (Tehran: Hermes, 1385/2006), 33.

42 Dabashi, *Masters and Masterpieces*, 108.

43 Ibid., 108–9.

44 Ghanoonparvar, *Iranian Film and Persian Fiction*, 48.

The film was banned for a while and gained screen permission only under the condition of adding a disclaimer, stating that the story had taken place about forty years earlier. This act of governmental censorship became, as Hamid Dabashi observes, "the opening shot of a whole history of relentlessly undertheorizing and overpoliticizing it at the expense of the narrative revolution it had occasioned in Iranian visual culture."[45] Indeed, overlooking Sa'edi and Mehrjui's ingenious creativity in exploring new layers of meaning, most critics at different times have tended to read the film as a political allegory. Michael C. Hillman points to how the film's screenplay (which was published in 1969 under Sa'edi's name alone) is "often (mistakenly) interpreted as a story pitting a village representing Iran against the suspicious outsiders representing the West."[46] Hamid Reza Sadr, for instance, emphasizes the metonymic reading of the villagers' dependence on the cow's milk as Iran's dependence on oil under the Shah: "The fear of a future without oil permeated all discussion, just as the fear of losing the cow taxed the villagers' faith."[47] Attempts have been made, however, also to attend to the complex dimensions of meaning and artistic creativity of the film. Just recently, for instance, Michelle Langford has questioned the metonymic relationship between the village and the nation and the cow milk and oil, stating that "[T]he connotative connection between the cow, its milk, the village and the nation's oil industry can only be made fleetingly."[48]

It is significant to note that, although *The Cow* is based on Sa'edi's short story, and even though Sa'edi had established himself as a *committed* dissident writer at the time of publishing his *The Mourners of Bayal* in 1964, the book was published without any strict note of censorship obligating the addition of a disclaimer similar to the one that was added to Mehrjui's film. Moreover, the short story collection has received less political attention (and less attention in general) than the film. Even those who insisted on Sa'edi's "Bayal" as an allegory for Iran directed such readings to the film as the work of "Sa'edi and Mehrjui" rather than either one's work alone. One could argue that it was with the adaptation of Sa'edi's short story into Mehrjui's film that Sa'edi's fictive world was rediscovered. Both Sa'edi and Mehrjui gained in this collaboration in re-mediating the former's work from literature to cinema. As Dabashi astutely observes, "Mehrjui achieved for Sa'edi what he could never attained on his own – a masterful visualization of his psychotic realism – while Sa'edi did for Mehrjui what he could never imagined on his own – a direct, and laser-beam accurate, access into the collective *embodiment* of his culture."[49]

Elsewhere Dabashi argues that "although modern Persian fiction continued to thrive long after the rise of Iranian cinema, one may still consider, on a historical scale,

[45] Hamid Dabashi, *Corpus Anarchicum: Political Protest, Suicidal Violence, and the Making of the Posthuman Body* (New York: Palgrave Macmillan, 2012), 167.
[46] Michael C. Hillman, "The Modernist Trend in Persian Literature and Its Social Impact," *Iranian Studies* 15, no. 1 (1982): 14.
[47] Hamid Reza Sadr, *Iranian Cinema: A Political History* (London: I.B.Tauris, 2006), 133.
[48] Michelle Langford, *Allegory in Iranian Cinema: The Aesthetics of Poetry and Resistance* (London: Bloomsbury, 2019), 33.
[49] Dabashi, *Corpus Anarchicum*, 167.

the emergence of Mehrjui's cinema as the death of the Persian author and the birth of the Iranian auteur."[50] I, however, think that particularly the collaboration between Sa'edi and Mehrjui in making *The Cow* promises not a death, but a rebirth of the Persian author. With the re-mediation of Sa'edi's work from fiction to film, Sa'edi found a new life; the "Fourth Story" (aka "The Cow") in his collection found a new life; Bayal and its villagers found new lives; and Persian fiction found not only a new life but also an "afterlife," in Benjamin's term. A discussion of how this afterlife of Sa'edi's work in Mehrjui's film becomes "universalized" is in order.

The First Afterlife: *The Cow* Travels Abroad

Shortly after production, the film found its way out of the country and was praised at several international film festivals. Although it had won the award for best screenplay at Sepas Film Festival in 1970, and even after the addition of the disclaimer mentioned earlier, the film was still denied a screening permit as well as an export permit. Yet, it eventually found its way out when a friend of Mehrjui managed to smuggle a copy in a suitcase. This was the start of the global presence of *The Cow*. The film was premiered at the 1971 Venice Film Festival, and although lacking subtitles, the film won the International Federation of Film Critics (FIPRESCI) prize: "Highly impressed by the work, Italian critics compared Mehrjui to Pier Paolo Pasolini, Akira Kurosawa, and Satyajit Ray."[51] In the same year, the film entered the Chicago Film Festival, where the lead actor Ezzatollah Entezami (1924–2018) won the best actor award. It was the first such international award for an Iranian actor. The film was also screened at Berlin Film Festival in 1972 and won the OCIC Award – Recommendation (Forum of New Film). In early 1970s, it was also screened in Los Angeles, becoming the first Iranian film screened in a commercial American cinema. After this global recognition brought international prestige for Iranian cinema, the government lifted the ban and the film enjoyed financial as well as critical success at home as well.

In accounting for the worldwide success of the film, many refer to the universal aspects of the story itself. The story-as-film's universal success is a reminder of what Zhang Longxi notes as the defining feature of a canonical work, that is, a work's "[appealing] to readers in very different social, political, cultural, and historical conditions beyond its national origin."[52] Even today, *The Cow* has been said to appeal to the global audience. Following the screening of a restored version of the film at UCLA in 2016, a *Cineaste* writer compares the film with Mark Twain's *Adventures of Huckleberry Finn* in terms of the place they have in the artistic history of their countries of origin:

[50]   Dabashi, *Masters and Masterpieces*, 111.
[51]   Naficy, *A Social History*, 346.
[52]   Longxi Zhang, "Canon and World Literature," *Journal of World Literature* 1, no. 1 (2016): 121.

If not the first, they mark the beginnings of both distinctly national *and* globally accessible artistic histories; both cast large shadows over their respective national literary and filmic histories and ... they speak to us today as resonantly as when they were created.[53]

He further emphasizes, condemning like Dabashi and Langford the over-political readings of the film, that such a reading "ignores its far more universal themes, which have endured through time and across even larger geographic as well as cultural barriers."[54] Likewise, Iran historian Golbarg Rekabtalaei points to *The Cow*'s being "praised as a film with global sentiments" and its "universal themes of hopelessness, marginalization, and loss."[55] She quotes a commentator's note on the film, at the time of the film's screening at Berlin Film Festival, who praises the humanism of Mehrjui's *The Cow* and compares the story "to modern tales of Kalileh and Demneh."[56] All such laudatory views of *The Cow* and its worldwide travel are arguably also simultaneously applicable to "The Cow."

Redeemer and Redeemed: *The Cow*, the Supreme Leader, and the School Textbooks

A few years after the production and the international success of Mehrjui's *The Cow*, one of the most significant events in the history of contemporary Iran took place: thousands of people rallied on the streets under the leadership of Ayatollah Khomeini and in February 1979 they overthrew the Pahlavi dynasty, forming an Islamic government. During the first few years of the Islamic Republic, cinema had a very unstable position. Part of the revolutionary forces, Islamic fundamentalists, were against the entire medium and considered it a Western instrument that could corrupt the society. Many studios had been closed and many movie theaters had been burnt. This situation went on until one night, by chance, Ayatollah Khomeini watched *The Cow* on television. "The next day he made a speech in which he said that we are not against the art of cinema at all. We are in favor of educational and cultural films such as *The Cow*."[57] Thus, a dissident writer who had been known for his political activism before the Revolution, and for writing vehemently against the forced Islamization of the country after the Revolution, the one who fled the country and wrote his play *Othello in Wonderland* as a satire criticizing the Islamic government, Saʿedi ironically

---

[53] Nafis Shafizadeh, "Limitless Humanity: Dariush Mehrjui's *The Cow*," *Cineaste* 41, no. 4 (2016): 11.

[54] Ibid., 12.

[55] Golbarg Rekabtalaei, "Cinematic Revolution: Cosmopolitan Alter-cinema of Pre-revolutionary Iran," *Iranian Studies* 48, no. 4 (2015): 576.

[56] Ibid.

[57] Dariush Mehrjui, "Dariush Mehrjui: Islamic Ideology and Post-revolutionary Intellectual Films," in *Iranian Cinema Uncensored: Contemporary Film-Makers since the Islamic Revolution, 79–100*, ed. Shiva Rahbaran (London: I.B.Tauris, 2016), 82.

catalyzed, with the cinematic afterlife of his own short story, the redemption of cinema and the art of filmmaking in postrevolutionary Iran. Had it not been for this film, Iranian cinema could have come to a halt, denying the country and world most if not all of the postrevolutionary masterpieces that form a significant part of the Iranian cultural identity.

Perhaps due to being praised by the highest authority of the new government, Saʿedi's short story secured a safe place within the literary discourse of the new government. It received considerably more attention than any other story in *The Mourners* of *Bayal*, and in another surprising event in the Islamic Republic, it was added to the official high school text books, this time being entitled "The Cow," instead of "The Fourth Story" as was the case in Saʿedi's collection, which can be an effect of its afterlife in Mehrjui's film. Although the inclusion of Saʿedi's work in school textbooks has been castigated by conservative voices, who point to Saʿedi's leftist background and to his distaste for the Islamic government the story still enjoys wide readership, being discussed in school curricula throughout the country. One can argue that what contributed to the inclusion of Saʿedi's short story in the conservative school system in the Islamic state, which the government expended a considerable amount of energy to control, is indeed the national and international prestige of the story's afterlife in Mehrjui's film both before and after the Revolution. This is ironic since what has appealed to the Islamic government is mostly the insistence of superficial and overpoliticizing discourses on the story's depiction of the poor village life in the Pahlavi era. The inclusion of "The Cow" as a canonical text of Persian literature and a must-read for the postrevolutionary generation, was a merit yet to be granted by the same apparatus to many other literary figures including the seminal poets Forough Farrokhzad and Ahmad Shamlou as well as acclaimed fiction writers such as Sadeq Hedayat and Sadeq Chubak.

The Second Afterlife: Saʿedi Communicates with the World

More than fifty years after the publication of Saʿedi's short story collection and the production of Mehrjui's film, Saʿedi's story and its adaptation find another afterlife, this time in Asghar Farhadi's *Forushandeh* (*The Salesman*, 2016). The story is about a young, educated couple, Emad and Rana, who live in Tehran. They are practicing for a play in which they play the roles of Willy Loman and Linda in Arthur Miller's 1949 play *Death of a Salesman*. After their flat is damaged, they move to an apartment once rented by a prostitute. One night, when Rana is at home alone, she buzzes in a caller she thinks is her husband, but who is in fact one of the former tenant's clients. The sudden assault dramatically changes the young couple's life and starts tensions between them as husband and wife. Emad is hesitant to call the police, feeling at first ashamed and then tempted to find the culprit and take revenge all by himself.

Emad's day job is teaching literature in high school. In one of the early scenes of the film, Saʿedi's short story is read in class as part of the students' textbook. After the reading, a student asks if the story is based on a true story. Emad answers no, but he adds that in Saʿedi's works the relationships between characters are realistic. Another student asks Emad if he could show the film in the class, which Emad welcomes. In one of the most significant prophetic moments of the film, a student asks, "How can a man turn into a cow?" At first, another student answers: "Have you looked at yourself in the mirror?" This answer provokes laughter. But when another student asks the same question again, Emad answers "Gradually!" This exchange of dialogue can be read as a foreshadowing of Emad's psychological transformation. Sa'edi's story of the metamorphosis of a poor villager into his dead cow "echoes Emad's gradual post-traumatic transformation from a rational and civilized man into a revenge-seeking, offended macho."[58] By astutely telling about the fate of the protagonist through a seminal literary work which has now found a canonical status in the cultural history of Iran, Farhadi attests to the universality of Sa'edi's work, emphasizing its humanistic aspects, which go beyond place and time.

Moreover, Farhadi forms a correlation between Persian literature and American literature in this very scene. Right after the class conversation on "The Cow," a student asks how Emad's own rehearsal is going, to which Emad answers that staging will start the next week. He mentions Miller's work when a student asks the name of the play, and after another student asks which role he is going to play, Emad replies "The Salesman." The question as to how such a metamorphosis as the one Sa'edi narrated is possible can thus also be "reminiscent of Willy's gradual changing,"[59] suggesting a correlation between Sa'edi's and Miller's protagonists, both invoked by Farhadi to prefigure the tragic tale of his modern-day protagonists.

Farhadi's perceptive use of Sa'edi's short story in critical moments of his film, and his drawing correspondence between Persian and American literatures tremendously contributed to the reestablishment of Sa'edi's place in world literature. Having consolidated his position as a significant figure in World Cinema with films such as *Darbareh-ye Eli* (*About Elly*, 2009), which won many international awards, including best screenplay and Jury Grand Prizes at Asia Pacific Screen Awards, and *Jodayi-ye Nader az Simin* (*A Separation*, 2011), which won the Academy Award for best international feature film, Farhadi shows in *The Salesman*, more than in all his previous films, concern for World Literature and World Cinema and their interconnections. His astute use of Sa'edi's short story and placing it in dialogue with Miller's play gives Sa'edi's story, in Hutcheon's words, "an afterlife it would never have had otherwise."[60] The film was screened at Cannes Film Festival in 2016 where it won the best screenplay and best leading actor awards, and it won Farhadi his second Oscar for the Best Foreign Language Film, a remarkable event in the history of Iranian cinema. Starting with the global recognition of *The Salesman*, the intertextual correlations within the film have been further attended to in the academic discourse and beyond. Consequently, Sa'edi's story has been discussed again. For instance, Godfrey Cheshire devotes two paragraphs

[58] Babak Tabarraee, "*Furushandih* [*The Salesman*]," *Journal of Islamic and Muslim Studies* 3, no. 1 (2018): 106.

[59] Naghmeh Rezaie, "Asghar Farhadi's *The Salesman*: A Border-Crossing Adaptation in a Border-Blocking Time," *Literature/Film Quarterly* 46, no. 4 (2018).

[60] Linda Hutcheon, *A Theory of Adaptation* (New York: Routledge, 2006), 176.

in his review to explaining Farhadi's reference to Saʿedi's story: "The key reference here will be unfamiliar to American viewers, so it's worth unpacking. Emad is assigning the short story 'The Cow' by Gholam-Hossein Saʿedi, a leading Persian 20th-century literary figure and political activist." Another critic notes connections between the film and Saʿedi's work in terms of realism: "The milieu that Farhadi creates in *The Salesman* is initially very close to reality, but like Saʿedi, he soon begins to combine the quotidian with the extraordinary, to varying degrees of success."[61] Most of Farhadi's films are remembered by one remarkable piece of dialogue, which can be a single statement or an exchange. In *About Elly* it is, "A bitter end is better than a never-ending bitterness." In *A Separation*, it is "He doesn't recognize me as his son, but I can recognize him as my father!"[62] As for *The Salesman*, given the frequency of its being cited in the reviews and scholarly works on the film, one can claim that the most memorable dialogue of the film is the student–teacher exchange on Saʿedi's story at class: "How can a man turn into a cow? – Gradually!"

Conclusion

The objective of this chapter has been to start a conversation between the neighboring fields of World Literature and World Cinema, and to demonstrate how the former can benefit from resonances of the contiguous field of the latter. As I have demonstrated in my close analysis of the case of Saʿedi's short story, the transmedial interrelations between modern Persian literature and Iranian cinema, manifested in the collaboration between Saʿedi and Mehrjui in adapting Saʿedi's short story to the screen, have started a remarkable cinematic wave in the history of Iranian cinema, bringing it international recognition and securing its place in the uncertain postrevolutionary cultural arena. As my investigation of the cinematic afterlife of Saʿedi's short story has indicated, such transmedial interrelations have also contributed to the formation of the modern Persian literary canon as well as to the development of Persian literature as World Literature.

Acknowledgments

I sincerely thank Michelle Langford for her thoughtful comments throughout the process of writing this chapter and for providing me with valuable resources. I am deeply grateful to Behnam M. Fomeshi for assisting me in developing my ideas at different stages of writing this chapter. I also thank Laetitia Nanquette, members

---

[61] Amir Abou-Jaoude, "Asghar Farhadi Captivates with Almost Perfect *The Salesman*," *The Stanford Daily*, January 31, 2017.

[62] Nader states this as a response to Simin's argument that his father has Alzheimer's and thus cannot recognize Nader, in order to encourage him to migrate.

of the Iranian Studies Network at UNSW, and anonymous reviewers of *Persian Literature as World Literature* for their constructive comments on earlier drafts of this chapter.

Bibliography

Abou-Jaoude, Amir. "Asghar Farhadi Captivates with almost Perfect *The Salesman*." *The Stanford Daily*, January 31, 2017. Web. Available at www.stanforddaily. com/2017/01/31/asghar-farhadi-captivates-with-almost-perfect-the-salesman (accessed May 10, 2020).

Bakhtin, Mikhail. "Discourse in the Novel." In *The Dialogic Imagination: Four Essays*. Ed. Michail Holquist. Trans. Caryl Emerson and Michael Holquist. 259–420. Austin: University of Texas Press, 1980.

Bassnett, Susan. "The Figure of the Translator." *Journal of World Literature* 1, no. 3 (2016): 299–315.

Bassnett, Susan. "Introduction: The Rocky Relationship between Translation Studies and World Literature." In *Translation and World Literature*. Ed. Susan Bassnett. 11–19. London: Routledge, 2018.

Benjamin, Walter. "The Task of the Translator." In *Illuminations*. Ed. Hannah Arendt. 69–82. New York: Schocken, 1968.

Cartmell, Deborah. "100+ Years of Adaptations, or, Adaptation as the Art Form of Democracy." In *A Companion to Literature, Film, and Adaptation*. Ed. Deborah Cartmell. 1–13. Sussex: Wiley-Blackwell, 2012.

Casanova, Pascale. *The World Republic of Letters*. Trans. M. B. DeBovois. Cambridge, MA: Harvard University Press, 2005.

Cheshire, Godfrey. "The Salesman." *RogerEbert*, January, 27, 2017. Web. Available at www. rogerebert.com/reviews/the-salesman-2017 (accessed May 10, 2020).

Dabashi, Hamid. *Corpus Anarchicum: Political Protest, Suicidal Violence, and the Making of the Posthuman Body*. New York: Palgrave Macmillan, 2012.

Dabashi, Hamid. *Masters and Masterpieces of Iranian Cinema*. Washington: Mage, 2007.

Damrosch, David. *What Is World Literature?* Princeton: Princeton University Press, 2003.

Farrokh, Faridoun, and Houra Yavari. "SA'EDI, Gholam-Hosayn." *Encyclopaedia Iranica*, December 6, 2012. Web. Available at www.iranicaonline.org/articles/saedi-gholam-hosayn (accessed May 10, 2020).

Ghanoonparvar, Mohammadreza. *Iranian Film and Persian Fiction*. Costa Meza: Mazda Publishers, 2016.

Haghighi, Mani, and Dariush Mehrjui. *Mehrjui: Karnameh-ye Chehel-Saleh* [*Mehrjui: Forty Years of Filmmaking Career*]. Tehran: Nashr-e Markaz, 1392/2013.

Hillman, Michael. "The Modernist Trend in Persian Literature and Its Social Impact." *Iranian Studies* 15, no. 1 (1982): 7–29.

Hutcheon, Linda. *A Theory of Adaptation*. New York: Routledge, 2006.

Javadi, Hassan. "Gholamhosseyn Sa'edi." *The Literary Encyclopedia*, April 10, 2017. Web. Available at www.litencyc.com/php/speople.php?rec=true&UID=13360 (accessed May 10, 2020).

Langford, Michelle. *Allegory in Iranian Cinema: the Aesthetics of Poetry and Resistance*. London: Bloomsbury, 2019.

Mehrjui, Dariush. "*Az Almas-e 33* ta *Dayereh-ye Mina* [From *Diamond 33* to *The Cycle*]." In *Dariush Mehrjui: Naqd-e Asar az Almas 33 ta Hamoun*. Ed. Nasser Zera'ati. 30–5. Tehran: Hermes, 1385/2006.

Mojabi, Javad. *Shenakhtnameh-ye Gholamhossein Sa'edi* [*A Reader's Guide to Gholamhossein Sa'edi*]. Tehran: Atiyeh, 1379/2000.

Moretti, Franco. "Conjectures on World Literature." *New Left Review* 1 (2000): 54–68.

Murphet, Julian, and Lydia Rainford. "Introduction." In *Literature and Visual Technologies: Writing after Cinema*. Ed. Julian Murphet and Lydia Rainford. 1–11. New York: Palgrave Macmillan, 2003.

Murray, Simone. "Materializing Adaptation Theory: The Adaptation Industry." *Literature/Film Quarterly* 36, no. 1 (2008): 4–20.

Naficy, Hamid. *A Social History of Iranian Cinema*, vol. 2: *The Industrializing Years 1941–1978*. Durham: Duke University Press, 2011.

Rahbaran, Shiva. "Dariush Mehrjui: Islamic Ideology and Post-revolutionary Intellectual Films." In *Iranian Cinema Uncensored: Contemporary Film-Makers since the Islamic Revolution*. Trans. Maryam Mohajer and Shiva Rahbaran. Ed. Shiva Rahbaran. 79–100. London: I.B.Tauris, 2016.

Rekabtalaei, Golbarg. "Cinematic Revolution: Cosmopolitan Alter-cinema of Pre-revolutionary Iran." *Iranian Studies* 48, no. 4 (2015): 567–89.

Rezaie, Naghmeh. "Asghar Farhadi's *The Salesman*: A Border-Crossing Adaptation in a Border-Blocking Time." *Literature/Film Quarterly* 46, no. 4 (2018). Web. Available at https://lfq.salisbury.edu/_issues/46_4/asghar_farhadis_the_salesman_adaptation.html (accessed May 10, 2020).

Sadr, Hamid Reza. *Iranian Cinema: A Political History*. London: I.B.Tauris, 2006.

Sa'edi, Gholamhossein. *Azadaran-e Bayal* [*The Mourners of Bayal*]. Tehran: Negah, 1349/1970.

Shafizadeh, Nafis. "Limitless Humanity: Dariush Mehrjui's *The Cow*." *Cineaste* 41, no. 4 (2016): 11–13.

Stam, Robert. "Introduction: The Theory and Practice of Adaptation." In *Literature and Film: A Guide to the Theory and Practice of Film Adaptation*. Ed. Robert Stam and Alessandra Raengo. 1–52. Malden: Blackwell, 2005.

Stam, Robert. *World Literature, Transnational Cinema, and Global Media: Towards a Transartistic Commons*. London: Routledge, 2019.

Tabarraee, Babak. "Furushandih [The Salesman]." *Journal of Islamic and Muslim Studies* 3, no. 1 (2018): 104–11.

The Cow. Dir. Dariush Mehrjui. Iran: Ministry of Culture and Arts, 1348/1969.

The Salesman. Dir. Asghar Farhadi. Iran: Filmiran, 1395/2016.

Zhang, Longxi. "Canon and World Literature." *Journal of World Literature* 1, no. 1 (2016): 119–27.

Part Three

The Transnational Turn

10

Until a Shirt Blossoms Red: Proto-Third Worldism in Ahmad Shamlou's *Manifesto*

Levi Thompson

This chapter introduces "proto-Third Worldism" as a rubric for bringing modern Persian literature into discussions about what constitutes World Literature. I take up an early poetic collection of Ahmad Shamlou (1925–2000) titled *Qatʿnameh* (*The Manifesto*, 1951),[1] which Anglophone criticism has for the most part ignored until now, as an example of Persian literature as world literature. As we will see, Shamlou's poetry develops as part of what scholars have recently dubbed the "planetary" movement of literature, a phenomenon Susan Stanford Friedman explores in *Planetary Modernisms*. Although I depend heavily on the term "transnational" below, I here invoke the more open, less-overdetermined "planetary" as Friedman conceives of it. That is, whereas "*transnational* suggests the ongoing tension between nation-states and globalized postnational political formations … [, p]lanetary … echoes the spatial turn in cultural theory of the twenty-first century. It is cosmic and grounded at the same time, indicating a place and time that can be both expansive and local … *Planetary* has an open-ended edge that *transnational* and *global* lack."[2] While Shamlou's poetry has an undeniable planetary dimension in its openness to shared humanity, nature, and time, the political realities it negotiates cannot escape the transnational tensions of the mid twentieth century.

The Manifesto announces Shamlou's rebirth into *taʿahhod* (political commitment) following the roundly dismissed and derided juvenilia of his first collection, *Ahang-ha-ye Faramush-shodeh* (*Forgotten Songs*, 1947).[3] *The Manifesto*'s poetic persona suddenly awakens from an earlier chauvinist Iranian nationalism—and, to have Shamlou himself explain it, the romanticism that accompanied it—to an acute realization of the poet's place in a nascent revolutionary Third World. The collection constitutes an early instance of transnational solidarity that predates and thus paves the way, literarily, for

---

[1] Ahmad Shamlou, *Qatʿnameh*, 4th ed. (Tehran: Morvarid, 1364/1985).

[2] Susan Stanford Friedman, *Planetary Modernisms: Provocations on Modernity across Time* (New York: Columbia University Press, 2015), 7–8. Italics in original.

[3] Ahmad Shamlou, *Ahang-ha-ye Faramush-shodeh*, 2nd ed. (Tehran: Morvarid, 1386/2007).

the Afro-Asian Bandung Conference held in Indonesia in 1955 and the Non-Aligned Movement, which began in earnest in 1961.[4] Although Iran was a participant in both, Mohammad Reza Shah's (r. 1967–79) alignment with the neocolonial West contrasts sharply with Shamlou's poetic vision of solidarity, which nonetheless draws heavily on Western literature—especially, in the case of *The Manifesto*, on the life and work of the Spanish poet Federico García Lorca (1898–1936). By approaching *The Manifesto* as world literature, my intention is to not only ensure the continued appreciation of the classics, which Shamlou openly depends on, but also to make room for literature that reflects on what it means to be of and in a globalized world that stretches across the planet and brings far-flung individuals together in an inescapable network of connections driven by capitalism.

What Is Proto-Third Worldism?

I propose the concept of proto-Third Worldism as a theoretical frame for bringing literatures Western academics often consider minor into our discussions of World Literature. The phrase "proto-Third Worldism" appears in a few places. Zeynep Çelik uses it when discussing Turkish modernist poet Nâzım Hikmet's (d. 1963) position vis-à-vis European imperialism.[5] Daniel Widener employs the term in his discussion of Black internationalism in the context of the Korean War.[6] Patrick Iber brings it up in his analysis of Jorge Amado's (d. 2001) brand of "Communist cultural criticism": "a combination of Latin American nationalism, indigenism, and a kind of Proto-Third Worldism."[7] Still, the concept has remained undertheorized as an analytical tool and an ideological space that writing might occupy. My goal here is to buttress proto-Third Worldism as a theoretical frame for use within the study of World Literature through my reading of Shamlou's *Manifesto*, to move our considerations of modern Persian literature beyond the realm of the national and into the transnational.

The roots of proto-Third Worldism reach down into a literary history existing on the margins of European metropoles. Connections across literary contexts and continents challenge us now in the Western academy, where it seems we cannot forget English (or French, or German, etc.) because the disciplinary boundaries of English departments, naturally, and Comparative Literature departments, unfortunately, and the gatekeeping functions that form them have largely proven too staid to allow for academic engagements

4   For many insights about the will for independence that spawned the Bandung Conference, see Richard Wright, *The Color Curtain: A Report on the Bandung Conference*, foreword by Gunnar Myrdal (Cleveland: The World Publishing Company, 1956).
5   Zeynep Çelik, "Speaking Back to Orientalist Discourse," in *Empires of Vision: A Reader*, ed. Martin Jay and Sumathi Ramaswamy (Durham: Duke University Press, 2014), 396.
6   Daniel Widener, "Seoul City Sue and the Bugout Blues: Black American Narratives of the Forgotten War," in *Afro Asia: Revolutionary Political and Cultural Connections between African Americans and Asian Americans*, ed. Fred Ho and Bill V. Mullen (Durham: Duke University Press, 2008), 77.
7   Patrick Iber, *Neither Peace Nor Freedom: The Cultural Cold War in Latin America* (Cambridge, MA: Harvard University Press, 2015), 60.

of other literatures on their own terms.[8] My conception of proto-Third Worldism as a politically conscious literary stance draws on Françoise Lionnet and Shu-Mei Shih's conception of "transnationalism-from-below," which they define in the introduction to their 2005 collection *Minor Transnationalism* as "the sum of counterhegemonic operations of the non-elite who refuse assimilation to one given nation-state."[9] They further define "transnationalism-from-below" in opposition to "transnationalism-from-above," or "the transnationalism of the multinational corporate sector, of finance capital, of global media, and other elite-controlled macrostructural processes."[10] I have elsewhere argued for the necessity of tweaking the definition of "transnationalism-from-above" in the case of Soviet Communist imperialism and its top-down approach to local Communist movements in the Third World.[11] In Shamlou's case, although he expresses his solidarity with Marxist revolutionaries across the planet, he neither toes a specifically Soviet line nor adopts wholesale Communist socialist realism in *The Manifesto*. I therefore look to the way he builds transnational solidarity in his poetry as an early instance of "transnationalism-from-below." In returning to the literary history of the twentieth century and reconsidering poetry in Iran as it relates to an ongoing and interconnected process of social, political, and economic development, I am taking my cue from Aarthi Vadde, who, in *Chimeras of Form*, argues for the simultaneous considerations of internationalism and global consciousness, though these trends are generally associated with either end of the twentieth century. "Rather than assert that globally oriented analytical terms such as *transnationalism, cosmopolitanism, planetary*, and *world-system* supersede older terms such as *empire, anticolonialism*, and *internationalism*," she explains, "I contend that they sublate them—that is, absorb their lessons in the process of claiming to move past them."[12] My first goal in analyzing an example of Third Worldist literature *avant la lettre*, then, is to begin, however modestly, writing a missing chapter in the history of World Literature. My second—in which I join other contributors to this book—is to make modern Persian literature part of the developing conversation about Persian literature as world literature.

The Third World, the Non-Aligned Movement, the Global South.[13] The terms for "the rest" of the world outside of the West have changed along with the prevailing

---

[8] You can find a trenchant critique of the formulation of world literature in the shadow of the colonial and decolonial experience and with the rise of "local bourgeoisies at least elements of which now consider themselves part of the global ruling class" in Aamir Mufti, *Forget English! Orientalisms and World Literatures* (Cambridge, MA: Harvard University Press, 2016), 243.

[9] Françoise Lionnet and Shu-Mei Shih, "Introduction: Thinking through the Minor, Transnationally," in *Minor Transnationalism*, ed. Françoise Lionnet and Shu-Mei Shih (Durham: Duke University Press, 2005), 5–6.

[10] Ibid., 6.

[11] Levi Thompson, "An Iraqi Poet and the Peace Partisans: Transnational Pacifism and the Poetry of Badr Shākir al-Sayyāb," *College Literature* 47, no. 1 (2020): 65–88.

[12] Aarthi Vadde, *Chimeras of Form: Modernist Internationalism Beyond Europe, 1914–2016* (New York: Columbia University Press, 2017), 30.

[13] "Third World" has its roots in an article written by Alfred Sauvy, in French, in the newspaper *L'Observateur* (August 14, 1952), where he referred to "*ce Tiers Monde ignoré, exploité, méprisé*" ("this ignored, exploited, scorned Third World") in a comparison between the exploited nations of the world and the dispossessed Third Estate at the beginning of the French Revolution (see "Seeing the World Differently: Rethinking the 'Third World,'" *The Economist* 395, no. 8686 [June 12, 2010]: 71–2).

world order. Following the outset of the Cold War, analysts split the world up into thirds: the First World of capitalism (the developed nations), the Second World of the Communist Bloc, and the Third World (nonaligned, undeveloped nations). As the Cold War heated up, Western powers and the Soviets alike sought to bring developing nations into their spheres of influence, thus providing the impetus for declarations of nonalignment from countries across the Middle East, Asia, Africa, and South America, beginning in 1961 and continuing until the fall of the Berlin Wall. The terms we use to refer to "the rest" have a historical basis, one that reaches back to the era of colonial domination and yet further. But what possibilities could we open up in order to consider the various sublations of older terms into newer ones? Vadde suggests that we can better understand the previous century not through "the usual narratives of rupture around 1945 (the end of World War II and the beginning of decolonization) or 1989 (the end of the Cold War)." Rather, Vadde offers as an alternative the possibility of "reenergizing the relationship between early and late twentieth-century thought," which "furnishes contemporary 'globalization talk' with a richer understanding of its own world-making vocabularies."[14] With Vadde's words in mind, I propose creating a literary history that takes into consideration instances of proto-Third Worldism; "proto" not because authors writing in the Third World were unaware of their subordinate position to the Great Powers, but because the term "Third World" had not yet become an organizing principle prior to the Bandung Conference. Yet, as I will show in my readings of Shamlou's early poetry, the poet was already actively engaged in imagining new futures for formerly colonized nations, a process that Adom Getachew also uses the term "worldmaking" to describe.[15] Shamlou's poetic world-making, then, might bring us to a new understanding of what the "world" of world literature could be. Finally, I retain the term "Third World" here not as a pejorative (though it certainly has been used as one), but instead to reclaim it as a term for collective solidarity across the Global South.

I use Shamlou's work as an exemplary case because of the nascent Third World consciousness that transformed his poetry as the internationally turbulent 1940s rolled into the domestic unrest of the 1950s in Iran. This attitudinal shift occurred largely due to the poet's encounter with Lorca's poetry and biography, thus offering us a remarkable case in which a Western poet becomes a revolutionary icon across the non-West. Once Shamlou learned about the circumstances of Lorca's execution, he gave up the centrality and individuality of his lyric "I" and devoted his poetic persona to a collective "you." This chapter positions Shamlou's *Manifesto* within broader transnational trends in the Global South and Third World at the dawn of the Cold War and in the midst of American aggression in Korea (1950–3). While I account for the indelible mark Lorca's poetry left on Shamlou's work, I also aim to provincialize traditional modernist centers—Paris and London positioned at the

---

[14] Vadde, *Chimeras of Form*, 30.
[15] Adom Getachew, *Worldmaking after Empire: The Rise and Fall of Self-Determination* (Princeton: Princeton University Press, 2019).

heart of empires and at the usual centers of modernist geographies—by reorienting our focus to lateral networks of literary exchange that operated beyond the reach and beneath the radar of Western metropoles as a Third World consciousness began to develop across the planet.

Proto-Third Worldism in Ahmad Shamlou's *Manifesto*

Let us now turn to Shamlou's *Manifesto* to see just how it presages the birth of Third Worldist solidarity in literature. The title of the first poem in the collection, "Until A Shirt Blossoms Red," metaphorically evokes the image of blood blossoming across the chest of a bullet victim and subtly alludes to transnational Communist commitment in its flowing red. It begins with a metapoetic reflection on the act of writing politically committed poetry:

سنگ می کشم بر دوش،
سنگ الفاظ
سنگ قوافی را.
و از عرق‌ریزان غروب، که شب را
در گود تاریکش
می کند بیدار،
و قیراندود می شود رنگ
در نابینائی تابوت،
و بی نفس می ماند آهنگ
از هراس انفجار سکوت،
من کار می کنم
کار می کنم
کار
و از سنگ الفاظ
بر می افرازم
استوار
دیوار،
تا بام شعرم را بر آن نهم
تا در آن بنشینم
در آن زندانی شوم...

I carry stones on my shoulders,
stones of words,
of rhyme
and from the sweating sunset that awakens
night
          in the pit of its darkness,
and becomes pitch black
in the blindness of a coffin

the song remains breathless
fearing an explosion of silence,
I work
    work
        and work
and from stones of words
           I steadily
construct
   a wall,
until I build the roof of my poetry over it
until I sit down inside it
and become a prisoner ...[16]

The poem starts with the persona carrying stones of words and rhymes, the building blocks of a poem, on his shoulders. He not only constructs a poem with them but also the walls that will eventually surround and entrap him. Language becomes not a refuge for the poet, but a prison. By trapping meanings in written or spoken words, poets might even land themselves in a real prison when those words are written or spoken under the watch of an autocratic political regime. The above lines would eventually prove prophetic, as Shamlou was arrested for his political poetry following the Shah's crackdown on leftists after the 1953 royalist and US and UK-orchestrated coup d'état against Prime Minister Mohammed Mosaddegh (d. 1967).

Alongside the revolutionary content of the above lines, Shamlou extends the formal poetic experiments of Nima Yushij (d. 1960), widely regarded as the founder of the modernist poetic movement in Persian. Shamlou here continues Nima's effacement of the lyric "I," which was a significant departure from earlier Persian poetry—especially from the premodern period—and signaled the genesis of modernist Persian poetry. In his distinctly modernist poems, such as "*Qu*" ("The Swan") and "*Qoqnus*" ("The Phoenix"), Nima introduced the figures of the swan and the phoenix as stand-ins for the poet's "I" and presented the poems in the third person. As the modernist movement grew and attracted younger poets like Shamlou, Nima further contributed to the displacement of the "I" with 1952's "*Morgh-e Amin*" ("The Amen Bird"), which, as the critic Ahmad Karimi-Hakkak explains, "features a bird with no known identity in Persian poetry or mythology, either as a real animal or a mythical creature. True to his habit of placing himself in his poems, often through the figure of a bird, Nima may have made up the bird's name by inverting the letters of his own pen name, thus: Nima → Amin." Karimi-Hakkak goes on to add that Nima uses the figure of the bird to proclaim a new vision for a happy future to the *mardom* (people) and *khalq* (masses),[17] thus highlighting the political stakes at play in poetry at the time in Iran.

---

[16] Shamlou, *Qat'nameh*, 37–8.
[17] Ahmad Karimi-Hakkak, *Recasting Persian Poetry: Scenarios of Poetic Modernity in Iran* (London: Oneworld, 2012 [1995]), 262.

While Shamlou does not replace the lyric "I" with another figure in the poems of *The Manifesto*, he subordinates it to his audience, a collective *shoma* (you) that parallels the *mardom* or *khalq* in both Nima's poem and Communist-inspired poems in other literary traditions. Whereas Nima plays on the premodern literary device of the *takhallos* (the incorporation of a pen name into the final lines of a poem) in "The Amen Bird" by rearranging the letters of his pen name, in this collection Shamlou foregoes centering the "I," thereby signaling his newfound political commitment. We might even consider this shift away from an "I" focused on mystical union with the divine or a beloved to one trained in the service of "the masses" as symbolic of an awakening Third World consciousness and a move toward solidarity across the Global South. In Shamlou's poetics, as I will show below, the effaced "I" makes space for an emergent collective "you": the toiling masses.

The displacement of the lyric "I" has significant consequences for the political import of Shamlou's poems. In the second poem of *The Manifesto*, "Song of a Man Who Killed Himself," Shamlou's new political commitment overflows in a violent renunciation of the romanticism in his *Forgotten Songs*. This second poem begins, "I gave him no chance / I said no prayer / I put a knife to his throat / and in prolonged agony / I killed him. / I told him, / 'You speak the enemy's language!' / And I / killed him."[18] The unnamed "him" is the "man" from the poem's title. In the following stanza, it becomes obvious exactly who this mysterious man speaking the enemy's language is—the speaker of *Forgotten Songs*: "He had my name / no one was closer to me than him, / and he alienated me / from you / from you whose yearning for bread / beats in every one of your impatient veins. / He alienated me / from myself."[19]

In these lines, the speaker declares his disillusionment with his lyric "I," which in *Forgotten Songs* alienated the experience of the individual "I" from that of the collective "you" to whom the now-committed speaker intends to dedicate his life. The romantic "I" attempts to subsume the experience of the collective within itself, but in doing so it discounts the heterogeneous voices that exist within the collective. The experience of the individual cannot stand in for everyone else's. Shamlou has the lyric "I" of *Forgotten Songs* speak in "Song of a Man Who Killed Himself" so that the speaker's "I" can respond to him: "'We are but ripples in a flag,' he told me, / 'the Urmian soldiers' flag.' / 'No,' I replied. / 'We are a knife / in their throat!'"[20]

The earlier lyric "I's" outburst in these lines could easily be considered a delayed reaction to Shamlou's experiences as a young man in Urmia, where he openly opposed the occupying Allied Forces (that is, the Soviets) during the Second World War. The romantic "I" takes refuge in the nationalist symbol of a flag waving in the wind, an image the now-committed poet rends to shreds. Shamlou specifically references the romantic nationalism found in many of the poems he wrote in *Forgotten Songs*. Consider these lines from "Flag-bearer!" written to a patriotic soldier led by Brigadier

---

[18] Shamlou, *Qat'nameh*, 57.
[19] Ibid., 58.
[20] Ibid., 61.

General Zangeneh, who resisted the Allies in Urmia towards the end of the war: "Ahoy, Flag-bearer! My comrade! ... / Be proud, proud ... you have thousands of years of history in your hands. / You carry a flag whose red we spilled our blood for."[21] In *The Manifesto*, however, Shamlou responds to the blind nationalism found in his *Forgotten Songs* with a simple, direct language that calls its reader to social engagement and lashes out against the lyric "I" who ignores the collective in favor of individual experience.

With "Song of a Man Who Killed Himself" Shamlou goes so far as to murder the lyric poet from *Forgotten Songs*. Estranged from his earlier poetry and awakened by his newly found political commitment, Shamlou rails against his earlier collection, calling it out by name to bury it in the past during a brutal scene of murder-suicide: "He cooed a forgotten song in his windpipe / and in prolonged agony / went cold / and blood dripped from his throat / to the ground, / one drop / after another! / The blood of forgotten songs / not the blood of 'No!'"[22]

Shamlou's Encounter with Lorca

In "Song of a Man Who Killed Himself," the poem's speaker further encourages Shamlou's poetic and political awakening to a budding Third World solidarity movement through an encounter with Lorca. The poem retells the story of the Spanish poet's death at the hands of Franco's fascists at the beginning of the Spanish Civil War (1936–9), which animated leftists across the planet. Shamlou writes,

فرانکو را نشانش دادم
و تابوت لورکا را
و خون تنتور او را بر زخم میدان گاوبازی.
و او به رؤیای خود شده بود
و به آهنگی می خواند که دیگر هیچ گاه
به خاطره ام باز نیامد.
آن وقت، ناگهان خاموش ماند
چرا که از بیگانگی صدای خود
که طنینش به صدای زنجیرِ بردگان می مانست
به شک افتاده بود.
و من در سکوت
او را کشتم.
آبش نداده، دعایی نخوانده
خنجر به گلویش نهادم
و در احتضاری طولانی
او را کشتم
—خودم را—

---

[21] Shamlou, *Ahang-ha*, 165–8.
[22] Shamlou, *Qat'nameh*, 59.

و در آهنگ فراموش شده اش
کفنش کردم،
در زیرزمین خاطره ام
دفنش کردم.

I showed him Franco,
Lorca's grave,
  and the blood of his iodine in the wound from the bullring[23]
He went into his own dream
and sang a song that would no longer
come to my mind.
He went silent suddenly, since
he had fallen into doubt
from the alienation of his own voice
echoing the sounds of slaves' chains.
And I silently
killed him.
I gave no chance, said no prayer
I put the knife to his throat
and in drawn out agony
I killed him
    —myself—
and I shrouded him in his forgotten song.
In the basement of my memory,
I buried him.[24]

The poetic persona forces the poet from Shamlou's *Forgotten Songs* to face the grave consequences of the thinking that shaped his first collection of poems as they contemplate Lorca's blood in the bullring. The scene amounts to an admission that his earlier poems evoked nationalism, even jingoism, and bordered on propaganda if not outright support of the Fascist ideology popular in Iran during the late 1940s. In the above lines, Shamlou has his poetic persona serve as teacher and guide to an earlier self, forcing him to witness Lorca's death at the hands of reactionary forces. Lorca, therefore, plays an important part in Shamlou's poetic development, as he did in that of many poets writing in what would become the Third World, and particularly in the Middle East broadly conceived.

---

[23] Shamlou paraphrases a line from Lorca's "Lament for the Death of Ignacio Sánchez Mejías" ("*Llanto por la muerte de Ignacio Sánchez Mejías*"), which goes "*cuando la plaza se cubrió de yodo*" ("when iodine covered the ring") (Federico García Lorca, *Selected Poems*, trans. Martin Sorrell [Oxford: Oxford University Press, 2007], 156).

[24] Shamlou, *Qat' nameh*, 62–3.

For instance, while a Westerner like Stephen Spender (d. 1995) could denounce (Western) Communists' instrumentalization of Lorca's death as "crude atrocity propaganda"—which he did in his repudiation of Communism in *The God That Failed*[25]—poets in the Arab Middle East looked to Lorca for political and poetic inspiration and developed his memory to mythic proportions. Elegies to Lorca appear among the poems of such Arab luminaries as Badr Shakir al-Sayyab (d. 1964), Abd al-Wahhab al-Bayati (d. 1999), and Palestine's late poet laureate Mahmud Darwish (d. 2008).[26] Sustained interest in Lorca and his poetry among these poets extends beyond the period of proto-Third Worldism during which Shamlou composed *The Manifesto*. We can therefore follow later poetic invocations of Lorca in the East as but one of many threads connecting a nascent feeling of Third World cohesion extending from Bandung all the way through official Third World solidarity movements like the Non-Aligned Movement.[27]

Furthermore, we might be too hasty should we tag Lorca's poetry as distinctly Western. Not only did Lorca draw on poetic influences coming from the margins of Spanish literary production, but he also hailed from a small town outside Granada, in what had been Moorish Andalusia. In his poetry, he often referenced the history of Andalusia, which had been a site of cultural exchange between Christians and Muslims for hundreds of years under Islamic rule. Modern Arab poets thus frequently see Lorca as a rebel, revolutionary, and martyr who "express[ed] his deep reverence for the Arabic civilisation which once flourished in Spain."[28] Lorca himself gestured to these connections to Spain's Islamic past in his poetry—particularly in the Arab-Andalusian inspired *gacelas* (*ghazals*) and *casidas* (*qasidehs*) of his *Tamarit Poems*.[29]

In the above stanza, the paraphrase of a line from Lorca's "Lament for the Death of Ignacio Sánchez Mejías" shows Shamlou to be attentive to this contemporary reception of Lorca's poetry. Indeed, the poem emerged out of a real scene of violent death. Lorca wrote "Lament" in 1934 following the bloody demise of his friend in the bullring. Scholar of Spanish literature Allen Josephs reports that before the fight even started "Lorca knew intuitively that the matador would be killed. When it proved true he told a friend: 'Ignacio's death is like mine, the trial run for mine.'"[30] Not long after, in 1936,

---

[25] Stephen Spender, "Stephen Spender," in *The God That Failed*, ed. Richard Crossman (New York: Columbia University Press, 2001), 249.

[26] Rasheed El-Enany provides a useful overview of Lorca's role in modern Arabic poetry in "Poets and Rebels: Reflections of Lorca in Modern Arabic Poetry," *Third World Quarterly* 11, no. 4 (1989): 252–64. Ahmad Abd al-'Aziz thoroughly investigates Lorca's influence on modern Arabic poetry in "Athar Fidiriku Jarthiya Lurka fi al-Adab al-'Arabi al-Mu'asir." ("Federico García Lorca's Influence on Modern Arabic Literature"), *Fusul: majallat al-naqd al-adabi* (*Fusul: Journal of Literary Criticism*), al-Adab al-Muqarin 2 (Comparative Literature Part 2) 3, no. 4 (1983): 271–99.

[27] As just one example of Lorca's transnational reach beyond Europe, the Americas, and the Middle East, Dai Wangshu (d. 1950)—who was "sympathetic with the anti-fascist Communist cause both in China and worldwide"—translated Lorca's poetry into Chinese (Jesús Sayols Lara, "Translating as Transculturating: A Study of Dai Wangshu's Translation of Lorca's Poetry from an Integrated Sociological-Cultural Perspective," PhD diss., Hong Kong Baptist University, 2015, 128).

[28] El-Enany, "Poets and Rebels," 260.

[29] Federico García Lorca, *The Tamarit Poems: A Version of Diván del Tamarit*, trans. Michael Smith (Dublin, Ireland: Dedalus Press, 2007 [first published posthumously in 1940]).

[30] "The Blood of a Genius," *The New York Times Book Review*, October 8, 1989.

Fascist rebels would assassinate Lorca outside Granada. Shamlou here brings Lorca's biography and poetry to bear on modern Persian poetry by creating a poetic parallel between Lorca's grief for the death of his friend and his own speaker's coming to terms with a new political commitment by "murdering" his past self.

The scene at Lorca's grave in the lines we saw earlier mirrors Shamlou's real-life encounter with Lorca's work and the transformation it caused in his poetry. A moment of reflection sends the poetic persona from *Forgotten Songs* "into his own dream," where he "sang a song that will no longer / come to my mind," that is, the now *Forgotten Songs*. After seeing Lorca's grave, Shamlou's earlier persona "went silent" and "fell into doubt." Unable to continue after being confronted with Lorca's poetry and biography, the old, alienating lyric "I" is killed, transformed, and reborn as the committed poet Shamlou's readers remember him as today.

Third World Commitments in *The Manifesto*

Having moved through the transitional moment of self-realization that followed his reception of Lorca's poetry and the circumstances of his death, the speaker in Shamlou's "Song of a Man Who Killed Himself" announces for the first time that the man he has murdered is an earlier version of himself: "I killed him / —myself—." With his past self now dead and buried, the speaker asseverates his rebirth into a new political commitment that extends beyond Iran into what would become the Third World. "He is dead / dead / dead … / And now / this is me / your worshiper / O Gods of my myths!"[31] The speaker turns to the collective "you" (*shoma*), declaring himself to be the "worshiper" of *shoma*, whom he further describes as the "Gods of my myths." Instead of declaring allegiance to God, country, or self—a declaration we find in the *Forgotten Songs* and some but not all other romantic poetry— Shamlou's lyric "I" now links himself with the collective, the masses to whom he will now attempt to give voice. Sloughing off the dead weight of national myths and the history of romantic nationalism, the lyric "I" is reborn through and in his newfound political commitment to the subjugated and forgotten.

A refrain rings out in the second half of "Song of a Man Who Killed Himself," "Now this is me!" Nine times the speaker declares his new existence as a committed poet after metaphorically burying Shamlou's romantic past and announcing the earlier poet's death:

اکنون این منم

با گوری در زیرزمین خاطرم

که اجنبی خویشتنم را در آن به خاک سپرده ام

در تابوت آهنگ‌های فراموش شده اش ...

اجنبی خویشتنی که

من خنجر به گلویش نهاده ام

---

[31] Shamlou, *Qat'nameh*, 63–4.

و او را کشته ام در احتضاری طولانی،
و در آن هنگام
نه آبش داده ام
نه دعائی خوانده ام!

اکنون
این
منم!

Now this is me
with a grave in the basement of my memory
whose foreign self I have buried in the earth there
in the coffin of forgotten songs ...
A foreign self whose
neck I have put a knife to
and have killed in drawn-out agony,
and at the same time
I have given him no chance
and I have said no prayer!

Now
this
is me![32]

In the process of burying his old poetic self along with the *Forgotten Songs,*
Shamlou metapoetically recreates himself in the pages of *The Manifesto* as an engaged
revolutionary poet ready to sacrifice himself to obtain justice for a collective "you."
His paratextual comments on *The Manifesto* provide yet more evidence to help us
understand his conception of the collection's place in relation to his earlier poetry. He
writes that its first two poems, "Until a Shirt Blossoms Red" and "Song of a Man Who
Killed Himself," are the "direct result of the regret and spiritual pain I felt after the
childish mistake I made publishing a handful of weak poems and worthless fragments
in a book called *Forgotten Songs.*"[33] By killing off his previous poetic persona, Shamlou
emphasizes his rebirth in *The Manifesto.*

While the first two poems of *The Manifesto* announce the poetic persona's devotion
to social justice for his own people, the third poem, "The Grand Anthem," contains the
most explicit example of proto-Third Worldism in the collection, reaching beyond the
borders of Iran to address a soldier in Korea. Shamlou dedicates the poem to one Shen
Chu, "an unknown Korean comrade."[34] Written on July 6, 1951, the poem addresses
Shen Chu as the speaker's *baradarak* (little brother) who is fighting against the United
States and United Kingdom in the Korean War. Although calling his addressee "little

---

[32] Shamlou, *Qatʿ nameh,* 66–7.
[33] Ibid., 89.
[34] Ibid., 69.

brother" may at first seem patronizing, it quickly becomes clear that the poetic persona only intends affection. In fact, the poem begins by immediately calling out to Shen Chu, and the speaker (that is, the lyric "I") waits to introduce itself until the eighth line, and then only as a possessive "my":

شن—چو!

کجاست جنگ؟

در خانهٔ تو

در کرّه

در آسیای دور؟

اما تو

شن

برادرک زردپوستم!

هرگز جدا مدان

زان کلبهٔ حصیر سفالین بام

بام و سرای من.

پیداست

شن

که دشمن تو دشمن من است

و ان اجنبی که خوردن خون تو راست مست

از خون تیرهٔ پسران من

باری

به میل خویش

نشوید دست!

Shen Chu!
>   Where's the war?
Is it in your house
in Korea
>   in far-off Asia?
As for you
>   Shen
>   my Asian brother!
Don't ever consider
that clay-roofed straw hut of yours
different from my roof and my palace.
It's clear
>   Shen
>   that your enemy is my enemy
and that foreigner who gets drunk from drinking your blood
will never
let go of
my sons' dark blood
on his own![35]

---

[35] Shamlou, *Qat'nameh*, 69–70.

The poem begins with this direct address to Shen Chu, followed by a series of questions and commands. The lyric "I" may be speaking here, but all we find are lines directed at Shen Chu, "you." Here, Shen Chu's individual "you" (*to*) replaces the collective *shoma* of the previous poems, yet this singular "you" continues to serve a similar function. The lyric "I" praises Shen Chu's "you" for fighting imperialism in Korea, even suggesting that it is there with him in "that thatch-roofed clay hut of yours / [not different from] my roof and my palace" resisting the same enemy. As the poem progresses, the speaker continues exhorting Shen Chu to fight imperialism. In the final stanza, the speaker encourages him to sing an anthem for the victims of fascism, connecting Nazi atrocities with the contemporary experience of war in Korea:

شن—چو

بخوان!

بخوان!

آواز آن بزرگ دلیران را

آواز کارهای گران را

آواز کارهای مربوط با بشر، مخصوص با بشر

آواز صلح را

آواز دوستان فراوان گمشده

آوازهای فاجعهٔ بلزن و داخاو

آوازهای فاجعهٔ وی یون

آوازهای فاجعهٔ مون واله ری ین

آواز مغزها که آدولف هیتلر

بر مارهای شانهٔ فاشیسم می نهاد،

آواز نیروی بشر پاسدار صلح

کز مغزهای سرکش داونینگ استریت

حلوای مرگ برده فروشان قرن ما را

آماده می کنند

آواز حرف آخر را

نادیده دوستم

شن—چو

بخوان

برادرک زردپوستم!

Shen Chu
    sing!
        Sing!
The song of those heroes
the song of weighty deeds
the song of deeds connected to mankind, particular to mankind

the song of peace
the song of all those friends lost
the songs of the Belsen tragedy, and Dachau[36]
the songs of the Haute-Vienne tragedy[37]
the songs of the Mont-Valérian tragedy[38]
the song of the brains that Adolf Hitler
gave to the snakes of fascism's shoulders
the song of the peacekeeping force of humanity
who are serving
the rebellious brains of Downing Street
as sweets at a funeral for the slave-traders of our century
the song of the last word
my unseen friend
Shen Chu
sing
my Asian brother![39]

As the poem comes to its end, the speaker employs an extended anaphora with the repetition of "song" or "songs" at the beginning of eleven lines, within which he makes three references to Nazi ethnic cleansing and violence in Europe. In a nod to ancient Iranian mythology, the poem also uses the story of Zahhak as a corollary for Hitler's murderous policies. Zahhak, a notorious villain in Zoroastrian literature whom we also find in Ferdowsi's *Shahnameh* (*The Book of Kings*, completed in 1010), was cursed with two snakes growing out of his shoulders. He had to feed the snakes human brains daily; otherwise, they would feast upon his own. The poem not only makes these references to reflect upon the terrible events of the Second World War but also draws a connection between the brutality and carnage of Hitler's Germany and the war that had recently begun in Korea. There, the British (represented in the poem by Downing Street) joined the United States, Canada, Australia, and several other countries against North Korea, China, and the Soviets. The final lines imagine a North Korean victory against this US-led coalition, whom the speaker derides as "the slave-traders of our century."

Continuing the collection's focus on Communist resistance against imperialism, the fourth and final poem, "Ode for the Man of the Month of Bahman," celebrates the

---

[36] The reference could also be to the 1939 transfer of Jewish citizens of Plzeň to the Dachau concentration camp and subsequent anti-Jewish violence from the local German population during the Nazi occupation of Czechoslovakia in the Second World War (Kim Wünschmann, *Before Auschwitz: Jewish Prisoners in the Prewar Concentration Camps* [Cambridge, MA: Harvard University Press, 2015], 218).

[37] On June 10, 1944, Nazis slaughtered 642 people in the central French department of Haute-Vienne "in what was the single worst massacre carried out by German troops during the four years of occupation" (Alan Riding, "Generation of Mourning: An Account of the Nazi Massacre at Oradour-sur-Glane and the Town's Fight for Justice," *New York Times Book Review*, February 28, 1999).

[38] The Nazis executed over one thousand members of the French Resistance by firing squad at Fort Mont-Valérian between 1941 and 1944.

[39] Shamlou, *Qat' nameh*, 74–5.

memory of Taqi Arani (d. 1940), a member of the group of fifty-three Communists arrested by the Shah's government in 1937. Arani was murdered in prison, and Shamlou's poem presents his bodily sacrifice as a revolutionary gate for future freedom fighters to pass through: "And each bullet hole in each body (*peykar*) / is a gate which three people (*nafar*), a hundred people, a thousand people, / which three hundred thousand people / pass through / going to the emerald tower of tomorrow."[40] In this fourth poem, the lyric "I" again recedes into the background as it praises Arani's heroism, appearing only once throughout the entire poem. The poem links the holes in Arani's body to the people his sacrifice will eventually free through the repeated rhyme of *peykar* (body) and *nafar* (literally a "person" or an "individual"), which appears four times in ever-growing number: "three people, a hundred people, a thousand people / ... three hundred thousand people."

Conclusion: *The Manifesto*, Proto-Third Worldism, and World Literature

In sum, *The Manifesto* marks a distinct moment both in Shamlou's poetic career and in the history of modernist Persian poetry. Having encountered the scene of Lorca's execution and witnessing the continued depredations and deprivations of formerly colonized and decolonizing countries throughout what would soon become the Third World, Shamlou transforms himself and his poetic persona, devoting both to the realization of social justice in lieu of what he himself called the "mistake" of his romanticism in *Forgotten Songs*. Shamlou wrote poetry for the rest of his life following *The Manifesto*, finally devoting himself to a multivolume investigation of the Persian language as used among the masses, *Ketab-e Kucheh* (*The Book of the Alley*).[41] While his magnum opus may reflect a redirection of focus inward to Iranian society, Shamlou kept working to bring foreign voices into modern Persian literature following his political awakening. Other than Lorca, Shamlou also translated into Persian Mikhail Sholokhov's (d. 1984) *And Quiet Flows the Don* (working from the French translation),[42] many poems by Langston Hughes (d. 1967),[43] and selections from the works of several other foreign writers.

These translation choices show Shamlou's motivation to bring the work of figures central to anti-imperial resistance to Iranian readers, despite the waning of his explicit Communist affiliation after he was thrown in prison following the 1953 coup. By that point, too, international politics were shifting in the aftermath of the Korean War as it

---

[40] Shamlou, *Qat'nameh*, 82–3.
[41] Ahmad Shamlou and Ayda Serkisiyan, *Ketab-e Kucheh: Farhang-e Loghat, Estelahat, Ta'birat, va Zarb al-Masal-ha-ye Farsi* (Tehran: Maziyar, 1377–/1998–).
[42] Mikhail Sholokhov, *Don-e Aram* [*And Quiet Flows the Don*], trans. Ahmad Shamlou (Tehran: Maziyar, 1382/2003).
[43] Langston Hiyuz, *Siyah Hamchun A'maq-e Afriqa-ye Khodam* [*Black Like the Depths of My Africa*], trans. Ahmad Shamlou (Tehran: Sazman-e Entesharati va Farhangi-ye Ebtekar, 1359/1980).

became apparent that the United States and the Soviets were each prepared to militarily intervene to both defend and extend their respective spheres of influence. Not long after, the Bandung Conference brought together the nations of the Third World, who sought to find their own way within the geopolitics of the Cold War.

The features of proto-Third World literature—notions of transnational solidarity, nascent political commitment, and a focus on current events taking place across the globe—carried over into the literature of the Third World, and indeed we can trace these qualities through to Fredric Jameson's thoughts on national allegory and Third World literature.[44] However, as I have made a point to avoid doing throughout this chapter, we should not anachronistically declare writers as representatives of Third World literature since the category did not yet exist. Hence, my suggestion of *proto-Third Worldism* as a category for literary works expressing a will toward transnational solidarity among colonized and decolonizing nations prior to the coining of the term "Third World" and before the self-organizing of many of these same nations at Bandung.

Shamlou's *Manifesto* came out only a few years before Bandung, but the poet was already at pains to present his readers with a robust Third World solidarity pitted against the neo-imperialism of the Cold War along with the emerging authoritarianism of the postcolonial nation-state. The collection is a prime example of political commitment in literature, announcing as much in its title that immediately reminds us of Marx and Engels's 1848 *Manifesto of the Communist Party*. Yet, however much the poetic persona of *The Manifesto* might stress his support for Communist revolutionaries, the poems themselves resist the strictures of socialist realism. Instead, Shamlou's verses tell the story of the poet's own political awakening through a rich combination of modernist style (irregular rhymes and metrical patterns) and intertextual references to both foreign and Iranian literature: Ferdowsi's *Shahnameh*, Lorca's "Lament for the Death of Ignacio Sánchez Mejías," and Shamlou's own first collection *Forgotten Songs*. In announcing his political rebirth in *The Manifesto*, Shamlou puts his lyric "I" in the service of his audience, whom he invites to consider the growing forces united against Western imperialism inside Iran and across the planet, and in Korea in particular.

To conclude, Shamlou's works and others by writers and translators from what would later become the Third World present us with a different conception of World Literature, one driven not by canon, prestige, economic power, or even faith in the postcolonial nation-state, but rather by a will for solidarity and resistance against the military and industrial might of the West. This literature challenges both the actual world order during the twentieth century as well as the concept of World Literature itself. Thus, formulating the category of proto-Third World Literature pushes us to recognize a more capacious world literature, one that engages works openly antagonistic to its current composition: the untranslated, uncanonized, parochial, or provincial literature that looks outside the West for its readers and critiques the

---

[44] Fredric Jameson, "Third-World Literature in the Era of Multinational Capitalism," *Social Text* 15 (1986): 65–88.

development of global capital from their perspective. By recognizing literary networks that operate outside those driven by the Western imagination we can create new ways to conceive of what a yet worldlier literature might be.

Bibliography

Abd al-ʿAziz, Ahmad. "Athar Fidiriku Jarthiya Lurka fi al-Adab al-ʿArabi al-Muʿasir" ("Federico Garcia Lorca's Influence on Modern Arabic Literature"). *Fusul: majallat al-naqd al-adabi (Fusul: Journal of Literary Criticism)*, al-Adab al-Muqarin 2 (Comparative Literature Part 2) 3, no. 4 (1983): 271–99.

Çelik, Zeynep. "Speaking Back to Orientalist Discourse." In *Empires of Vision: A Reader*. Ed. Martin Jay and Sumathi Ramaswamy, 395–414. Durham: Duke University Press, 2014.

El-Enany, Rasheed. "Poets and Rebels: Reflections of Lorca in Modern Arabic Poetry." *Third World Quarterly* 11, no. 4 (1989): 252–64.

Friedman, Susan Stanford. *Planetary Modernisms: Provocations on Modernity across Time*. New York: Columbia University Press, 2015.

Getachew, Adom. *Worldmaking after Empire: The Rise and Fall of Self-Determination*. Princeton: Princeton University Press, 2019.

Hughes, Langston. *Siyah Hamchun Aʿmaq-e Afriqa-ye Khodam* [*Black Like the Depths of My Own Africa*]. Trans. Ahmad Shamlou. Tehran: Sazman-e Entesharati va Farhangi-ye Ebtekar, 1359/1980.

Iber, Patrick. *Neither Peace Nor Freedom: The Cultural Cold War in Latin America*. Cambridge, MA: Harvard University Press, 2015.

Jameson, Fredric. "Third-World Literature in the Era of Multinational Capitalism." *Social Text* 15 (1986): 65–88.

Josephs, Allen. "The Blood of a Genius." *The New York Times Book Review*, October 8, 1989. Web. Available at www.nytimes.com/1989/10/08/books/the-blood-of-a-genius. html (accessed June 10, 2020).

Karimi-Hakkak, Ahmad. *Recasting Persian Poetry: Scenarios of Poetic Modernity in Iran*. London: Oneworld, 2012 [1995].

Lara, Jesús Sayols. "Translating as Transculturating: A Study of Dai Wangshu's Translation of Lorca's Poetry from an Integrated Sociological-Cultural Perspective." PhD diss., Hong Kong Baptist University, 2015.

Lionnet, Françoise, and Shu-Mei Shih. "Introduction: Thinking through the Minor, Transnationally." In *Minor Transnationalism*. Ed. Françoise Lionnet and Shu-Mei Shih. 1–23. Durham: Duke University Press, 2005.

Lorca, Federico García. *Selected Poems*. Trans. Martin Sorrell, introduction and notes by D. Gareth Walters. Oxford: Oxford University Press, 2007.

Lorca, Federico García. *The Tamarit Poems: A Version of Diván del Tamarit*. Trans. Michael Smith. Dublin: Dedalus Press, 2007 [1940].

Mufti, Aamir. *Forget English! Orientalisms and World Literatures*. Cambridge, MA: Harvard University Press, 2016.

Riding, Alan Riding. "Generation of Mourning: An Account of the Nazi Massacre at Oradour-sur-Glane and the Town's Fight for Justice." *New York Times Book*

Review, February 28, 1999. Web. Available at www.nytimes.com/books/99/02/28/
reviews/990228.28riding.html (accessed June 10, 2020).

Shamlou, Ahmad. *Ahang-ha-ye faramush shodeh [Forgotten Songs]*. 2nd ed. Tehran:
Entesharat-e Morvarid, 1386/2007.

Shamlou, Ahmad. *Qat' nameh [Manifesto]*, 4th ed. Tehran: Entesharat-e Morvarid,
1364/1985.

Shamlou, Ahmad, and Ayda Serkisiyan. *Ketab-e Kucheh: Farhang-e Loghat, Estelahat,
Ta' birat, va Zarb al-Masal-ha-ye Farsi [The Book of the Alley: A Dictionary of Persian
Words, Idioms, Metaphors, and Proverbs]*. Tehran: Maziyar, 1377–/1998–.

Sholokhov, Mikhail. *Don-e Aram [And Quiet Flows the Don]*. Trans. Ahmad Shamlou.
Tarjomeh az bargardan-e faransavi-ye Antovan Vitiz [Translated from the French
version, by Antoine Vitez]. Tehran: Maziyar, 1391/2012 [1382/2003].

Spender, Stephen. "Stephen Spender." In *The God That Failed*. Ed. Richard Crossman.
229–73. New York: Columbia University Press, 2001.

Thompson, Levi. "An Iraqi Poet and the Peace Partisans: Transnational Pacifism and the
Poetry of Badr Shākir al-Sayyāb." *College Literature* 47, no. 1 (2020): 65–88.

Vadde, Aarthi. *Chimeras of Form: Modernist Internationalism beyond Europe, 1914–2016*.
New York: Columbia University Press, 2017.

Widener, Daniel. "Seoul City Sue and the Bugout Blues: Black American Narratives of the
Forgotten War." In *Afro Asia: Revolutionary Political and Cultural Connections Between
African Americans and Asian Americans*. Ed. Fred Ho and Bill V. Mullen. 55–87.
Durham: Duke University Press.

Wright, Richard. *The Color Curtain: A Report on the Bandung Conference*. Cleveland: The
World Publishing Company, 1956.

Wünschmann, Kim. *Before Auschwitz: Jewish Prisoners in the Prewar Concentration
Camps*. Cambridge, MA: Harvard University Press, 2015.

11

Translocal Dreams of Justice and Mobility: Fariba Vafi's *Tarlan* and Ali Mirdrekvandi's *No Heaven for Gunga Din*

Gay Jennifer Breyley

> *In the birds' eyes*
> *west is*
> *where the sun sets*
> *and east is*
> *where the sun rises;*
> *that's it.*[1]

Introduction

The history of the novel in Persian "is generally divided into three periods: the pioneers (1895–1941), the middle generations (1953–79) and the post-revolutionary novels (1979 and after)."[2] Omid Azadibougar explains that, in the pioneers' period, historical and social novels dominate, motivated respectively by "a rising nationalism" and "the will to display the negative impacts of modernization on Iran." The middle generations are characterized by "the concept of committed literature that called for revolution," while the emergence of post-revolutionary novels coincides with "the ascendance of the novelistic in the literary space."[3] Azadibougar adds to these conventional categories those of the translated novel and popular and romance novels.[4] Within this history, Fariba Vafi's *Tarlan* sits clearly in the category of postrevolutionary novels,[5] while

---

[1]   Abbas Kiarostami, *A Wolf Lying in Wait: Selected Poems*, trans. Karim Emami and Michael Beard (Tehran: Sokhan, 2005), 86.

[2]   Omid Azadibougar, *The Persian Novel: Ideology, Fiction and Form in the Periphery* (Leiden: Rodopi | Brill, 2014), 154; Houra Yavari, "The Persian Novel," *Encyclopaedia Iranica*, January 26, 2012, accessed August 19, 2019.

[3]   Azadibougar, *The Persian Novel*, 154.

[4]   Ibid.

[5]   Fariba Vafi, *Tarlan* (Tehran: Nashr-e Markaz, 1382/2003).

Ali Mirdrekvandi's *No Heaven for Gunga Din* sits outside the schema, as it was not originally written in Persian.[6] The latter also emerges in the gap in the history, as it was written from 1944 to 1945, as a direct consequence of the military occupation of Iran by the UK, the then USSR and, in 1945, the United States. Although, or perhaps because, it is difficult to categorize *No Heaven for Gunga Din*, it serves as a useful example of the diverse ways literature written in Iran, by speakers of Persian, may be read as world literature. Despite the significant differences between *Tarlan* and *No Heaven for Gunga Din* as literature, and as historically situated novels, they both address universal themes, such as justice and inequality, freedom and captivity, connection and separation, camaraderie and solitude, imagination and reality, love and its absence, and peace and war. In addition, both novels address these themes through narratives rich in translocal significance.

Michael Peter Smith understands translocality as "a mode of multiple emplacement or situatedness both *here* and *there*," or characterized by "situated yet mobile subjectivities."[7] Drawing on Walter Benjamin's analysis of ideas as constellations, that is, concerned with the perception of relationships and positioning rather than with isolated "stars," Gisela Brinker-Gabler develops a related model of "translocal constellation" to examine "border-crossing literature with seemingly antagonistic conditions of manifold practices of mobility as well as cultural expressions of emplacement."[8] Brinker-Gabler's model "situates cultural practice continuously within and across 'locales' without confining them to the boundedness of one single nation, one single culture and moreover without limiting them within the antipodes of East and West, North and South."[9] Similarly, in the field of music, Hyunjoon Shin and Keewoong Lee describe the translocal as "widely dispersed but closely encountered."[10] Also focusing on musical encounters, Richard Peterson and Andy Bennett observe that "local music scenes that focus on a particular kind of music are in regular contact with similar local scenes in distant places … These we call translocal scenes because, while they are local, they are also connected with groups of kindred spirits many miles away."[11] In their different ways, the above applications of notions of translocality are all

---

[6] Ali Mirdrekvandi [Gunga Din], *No Heaven for Gunga Din* (Costa Mesa: Mazda Publishers, 2018).

[7] Michael Peter Smith, "Translocality: A Critical Reflection," in *Translocal Geographies: Spaces, Places, Connections*, ed. Katherine Brickell and Ayona Datta (London: Routledge, 2016), 181.

[8] Gisela Brinker-Gabler, "Translocal Constellations: Navigations of Mobility and Emplacement and Emine Sevgi Özdamar's Story 'The Courtyard in the Mirror," in *The Many Voices of Europe: Mobility and Migration in Contemporary Europe*, ed. Gisela Brinker-Gabler and Nicole Shea (Berlin: De Gruyter, 2020), 73–84. See also Walter Benjamin, *The Origin of German Tragic Drama*, trans. John Osbourne (London: Verso, 1998).

[9] Brinker-Gabler and Nicole Shea, "Introduction," in *The Many Voices of Europe*, 1–12.

[10] Hyunjoon Shin and Keewoong Lee, "The Question of Geographic Scale in Asian Popular Music: Global, Local, Regional, and Translocal," *Korean Journal of Popular Music* 25 (2020): 197.

[11] Richard Peterson and Andy Bennett, "Introducing Music Scenes," in *Music Scenes: Local, Translocal, and Virtual*, ed. Andy Bennett and Richard Peterson (Nashville: Vanderbilt University Press, 2004), 8–9.

concerned with the relations formed by mobilities, often in contexts of migration, and their effects on cultural practices, emotions, tastes, and attitudes.[12]

In this chapter, my application of translocality draws on the above models, especially Benjamin's constellatory focus on relations and positionality, but it differs slightly. My reading of *Tarlan* and *No Heaven for Gunga Din* focuses on a constellation of local narratives that are closely connected in their evocations of individual and collective struggles to fulfill dreams and to survive within and beyond illogical power structures. In the context of parallel—or constellatory—local histories around the world and across temporal boundaries, these narratives connect "groups of kindred spirits," in Peterson and Bennett's words, "many miles away" and many decades apart. The respective protagonists of *Tarlan* and *No Heaven for Gunga Din* present "situated yet mobile subjectivities." Neither protagonist migrates from one nation to another, but both are highly mobile in their searches for employment, knowledge, and meaning, their multilingual and cross-hierarchical relationships, and their reflections on the effects of world histories on local lives. The juxtaposition of *Tarlan* and *No Heaven for Gunga Din* enables an analysis of the possibilities for connection across seemingly rigid boundaries, as well as an understanding of the complexities of world literature emanating from Iran. This chapter explores the respective settings and protagonists of the two novels, before examining the translocal nature of their narratives and their representations of mobility and the desire for mobility. It then turns to the theme of knowledge of self and others—and the ways both novels link such knowledge to the possibilities of language, especially the translocal relations constructed and evoked by language use. Finally, the chapter analyzes aspects of the reception of Vafi's and Mirdrekvandi's work, focusing on different responses to the translocal nature of the novels' respective narratives.

The Protagonists: Tarlan and Gunga Din

Both *Tarlan* and *No Heaven for Gunga Din* have protagonists with a passion for language and different forms of literature, who find themselves in the lowest positions of military power structures. The differences and similarities between the two settings, both in Iran, but at different historical moments and with different groups holding power, point to intersections with military and other power structures around the world and in various historical contexts, and with the diverse literature addressing these themes. *Tarlan* is mostly set in the feminine world of a policewomen's training center in postrevolutionary Iran, with a focus on interactions between the protagonist,

---

[12] For other readings and applications of translocality, see Arjun Appadurai, "Disjuncture and Difference in the Global Cultural Economy," *Theory, Culture & Society* 7, nos. 2–3 (1990): 295–310; David Conradson and Deirdre McKay, "Translocal Subjectivities: Mobility, Connection, Emotion," *Mobilities* 2, no. 2 (2007): 167–74; and Ulrike Freitag and Achim von Oppen, eds., *Translocality: The Study of Globalising Processes from a Southern Perspective* (Leiden: Brill, 2010).

nineteen-year-old Tarlan, and the other young women, from various parts of Iran, in her dormitory. Tarlan's internal thought processes and feelings are articulated carefully, in contrast with the ironic, protagonist-effacing approach taken by Mirdrekvandi in *No Heaven for Gunga Din*. The novel is set in the 2080s and 2090s, in the Milky Way—Mirdrekvandi's imagined space between Earth and Heaven—but its characters and language are drawn from English-speaking military contexts in 1940s Iran. Within its fantasy framework, the novel's setting is the masculine world of male military officers living in close quarters and engaging in competitive strategy formation, while "affectionately" exploiting a mostly silent servant. Mirdrekvandi presents the low hierarchical standing of his protagonist, Gunga Din—and the injustice of this position—not by articulating Gunga Din's thoughts and feelings, but by largely omitting them from the narrative. As Gunga Din's internal life is ironically implied, rather than observed, it can be read in very different ways, with some readers apparently missing much of Mirdrekvandi's irony. Even the book's editor and Mirdrekvandi's former employer, John Hemming, describes the author in his Introduction to *No Heaven for Gunga Din* as "child-like," while Mirdrekvandi's other former employer, R. C. Zaehner, describes his former "houseboy" at the British Embassy as "naïve" and his English as "touching."[13] Both Hemming and Zaehner were, of course, part of the colonial apparatus in Iran from 1941 to 1945, when, in Brian Spooner's words, "Iran was reduced to the most abject state of dependence of its modern history."[14] Ensuing from this context, Mirdrekvandi's novel shares some characteristics with a range of world literature identified as postcolonial.[15]

Mirdrekvandi and Vafi both present protagonists who, while keenly observant themselves, suffer from nonrecognition, a familiar trope in world literature. *Tarlan* and *No Heaven for Gunga Din* are both narrated in the third person. In keeping with Mirdrekvandi's presentation of his fictional Gunga Din as an overlooked, unappreciated figure, he provides no explicit back story for his protagonist. However, the author of *No Heaven for Gunga Din* is identified as "Ali Mirdrekvandi [Gunga Din]," inviting the reader to imagine intersections between the fictional character and his creator. A United States officer gave Mirdrekvandi the nickname "Gunga Din" (after Rudyard Kipling's 1890 poem and the 1939 film adaptation) and both Zaehner and Hemming refer to him as "Gunga."[16] Hemming recalls encouraging "Gunga" to write "a story,"

[13] John Hemming, "Introduction," in *No Heaven for Gunga Din*, by Ali Mirdrekvandi, 23; Robert Charles Zaehner, "Foreword," in *No Heaven for Gunga Din*, by Ali Mirdrekvandi, 7. For more on Zaehner's academic interests and his relationship with Mirdrekvandi and his work, see Philip G. Kreyenbroek's Introduction to the following source: Robert Charles Zaehner, "Zoroastrian Survivals in Iranian Folklore II," *Iran* 30, no. 1 (1992): 65–75. On Zaehner's role in the 1953 coup and as Special Operations Executive (SOE) for MI6 in Tehran, see Ervand Abrahamian, *The Coup: 1953, The CIA, and the Roots of Modern U.S.-Iranian Relations* (New York: The New Press, 2013).

[14] Brian Spooner, "Introduction," in Simin Daneshvar, *Savushun: A Novel about Modern Iran* (Washington, DC: Mage, 2001), xiv.

[15] On the circumstances of Mirdrekvandi's life and work, see the documentary film *No Heaven for Gunga Din* (*Baraye Gunga Din Behesht Nist*, 2012). For an analysis of debates around postcolonialism and world literature, see Stefan Helgesson, "Postcolonialism and World Literature," *Interventions* 16, no. 4 (2014): 483–500.

[16] Zaehner, "Foreword," 8; Hemming, "Introduction," 19–23.

resulting in Mirdrekvandi writing his first novel, *Nur-afkan* (*Irradiant*), and explains that he began *No Heaven for Gunga Din* "for the entertainment of the officers" for whom he worked in 1944–5.[17] Indeed, humorous observations of the officers' personalities and language are evident throughout the novel. Hemming includes in his Introduction a letter Mirdrekvandi wrote to him in 1944, in which he recounts his anger about the harsh conditions suffered by his family under British occupation:

> Reihan is a village in which my brothers and sisters are living and it is my native place. When I visited my brothers and sisters, I saw that they were wearing nothing. They are so poor that they are eating named ballowt instead of wheat bread. When I saw so I was very angry. I made a big fire and put all my dictionaries into it and then sat down gravely. When all my dictionaries were burnt and were changed with ashes, I sweared and agreed I shall learn English no more.[18]

Mirdrekvandi's resolve to give up his preoccupation with learning English was short-lived, but the anger expressed in this letter is arguably an undertone to *No Heaven for Gunga Din*. Hemming, however, does not comment on this aspect of Mirdrekvandi's letter or his novel.

Vafi introduces her protagonist, Tarlan, as a jobseeker, filling out an application form, like jobseekers around the world, having to divulge all sorts of personal details, while getting nothing in return. At home, only her brother shows any interest in her dreams and acknowledgment of her agency. Tarlan wants to be a writer and is also interested in teaching and acting, but the only position available to her is that of trainee policewoman, which requires her to leave her hometown Tabriz for the first time and move to the barracks in Tehran, where "training" entails strict discipline and detachment from the outside world. Unlike Mirdrekvandi's character Gunga Din, who is alone in his "inferior" position in the military hierarchy, Tarlan shares her lowly position in the police hierarchy with a broad range of other young women, who all have different interests, fears, and hopes for the future. *Tarlan* could be read as a collective Bildungsroman, in which young women learn to understand others as they learn to understand themselves, along with the injustices and rare pleasures of the world. For the character Tarlan, a primary pleasure is literature. She reads Chekhov, Hikmet, Shamlou, Molière, Tolstoy, Dostoevsky, Sholokhov, Gorki, Goethe, and Rolland, among many others. Tarlan's imaginary world is so full of these writers that they and their fictional characters sometimes seem more real to her than members of her family. Meanwhile, Tarlan's own writing in the barracks brings violent punishment from her "commander."[19] This trope of the young woman in trouble for expressing herself in a strict institutional context is another that recurs in world literature.

Mirdrekvandi does not represent his character Gunga Din as a writer, but rather as an obedient servant whose communication consists almost entirely of receiving orders

---

[17] Ibid., 20.
[18] Ibid., 15.
[19] Vafi, *Tarlan*, 2, 3, 19, 171.

from the officers, whose shoes he repeatedly cleans. Gunga Din has only two extended pieces of dialogue in the novel. In the first, he addresses the "Fate Commander" in the "Holy House" on what the British and American officers hope is the way to "Heaven":

> You caused me many troubles during my living down on earth. I was not worried and I held my patience firmly, but one grievous thing that made me and yet makes me very worried and sad is this. I wanted to serve both the British and American Forces with an infinite manner during the Harvesting-Living-War according to the greatest decision which I had taken during the half-peace-half-fear-time. But regretfully when the Harvesting-Living-War started, I could not reach the British Army, neither could I reach the American Army. So I could not serve either and my greatest decision was turned into a drift of sorrow-fire in my heart, which burns me yet.[20]

This fervor to work with English-speaking officers is reminiscent of Mirdrekvandi's letters, which articulate his problematic passion for the language. Equally significantly for a reading of *No Heaven for Gunga Din* as world literature, Gunga Din identifies the most recent war as "the Harvesting-Living-War," focusing on the universal desire for resources and survival rather than naming any nations that might be involved in the war. Similarly, he describes the peace as "half-peace-half-fear-time," a description recognizable in any post-war context around the world. However, only Gunga Din and the Fate Commander refer to the peace in this way. The British and American officers, whose power in this world depends on war and fear, do not reflect on the peace. In the "Judgement Field" before "Heaven," the officers fail to recall the times they slighted their servant Gunga Din. Paradoxically, these officers, whose work and privilege depend on war, are forgiven their "sins" because "they were prepared to sacrifice themselves for Freedom," while Gunga Din is condemned to "Hell" because "his great and wicked desire was that he wished that the Harvesting-Living-War would happen soon," a desire based on his wish "to work for the British and American forces again."[21] While set in an imagined chronotope and based on specific experiences and observations in 1940s Iran, Mirdrekvandi's novel is translocal in its scope and sensibility. In many parts of the world, local memories and social histories of the 1940s include the effects of the presence of officers from the UK and the United States.

Translocality and Mobility

Michael Rothberg suggests that:

> transnational memory studies oriented by a politics of location and aware of its own locatedness in an uneven world can move between the too-abstract poles of

---

[20] Mirdrekvandi, *No Heaven*, 72.
[21] Ibid., 104–5, 112, 115.

the local and the global and instead uncover the rich terrain in between. This is the realm of what anthropologist James Clifford calls "big-enough," more-than-local narratives: histories that travel and translate, but without cumulating in a coherent destiny.[22]

Transnational memory studies is one of several fields in which world literature written in Iran might be read, but this description of "histories that travel and translate" resonates with the translocal work of Vafi and Mirdrekvandi. This work connects and points to intersections among local histories in multiple sites around the world, rather than histories defined by national boundaries. Like Mirdrekvandi, Vafi does not focus on naming nations in *Tarlan*. Rather, on one level, she refers to translocally symbolic figures such as the Irish hunger striker Bobby Sands,[23] and on another level, she carefully observes the differences and similarities between her characters, young women with different first languages, songs, food, habits and approaches to life, formed and developed in the diverse provinces of Iran. Vafi's protagonist Tarlan is an idealistic, well-read, and open-minded young woman, whose heart is with "the oppressed masses," from Iran's own revolutionaries to those of Latin America and North Africa. However, Tarlan admits to initial feelings of insecurity in her real-life proximity to "threatening" groups of unfamiliar people, even her fellow trainees, who are in the same position as her, a long way from "home":

> They are all strangers, all in black. Tarlan does not understand their words, as they speak quickly and roughly, making the girls sound as if they are speaking German or Chinese rather than Persian. The mob of unruly girls frightens Tarlan. They are like the workers who noisily congregate on the streets at night. It is not the first time that large amorphous groups of people have worried her. This feeling of insecurity has often come upon her at demonstrations, although she knows very well that masses are made up of individual beings.[24]

The young police trainees in *Tarlan* include speakers of Azeri, Lori, Kurdish, and other languages, and girls from Abadan, Ahvaz, Mashhad, and many other cities and towns across Iran. In *No Heaven for Gunga Din*, Mirdrekvandi presents his version of cosmopolitan 1940s Iran, with narratives involving an "Arab-man," a "Persian young man," and a Jewish "beautiful girl" who has studied English, French, German, Russian, Arabic, Armenian, and Persian and an "American boy."[25] The only border mentioned in *No Heaven for Gunga Din* is the border of Heaven, which the officers and Gunga Din seek to cross.[26] Here, Heaven is the universally desired imaginary space, the space

[22] Michael Rothberg, "Afterword: Locating Transnational Memory," *European Review* 22, no. 4 (2014): 654. Rothberg refers to James Clifford, *Returns: Becoming Indigenous in the Twenty-First Century* (Cambridge, MA: Harvard University Press, 2013).
[23] Vafi, *Tarlan*, 5.
[24] Ibid., 18–19 (my translation from Persian).
[25] Mirdrekvandi, *No Heaven for Gunga Din*, 61–6.
[26] Ibid., 94–5.

civilians dream of and military men invade. When Gunga Din's officers are not granted "Freedom Passes" to enter Heaven peacefully, they repeatedly attack.

Translocal approaches to narratives of power relations and personal and collective struggles attend to differences within nations and other localities and commonalities across nations and other boundaries. In these contexts, who holds power is less important than how individuals and groups may negotiate their personal and collective positions within power structures. The kinds of mobility desired in such narratives range from shifts and developments in attitude and knowledge to physical moves from one location to another and metaphysical moves from forms of captivity to the "freedom" of entry into an imagined "Heaven." Vafi's protagonist Tarlan desires mobility in all these forms, with each one relating to writing. She deeply desires experience, even the harsh experience of the police barracks, to give her insight and increase her understanding of the human condition, which will enable her to write effectively, her mode of "freedom." Similarly, the character Gunga Din wants to work in the unappreciated position of servant to the British and American officers because of his love of knowledge and language and a desire for communication with those holding power. This desire for communication is effectively fulfilled only when the injustices around Gunga Din have culminated in the extreme division between "Heaven," where the officers finally live, "all happy, all lucky, all pleased and all exceedingly glad," and "Hell," where their former servant is killed every night and revived every morning for another day of pain and misery. Gunga Din's second and final extended piece of dialogue in the novel occurs in Hell, after the officers' happiness is interrupted one night by dreams of their former faithful servant, and they arrange to visit him in Hell. Perhaps for the first time, the officers listen to Gunga Din for three hours, as he outlines the extreme suffering endured by him and his thirty million and one fellow inmates, most of them "Communists." Gunga Din's description of this suffering is reminiscent of any description of war as experienced by civilian populations, repeatedly having to be "back in our own rooms before Hell-Fire attacks."[27]

In this novel, Gunga Din's desire to move from "Hell" to "Heaven" primarily represents a desire for the justice that has never been available to him and his voiceless people throughout the narrative. While the novel closes without the desired justice being attained, Gunga Din succeeds in convincing the officers of his cause, leading to demonstrations in Heaven: "'Be destroyed Hell! Be destroyed Purgatory! Be destroyed the Judge!' And so they shouted with loud voices as they marched through Heaven." Although written in the 1940s, these slogans remind the reader of Iran's streets in the late 1970s and of the regular marches and demonstrations in postrevolutionary Iran and elsewhere. Just as Vafi reflects on the paradoxes of Tarlan's personal experience of demonstrations in Tabriz, so too Mirdrekvandi employs his characteristic ironic humor to recount the demonstration's aftermath: "And some of the angels said with a loud voice, 'The Children of Man seem to have become crazy this morning!' And the

---

[27] Ibid., 120, 125.

Children of Man were very hard angry when they heard the words that came out of the angels' mouths. And they attacked the angels and beat them and there was almost a pell-mell fight between them."[28] Such righteous but violent anger is a familiar trope in Iran's prerevolutionary popular cinema known as *filmfarsi*[29] and in related narratives of the battler's struggle for justice around the world. In *No Heaven for Gunga Din*, despite the altercation in Heaven, a ceasefire is negotiated and the "Hell-Fire" stops, leaving Gunga Din and his fellow "Hellishes" to "live [in Hell] like prisoners on Earth."[30] Mobility remains a fantasy.

Knowledge of Self and Others

Academic approaches to World Literature have arguably been dominated by Western perspectives.[31] To counter some of the less productive debates around term, Mridula Nath Chakraborty[32] draws on the work of Rabindranath Tagore, particularly his 1907 paper "Visva-sahitya ki?" ("What Is World Literature?"), in which he addresses three kinds of "bonds with truth": those of reason, necessity, and joy. On the "bond of joy," Tagore writes: "The bond of beauty or joy erases all distance: there is no more self-conceit; we do not hesitate to surrender ourselves to the small and the weak ... What is this bond of joy? It is nothing but knowing others as our own and our own selves as other."[33] As Chakraborty observes, the "interconnectedness of the 'local' and the 'global' and how the particular infuses and informs the universal are a consistent thread in these writings." Tagore's vision of World Literature, she continues, is "determinedly located in an anticolonial *and* antinationalist ethic."[34] This resonates with Hamid Dabashi's assertion that "re-worlding Persian literary humanism means rescuing it from both Orientalism and nativist nationalism, and thus restoring the cosmopolitan worldliness of its historic experiences."[35] The work of Vafi and Mirdrekvandi—and the

---

[28] Ibid., 127.

[29] See G. J. Breyley and Sasan Fatemi, *Iranian Music and Popular Entertainment: From Motrebi to Losanjelesi and Beyond* (London: Routledge, 2016); Golbarg Rekabtalaei, *Iranian Cosmopolitanism: A Cinematic History* (Cambridge: Cambridge University Press, 2019).

[30] Mirdrekvandi, *No Heaven for Gunga Din*, 127–8.

[31] For differing analyses, see David Damrosch, "The World in a Journal," *Journal of World Literature* 1, no. 1 (2016): 1–7; Keya Ganguly, "World Cinema, World Literature, and Dialectical Criticism," in *The Cambridge Companion to World Literature*, ed. B. Etherington and J. Zimbler (Cambridge: Cambridge University Press, 2018), 211–26; and Aamir Mufti, "Orientalism and the Institution of World Literatures," *Critical Inquiry* 36, no. 3 (2010): 458–93.

[32] Mridula Nath Chakraborty, "Rabindranath Tagore and 'World Literature,'" in *Perspectives on Literature and Translation: Creation, Circulation, Reception*, ed. Brian Nelson and Brigid Maher (New York: Routledge, 2013), 117–33.

[33] Rabindranath Tagore, *The Essential Tagore*, ed. Fakrul Alam and Radha Chakravarty (Cambridge, MA: Harvard University Press, 2011), 139.

[34] Chakraborty, "Rabindranath Tagore and 'World Literature,'" 128, 130.

[35] Hamid Dabashi, *The World of Persian Literary Humanism* (Cambridge, MA: Harvard University Press, 2012), 321.

narratives of their respective protagonists, Tarlan and Gunga Din—find a home within this vision, where language and literature form a joyful path to knowledge of self and others, and of self with others.

Chakraborty elaborates on Tagore's notions of unity, explaining that he understood literature "as *Sahitya* (from the Sanskrit *sahit*, 'to be with'), a functional union of word and meaning that evokes the *sahridaya* (from the Sanskrit *hridaya*, 'one with heart')," and that he argued for "the commonality and commensurability of all literatures from around the world through the only possible mode of 'being with' and 'in heart with' their sociohistorical specificities and contextual lineages."[36] As they desire different kinds of mobility, the fictional characters Tarlan and Gunga Din also desire a shift from solitude to the complex forms of unity, encompassing "truth" and mutual recognition, intimated by Tagore. Tarlan reflects explicitly on the meanings of literature, reading, and writing, reaching similar conclusions to Tagore's. For her, writing is not only about truth and responsibility, but about being and becoming, entering into "the light" and becoming "free."

In the spirit of Tagore's notions of literature as creating bonds of knowledge, connection and joy, Omid Azadibougar and Esmaeil Haddadian-Moghaddam recall that "translated literature made it possible for us [postrevolutionary Iranians] to think of the world in other ways: situations that were not ours and in which we did not participate gave us perspective on our own condition."[37] This capacity of translated literature is also true for readers of Vafi and Mirdrekvandi in translation. In Vafi's case, this applies especially to readers concerned with or identifying as women immobilized in restrictive structures. Vafi's novels have been translated into English, Italian, German, Spanish, Russian, Arabic, Japanese, French, Icelandic, Norwegian, Swedish, Azeri, Turkish, and Kurdish. Their reception has been especially strong in Scandinavia. *No Heaven for Gunga Din* was translated into Hindi, Japanese, Swedish, French, German, and Persian. It was especially popular in the United States and the United Kingdom. Vafi has commented that she would like to write in her first language, Azeri: "When I write in Persian, I notice sometimes that a few things that I could express in my first language slip through my fingers. Like a dream that loses a section in the telling. There's always something missing."[38] The dialogue in *Tarlan* would, if represented realistically, be multilingual, with Persian as the language used by authorities and the common language used by characters with different first languages. In this sense, the original novel, in Persian, already contains elements of translation.

Mirdrekvandi's use of English in *No Heaven for Gunga Din* is *realistic* in the sense that English was the language used by officers from the UK and the United States in Iran in the 1940s. Of course, while Mirdrekvandi captures several idioms, such as the officers' repeated exclamations of "Hell" and phrases such as "We must fix these

---

[36] Chakraborty, "Rabindranath Tagore and 'World Literature'," 127.

[37] Omid Azadibougar and Esmaeil Haddadian-Moghaddam, "From Persian to World Literature," *Journal of World Literature* 1, no. 1 (2016): 11.

[38] Maryam Aras, "Interview with the Iranian author Fariba Vafi," *Qantara*, September 12, 2015, accessed July 12, 2020. My translation from German.

damned M.P.'s up,"[39] the author does not consistently use standard English grammar. Arguably, this is also *realistic*, presenting the narrator's voice as that of the servant communicating in his *masters'* language. Mirdrekvandi's English is informed by his first languages, including Lori and Persian, as is evident in many of his expressions and grammatical constructions. His original text, in English, does not *benefit* or *suffer*, depending on the English-speaking reader's perspective, from the skills and preconceptions of a professional translator. As Azadibougar and Haddadian-Moghaddam observe in the context of postrevolutionary Iran, "translated literature was often re-coded in what the translator(s) considered acceptable as literature, even if it meant rendering radical changes in the translated material."[40] To a lesser extent, editing can have similar effects. However, Mirdrekvandi's choice to write *No Heaven for Gunga Din* in English has contributed to the particular challenges the novel poses for both editors and translators. The author's idiosyncratic use of English reflects both his disadvantage and his agency—his subordinate position in the military hierarchy in 1940s occupied Iran, and his control of some forms of knowledge through his language acquisition and choices. As Zaehner reflects, "you wondered all the time whether he was not secretly laughing at you himself."[41]

Elsewhere, Zaehner expresses frustration with his own inability to understand aspects of Mirdrekvandi's work, particularly his epic story *Nur-afkan* (*Irradiant*), and wishes he had written in Persian, which Zaehner imagines he would have found easier to understand and thus to translate accurately:

> We are fortunate in knowing that Irradiant's real name is *Nurafgan* and Chandelier's *Chehel-cheragh*. For most of the others we are completely in the dark. Some are translated and go easily back into Persian; Crazy Hero is presumably *pahlavan-e divaneh* or *pahlavan-e majnun*, Heroine Girl *dokhtar-e pahlavan*, Pearlia *keshvar-e dorr*, and so on. Others are recognisably Persian, such as Aladdin (Ala' ud-din), Aboud, Elias, Ethiop Sadi (Saʿdi-e habashi), Khagan, Jowshan Kabir, Changiz and Kuhzad. But there are also proper names which seem to me neither Persian, Turkish nor Arabic, such as Comle, Comelous, Argon, Greigow, Dartognek and Ketchy. For these I can offer no explanation at all ... As a scholar, I would have preferred that the work had come into my hands in Persian rather than in English and that it had been transmitted by someone less imaginative and less inventive than Ali Mirdrakvandi [*sic*].[42]

Zaehner's perplexity illustrates some of the complications that arise when writing from what some see as the "periphery" enters the "center."[43] As a speaker of Persian writing in

---

[39] Mirdrekvandi, *No Heaven for Gunga Din*, 89.
[40] Azadibougar and Haddadian-Moghaddam, "From Persian to World Literature," 11.
[41] Zaehner, "Foreword," 7.
[42] Zaehner, "Zoroastrian Survivals in Iranian Folklore II," 75.
[43] See also Emily Apter, *Against World Literature: On the Politics of Untranslatability* (London: Verso, 2013); Azadibougar, *The Persian Novel*; and Amirhossein Vafa, *Recasting American and Persian Literatures: Local Histories and Formative Geographies from* Moby-Dick *to* Missing Soluch (New York: Palgrave Macmillan, 2016).

English,[44] as a citizen of Iran writing under military occupation, and as a member of a family and clan with a history of persecution by Iran's monarchic rulers, Mirdrekvandi employs an ironic approach that is both powerful and bitter. His character Gunga Din responds, in effect, to the occupiers' demands that Gunga Din and his people "give up" their modes of communication and mobility by demonstrating how the occupiers "lose," at least on some levels, along with their servants. Gunga Din—and his creator Mirdrekvandi—may have much taken from them, but their language choices enable them to control what knowledge they share, how it is communicated and with whom it is shared.

Vafi's protagonist Tarlan also takes on the work of using language to take control of her circumstances and relationships. Rebecca Gould observes that "[f]rom Boethius to Gramsci, incarcerated writers have regularly linked the act of writing to the quest for freedom. They have rendered the uniqueness of their experience in words, and linked their subjective suffering to wider political themes."[45] The fictional Tarlan and Gunga Din are not literally incarcerated, but they both survive in a "world of boots and shoe polish"[46] and both link writing to freedom from their respective forms of captivity. When asked about the translation and dissemination of her work around the world, Vafi responds, "When you go beyond your limits and find new readers, you enter the space of people who are from another world. That, of course, influences your own work. You become acquainted with others' way of thinking, thereby gaining new knowledge. That, in my opinion, is important to any writer."[47] This ongoing translocal, reciprocal communication extends the literary relationships begun when young people, such as the young Vafi and the fictional Tarlan—and, indeed, Mirdrekvandi and his fictional Gunga Din—first discover literature and other forms of storytelling.

Translocal Reception

As Azadibougar and Haddadian-Moghaddam observe, "whether or not a discourse is political largely depends on how and where it is received."[48] How and where literary discourse is received is, of course, related to how and where texts are published and circulated. The different ways in which Vafi's work and Mirdrekvandi's work have been understood politically relate to differences of language, genre, and historical period, among other things. The differences in reception arguably have as much to do with translocal differences and similarities as with national differences. For example, Vafi's

---

[44] On "minor literature," see Gilles Deleuze and Félix Guattari, *Kafka: Toward a Minor Literature* (Minneapolis: University of Minnesota Press, 1986), 16.

[45] Rebecca Gould, "Literature as a Tribunal: The Modern Iranian Prose of Incarceration," *Prose Studies* 39, no. 1 (2017): 19.

[46] Vafi, *Tarlan*, 170. My translation from Persian.

[47] Vafi, cited in Sabine Oelze, "Author Fariba Vafi: Writers Struggle for Influence in Iran," *Deutsche Welle*, February 19, 2018, accessed July 12, 2020.

[48] Azadibougar and Haddadian-Moghaddam, "From Persian to World Literature," 11.

translocal plots, in *Tarlan* and other novels, serve to counter narratives that have dominated popular political thought in many parts of the world.[49] Especially in the English-speaking world, which itself may be understood as a translocal entity, no longer defined by national boundaries, in the context of corporate domination of multinational media and in the wake of the Iranian American women's memoir boom of the early twenty-first century, popular political narratives have tended to represent "freedom" as a "Western" commodity and contemporary Iran as a site that women, in particular, wish to "escape."[50] Vafi's nuanced narratives of women in Iran who are well informed about the world, and who contemplate their respective possibilities to live meaningful lives, counter such popular constructions. As Maryam Aras puts it, one of Vafi's "recurring motifs present in *Tarlan* is the motif of inner and outer exile, of the quest for identity."[51] Vafi herself elaborates:

> I concentrate in my novels on crises inside the social network of the family, whether traditional or modern. On structures that destroy interpersonal relationships. I try to grasp them in their essence and criticize them. Within this community that we call family, women seek to resist the suppression and violence that they often face, to attain, in some way, an independent identity. These women see the roles that are prescribed to them clearly and they try to seek out their own roles.[52]

This focus is clearly one that transcends national and political borders, one that may be understood in any local context around the world. However, it is precisely this translocality that can disappoint readers who come to Vafi's work expecting and desiring narratives that support their preconceived ideas about contemporary Iran. For example, one anonymous review of Vafi's novel *My Bird* exposes that reader's preconceptions about what constitutes "new perspectives": "this slender book will likely disappoint Western readers interested in new perspectives on the lives of contemporary Iranian women."[53] However, the same review confirms the translocal nature of Vafi's novel, its characters and settings: "the writing is so thoroughly introspective that the book could have been set in any grimy working-class neighborhood with loud neighbors, marital discord and selfish, demanding relatives ... the narrative is unnervingly myopic and

---

[49] See also Mostafa Abedinifard, "Graphic Memories: Dialogues with Self and Other in Marjane Satrapi's *Persepolis* and *Persepolis 2*," in *Familiar and Foreign: Identity in Iranian Film and Literature*, ed. Manijeh Mannani and Veronica Thompson (Edmonton: Athabasca University Press, 2015), for an analysis of Marjane Satrapi's graphic novels; Mohammad Mehdi Khorrami, *Literary Subterfuge and Contemporary Persian Fiction: Who Writes Iran?* (New York: Routledge, 2014); and Farzaneh Milani, *Words, Not Swords: Iranian Women Writers and the Freedom of Movement* (Syracuse: Syracuse University Press, 2011).

[50] See Amy Motlagh, "Towards a Theory of Iranian American Life Writing," *MELUS* 33, no. 2 (2008): 17–36; Amy Motlagh, "Autobiography and Authority in the Writings of the Iranian Diaspora," *Comparative Studies of South Asia, Africa and the Middle East* 31, no. 2 (2011): 411–24.

[51] Maryam Aras, review of *Tarlan*, by Fariba Vafi, *Anthropology of the Middle East* 11, no. 2 (2016): 118.

[52] Aras, "Interview with the Iranian Author Fariba Vafi." My translation from German.

[53] Anonymous Review of Vafi's *My Bird*, *Publishers Weekly*, September 28, 2009, accessed July 12, 2020.

mostly notable for its inertia."[54] This failure to read Vafi's text from a "new," translocal perspective is reminiscent of Hemming's and Zaehner's respective limited—or, at least, selective—readings of their "friend" Gunga Din's work. Like Hemming and Zaehner, this anonymous reviewer appears to miss not only the text's translocal ironies but also the novelist's careful depiction of "structures that destroy interpersonal relationships," in Vafi's words.[55]

To conclude, *Tarlan* and *No Heaven for Gunga Din* are two texts written in Tehran that have circulated around the world in perhaps unexpected ways. *Tarlan* is popular among readers in Iran and acclaimed in a range of local contexts around the world. *No Heaven for Gunga Din* is loved by a very small and localized group of readers in Iran and acclaimed by an eclectic base of readers elsewhere, especially in the English-speaking world. Both novels' unpredictable patterns of circulation and popularity are related to the translocal nature of their respective narratives, which address themes that cross temporal and geographical boundaries. The two novels are read and understood in many different ways, but they both primarily concern the human condition, the im/possibilities of freedom, and the power of communication. While particular local circumstances of Iran's turbulent history over the last century, including Iran's transnational relations, shape the details of both novels' narratives, the characters are recognizable as young people desiring to move from situations experienced as "hellish" to spaces imagined as "heavenly."

Acknowledgments

Many thanks to the anonymous reviewers for their helpful comments, to Omid Azadibougar, Amirhossein Vafa, and Mostafa Abedinifard for their support and patience, and to Maryam Aras for prompting me to read *Tarlan*.

Bibliography

Abedinifard, Mostafa. "Graphic Memories: Dialogues with Self and Other in Marjane Satrapi's *Persepolis* and *Persepolis 2*." In *Familiar and Foreign: Identity in Iranian Film and Literature*. Ed. M. Mannani and V. Thompson. 83–109. Edmonton: Athabasca University Press, 2015.

Abrahamian, Ervand. *The Coup: 1953, the CIA, and the Roots of Modern U.S.-Iranian Relations*. New York: The New Press, 2013.

Appadurai, Arjun. "Disjuncture and Difference in the Global Cultural Economy." *Theory, Culture & Society* 7, nos. 2–3 (1990): 295–310.

---

[54] Ibid.

[55] For a more effective reading, see Sharareh Frouzesh, "The Use and Abuse of Guilt," PhD diss. University of California, Irvine, 2013, 209–17.

Apter, Emily. *Against World Literature: On the Politics of Untranslatability*. London: Verso, 2013.

Aras, Maryam. "Interview with the Iranian Author Fariba Vafi." *Qantara*, September 12, 2015. Web. Available at en.qantara.de/node/22051 (accessed July 12, 2020).

Aras, Maryam. Review of *Tarlan*, by Fariba Vafi. *Anthropology of the Middle East* 11, no. 2 (2016): 116–19.

Azadibougar, Omid. *The Persian Novel: Ideology, Fiction and Form in the Periphery*. Leiden: Rodopi | Brill, 2014.

Azadibougar, Omid. "Translation Norms and the Importation of the Novel into Persian." *International Journal of Society, Culture & Language* 2, no. 2 (2014): 89–102.

Azadibougar, Omid, and Esmaeil Haddadian-Moghaddam. "From Persian to World Literature." *Journal of World Literature* 1, no. 1 (2016): 8–15.

Benjamin, Walter. *The Origin of German Tragic Drama*. Trans. John Osbourne. London: Verso, 1998.

Breyley, G. J., and Sasan Fatemi. *Iranian Music and Popular Entertainment: From Motrebi to Losanjelesi and Beyond*. London: Routledge, 2016.

Brinker-Gabler, Gisela. "Translocal Constellations: Navigations of Mobility and Emplacement and Emine Sevgi Özdamar's Story 'The Courtyard in the Mirror.'" In *The Many Voices of Europe: Mobility and Migration in Contemporary Europe*. Ed. Gisela Brinker-Gabler and Nicole Shea. 73–84. Berlin: De Gruyter, 2020.

Brinker-Gabler, Gisela. "Introduction." In *The Many Voices of Europe: Mobility and Migration in Contemporary Europe*. Ed. Gisela Brinker-Gabler and Nicole Shea. 1–12. Berlin: De Gruyter, 2020.

Chakraborty, Mridula N. "Rabindranath Tagore and 'World Literature.'" In *Perspectives on Literature and Translation: Creation, Circulation, Reception*. Ed. Brian Nelson and Brigid Maher. 117–33. New York: Routledge, 2013.

Clifford, James. *Returns: Becoming Indigenous in the Twenty-First Century*. Cambridge, MA: Harvard University Press, 2013.

Conradson, David, and Deirdre McKay. "Translocal Subjectivities: Mobility, Connection, Emotion." *Mobilities* 2, no. 2 (2007): 167–74.

Dabashi, Hamid. *The World of Persian Literary Humanism*. Cambridge, MA: Harvard University Press, 2012.

Damrosch, David. "The World in a Journal." *Journal of World Literature* 1, no. 1 (2016): 1–7.

Deleuze, Gilles, and Félix Guattari. *Kafka: Toward a Minor Literature*. Trans. Dana Polan. Minneapolis: University of Minnesota Press, 1986.

Freitag, Ulrike, and Achim von Oppen, eds. *Translocality: The Study of Globalising Processes from a Southern Perspective*. Leiden: Brill, 2010.

Frouzesh, Sharareh. "The Use and Abuse of Guilt." PhD diss. University of California, Irvine, 2013.

Ganguly, Keya. "World Cinema, World Literature, and Dialectical Criticism." In *The Cambridge Companion to World Literature*. Ed. Ben Etherington and Jarad Zimbler. 211–26. Cambridge: Cambridge University Press, 2018.

Gould, Rebecca. "Literature as a Tribunal: The Modern Iranian Prose of Incarceration." *Prose Studies* 39, no. 1 (2017): 19–38.

Helgesson, Stefan. "Postcolonialism and World Literature." *Interventions* 16, no. 4 (2014): 483–500.

Hemming, John. "Introduction." In *No Heaven for Gunga Din: Consisting of The British and American Officers' Book*. 9–23. Costa Mesa: Mazda Publishers, 2018.

Khorrami, Mohammad Mehdi. *Literary Subterfuge and Contemporary Persian Fiction: Who Writes Iran?* London: Routledge, 2014.

Kiarostami, Abbas. *A Wolf Lying in Wait: Selected Poems*. Trans. Karim Emami and Michael Beard. Tehran: Sokhan, 2005.

Kipling, Rudyard. "Gunga Din." First published in the *New York Tribune* on May 22, 1890 and in the *Scot's Observer* on June 7, 1890. ORG No. 460.

Milani, Farzaneh. *Words, Not Swords: Iranian Women Writers and the Freedom of Movement*. Syracuse: Syracuse University Press, 2011.

Mirdrekvandi, Ali [Gunga Din]. *No Heaven for Gunga Din: Consisting of The British and American Officers' Book*. Costa Mesa: Mazda Publishers, 2018 [London: Gollancz, 1965].

Mirdrekvandi, Ali [Gunga Din]. *Nur-afkan [Irradiant]*. Unpublished manuscript MS. Ind. Inst. Misc. 35/1, bequeathed to the Bodleian Library, Oxford, by John Hemming in 1996.

Motlagh, Amy. "Autobiography and Authority in the Writings of the Iranian Diaspora." *Comparative Studies of South Asia, Africa and the Middle East* 31, no. 2 (2011): 411–24.

Motlagh, Amy. "Towards a Theory of Iranian American Life Writing." *MELUS* 33, no. 2 (2008): 17–36.

Mufti, Aamir. "Orientalism and the Institution of World Literatures." *Critical Inquiry* 36, no. 3 (2010): 458–93.

No Heaven for Gunga Din (Baraye Gunga Din Behesht Nist) [film]. Dir. Gholamreza Nematpour and Laleh Roozgard. Iran: H.O.C.I.G, Lorestan, 2012.

Oelze, Sabine. "Author Fariba Vafi: Writers Struggle for Influence in Iran." *Deutsche Welle*, February 19, 2018. Web. Available at http://p.dw.com/p/2sgGs (accessed July 12, 2020).

Peterson, Richard, and Andy Bennett. "Introducing Music Scenes." In *Music Scenes: Local, Translocal, and Virtual*. Ed. Andy Bennett and Richard Peterson. 1–15. Nashville: Vanderbilt University Press, 2004.

Rekabtalaei, Golbarg. *Iranian Cosmopolitanism: A Cinematic History*. Cambridge: Cambridge University Press, 2019.

Rothberg, Michael. "Afterword: Locating Transnational Memory." *European Review* 22, no. 4 (2014): 652–6.

Shin, Hyunjoon, and Keewoong Lee. "The Question of Geographic Scale in Asian Popular Music: Global, Local, Regional, and Translocal." *Korean Journal of Popular Music* 25 (2020): 181–211.

Smith, Michael Peter. "Translocality: A Critical Reflection." In *Translocal Geographies: Spaces, Places, Connections*. Ed. Katherine Brickell and Ayona Datta. 181–98. London: Routledge, 2016.

Spooner, Brian. "Introduction." In *Savushun: A Novel about Modern Iran*. Simin Daneshvar. Trans. Mohammad Ghanoonparvar. xi–xvi. Washington, DC: Mage, 2001.

Tagore, Rabindranath. *The Essential Tagore*. Ed. Fakrul Alam and Radha Chakravarty. Cambridge, MA: Harvard University Press, 2011.

Vafa, Amirhossein. *Recasting American and Persian Literatures: Local Histories and Formative Geographies from Moby-Dick to Missing Soluch*. New York: Palgrave Macmillan, 2016.

Vafi, Fariba. *My Bird*. Trans. Mahnaz Kousha and Nasrin Jewell. Syracuse: Syracuse University Press, 2009.

Vafi, Fariba. *Parandeh-ye Man [My Bird]*. Tehran: Nashr-e Markaz, 1381/2002.

Vafi, Fariba. *Tarlan*. Tehran: Nashr-e Markaz, 1382/2003.

Vafi, Fariba. Anonymous Review of Vafi's *My Bird*. *Publishers Weekly*, September 28, 2009. Web. www.publishersweekly.com/978-0-8156-0944-5 (accessed July 12, 2020).

Yavari, Houra. "The Persian Novel." In *Encyclopaedia Iranica*, 2012. Web. Available at www.iranicaonline.org/articles/fiction-iibthe-novel (accessed August 19, 2019).

Zaehner, Robert Charles. "Foreword." In *No Heaven for Gunga Din: Consisting of The British and American Officers' Book*. 7–8. Costa Mesa: Mazda Publishers, 2018.

Zaehner, Robert Charles. "Zoroastrian Survivals in Iranian Folklore II." *Iran* 30, no. 1 (1992): 65–75.

12

The Purloined *Letter*: Reconsidering Simin Daneshvar's *Dagh-e Nang* and the Politics of Translation in the Landscape of World Literature

Amy Motlagh

The past three decades have witnessed not only the rise of *translation* as a major critical paradigm in academia but also an institutionalized one. Centers for Translation Studies have been established, fields of specialization have been designated, and journals dedicated to this area of inquiry. Consequently, a cadre of professionals trained in a variety of disciplines has developed whose job it is not to translate, per se, but to theorize and study the practice of translation. The rise of contemporary translation studies grew alongside, and has been an important aspect of, the development of the field of comparative literature in the United States. Since comparative literature itself grew out of the exilic situation of post-war European intellectuals, the field was initially limited to questions of translatability and literary heritage among predominantly western European languages and literatures, and efforts to expand the scope of comparative literature met with institutional resistance (see, e.g., the Bernheimer Report). However, the attacks on the World Trade Center on September 11, 2001, and the subsequent US immersion in an extended period of wars in West and Central Asia brought new attention to the languages of the "Middle East," particularly Arabic, and not only gave new urgency to the need for translation to happen fast but also raised new ethical questions about the role of translators.

In what at first may seem like a contradiction, the rise of translation studies coincided with the decline of foreign-language study in the United States.[1] At the same time, and possibly owing to the same genesis, the new subfields of transnational American Studies and World Literature (an academic field that takes translation of texts in English as its primary requirement) were developing as corollaries to the interest in translation. Concomitant with the rise of these areas of inquiry has been a contrarian notion, that

---

[1] A study by the Modern Languages Association (MLA) found a 6.7 percent drop between 2009 and 2013 and a 9.2 percent drop between 2013 and 2016. Enrollment in advanced courses for languages show even steeper declines, indicating that most students enrolled in languages in US universities do not continue past the intermediate level. See Colleen Flaherty, "L'œuf ou la Poule?" *Inside Higher Ed*, March 19, 2018.

of *untranslatability*. Discussed most famously by Francophone specialist, and ardent critic of World Literature, Emily Apter in *The Translation Zone*,[2] *untranslatability* is a term flagging those parts or aspects of a text whose meaning is not easily rendered into the target language. Ironically, *untranslatability* has the consequence not only of fetishizing translation but also fetishizing its perceived limits.

One problem with the notion of untranslatability as Apter discusses it in *The Translation Zone* and later in *Against World Literature* (2013) is that, when she turns to Arabic (a language that she does not read), so much depends on her perception of its sacrality.[3] Discussing this interpretation, Shaden Tageldin avers that "Apter ties untranslatability to the theological—to the insistence that a sacred text *not* be, even *cannot* be, translated—and takes seriously its sacral dimension. She hints that sacrality clings with particular force to (Qur'anic) Arabic" and goes on to suggest that "untranslatability fascinates [Euro-American] comparative literature today because the idea teeters on the threshold between the imagined absolutism of the theological and the imagined relativism of the worldly, cross-contaminating both."[4]

It is this paradox of the untranslatable, and the misattribution of a sacred quality to modern Persian and Arabic, that haunts Jeffrey Einboden's *Nineteenth-Century American Literature in Middle Eastern Languages*.[5] Although he never cites Apter and generally seems to eschew engagement with the scholarly milieu of translation studies in which his work is situated, Einboden's work is certainly a product both of the increased attention to "Middle Eastern languages" (Einboden's term) that followed 9/11 and the fact that such increased attention has created new subfields of academic inquiry. The remarkable feat Einboden attempts in this work—to interpret and judge the quality and cultural significance of translations of major American Romantic works by Whitman, Melville, and Hawthorne, among others, into Arabic, Hebrew, and Persian—is a project of vertiginous scale. It not only requires near-native fluency in three very different foreign languages that Einboden collectivizes under the category "Middle Eastern," but also likely a degree of cultural immersion or familiarity that would be difficult to achieve for even one of these linguistic contexts, let alone the vast range of geography these three languages span. This project, Einboden's first monograph, would be the beginning of a career spent in translating/interpreting "Middle Eastern" languages (which at the historical moment of Einboden's career

2   Emily Apter, *The Translation Zone* (Princeton: Princeton University Press, 2005).

3   Apter is, like so many Francophone scholars, fascinated by North Africa and other regions that have long enthralled Europeanists, but where they linguistically fear to tread. Like most Francophone scholars, Apter has not learned Arabic, the official language of those nations, and reads literature and theorists from this region in French only. Similarly, although she is fascinated by the experiences of Leo Spitzer and Erich Auerbach in Turkey, she has not (like Auerbach) learned that country's language, either.

4   Shaden Tageldin, "Untranslatability." American Comparative Literature Association "State of the Discipline Report 2014–2015." March 3, 2014.

5   Jeffrey Einboden, *Nineteenth-Century US Literature in Middle Eastern Languages* (Edinburgh: Edinburgh University Press, 2013). An earlier version of the chapter on *Dagh-e Nang* was published as "Composing a Persian Letter: Simin Daneshvar's Rendition of Hawthorne," *Nathaniel Hawthorne Review* 34, nos. 1–2 (2008): 81–102.

essentially means "languages from Muslim-majority nations"), and has been followed by *Islam and Romanticism: Muslim Currents from Goethe to Emerson* (2014), *The Islamic Lineage of American Literary Culture* (2016), *The Qur'an and Kerygma* (2019), and *Jefferson's Muslim Fugitives* (2020).[6]

A broader critique of Einboden's project and the disciplinary and political circumstances that have enabled it by scholars of the languages he engages (Arabic, Hebrew, Persian) is certainly overdue, but regrettably, engagement with all three of those languages is beyond the scope of this chapter (or this author). In what follows, I focus on Einboden's critique of Iranian author and translator Simin Daneshvar's 1955 Persian translation of Nathaniel Hawthorne's *The Scarlet Letter*, published as *Dagh-e Nang*, to consider the pitfalls of what we might call the "translational turn" in American scholarship.[7] This "translational turn" had broad effects, but for my purposes here, I concentrate on its impact on American Studies (specifically, on transnational American Studies) and Comparative Literature, particularly the subfield of World Literature. I am interested not only in the unwitting imperialism and exceptionalism that characterizes not only Einboden's project but also the way in which (ironically) greater interest in translation facilitated these new movements in scholarship. I situate Einboden's critique of *Dagh-e Nang* at the intersection of the diminution of American investment in language acquisition, the development of an academic culture of World Literature in the United States in the 1990s (which was supported by the rise of Translation Studies), and the flourishing of the "new" and "transnational" schools of Americanist scholarship. Einboden's misapprehension of Daneshvar's translation is, regrettably, not exceptional, but represents the culmination (or perhaps the extreme) of these scholarly practices.[8]

While the intent of the so-called "New Americanists" was to redefine the boundaries of Americanist inquiry beyond the conventional areas delineated by previous generations of Americanists, and to question the shibboleth of American exceptionalism, such projects have often, inadvertently, ended up reaffirming American exceptionalism and had ironically imperialist tones. As John Carlos Rowe, one of the most eminent New Americanists, himself cautioned, "In re-conceptualizing the global

---

[6] See also Einboden's "Harriet Beecher, from Beirut to Tehran: Raising the Cabin in the Middle East," in *Uncle Tom's Cabins: The Transnational History of America's Most Mutable Book*, ed. Tracy Davis and Stefka Mihaylova, 343–65 (Ann Arbor: University of Michigan Press, 2018).

[7] Two editions of Daneshvar's translation of *The Scarlet Letter* are referenced in this chapter: *Dagh-e Nang*, trans. Simin Daneshvar (Tehran: Nil, 1334/1955); *Dagh-e Nang*, trans. Simin Daneshvar (Tehran: Kharazmi, 1369/1990).

[8] In the 1980s, a rift within the field of American Studies became public when, in a now famous 1988 article in the *NYRB*, Frederick C. Crews called the trend to rethink the certain foundations of the American canon the work of the "new americanists" (Frederick C. Crews, "Whose American Renaissance?" *New York Review of Books*, October 27, 1988, 68–81). This epithet would be taken up as a badge of honor by its practitioners, most notably, Donald Pease and John Carlos Rowe (see, e.g., Donald Pease, "New Americanists: Revisionist Intervention into the Canon," *Boundary 2* 17, no. 1 [1990]: 1–37). This "New" Americanism later gave rise to an offshoot, "transnational" American Studies, a subfield that seeks out reception of American cultural products and policies in other national sites. A new generation of scholars trained in the wake of this reformist spirit attempted to broaden the scope of American Studies.

scope that American Studies must undertake to respond to US neo-imperialism, we must remain vigilant regarding the specific ways knowledge and power have been coordinated historically."[9] In other words, there was in this type of study a danger of reinscribing American exceptionalism as scholars broadened their analysis to include new aspects of American culture in examinations of American literature and history, and in turn examined the lives and afterlives of American cultural products abroad. Einboden's projects capitalize on a period of American scholarly fascination with the transformation of American cultural products abroad while not being able to fully investigate the actual repercussions of these translations in their indigenous linguistic contexts. In the United States, no language acquisition (beyond, perhaps, French or German as reading languages) is required of students specializing in American Studies or American literature, and among Americanists, Einboden's facility with languages is viewed as remarkable.[10] His effort to look at American literature through the lens of its engagement in Arabic, Persian, and Hebrew has been given special attention and funding. Yet, at least partially because his work was not subjected to the peer review of critics from these linguistic fields, his work exceptionalizes the afterlives of works like *The Scarlet Letter*, overprivileging their influence in local literary and cultural landscapes which only vaguely took notice of them.

Perhaps unsurprisingly, these new Americanisms coincided with the move in American academia toward a commercialized and institutionalized study of World Literature, best epitomized by the efforts of the distinguished American scholar David Damrosch, whose work on the "discovery" of Gilgamesh in the nineteenth century itself led to a rediscovery of that text in American curricula, and whose writings on world literatures, however contested, have defined the American approach to that topic.[11] Against the views of others in the field (e.g., Gayatri Spivak), Damrosch is well known for his commitment to translation as an invariable good.[12] In a 2013 article, however, Damrosch expressed a somewhat surprising observation—namely, that American literature has itself been marginalized within the study of both English literature in the United States and in the study of World Literature. While the New Americanists'

[9] John Carlos Rowe, *The Cultural Politics of the New American Studies* (Ann Arbor: Open Humanities Press, 2012), 101.

[10] Reviews of *Nineteenth-Century US Literature in Middle East Languages* were overwhelmingly positive, and entirely undertaken by Americanist scholars (see, e.g., Saleh D. Hassan, "Enemies and Intimacies: Rethinking US-Middle East Cultural History," *American Literary History* 27, no. 4 [2015]: 788–99; Jacqueline Jondot, "Review of *Nineteenth-Century US Literature in Middle Eastern Languages*," *Transatlantica* 1 [2014]); Brian Yothers, "Review of *Nineteenth-Century US Literature in Middle Eastern Languages*," *Translation & Literature* 24, no. 1 [2015]: 112–16). Einboden received a prestigious National Endowment for the Humanities grant for his monograph *The Islamic Lineage of American Literary Culture: Muslim Sources from the Revolution to Reconstruction*.

[11] David Damrosch, "How American Is World Literature?" *The Comparatist* 33 (2009): 13–19. See also *What Is World Literature?* (Princeton: Princeton University Press, 2003), and the more recent *How to Read World Literature* (New York: Wiley-Blackwell, 2018).

[12] See their conversation about world literature and translation in "Comparative Literature/World Literature: A Discussion with Gayatri Chakravorty Spivak and David Damrosch," *Comparative Literature Studies* 48, no. 4 (2011): 455–85.

concern was that the canon had privileged the work of a few, Damrosch is interested in the repositioning of American literature within the broader (and longer) scheme of the "world" of World Literature, and points to New Americanists like Wai Chee Dimock and Djelal Kadir as representing a positive and novel strain of Americanist. For Damrosch, Dimock's and Kadir's representations of American literature as part of longer and larger worldly timelines complicates conventional genealogies of literary progress/development in the United States.[13] Yet, at the same time, cautions Damrosch, Americanists must be careful that in correcting the marginalization of American literature in the schema of World Literature, Americanists must not become unwitting imperialists. There is a danger in overprivileging the American canon when one moves to correct the bounds of study.

Drawing on works that conform to F. O. Matthiesen's definition of the American canon in his 1941 magnum opus *American Renaissance: Art and Expression in the Age of Emerson and Whitman*, and evincing a very limited familiarity with the literary milieus of the translators whose works he considers, Einboden's work is a strange hybrid.[14] It not only reinforces views of American exceptionalism but also espouses the unwitting neo-imperialism Rowe warns against. Through a very superficial engagement with Simin Daneshvar's translation of *The Scarlet Letter* (*Dagh-e Nang*) and her other work (both translations and her original writing), Einboden paints a picture that may be compelling from the point of view of Americanists, in that it suggests that American cultural products like *The Scarlet Letter* have had a profound and enduring impact on world literature and Persian literature in particular, but which is fundamentally untrue.

Throughout his analysis of *Dagh-e Nang* and his interpretation of its broader effect on the Persian language and Iranian society, Einboden insists on three major points: (1) the inability of "Middle Eastern" translators to successfully translate the central metaphor of the novel, the scarlet "A"; (2) the difficulty Daneshvar had in translating "Christian" language for "Muslim" readers; and (3) her general misapprehension of key points within *The Scarlet Letter*, which, in his view, derived from her unfamiliarity with the American cultural milieu (specifically, nineteenth-century New England) and led her to translate terms and ideas incorrectly and in ways that fundamentally change the meaning of Hawthorne's novel.[15]

Consider the following passage, in which the terms Einboden uses to build his interpretative framework first show the problems:

---

[13] Indeed, in comparison to a work like Wai Chee Dimock's *Through Other Continents: American Literature across Deep Time* (Princeton: Princeton University Press, 2009), the scope of Einboden's work might even seem modest. Dimock suggests that instead of thinking of American literature as a national construct, it must be considered in terms of the hemispheric and in a seemingly endless expanse of time, reaching back into antiquity. Dimock's flawed engagement with Hafez (whom she largely misunderstands, pulling him willy-nilly into the history of Nation of Islam, jazz, and American literature via her theory of "deep time") is one I leave aside here."

[14] Francis Otto Matthiesen, *American Renaissance: Art and Expression in the Age of Emerson and Whitman* (New York: Oxford University Press, 1941).

[15] Einboden, *Nineteenth-Century*, 76–7, 79, 89–95.

The transfer of any novel across the boundaries of language raises difficult questions regarding the most effective means of rendering a literary symbol and fictional character. The translation of *The Scarlet Letter* into a Middle Eastern vernacular, however, also raises the problem of religious difference, challenging translators to find ways of expressing Christian content through language shaped by Islamic culture and history.[16]

Although the term "Middle East" is, of course, commonly used in colloquial speech, politics, and journalism, it seems odd to group translations into Persian, Arabic, and Hebrew together in one study, not least because the nations on which Einboden focuses have had such mutually alienating experiences of language in the twentieth century, growing further apart rather than closer together—except, perhaps, through the globalization of English.[17] Therefore, in using "Middle Eastern" as a qualifying rubric for the texts he selects, Einboden inadvisedly groups together a body of *litterarateurs* and translators working in three languages with very different national and literary traditions.[18]

The languages that Einboden engages in his monograph include Persian, the language in which Daneshvar wrote and primarily read; Arabic, a language Daneshvar would likely not have had reading knowledge of beyond the scriptural; and Hebrew, which had been until the twentieth century a largely liturgical language (diasporic Jews would have spoken Yiddish, Ladino, Judeo-Persian, Judeo-Arabic, and other regional variants) that was reinstated as a modern language with the establishment of the state of Israel in 1948. Although she did once visit Israel with her husband, Daneshvar did not learn Hebrew (very few people in Iran at that time or at present would have).[19] Moreover, it's unlikely that she would have thought of herself as a "Middle Eastern" or even a "Muslim" translator. (She did, on occasion, call herself an "Eastern" writer or woman, in contrast to the "West" that was asserted as having a specific literary and cultural heritage, and a liberal moral outlook). If she felt the need to characterize herself within any national or geographic identity, Daneshvar's writings reveal that she thought of herself primarily as an Iranian, or perhaps in even more local terms, as a Shirazi. Einboden's insistence on categorizing her within the terms "Middle Eastern" and "Muslim" suggests both a totalizing perspective as well as a lack of familiarity with her writing. Further, it flattens out the analysis, assuming that because Daneshvar was an Iranian, she was an observant Muslim, or that being a Muslim was an important

---

[16] Ibid., 89.

[17] The severing of existing cultural ties among the nations of the "Middle East" through language reform in the late nineteenth and early twentieth centuries is well documented by historians. For a brief account of this history in the Iranian context, see Mehrdad Kia, "Persian Nationalism and the Campaign for Language Purification," *Middle Eastern Studies* 34, no. 2 (1998): 9–36.

[18] Regrettably, Einboden continues to use the category "Middle Eastern languages" in later writings. See his *Jefferson's Muslim Fugitives* (New York: Oxford University Press, 2020) for multiple examples.

[19] Daneshvar and Al-e Ahmad visited Israel in 1963, and Al-e Ahmad was so impressed and interested in the project of the new nation that he wrote a travelogue based on the experience called *Safar beh Velayat-e Ezra'il* [*Journey to the State of Israel*] (Tehran: Majid, 1374/1995).

part of her identity as a writer. Similarly, his analysis assumes that because she lived in Iran, she considered herself part of an entity called the "Middle East." For Einboden, Daneshvar is a type: the Muslim Middle Eastern Woman Writer, who will necessarily write and think (and most important for his purposes, translate) in particular ways.

Would Daneshvar have thought of herself as a Muslim in the way that Einboden characterizes her as one? For Daneshvar and her husband and major interlocutor, Jalal Al-e Ahmad (1923–69), the idea of being Muslim was deeply fraught: Al-e Ahmad came from a religious and clerical family, and had broken with his family to marry someone from a very different (and secular) background. Though he eventually espoused a kind of revolutionary Shi'ism, this was not a view that Daneshvar shared; she saw it as a politicized reading of religion, and in general, saw herself as being stringently apolitical.

A letter written to Al-e Ahmad written during her Fulbright year (1952–3) in Palo Alto is suggestive of some of the ways in which Daneshvar was interested in religious practice. Daneshvar observes a Quaker meeting taking place in the Palo Alto woods. She sees the Quakers as marginal to American and Christian societies, and invested in a nonorthodox version of Christianity; perhaps on the basis of this comparativism, she makes a (perhaps mistaken) conclusion that they occupy a similar place in American religions to that of Sufis in Iran. Indeed, she suggests that they are like "our own *darvishe*s [Sufis]."[20] This kind of comparative syncretism makes Einboden's reading of "Islam" seem cartoonish; his finalizing and monolithic category of "Muslim" clearly has little to do with Daneshvar's own way of conceptualization of that term.

If Daneshvar's notions about what it means to be a Muslim are broader and more complicated than Einboden would make out, what of his insistence on the sacred nature of the Arabic alphabet, and its inability to convey Christian meaning? Is the "A" indeed untranslatable? Perhaps by way of answering, we might begin by considering the difference between *letters* and *symbols*. Einboden, oddly, refers to the letter "A" in *The Scarlet Letter* alternately as "letter," "symbol," and "glyph," insisting that because Daneshvar cannot find an adequate translation in Persian (using Arabic characters) for the "A," the scarlet letter worn by Hester Prynne becomes for "Iranian readers," "Persian readers," and "Middle Eastern readers" (he uses the terms interchangeably in this chapter) only a signifier without a signified—a floating signifier. In the process, the "A" becomes meaningless, thus erasing the novel's central metaphor. Calling it alternately both a "glyph" and a "letter," Einboden proposes that Daneshvar sees the "A" through a "Muslim" lens, effacing its fundamentally Latinate and Christian nature.

For Einboden, Hawthorne's "A" is an irreducible symbol of something that can only be properly understood by Christian readers, presumably Protestant Christian readers in the United States, but possibly also Christian readers more generally. Focusing on the singularity of the "A," Einbdoden fetishizes its presence and focuses on the difficulty of translating it into Arabic characters, rather than looking comparatively at

---

[20] Simin Daneshvar and Jalal Al-e Ahmad, *Nameh-ha-ye Daneshvar va Al-e Ahmad* (*The Letters of Simin Daneshvar and Jalal Al-e Ahmad*), ed. Masud Jafari-Jazi (Tehran: Nilufar, 2004), 158–9.

how other translators of other non-Latin languages have treated it. We hear echoes of Apter's assertion of untranslatability here, and of the assumed "sacrality" of the Arabic alphabet.

The case of Turkish brings to the fore the problem with Einboden's use of the term "Middle Eastern languages" and the characteristics he attributes to them. One of the nations that Einboden subsumes into the category of "Middle Eastern,"[21] Turkey is, of course, a Muslim-majority country, but its national language is both non-Semitic and not an Indo-Iranian language (it is from the Ural-Altaic family) and, since 1929, it has used the Latin alphabet. What might Einboden have learned if he had considered how Turkish translators deal with *The Scarlet Letter*'s "central symbol" in their translations?[22] And what if, to lend greater credence to his assertions about the particularity of the Arabic alphabet and the impossibility of translating the "A" into it, he had considered how, say, Polish translators deal with the letter?

Einboden seems to insist that only Christian readers can understand the Latinate nature of Hester's "A," but Polish, for example, *is* written in Latin characters and is spoken in a majority Christian country; however, it is a Slavic language and has a very different grammar and vocabulary from Romance languages, most of which share a similar word for adultery (*adultere, adulterio*, etc.), all of which begin with "A." In contrast, the word for adultery in Polish begins with a "c." Further, Poland is not a *Protestant* Christian context. Is it as complicated to translate the "A" in Turkish or Polish as Einboden considers it to be in Persian or other non-Latinate alphabet languages in non-Protestant majority nations? What about Greek, or Chinese—spoken in lands where there are large Christian populations—albeit with very different histories from that of Puritan New England? What might we learn from the fact that translations of *The Scarlet Letter* in China have been so successful and the novel of so much interest that it has been translated multiple times and embraced both by critics and popular audiences? In a discussion of the three translations undertaken in Chinese at the time of the essay's publication, critic Xiao-Huang Yin does not mention the problem of translating the symbol of the "A" at all, but instead notes the popularity of all of the translations of *The Scarlet Letter*, which have been given titles as various as *Song of the Rustic Poor*.[23] Is *The Scarlet Letter* truly only legible (in every sense of the word) to Anglophone readers and western Europeans?

Toward the end of his chapter on *Dagh-e Nang*, Einboden turns to what he believes is the extensive and enduring impact of *The Scarlet Letter* on Iranian culture:

---

[21] Einboden, *Nineteenth-Century*, 77.

[22] The Turkish titles of existing translations of *The Scarlet Letter* are *Kizil Damga* and *Kizil Harf*. One chooses "damga" ("mark," "brand," "stamp"—a similar choice to the Persian *dagh* in Daneshvar's translation) and the other *harf* ("letter"). See *Kizil Damga*, trans. Z. Gülümser Ağırer Çuhadar (Istanbul: Arıon Yayınevi, 2002).

[23] See Xiao-Huang Yin, "The Scarlet Letter in China," *American Quarterly* 39, no. 4 (1987): 551–62. Einboden refers in passing (in an endnote) to research on translations of *The Scarlet Letter* into German and Chinese, but he does not engage these.

Searching for Hawthornean intersections within Iranian circles—from scholarship, to poetry, to film—is potentially endless. Such a search risks, however, inadvertent acts of over-reading, mistaking mere coincidence for genuine overhearing across cultures: to what extent may artistic correspondence of theme and phrase, American and Persian, be credited with significance? Despite these hazards, it remains clear that *The Scarlet Letter*'s incarnation, and reincarnations, as *Dagh-e Nang* has worked to "rebrand" the novel, allowing this US classic to speak language reminiscent now of feminist activism in Iran—an outcome unanticipated by Hawthorne, and perhaps, by Daneshvar herself.[24]

Acknowledging that Daneshvar herself went on to become one of Iran's most distinguished writers of fiction, Einboden proposes that this translation "launched" Daneshvar's literary career in Iran and indeed shaped her later magnum opus, *Savushun* (1969).[25] But he does not stop there. In the quote above, he asserts that the translation has had far-reaching consequences for Persian letters. Yet he only goes as far as to *gesture* toward a possible reception, using only sources in English (online newspaper resources and a smattering of anthological works) to support his point.[26] Because Einboden's understanding of Daneshvar's career and the importance of *Dagh-e Nang* in Iran rests on sources in English, it is extremely partial and misleading. On Daneshvar's reputation and importance in the Persian literary canon, he cites only one source total—US-based literary scholar Farzaneh Milani's 1992 monograph— while his assessment of *Dagh-e Nang*'s influence on other Iranian culture and letters is based, oddly, on two points: (1) his perception that Daneshvar's masterwork *Savushun* "overlap[s] in detail and diction" with *The Scarlet Letter*,[27] and (2) what he sees as *Dagh-e Nang*'s influence on another famous Iranian woman writer (one of the few to be widely translated into English, and to have achieved an international reputation), Forugh Farrokhzad. According to Einboden, because another US-based critic (Hamid Dabashi) characterizes Farrokhzad as wearing "a scarlet letter,"[28] and because Farrokhzad used the phrase *dagh-e nang* in a minor poem, she, too, must have been influenced by Daneshvar's translation (Farrokhzad, of course, became [in]famous in her time at least partly because she was openly having an affair with a married man, Ebrahim Golestan).

---

[24] Einboden, *Nineteenth-Century*, 97.
[25] Ibid., 76, 95. *Savushun* has itself twice been translated into English: once in 1990 by M. R. Ghanoonparvar as *Savushun* (Washington, DC: Mage Publishers, 1990) and again by Roxane Zand in 1992 as *A Persian Requiem* (New York: G. Braziller, 1992).
[26] Einboden's engagement with the Iranian or Persophone reception of *Dagh-e Nang* is startlingly superficial and incongruous. Every time he sees the term *dagh-e nang*, he assumes it can be attributed in some way to Daneshvar's translation. For full references, see Einboden, *Nineteenth-Century*, 198.
[27] Einboden, *Nineteenth-Century*, 95–6.
[28] Dabashi is certainly a very well-known scholar of Iran in the United States. He completed his post-graduate education in the United States and has lived here for the past forty years or more. The same is true of Milani. I doubt that either one of them would suggest resting an assessment of either Daneshvar's career or *The Scarlet Letter*'s influence in Iran on their work.

Following his own scholarly milieu, Dabashi's assertion simply demonstrates the use of "scarlet letter" in English to describe publicly recognized adultery. And while Einboden suggests specifically that Farrokhzad's poem "A Poem for You" ("She'ri baraye To") makes a reference to Daneshvar's translation because it uses the expression *dagh-e nang*, this is likely not the case.[29] Daneshvar did not coin the term for purposes of naming her translation—it was a common expression long before, which is probably why it made a good title for the translation, however much it transformed the letter more literally into a symbol.[30] By looking at the broader semantic range and usage of *dagh-e nang* that precedes Daneshvar's translation, we can safely assume that every time the phrase is invoked, it need not refer in some way to Daneshvar's translation of Hawthorne. While Daneshvar and Farrokhzad knew each other, and may have read each other's work, there is no textual or documentary evidence that they influenced one another.

This is not to say that feminism does not play a role in the translation—just not in the way that Einboden believes. Had Einboden looked at the first introduction that Daneshvar included with her 1955 translation (which is also reproduced in later editions), "Nathaniel Hawthorne and His Work," he might also have found something that could have been the basis for a different and more substantial argument about the importance of *Dagh-e Nang* to the modern Iranian cultural tradition. Daneshvar notes, "the writer of this story has hopes of a better world for women ... Hawthorne dreams of a new woman as the prophet of the future of this world," asserting that she hopes for a feminist figure in Iranian literature like Hester.[31] For Daneshvar, the translation of this work of American Romanticism into Persian was at least partially motivated by her own critique of the plight of women in Iran.

It becomes clear that Einboden has actually not looked at the reception of the novel in Persian at all. His assessment of the work's influence on Daneshvar is to assert that Daneshvar was so influenced by her translation work that it is "embroidered" on the text of her most famous and best-selling novel, *Savushun*.[32] He suggests that they overlap in "diction" and "style," but it is hard to see how Einboden could know this, since he is clearly citing an English translation of Daneshvar's novel. In his assertion of an "echo" of *The Scarlet Letter* in *Savushun*, Einboden describes what he understands

---

[29] Forugh Farrokhzad, *Another Birth*, trans. Hassan Javadi and Susan Sallee (Emeryville: Albany Press, 1981).

[30] A basic search for *dagh-e nang* in the online and easily accessible catalog of the National Library of Iran reveals a substantial body of criticism on Hawthorne and *The Scarlet Letter*, including a 2011 article by two Iranian scholars (in English) comparing two Persian translations of *The Scarlet Letter*—Daneshvar's canonical translation, and a more recent translation (*Zani ba Neshan-e Qermez*, trans. Mohammad Sadeq Shariati [Tehran: Rowshangaran, 2004]). Einboden might also have come across the film *Dagh-e Nang* (1965), which has nothing to do with Hawthorne or his novel, but was written by Ahmad Shamlou, a poet and contemporary of Daneshvar.

[31] Simin Daneshvar, "Nataniyel Hawtorn va Asar-e U," in *Dagh-e Nang*, trans. Simin Daneshvar (Tehran: Nil, 1955), 8.

[32] Einboden transcribes this as *Sovashun*, but because Daneshvar was from Shiraz, where the pronunciation of this word was Savushun, translators have often chosen to transcribe the word accordingly. Daneshvar frequently used Shirazi dialect in her stories and novels.

to be an overheard conversation between two "sisters"; it ends with the story of a young servant who has been impregnated by either the husband or the son of one of the speakers. It is certainly a shameful event, and there is mention of the servant being branded (using the verb *dagh kardan*) as a punishment:

> Read solely within the context of *Sovashun*, this episode seems a minor tangent, merely another instance of cruelty suffered by women, a theme emphasized throughout the novel. If read within the broader context of Daneshvar's career, however, this brief moment, overheard between chambers, begins to sound more distinct, speaking in a remarkably Hawthornean accent.[33]

Seeing the word *dagh* might certainly be suggestive. However, the two women are *not* in fact sisters. They are two women from aristocratic families of Shiraz who have known each other from childhood, and about the disappointments of their lives as wives and mothers. Owing to their long friendship, they call each other "sister," although there is no blood kinship. This is hard to miss (even in translation—both translations of *Savushun* in English make it pretty clear), since the women belong, respectively, to the families of the protagonist and antagonist. Yet Einboden hangs a major conclusion about Daneshvar and the impact of *The Scarlet Letter* on his misinterpretation of this passage. Similarly, because Ezzat al-Dowleh, the woman speaking in the chapter, says she "branded" (*dagh kardam*) the servant as a punishment, Einboden believes this, too, must be an indirect reference to *The Scarlet Letter*. In the context of *Savushun*, Ezzat al-Dowleh commits this cruelty because, according to her, she cannot tell whether she has been a betrayed wife or a bad mother, and is in any case ashamed that she has allowed a dependent to be abused by a member of her household; it is characteristic that she perversely punishes that dependent victim rather than the perpetrator.

But must this have something to do with *The Scarlet Letter*? The character punished, the servant girl Ferdows has little or no role in the novel, and it is hard to see how she could be an indirect reference to Hester because she has been branded. *Dagh kardan* is a verb that has long been used in Persian language and literature to describe, literally and metaphorically, things that are burned on you—which is much the same way that "branded" is used in English. Giving Hawthorne or Daneshvar credit for this seems a stretch, to say the least.

As those acquainted with Daneshvar's oeuvre and life are aware, she was a copious letter writer, and many of her letters—especially those to other prominent intellectuals and writers, including her husband Jalal Al-e Ahmad—have been published over the last twenty years. Of particular interest here are these letters, published as *Nameh-ha-ye Simin-e Daneshvar va Jalal-e Al-e Ahmad* (*The Letters of Simin Daneshvar and Jalal Al-e Ahmad*),[34] Volume One of which comprises the letters Daneshvar wrote to Al-e Ahmad during her Fulbright year, the year in which she worked with Wallace

---

[33] Einboden, *Nineteenth-Century*, 95–6.
[34] Daneshvar and Al-e Ahmad, *Nameh-ha*.

Stegner (among others) at Stanford, and generally tried to become a professional writer. She spent a great deal of time thinking about translation, her own writing, and how to market her husband's writings to an American audience. They were, at least by American standards, poor. Although she was from a middle-class, educated family in Shiraz, Daneshvar had chosen to marry a man with few means and from a religious background very different from her own, whose family had initially severed ties with him when he chose to marry her. Daneshvar and Al-e Ahmad were forced to spend much of their married life thinking about how to make ends meet, and her work as a translator would oftentimes support them.

Therefore, while, for Einboden, Daneshvar's translation of Hawthorne seems like a singular and important event, it was neither the "launch" of her literary career, nor was it even her first translation.[35] Daneshvar made her living primarily as a translator and teacher, not as a writer, and before she published her translation of *Dagh-e Nang*, she had published a collection of Chekhov short stories (1951), *The Secret of Successful Living* by Dale Carnegie (1951), another Chekhov story (1952), *Beatrice* by Arthur Schnitzler (1953), and *The Human Comedy* by William Saroyan (1954).[36] She had also published a collection of her own short stories, which she later disowned and asked her publisher not to reprint, entitled *Atash-e Khamush* [*The Extinguished Fire*, 1327/1948]. Possibly we could look for "echoes and intersections" of these works in her own, and perhaps we would find them.

What we know for certain is that translation, unlike writing, was (and is) a paying job in Iran, and Daneshvar laments this circumstance in a preface to a later edition, which is dated, by the author, Mehr 20, 1358 (October 12, 1979) and included in the 1990 fourth edition, "Harf-e Akhar" ("Final Remarks") which Einboden himself refers to in this chapter.[37] Here again, however, he misunderstands her comments. Einboden characterizes her preface as a discussion of the "vanity of all translation," and sees her as bemoaning her own weakness in this regard.[38] But what this preface is actually about is the fact that so many talented writers of her generation in Iran have, for economic reasons sacrificed their time and talent translating works from foreign (European) languages into Persian instead of focusing on their own work.[39] That is the "trap" (or "snare," as Einboden translates it) of translation—it is a commercial one, heavily influenced by the exigencies of capitalism and imperialism that determined

---

[35] Einboden, *Nineteenth-Century*, 76.
[36] Einboden mentions these in passing (*Nineteenth-Century*, 78) and gives some of their titles in Note 10 (via a reference to Farzaneh Milani's English-language monograph *Words and Veils*) but does so with acknowledging their chronology, that is, that several of them preceded *Dagh-e Nang*, making it difficult to see that work as the "launch" of her career.
[37] This is mistranscribed by Einboden as "harf-e akhīr." Building on this misinterpretation, Einboden mistakenly suggests that "harf-e akhir" could mean either the "last word" or "another word" (the latter in Persian would be "harf-e *digar*"). While this mistake is trifling, Einboden goes on to develop an entire (and incorrect) argument about Daneshvar's views on translation based on the misinterpretation, and compounds this small error with further misunderstandings of Daneshvar's comments (Preface to *Dagh-e Nang*, Kharazmi, 1990).
[38] Einboden, *Nineteenth-Century*, 77.
[39] Daneshvar, "Harf-e Akhar," 5–6.

so much about Daneshvar's life as a writer, on which she was reflecting in the midst of the 1979 Revolution. Despite her fascination with the United States—one shared by many intellectuals of her generation—Daneshvar was an adamant anti-imperialist, which becomes clear if one reads any of her (untranslated) work in Persian.[40] Einboden is absolutely right in suggesting that translation can efface a great deal—in Daneshvar's case, the translation of her work into English oftentimes effaces its radical potential, and seeing her from a distance enables us to see her just as "the first Iranian woman novelist," and not as the leftist intellectual she actually was.

The "trap" of translation is one that Daneshvar in fact had to live with for the rest of her life, and while she continued to translate works into Persian (always from English— she was not, as Einboden implies, fluent in Russian and German; her translations of Chekhov and other writers from non-Anglophone contexts were always done from an intermediary translation in English), and lived primarily off her salary as a translator and teacher.[41] She sometimes had to translate works that would be commercially successful, rather than ones that had literary value. In addition to those named above, Daneshvar counted among her translations another Carnegie work, *How to Make Friends and Influence People*, as well as other self-help books like *Men Are from Mars, Women Are from Venus*.

If part of Einboden's quibble with Daneshvar is that she knew very little of the nineteenth-century America in which Hawthorne wrote, we might make the same critique of Einboden's own "translation" (or in his words, "rendition") of Daneshvar's translation. Einboden makes some very odd and elementary interpretative errors, complaining that Daneshvar's choice of translation for Pearl the "elf child" both effaces the "biblical" meaning of "pearl" (Daneshvar translates the name into Persian, since it is used as a name in Iran, too: Morvarid), and also gives the wrong interpretation to "elf child." But *bachcheh-ye sheytan*, Daneshvar's choice for Pearl the "elf child," doesn't in fact mean "satan child." Here, it certainly means a "mischievous child," which is, arguably, what "elf child" likely means to most readers of English. Another troubling example of misinterpretation is Einboden's assertion that the word *pezeshk*, commonly used for "doctor" or "physician," might also be read in the context of the translation as *pazashk*, an archaic and little-used synonym for "owl." Einboden believes that this is how Daneshvar made sense of Chillingsworth, the physician/leech of Hawthorne's *Scarlet Letter*. In modern Persian, two other words are more commonly used for owl: *joghd* and *buf*. Are these quibbling criticisms? Possibly. But they echo Einboden's own manner of critique, and in each of these cases, we might turn Einboden's critique back at him and suggest that *sheytan* here is not Satan in the way that we know him in the Christian tradition; that the differences between *pazashk, joghd,* and *buf* involve

---

[40] While there are many excellent translations of Daneshvar's work in English, many of them tend to efface specificities of language, choosing to render historically and culturally specific words into English idioms without any notation regarding those differences.

[41] Daneshvar also worked at the University of Tehran for twenty years, but was not tenured and eventually left her post. She attributed the end of her professorial career to her outspoken politics and the control of the university by the Pahlavis and their sympathizers.

substantive nuances that could "only" be known to a Muslim who lived in Iran in the mid twentieth century, much as the only translator of *The Scarlet Letter*, according to Einboden, must be a Christian who lived at the same time and in the same place as Hawthorne, or else is a historian of the period.[42]

But we might consider the matter differently, and suggest that the Iran of the 1950s— or today—is knowable (or at least visible) to scholars, if they will look. Einboden's approach to, and misreading of, *Dagh-e Nang* and the context of the translation and its translator diminish and flatten the richness and syncretic nature of Iranian literary, intellectual, and political culture of the 1950s. To look both ways, to think about the specificity of *The Scarlet Letter* and its singular importance in the American canon and the world canon through its "crossing of borders," and to reconsider *Dagh-e Nang* in the broader context of Daneshvar's life, writing, and literary milieu, is a step toward reconsidering our conception of World Literature as well as toward seeing an author often marginalized by her Otherly "firstness" in a non-Western canon as a practitioner of "world literature" *avant la lettre*.[43]

Bibliography

Al-e Ahmad, Jalal. *Safar beh Velayat-e 'Ezra'il (Journey to the State of Israel)*. Tehran: Majid, 1995.
Apter, Emily. *Against World Literature: On the Politics of Untranslatability*. New York: Verso, 2013.
Apter, Emily. *The Translation Zone*. Princeton: Princeton University Press, 2005.
Crews, Frederick C. "Whose American Renaissance?" *New York Review of Books*, October 27, 1988: 68–81.
Damrosch, David. "How American Is World Literature?" *The Comparatist* 33 (2009): 13–19.
Damrosch, David. *How to Read World Literature*. New York: Wiley-Blackwell, 2018.
Damrosch, David. *What Is World Literature?* Princeton: Princeton University Press, 2003.

[42] Here, too, we might say that anyone with an acquaintance, however passing, with the Persian literary tradition would recognize both of these words as having a specific resonance with one of the most famous Iranian novels ever written, which was authored by one of Daneshvar's near contemporaries, Sadeq Hedayat, in 1937. *Buf-e Kur*, translated in English by D. P. Costello in 1957 under the title *The Blind Owl*, is perhaps the most enduring modern Persian literary product, and the only Iranian novel that can be said to be part of a "world literary" tradition, à la Damrosch. Sadeq Hedayat, *Buf-e Kur* (Tehran: Elmi, 1316/1937). It is published in English as *The Blind Owl*, trans. D. P. Costello (New York: John Calder, 1957).

[43] In Iran, which is not a signatory to the Bern Convention or other international copyright agreements, there is no bar to a work being translated many times: consider, for example, Gabriel Garcia Marquez's *Love in the Time of the Cholera* or *One Hundred Years of Solitude*, both of which have been translated at least twice each, in spite of their relative newness when compared to works like *The Scarlet Letter*. Since Daneshvar, only one other translator has attempted to render *The Scarlet Letter* into Persian—more than sixty years after Daneshvar's attempt. The press and readers have largely ignored this translation, and Daneshvar's translation remains the canonical one.

Daneshvar, Simin. "Harf-e Akhar." Introduction to *Dagh-e Nang*. Kharazmi, 1369/1990.
Daneshvar, Simin. "Nataniyel Hawtorn va Asar-e U." Introduction to *Dagh-e Nang*. 3–8. Tehran: Nil, 1955.
Daneshvar, Simin. *A Persian Requiem*. Trans. Roxane Zand. New York: G. Braziller, 1992.
Daneshvar, Simin. *Savushun*. Tehran: Kharazmi, 1348/1969.
Daneshvar, Simin. *Savushun*. Trans. M. R. Ghanoonparvar. Washington, DC: Mage Publishers, 1990.
Daneshvar, Simin, and Jalal Al-e Ahmad. *Nameh-ha-ye Daneshvar va Al-e Ahmad (The Letters of Simin Daneshvar and Jalal Al-e Ahmad)*. Ed. Masud Jafari-Jazi. Tehran: Nilufar, 1383/2004.
Dimock, Wai Chee. *Through Other Continents: American Literature across Deep Time*. Princeton: Princeton University Press, 2009.
Einboden, Jeffrey. "Composing a Persian Letter: Simin Daneshvar's Rendition of Hawthorne." *Nathaniel Hawthorne Review* 34, nos. 1–2 (2008): 81–102.
Einboden, Jeffrey. "Harriet Beecher, from Beirut to Tehran: Raising the Cabin in the Middle East." In *Uncle Tom's Cabins: The Transnational History of America's Most Mutable Book*. Ed. Tracy C. Davis and Stefka Mihaylova. Ann Arbor: University of Michigan Press, 2018.
Einboden, Jeffrey. *The Islamic Lineage of American Literary Culture: Muslim Sources from the Revolution to Reconstruction*. Oxford: Oxford University Press, 2016.
Einboden, Jeffrey. *Nineteenth-Century US Literature in Middle Eastern Languages*. Edinburgh: Edinburgh University Press, 2013.
Farrokhzad, Forugh. *Another Birth*. Trans. Hassan Javadi and Susan Sallee. Emeryville: Albany Press, 1981.
Flaherty, Colleen. "L'œuf ou la Poule?" *Inside Higher Ed*, March 19, 2018. Web. Available at www.insidehighered.com/news/2018/03/19/mla-data-enrollments-show-foreign-language-study-decline (accessed June 15, 2020).
Hassan, Saleh D. "Enemies and Intimacies: Rethinking US-Middle East Cultural History." *American Literary History* 27, no. 4 (2015): 788–99.
Hawthorne, Nathaniel. *Dagh-e Nang*. Trans. Simin Daneshvar. Tehran: Nil, 1334/1955.
Hawthorne, Nathaniel. *Dagh-e Nang*. Trans. Simin Daneshvar. Tehran: Kharazmi, 1369/1990.
Hawthorne, Nathaniel. *Kizil Damga*. Trans. Z. Gülümser Ağırer Çuhadar. Istanbul: Arıon Yayınevi, 2002.
Hawthorne, Nathaniel. *The Scarlet Letter*. Ed. Leland S. Person. New York: W. W. Norton & Co., 2004.
Hawthorne, Nathaniel. *Zani ba Neshan-e Qermez*. Trans. Mohammad Sadeq Shariati. Tehran: Rowshangaran, 1383/2004.
Hedayat, Sadeq. *Buf-e Kur*. Tehran: Elmi, 1316/1937.
Hedayat, Sadeq. *The Blind Owl*. Trans. D. P. Costello. New York: John Calder, 1957.
Jondot, Jacqueline. Review of *Nineteenth-Century US Literature in Middle Eastern Languages*, by Jeffrey Einboden. *Transatlantica* 1 (2014). Web.
Kia, Mehrdad. "Persian Nationalism and the Campaign for Language Purification." *Middle Eastern Studies* 34, no. 2 (1998): 9–36.
Matthiesen, F. O. *American Renaissance: Art and Expression in the Age of Emerson and Whitman*. New York: Oxford University Press, 1941.
Milani, Farzaneh. *Veils and Words: The Emerging Voices of Iranian Women Writers*. Syracuse: Syracuse University Press, 1992.

Pease, Donald. "New Americanists: Revisionist Intervention into the Canon." *Boundary 2* 17, no. 1 (1990): 1–37.

Rowe, John Carlos. *The Cultural Politics of the New American Studies*. Ann Arbor: Open Humanities Press, 2012.

Spivak, Gayatri, and David Damrosch. "Comparative Literature/World Literature: A Discussion with Gayatri Chakravorty Spivak and David Damrosch." *Comparative Literature Studies* 48, no. 4 (2011): 455–85.

Tageldin, Shaden. "Untranslatability." American Comparative Literature Association's "State of the Discipline Report 2014–2015," March 3, 2014. Web. Available at https:// stateofthediscipline.acla.org/entry/untranslatability (accessed June 15, 2020).

Yin, Xiao-Huang. "The Scarlet Letter in China." *American Quarterly* 39, no. 4 (1987): 551–62.

Yothers, Brian. Review of *Nineteenth-Century US Literature in Middle Eastern Languages*, by Jeffrey Einboden. *Translation and Literature* 24, no. 1 (2015): 112–16.

13

World Literature as Persian Literature

Navid Naderi

Reality, however, went in the opposite direction.
— Quote that may be found in more than one place[1]

1

Nord und West und Süd zersplittern,	North and West and South up-breaking!
Throne bersten, Reiche zittern,	Thrones are shattering, Empires quaking;
Flüchte du, im reinen Osten	Fly thou to the untroubled East,
Patriarchenluft zu kosten,	There the patriarchs' air to taste!
Unter Lieben, Trinken, Singen	What with love and wine and song
Soll dich Chisers Quell verjüngen.	Chiser's fount will make thee young.
Dort, im Reinen und im Rechten,	There, 'mid things pure and just and true,
Will ich menschlichen Geschlechten	The race of man I would pursue
In des Ursprungs Tiefe dringen,	Back to the well-head primitive,
Wo sie noch von Gott empfingen	Where still from God did they receive
Himmelslehr' in Erdesprachen,	Heavenly lore in earthly speech,
Und sich nicht den Kopf zerbrachen.	Nor beat the brain to pass their reach.

Johann Wolfgang von Goethe
December 1814, translated by Edward Dowden[2]

When Goethe (1749–1832) was taking a spiritual flight to the East out of the Napoleonic Wars (1803–15), the first-person pronoun in his poem was not only

---

[1] I quote it from Kojin Karatani, *Nation and Aesthetics: On Kant and Freud*, trans. Jonathan Abel, Darwin Tsen, and Hiroki Yoshikuni (Oxford: Oxford University Press, 2017), 29.

[2] The quote is from the opening poem of "Moganni Name: Buch des Sänger," which is the first book of the *West-östlicher Divan*. The German text is quoted from Johann Wolfgang von Goethe, *West-östlicher Divan* (Stuttgart: Cottaischen Buchhandlung, 1819), 3; the English translation from Johann Wolfgang von Goethe, *West-Eastern Divan*, trans. Edward Dowden (London: J. M. Dent & Sons, 1914), 1. All quotations in the beginning of the following sections are from the same poem and the same editions.

inviting his addressee to another place but also to another time. The temporality of this flight *back in time to another place* is, of course, registered in the metaphors of "youth" and "depth" (*Tiefe*), but more significantly, it manifests itself in the sudden shift of tense in the second stanza (the present *dringen*, as opposed to the past tense *empfingen* and *zerbrachen*), as well as the tension between the spatial and temporal adverbs (*wo* and *noch*). John Weiss, the first English translator of the *West-östlicher Divan* (1819),[3] in his 1877 introduction to the book, which is mostly dedicated to a description of the tumultuous political atmosphere of "Germany" before, during, and after the Napoleonic Wars—as well as Goethe's "indifference" to national politics in general, even though he was thoroughly involved in it due to "personal friendships" and "with a shade of chagrin"[4]—invokes the same desire for spatiotemporal distance, as Goethe's main motivation not only in writing the *Divan*, but more generally, in dedicating his time to Oriental (and other sorts of scientific) scholarship: "The poet recoiled from this feeling of his own nation, and, as if to put as many degrees of *longitude* as possible between himself and the uproar of the *times*, he retreated into the study of the Chinese and other Oriental literatures."[5] And a few pages later: "he settled down in Teplitz and buried himself in Chinese, as if to put *two thousand years* between his mind and his country."[6] So, significantly opening his "Eastern Divan" with a poem titled "Hegire," the "Western author" was in fact inviting his readers to leave a war-torn Europe for a rejuvenating Orient, imagined as a place *in* time.[7]

As already signified by the French title of the opening poem, the way to this other time-space—at least for the early nineteenth-century German-speaking literati and intelligentsia—generally passed through the French (language). Goethe, too, as he explained himself in the last of his scholarly notes to the *West-östlicher Divan*, "was chiefly led into those areas" "under French escort [*Unter französischem Geleit*]"— referring mainly to Barthélemy d'Herbelot's *Bibliothèque orientale* (1697) with that military metaphor. "Oriental words and names," Goethe went on to explain, had entered the German language by way of French scholarship, and already "adapt[ed] ... to French pronunciation and phonic expectations." That is why, even though the German word "*Hedschra*" did exist at the time, Goethe—as the national "we" he invoked—"prefer[red] to say 'Hegire'" and found the French word "more pleasant and more familiar."[8] Not

---

[3] As indicated by the date of the first poem, Goethe had already begun writing the *West-östlicher Divan* in 1814.

[4] John Weiss, "Introduction," in *Goethe's West-Easterly Divan*, by Johann Wolfgang von Goethe, trans. John Weiss (Boston: Roberts Brothers, 1877), viii.

[5] Ibid., v. All italics are mine unless otherwise indicated.

[6] Ibid., xiv.

[7] Reference is to the frontispiece of the first German edition (1819), which gave a significantly different name to the book in Arabic: «الديوان الشرق للمؤلف الغربي», "The Eastern Divan by the Western Author."

[8] Johann Wolfgang von Goethe, *West-East Divan: The Poems, with "Notes and Essays": Goethe's Intercultural Dialogues*, trans. Martin Bidney (Albany: State University of New York Press, 2010), 287. Martin Bidney's 2010 translation is the first to include Goethe's original "Notes and Essays" in English. "Notes and Essays" has been translated together with Peter Anton von Arnim. In Bidney and Arnim's translation, the note referred to here is the penultimate note; it is the last note in the original German.

only did Goethe open his "Eastern Divan" in French, he also sealed it at the end with a dedication in German and Arabic to Silvestre de Sacy,[9] that is, his contemporary French philological authority whose work had allowed him to escape from the present time of the Napoleonic Wars to the very depths of the *Ursprung* in the "untroubled" East.

That all the four English translators of the *Divan* referenced here have decided to replace the French "Hegire" with the English "Hegira" (Weiss and Bidney), "Hejira" (Dowden), or "Hijra" (Rogers), doesn't say as much about their disregard for Goethe's preference, as it signifies the status of the English as the owners of another scholarly language who, like the French, "have reasonably acquired the right to pronounce and to write Oriental names in their way."[10] The leading role of the French and British philologists, however, should not have us forget the pan-European nature of Orientalist scholarship, to which, as is well known, many German Romantics contributed dearly. Orientalist scholarship, as a European phenomenon, provided the European imagination with a chronotope which, appropriating Goethe's words in his 1813 letter to Heinrich Meyer, would allow the man of letters to "rescue himself from the *present*."[11] Or in Elizabeth Dickinson Dowden's apt words, "in the epoch of the Byron *Welt-Schmerz*," Orientalist imagination would allow the European man of letters to take refuge in an "Indian summer," and be "free from all traces of self-torturings or of immersion in subjectivity."[12] The title of the opening poem of the *West-östlicher Divan* has more than often been read by means of this chronotope. Alexander Rogers, for example, writes that the title "signifies the flight of Goethe's spirit from the disturbed state of Europe, in which thrones were falling, etc., to the tranquil rest of the East."[13] That Rogers, who, as a late nineteenth-century official of the Indian Civil Service, definitely should have had a very different experience of "the East" than Goethe, would still describe "the East" as reveling in a state of "tranquil rest," says much about the imaginative power of this chronotope. Orientalist imagination made it possible—as it still does—to not only avoid the present time of Europe but also to close one's eyes on the present situation in the East. The Orient, in other words, as we should have already learned from Edward Said, is not really a place, but a commonplace, more exactly, a topos.

2

Wo sie Väter hoch verehrten,
Jeden fremden Dienst verwehrten;
Will mich freun der Jugendschranke:
Glaube weit, eng der Gedanke,

---

9 See Goethe, *West-östlicher Divan*, 555.
10 Goethe, *West-East Divan*, 287.
11 Cited in Weiss, "Introduction," xiv.
12 See her "Foreword" to Goethe, *West-Eastern Divan*, xvi.
13 Johann Wolfgang von Goethe, *Goethe's Reineke Fox, West-Eastern Divan, and Achilleid*, trans. Alexander Rogers (London: George Bell and Sons, 1890), 199 fn. 2.

Wie das Wort so wichtig dort war,
Weil es ein gesprochen Wort war.

Where ancestors were held in awe,
Each alien worship banned by law;
In nonage-bounds I am gladly caught—
Broad faith be mine and narrow thought;
As when the word held sway, and stirred
Because it was a spoken word.

Orientalist imagination introduced into the world the vision of a time arrested in a particular topos. Here I attempt to understand the conditions of possibility of this particular chronotopical configuration.

Michel Foucault describes the emergence of the modern *episteme* in the nineteenth century as a toppling of the "space of Western knowledge": the replacement of the horizontality of "taxonomia" with the "obscure verticality" of a "primitive and inaccessible nucleus, origin, causality, and history"—all figures of a somewhat mystical "depth," a "nether darkness," an *Ur*, from which "visible forms" emerge "in an already composed [read: reified, or in more Foucauldian terms, objectified] state, already articulated ... *with time*."[14] By way of a comparative consideration of the transformations of the "analysis of wealth" into "economics," "natural history" into "biology," and "general grammar" into "philology," Foucault describes the nineteenth-century process through which all these disciplines are reorganized—albeit to different and even opposing ends—according to a principle of inner historicity. Just in the same way that positing labor at the origin of all value enables "the possibility of a continuous historical time," because value is created and increased by way of "accumulation in series";[15] and just as life, understood as a violent, disintegrating force, opens "the being of things" up to an immanent death that comes from their interior darkness as a possibility of regeneration;[16] language too, in this period, acquires its own interior historicity. From this moment on, language, now conceived as a (reified) object, changes due, and according, to the operations of its own internal laws; and philology, whose "birth," according to Foucault, "has remained much more hidden from Western consciousness than that of biology and that of economics,"[17] is the name of the discipline that *posits and studies* those laws. In *The Order of Things*, however, Foucault uses the word "philology" as more or less synonymous with what is called "historical-comparative linguistics" today—hence his choice of Franz Bopp (1791–1867) as a representative figure. He further suggests that the modern conception of language as "the locus of tradition" was a "compensation for [the] demotion of language" to the

---

14 Michel Foucault, *The Order of Things: An Archaeology of the Human Sciences* (New York: Vintage, 1994), 251–2.
15 Ibid., 255.
16 Ibid., 278–9.
17 Ibid., 282.

status of an object of knowledge.[18] Historical-comparative linguistics itself, however, grew out of a broader notion of philology. Let us take our lead from the same text. As the modern division of (intellectual) labor—or again in more Foucauldian terms, the modern "[fragmentation of] the epistemological field"[19]—would have it, philology, Foucault tells us, developed alongside the particular "'philosophy' that suits it," which is not the same as the modern "philosophy" of economics or biology. Philology's particular philosophy is "a philosophy of cultures, of their relativity, and their individual power of expression."[20]

The emergence of the idea of cultures as self-coherent and expressive entities, as ultimately incomparable and relative phenomena that have to be evaluated according to their own inherent notions of the true, the beautiful, and the good, is generally associated with Romanticism, and particularly, with German Romanticism. In literary-historical terms, the emergence of this idea is understood as a reaction to the normative force exerted by French Classicism and Enlightenment universalism over the European World of Letters during the eighteenth and nineteenth centuries.[21] If cultures contain their own intrinsic criteria according to which their achievements have to be judged and evaluated, then it follows logically that they can neither be subordinated to each other, nor can there be any universal ideal of culture. What is universal is that *there is culture*. There can be no human community without culture. But the development of each community's culture is *proper* to itself, and is imagined as the temporal unfolding of that community's consciousness of itself as a human community. German Romantics conceived of this movement as the historical and organic poiesis of each community's "national spirit." "Poetry," in a broad sense that could include "all modes of civilized behavior," was imagined as the universal language of the human race, and what we call languages, imagined as the particular forms that this mother tongue of the human race has taken in the process of its historical unfolding.

The homogenizing force that Enlightenment rationality exerted over Europe, or really the World, was then taken to be aborting the historical unfolding of national spirits and thus withering "the most natural flowering of mankind's creative powers." "The Idea of the National Spirit"—all the bigotry it has historically caused aside—as the title of a 1955 essay by Erich Auerbach reminds us, is the very "Source of the Modern Humanities." That is, the source of our still—hopefully—current "hermeneutical

---

[18] Ibid., 297.

[19] Ibid., 346. That what Foucault calls the fragmentation of the epistemological field in the nineteenth century is translatable to the language of division of labor and its attendant notions of "alienation" and "reification" is perhaps best attested by Foucault's own description of the overlapping areas between the "three dimensions" of this now fragmented field: that all these dimensions ultimately meet in what is "mathematicizable" is not insignificant. See the section titled "The Three Faces of Knowledge" (344–8).

[20] Ibid., 279.

[21] See Erich Auerbach, *Time, History, and Literature: Selected Essays of Erich Auerbach*, ed. James I. Porter, trans. Jane O. Newman (Princeton: Princeton University Press, 2014), 57; Pascale Casanova, *The World Republic of Letters*, trans. M. B. DeBevoise (Cambridge, MA: Harvard University Press, 2004), 67–81.

perspectivism, on which all historical humanistic disciplines are based"; and it "explains the origins of the almost automatic expectation we now have ... that we understand the phenomena we study in terms of the specific assumptions of the times and social context out of which they arose." Philology in Auerbach's account grew out of "Romantic historicism," and not only did it give rise to the historical-comparative study of language, literature, and jurisprudence—and we should definitely add religion—but also to history itself: "history as a discipline," Auerbach does not hesitate to suggest, is a "product of historical philology, or if you prefer, of philology as history."[22]

The name of Johann Gottfried Herder (1744–1803) has become almost synonymous with this historicist, perspectival turn in the study of culture. And for Herder, everything began in the Orient, and with the "spoken word." Fascinated with the Hebrew Bible, which he conceived of as "Oriental poetry," Herder could still *hear* in it an "echo of the most ancient times." Hebrew, for him, conveyed, invisibly, a divine message to humanity that was really the same as that ancient echo. And it did so by the subtlest of devices, that is, by omitting the vowels from its alphabet. For Herder, the consonantal alphabet, which graphically leaves out the "primary and most vital" element of "all language" (i.e., the vowels), negatively mirrored the invisibility of the Abrahamic God.[23] What was not written down would in turn "[captivate] the ear" when read aloud—and reading aloud was of utmost importance for Herder. Indeed, he predicated the "art of writing" on the "art of hearing."[24] The fact that the Hebrew alphabet did not represent the vowels was thus turned by Herder into an occasion to assert the primacy of vocalized language, or the spoken word, as sensorially captivating. He thought, or maybe felt, that "nothing is more national [*nationeller*] and more individual as the pleasure of the ear."[25] Herder further sensibilized language by establishing a temporal relation between "word roots" and visual data: the older a language, the more "images and sensuous expressions" contained within its word roots.[26]

Like Enlightenment thinkers, Herder conceived of human history in terms of rational progress. He indeed saw humans as always-already capable of rationality, because they have always-already been capable of language, which for him was that which "sets limits and outline for the whole of human cognition"; and that which provides "the form of the sciences, not only in which, but also in accordance with which, thoughts take shape."[27] But he also saw the forward movement of reason as a progressive loss of sensory contact with "nature." "The oldest languages," of which Oriental languages including Hebrew, Arabic, Chinese, and Egyptian were prime examples, according to Herder were "formed immediately according to living nature."

---

[22] Auerbach, *Time, History, and Literature*, 56–9.

[23] Herder, cited in Maurice Olender, *The Languages of Paradise: Race, Religion, and Philology in the Nineteenth Century*, trans. Arthur Goldhammer (Cambridge, MA: Harvard University Press, 1992), 32.

[24] Herder, cited in John D. Baildam, *Paradisal Love: Johann Gottfried Herder and the Song of Songs* (Sheffield: Sheffield Academic Press, 1999), 84.

[25] Herder, cited in Baildam, *Paradisal Love*, 83.

[26] Olender, *The Languages of Paradise*, 33.

[27] Johann Gottfried Herder, *Herder: Philosophical Writings*, trans. Michael N. Forster (Cambridge: Cambridge University Press, 2002), 48–9.

They were directly addressed to the senses, more precisely, to the ear and the eye: "the first language painted ... : things which struck the senses through motion, for the ear; things which became intelligible through visual observation, for the eye." It was only later on that "modern languages" lost this original sensuality and came to be formed "according to arbitrary, dead ideas."[28] However, even in these modern languages, in "the case of all sensuous concepts," and also in literature, language remained, or really *ought to remain*, expressive.[29]

In Herder's text the Orient emerges as a site of what Kojin Karatani calls "sensibilization" or "aestheticization" of reason and language.[30] What runs *counter* to the Enlightenment in Herder's thought is not that he is anti-reason, but that he is against a certain universal notion of Reason (i.e., reason as linguistically and culturally unmediated). If reason is predicated on linguistic abstraction, and if each language has its own peculiar form of abstraction, that is, *originally* tied to the particular sensibility of that language, then there are as many forms of reason as there are human languages. Human rationality for Herder is located precisely in the same place as human sensibility, that is, in language-as-origin. That is why the only way "to *understand* ... far-off nations," or for that matter "times," is to "*sympathize*" with those nations and times.[31]

The human community of which Herder conceived most enthusiastically was of course not a community created through conscious association of free individuals who come together for a particular purpose; nor was it a community constituted in a particular historical situation. It was rather a community that had always-already been in formation—a community overdetermined by a spiritual essence that echoed backwards toward an aural darkness, just as it unfolded in plain sight. His concept of the *Volk* as the expression of this community "involved religion, nationality, culture, society, and politics, all bound together by a common language." So, language for Herder was not only an expression of some mystical notion of a poetic human nature but also "the primordial instrument of political association." And again "the Hebrews," whose poetics, he thought, was exactly the same as their politics, "were the quintessential *Volk*."[32] Grounding political community in a poetic notion of language which is at once the mystical locus of reason and sensibility, so that each member is rationally able to penetrate the depth of every other member's feelings, substantializes community in the form of the nation in the violent, nationalist sense of that term—which is our only sense of it anyway. The subject is objectively condemned to a community where everyone penetrates every other's inner sanctum: a community of language-as-unfolding-origin.

It is important, if we are to remain true to historical perspectivism, that this notion of poetico-political community is being thought precisely at the moment when commodity exchange and its concomitant calculating reason are on the verge

---

[28] Ibid., 60–1.
[29] Ibid., 48.
[30] See Karatani, *Nation and Aesthetics*, esp. 16–22.
[31] Olender, *The Languages of Paradise*, 40.
[32] Ibid., 37.

of dissolving the communal ties constituted by reciprocal exchange—and indeed as an early reaction to that dissolution. As Karatani writes, "the nation is nothing but an 'imagined' recovery of the community that was destroyed by the economy of commodity exchange."[33] The value attributed to the sensibilized spoken word also has to do with this imagined recovery. The rise of the vernaculars as national languages—so often described with sensory metaphors like "sweet"—is usually imagined as resulting from the national awakening of a people who insisted on their right to read and write in *their own* languages as opposed to the languages of learning in precapitalist world empires; but Karatani reminds us that the vernaculars themselves were "translated" from the *linguae francae* of world empires: it was Luther's translation, or as he called it *Verdeutschung*, of the Bible (1522 & 1534)[34] that made the establishment of High German as a national language possible. Herder was indeed sharply aware of this fact. Of Luther he wrote: "It was he who overturned academic verbiage, just like those moneychangers' tables"—and this, in John Baildam's words, had allowed "a whole nation ... to *think and feel*."[35] In order for the vernacular to become truly nationalized, then, its translational character (i.e., the fact of its having been *carried over* (translated) to the nation from the written language of the Empire) has to be mystified. The process of the nationalization of the vernacular "is complete ... when it is assumed [or imagined, or really, *felt*] to be derived directly from sentiments or interiority."[36] When a state is established, this mystification is institutionalized through national education. In this way, the community of language is "represented," primarily to itself, "as if [it] were older than [its] own origin, which is forgotten."[37]

Karatani reminds us that this imagined recovery of community in the form of the nation is not just a psychological compensation; rather, it is "imagination that mediates and synthesizes the state and market society." As I have already mentioned, *sympathy* was for Herder the only way to *understand* other nations. Sympathy, however, was a British economic notion that was aestheticized by the Germans beginning in the eighteenth century. For Adam Smith (1723–90), sympathy was the "moral sentiment" that allowed one to *imagine* oneself in the other's place. This, however, did not mean for Smith that one would penetrate the other's feelings; it would rather help one to "form some *idea* of his sensations." In other words, sentiment mediated by imagination would allow one to *understand* the other's situation. Having not witnessed the unprecedented

---

[33] Karatani, *Nation and Aesthetics*, 7. Just to prevent Romantic readings, I have to emphasize that "reciprocity" is a violent, and not at all egalitarian, form of exchange which keeps one infinitely indebted to others, and in which those with a higher power to give will occupy hegemonic positions that allow them to control the community politically and economically.

[34] The 1522 version includes only the New Testament; the 1534 version includes the old and the new testaments and the apocrypha.

[35] Baildam, *Paradisal Love*, 86.

[36] Karatani, *Nation and Aesthetics*, 26. In the same vein, Pascale Casanova has argued in the case of French that in order for the vernacular to assume the position and prestige of a national language it needed to be "enriched" by translating, "devouring," and otherwise appropriating the learned capital of Ciceronian Latin. See Chapter 2, "The Invention of Literature," in Casanova, *The World Republic of Letters*, 45–81. Also, see the section "Translation as *Littérarisation*."

[37] Karatani, *Nation and Aesthetics*, 7.

class difference that followed the rise in the rates of exploitation after the Industrial Revolution, Smith thought that given the working of moral sentiments, free exchange could help produce a moral world. What is important for our discussion, however, is the relation posited here between the *sentiment* and the *idea* mediated by *imagination*. Sentiments, regarded as deceptive premodernity, were thus elevated to another plane where they could be rationally productive. It was in the German language that this was formulated as a philosophical problem. There, an argument emerged that posited sentiment not only as rationally productive but also as "[exceeding] understanding and reason. This argument," Karatani tells us, "is called aesthetics." And even though this argument was critiqued by Kant, who tried to reestablish imagination as that which mediates between sensibility and understanding, it proved more forceful; and as we have already seen in the case of Herder, "the Romantic philosophers … began with the presupposition of the unity between nature and freedom, or subject and object." Of course, in Karatani's account too, "it was Herder, Kant's disciple, who first tried to overcome his master's dualism"[38] of subject and object. The point is, that when subject and object are one, political community is not something to be created, not even something to be consciously imagined, but an imaginary something that presents itself as *having always-already been* objectively real, that is, as substantial. Herder thought that folk-poetry was "the body of the nation [*Körper der Nation*]."[39] Romantic monism thus poeticizes political community and subsumes it under the form of the nation.

3

Will mich unter Hirten mischen,
An Oasen mich erfrischen,
Wenn mit Caravanen wandle,
Schawl, Caffee und Moschus handle.
Jeden Pfad will ich betreten
Von der Wüste zu den Städten.

Bösen Felsweg auf und nieder
Trösten Hafis deine Lieder,
Wenn der Führer mit Entzücken,
Von des Maulthiers hohem Rücken,
Singt, die Sterne zu erwecken,
Und die Räuber zu erschrecken.

Where shepherds haunt would I be seen,
And rest me in oases green;
When with the caravan I fare,

---

[38] Ibid., 11, 13, 16, 18, 20.
[39] Baildam, *Paradisal Love*, 88.

Shawl, coffee, musk, my chapman's ware,
No pathway would I leave untraced
To the city from the waste.

And up and down the rough rock ways
My comfort, Hafez, be thy lays,
When the guide enchantingly,
From his mule-back seat on high,
Sings, to rouse the stars, or scare
The lurking robber in his lair.

Just two days before his now famous pronouncement of national literature's loss of meaning and the coming of "the epoch of World literature," which seemed to Goethe to be "at hand," and thus "every one must strive to hasten its approach,"[40] in the evening of January 29, 1827, Goethe had another conversation with Johann Peter Eckermann (1792–1854). Frédéric Soret had been there and they had also been talking, in French, about the contemporary French poet Pierre-Jean de Béranger, the satirical character of whose poetry reminded Goethe of Horace and Hafez. After Soret's leaving, the conversation was carried on in German, and Goethe presented to Eckermann the final manuscript of *Helena*, an act of *Faust II* that was going to be published separately. Goethe mentioned that he had been working on this piece for a long time, but now he was happy to let it go "meet its proper destiny." He added that his "comfort [was] that the general culture of Germany stands at an incredibly high point; so that [he] need not fear that such a production will long remain misunderstood and without effect." Eckermann appreciated that there was "a whole antiquity" in Goethe's text, to which Goethe responded approvingly, adding that "the philologists will find work." Eckermann, who thought that the first going "forth into the world" of "the intellectual creation of a great master" was similar to "a newly built vessel ... first [going] to the sea," was, however, a little anxious, and not so much "about the antique part," than about "the modern romantic part" which he thought would make "heavy demands ... upon the reader," "for half the history of the world lies behind it." He was as if demanding that Goethe would add some explanatory notes to help his readers, and to help this intellectual vessel find its way in the world. Yet, Goethe thought that the difficulty would not be a problem: "It all appeals to the senses, and on the stage would satisfy the eye ... Let the crowd of spectators take pleasure in the spectacle; the higher import will not escape the initiated."[41]

When all communities of language are aestheticized and substantialized in the poetico-political form of the nation, then sympathy, which needs to be mediated by reason and conscious imagination, becomes the modality of international literary exchange. Within the nation, the work of art can "appeal to the senses." There, one

---

[40] Johann Peter Eckermann and Johann Wolfgang von Goethe, *Conversations with Eckermann: Being Appreciations and Criticisms on Many Subjects*, trans. John Oxenford (New York: M. Walter Dunne, 1901), 175.

[41] Eckermann and Goethe, 169–70.

does not need "sympathetic identification" with the other; one has always-already been identical with every other—even if in an unconsciously imaginary, that is illusory, or really mystical, way. But "historical sympathy ... *Einfühlung*," which Said characterizes as constitutive of "what today we call historicism," and as an "eighteenth-century element preparing the way for modern Orientalism," is the only way for "an outsider [to] penetrate" another culture, when "all cultures [are] organically and internally coherent, bound together by a spirit, genius, *Klima*, or national idea."[42] In this section, I will demonstrate how the *transnational*, that is to say *translational*, economy of such historicist sympathy has paved the way for the emergence of *both* National and World Literature as paradigms of literary study and creation.

That sympathetic identification with other textual traditions conceptualized as "literature" belonging to other "nations"[43] was as much literary and historical, as it was economic, is perhaps best attested to in Goethe's many economic metaphors in the *West-östlicher Divan*. Not only did Goethe, the coiner of *Weltliteratur*—whose *West-östlicher Divan* is an exemplary document of sympathetic identification—imagine himself, in those rather schmaltzy images, as an Oriental trader, but also, and more importantly, he conceived of his international literary and scholarly practice in terms of foreign trade. He wrote in the introduction to his "Notes and Essays for a Better Understanding of the *West-East Divan*"[44] that he

> would like best ... to be regarded as a traveler who will be worth hearing if he eagerly assimilates the ways of life of a strange country, tries to appropriate its forms of speech, and learns how to share views and comprehend customs. He will be forgiven if he succeeds only in part, if he still continues to be identifiable as a foreigner because of a distinctive accent or a resistant inflexibility in his national character [*unbezwinglichen Unbiegsamkeit seiner Landsmannschaft*] ... Also, to let his countrymen [*Seinigen*] enjoy more readily whatever he brings back, the traveler takes on the role of a merchant, who displays his goods appealingly and tries in many ways to make them pleasing [*übernimmt er die Rolle eines Handelsmanns der seine Waaren gefällig auslegt und sie auf mancherley Weise angenehm zu Machen sucht*].

Goethe was rather new to this sort of trade, which also had its own particular requirements. He mentioned in the same introduction that the *Divan* was different from all his previous, and apparently future, works in that it was the first time that he felt the need to add explanatory notes to his "little book." He had always "sent" his writings "into the world without a preface, without even indicating what they were intended for ... because [he] trusted that the nation [*die Nation*] would sooner or later make

---

[42] Edward W. Said, *Orientalism* (London: Penguin Books, 2003), 118. N.b. that *Klima* figures culture spatially.

[43] See Aamir R. Mufti, *Forget English!: Orientalisms and World Literatures* (Cambridge, MA: Harvard University Press, 2016).

[44] In the 1819 German edition, this section is simply called "Besserem Verständniß."

use of" them. But this time, even though with "regard to morality and aesthetics [*im Sittlichen und Aesthetischen*]" he had "made it [his] duty to keep this work within everyone's grasp," by "[using] the plainest language, the easiest, most understandable cadences of [his] vernacular [*Mundart*]," he still found it necessary to "clarify, explain, and illustrate, in every way [he] could think of, what would help readers attain immediate comprehension, even if they had little familiarity with the Orient." This was less than eight years before Goethe called upon everyone to hasten the approach of World Literature, and he was already in haste to make "a good immediate impression" on his folks [*Seinigen*].[45] He could not let the text be grasped differently by the "initiated" and the rest who might just be sensorially impacted. In fact, the sensory import itself needed philological mediation. The nation had to be philologically initiated into another sensorium. So, Goethe took it upon himself to do the work and help *trans-late* the nation to the "poet's land," which in this case was also "poetry's land."[46]

Even if Goethe was not following Herder's advice in adding the explanatory "Notes and Essays" to his *Divan*, his decision to do so was already anticipated by Herder's *Fragments: On Recent German Literature* (1767–8). There had been a crisis of German "genius" for a while by that time. Germany, as the late Pascale Casanova has described its dynamics persuasively, was suffering from acute shortage of literary capital under French literary domination.[47] Herder's book, mainly dealing with questions of translation, was a direct response to that situation, and written just when "the heat of the battle" between the representatives of French Classical taste (mainly represented through the figure of Gottsched) and the Moderns (of which Herder and Goethe were exemplary figures) had "passed," and it was the time "no longer to laugh, but to examine."[48] In an essay in the second collection of his *Fragments*, Herder reflected on the question of enriching German language and literature through Oriental import. The problem in the German literary space was the "lack of *originals*, of *geniuses*, of *inventors*," and among the German poems "some of [the] best [were] half-oriental [*halb Morgenländisch*]," and so became "original works [*werden sie Originale*]," if not *new* ones," through borrowing "*mores* and *taste* [*Sitten und Geschmack*]" from the people of the Morn," and providing "images, attitudes, and products of imagination *from afar*." This sense of *distance* is the main problematic that Herder's essay reflects on. If these half-Oriental poems, with all their shortcomings, *became* "original," it was because they were not reducible to imitation—and imitation, particularly from the French, was considered the plague of German literature. As the hyphen in the title of the essay, "On the German-Oriental [*Deutsch-Orientalischen*] Poets," already signifies, imitation

---

[45] Goethe, *West-East Divan*, 175–6.

[46] Goethe, *West-östlicher Divan*, 241.

[47] Casanova, *The World Republic of Letters*, 75–81.

[48] Johann Gottfried Herder, *Selected Early Works, 1764–1767: Addresses, Essays, and Drafts; Fragments on Recent German Literature*, ed. Ernest A. Menze and Karl Menges, trans. Ernest A. Menze and Michael Palma (University Park: Pennsylvania State University Press, 1991), 113. All italics in my citations of this text are in the original. The German text in brackets is taken from the 1767 edition, available online through "Deutsches Textarchiv."

was here "mixed with [German] *beliefs.*" The question, however, was whether German poets could pass the phase of imitation and begin to "emulate the people of the Morn" (i.e., to develop their own "original" poetry), and no more "mimic miserably."[49]

Distance caused aesthetic problems. For the Germans, to emulate the poetic originality of the Orient, sensual inspiration would not suffice—not least, because German "poetical sense" had become thoroughly philosophized, and even to be "stirred" Germans needed "contemplation." To simply imitate Oriental sensuality could only result in "ridiculous" poetry. Germans rather needed to *understand* and *explain* the Orient. To overcome the "historical and geographical" barriers, the German "public" needed "an endless commentary [*ewigen Commentar*]" that could act as a "telescope" to let them see "aspects of beauty" in Oriental poetry. To "translate and emulate" Oriental poetry, the German poet first needed to be able to "*explain*" their poetry on the basis of their national history [*Könnten wir doch nur erst ihre Gedichte aus ihrer Nationalgeschichte ganz erklären; alsdenn übersetzt und ahmt nach!*]." Orientalist philology here presented itself as a mode of importing originality into the German literary space. If Oriental studies could provide an *origin* for German literature, it was because the Orient itself was conceived as a reserve of original material. "All peoples of the Morn," Herder believed, "possess[ed] a rich abundance," or *overflow* [*einen sehr reichen Ueberfluß*], of "national assets [*Nationalvortheile*]," and due to their "sensuous" nature, they kept "[passing] down from the earliest times" what they had learned "with the first utterances of language." What the Germans could learn from the *study* of the Orient was the very principle of Romantic historicism: they could learn that "the taste of peoples," and also "of each *age*, grows precisely out of *mentality* and *mores*" of that people or time, and this could teach Germans to "study their [own] beliefs and the myths of the ancestors." The Orient was imagined precisely as a stockpile of tradition whose appropriation through rational understanding could bring about "a new epoch of [German] literature"[50]—and it did so, by bringing about, at the same time, the paradigm of *Weltliteratur.* But it was also precisely this stockpile of tradition that was later on gifted and sold to the colonized as a philological fund for self-Orientalization— that is, for *placing* oneself in a prior *time*.

Herder had begun his essay by acknowledging his critical debt to Johann David Michaelis (1717–91) whose philological labor had enabled Herder to write about the German-Oriental poets. Prior to this, in the seventh fragment of his first collection of *Fragments*, Herder had wished that Michaelis, who had a good "feeling for the East," should have also had a better sense of "versification." Now, in the seventh fragment of this essay, Herder "stated a *pium desiderium.*" What he desired was for "oriental philology which [had] flourished in our Germany for some time," to be "joined to taste." He desired the emergence of "a translator who is at once philosopher, poet, and philologist." This translator would then write a book for which Herder had already suggested an elaborate eighteenth-century style title: "Poetic translation of the poems

---

[49] Ibid., 171, 175, 186.
[50] Ibid., 176–81, 185–7.

of the Morn in which they are explicated on the basis of the land, the history, the attitudes, the religious life, the condition, the customs, and the language of their nation, and transplanted [*verpflanzt werden*] into the genius of our day [*unsrer Zeit*], our mentality, and our language." He even suggested parts of what should be written in its foreword. But most importantly, it would be this translator who "shall be the morning star in a new epoch of our literature!" He would translate Germany into literary originality by transplanting an origin into the "genius" of *its time*, which would then allow Germany to enter poetry's *land*, or the European space of letters, *on its own*, as it were. And even though this "origin" apparently belonged to a previous time, the work of this translator should allow the German nation to finally *come to know* this original nation that they "*ought to have known* face to face [*von Gesicht kennen sollten*]" (my emphasis).[51]

Here, philology emerges as a burning desire for understanding and closing distance, for global mystical interpenetration that unifies the world by rationally translating spatial distance into a sensibilized temporal hierarchy, and also as the historical site of all colonial mimicry. In the periphery of World Literature, we should do the critical work to insist, alongside Édouard Glissant, on our fundamental right to opacity[52]—not in any identitarian sense, but precisely as a universal right to untranslatability to the chronotope of colonial desire.[53]

4

The intellectual labor of the translator-philosopher-poet-philologist that Herder belatedly wished for—for he was already well on his way—is the condition of possibility of *both* National Literature, and its dialectical opposite, World Literature, as paradigms of literary study and creation. Because the work of this wished-for translator not only should have provided German literature with its own particular *historical* "origin," and thus should have set "apart the frontiers of foreign peoples from our own,"[54] but also should have carried German literature over into what Casanova calls the European literary *space*, as a literature that, having acquired its own particular "genius" (read: capital), could now compete with French and English literatures as the owners of most accumulated literary capital in Europe, which is to say, the World. The essay on German-Oriental poets was in fact part of a much larger literary-economic argument

---

51 Ibid., 117, 186–7.
52 See Édouard Glissant, *Poetics of Relation*, trans. Betsy Wing (Ann Arbor: University of Michigan Press, 1997).
53 The chronotope of colonial desire is basically the other side of what Aamir Mufti calls "the *chronotope of the indigenous*"—it is the same chronotope looked at from another angle. Mufti traces the chronotope of the indigenous back to William Jones (1746–94) and also to Herder, defining it as "spatiotemporal figures of habitation (in a place) in deep time" that yield "*a notion of indigeneity as the condition of culture*," in which "Orientalist theories of cultural difference are *grounded*" (Mufti, *Forget English!*, 74–5, 37).
54 Herder, *Early Works*, 187.

that was carried on by Herder in the European literary space, where he sided with Britain against France. And this argument contains an important reflection on the *planetary* economy of translation that allows national literatures to be established as such.

The general preamble to the argument is as follows: translation has been suggested as the most effective way to compensate for the shortage of literary capital in the German linguistic state. It has been suggested that the purpose of translation is to raise the reader in the target language "to the rank of an author and [turn] the little grocer into the merchant who really enriches the state." Generally, the idea is to translate from "a more perfect language" to enrich one's "mother tongue." Translating from a "superior language," that is "Greek and Latin," and also "a few more recent foreigners, whose genius is proven," will present the inferior target language with "concepts for which [it] must seek terms." This is of course profitable intellectually, yet also sensorially, because a "nicely shaped sentence" helps "the ear" to better appreciate "euphony." These recent foreigners with proven genius, Herder tells us, are "undoubtedly the French and the English." Herder's judgment is that Germans can gain much through translation from English, but all they have done so far has been bad translation. It even might be the case that Germans should "occupy the place [their] nation merits, to write the *prose of good common sense* and *philosophical poetry* ... when [they] cease to disfigure the finest English writers by translations." With regard to the French, there is almost "nothing to learn" from them. French is inferior to German with regard to "the barbaric in ... language, to the inversions, and to the meter," and also "with regards to order" and philosophical accuracy. There might only be place for some "French prose of social intercourse" and maybe some "critical observation concerning language."[55] With regard to Greek and Latin, things are a bit complicated, as there are syntactic problems in translating from Latin and metrical problems in translating from Greek, but of course there are things to be learned from them.

There is, however, another argument leveled against the idea that the emerging linguistic state should be enriched *only* through translating from presumably more advanced languages. Literature is made of language, Herder tells us, and languages originate in a sensory poetic situation and grow toward a prosaic philosophical state— as they gain in conceptual precision, they lose their expressive force. The German language, like other "European tongues," of course, "serve[s] contemplation more than the senses and the power of imagination." So, purely poetic forms of expression are rather unbecoming for it, and it needs a sort of literary prose that ought to be developed through "translation and reflection." Translation "borrows" new material, and "philosophical reflection" is used to "apply [them] frugally." Through translation "from the *sensuous* languages" the German language should acquire, within its "body," "new citizens" that are at the same time "foreign colonies" that "serve only to make up the shortcomings of [its] state." In this state, there is a certain clash of interest between the poet and the philosopher over the available "fund of words": the former

---

[55] Ibid., 118–19, 128, 134, 136, 145, 149, 150.

needs a "rich" language and the latter wishes to get rid of the "excesses" ("*synonyms …
metaphors … figurative* words, *inversions, and idioms*"). This is basically the clash of
interest between Enlightenment universalism and national particularism: a language
that loses its excesses, loses its "particularity." So, in this regard, it is similar to the
rule of French taste in Germany (and, as Casanova has argued, all over Europe): it is
the same as telling someone they "cannot become a writer" if they have "not read the
ancients"—it deprives the nation of originality, of the "patronymic beauties … woven
into the genius of [its] language." What also distinguishes the English writers (and even
the Swiss), and most important among them, Shakespeare, is precisely their relation to
such national reserves of beauty.[56]

   Herder's seventh fragment, to which he would later refer in his essay on German-
Oriental poets, is a reflection on the planetary economy of literary translation at the
dawn of colonial market capitalism. To emphasize the economic import, or excess,
of this fragment, I will cite it from two different English translations, always opting
for the one that prefers the strong economic reading.[57] As already mentioned, Herder
holds, as do many others, that the sensory and poetic "riches" of a language diminishes
as its philosophical "accuracy" grows.[58] Now, the difference between the "oldest"
languages, such as "Hebraic or Arabic," and European languages, is comparable to
the difference of the "domestic economies [*Haushaltung*] of those regions and ours."[59]
While the former are mainly slaveholding, cattle economies, the latter "*bourgeois*
world's*" economy is predicated on the accumulation of "gold and household goods."[60]
Thus, while the language of the former is "rich in *livestock*," the language of the
latter whose "gentlemen" pay no attention to "shepherds' knowledge" and whose
"natural philosophers live among … Latin books"[61] is replete with "technical terms
[*Kunstwörter*]"[62] and "bourgeois expressions [*bürgerliche Ausdrücke*]." This economic
difference explains why, for example, a Robert Lowth would characterize the use of
"*synonyms*" in Oriental poetry as "tautologies." In fact, they are not tautologies, but
they each add a new "color" to what was said, and make "the presented picture new with
nuances." But "our philological *prophet* in Oriental languages"[63] does not understand
this because he, like the "frugal [*haushälterische*] philosopher"[64] who wants to "give
most idle synonyms work and determinate posts," finds the slavish synonyms excessive
even in poetry. He does not understand that poetry, unlike bourgeois philosophy,

---

56 Ibid., 105–7, 109–12.
57 These are Ernest Menze and Michael Palma's translation in Herder, *Early Works*, 114–18, and
    Michael Forster's translation in Herder, *Philosophical Writings*, 33–7. All italics are in the originals.
    The justification for citing the text from two different translations lies in Herder's line of argument
    about synonyms and nuances.
58 Herder, *Early Works*, 114.
59 Herder, *Philosophical Writings*, 33.
60 Herder, *Early Works*, 115.
61 Herder, *Philosophical Writings*, 33.
62 Herder, *Early Works*, 115.
63 Herder, *Philosophical Writings*, 34–5.
64 Herder, *Early Works*, 118.

does not always want to compartmentalize words under concepts. The poet rather "lives from *superfluity* [*er lebt vom Ueberfluß*]" and given the pastoral origins of his profession, he can always accumulate more labor force.

Herder's final judgment on this conflict of linguistic interest within the German linguistic state, is that even though conceptual exactitude is not to be given up as an ideal—it is at the end the "nature" of the German language—the "philological philosopher [*philologische Weltweise*] … must not become a legislator *throughout*." Because, first of all, such a philosophical ideal cannot be imposed on "everyday language," which will keep using what the "grammatical philosopher" will throw out. Secondly, that will lead to a sort of civil war with the "furious" poet who will not accept philosophical "jurisdiction" over his "land,"[65] not least because under such jurisdiction "*fine* prose and *fine* poetry [*Poesie*] disappear," and "everything turns into a rosary of calculated technical terms [*abgezählter Kunstwörter*]." Lastly, such total jurisdiction of abstract language will cause a radical aesthetic crisis: both excessive poetic words and exact concepts are "coined deliberately,"[66] and also "enter general circulation"[67] "on the basis of a deliberately set value [*Beide werden willkührlich geprägt, und durch einen willkührlich festgesetzten Werth gäng und gäbe*]."[68] So, none could claim a higher ground because they are both ultimately based on (the same) will. Now, if a language "strives to collect instead of slaves, [only] gold and coins," when the "imagined value" [*eingebildete Werth*] of a word, that is, the willfully decided value on the basis of which it has gained its worth in general circulation, "evaporates," the only thing that remains for it will be its "natural value"[69]—that is, it becomes a slave, a synonym that should be either assigned to another fixed position, or it could be poetically twisted: made new with nuance [*mit Nebenzügen neu Gemachte*]. Yet, since the overconceptualization, or compartmentalization, of language deprives it of the necessary overflow of words—or to use a more apt metaphor, the "sanguine ferment"[70] of its *national assets*—that language will gradually lose its poetico-political force and would not be able to renew its fund of words with nuances. In that situation, not only poetry but also philosophy would be at a loss (even though Herder seems to be caring only about poetry here). Because such a loss of currency happens not only to sensory words but also to abstract concepts, which when their imaginative value evaporates, "only count insofar as

---

[65] Herder, *Philosophical Writings*, 35–7.
[66] Herder, *Early Works*, 117–18.
[67] Herder, *Philosophical Writings*, 36.
[68] Herder, *Early Works*, 118.
[69] Herder, *Philosophical Writings*, 36–7.
[70] Herder, *Early Works*, 178. On the vital relation of "sanguine ferment" to nation, state, and capital, see Gil Anidjar, *Blood: A Critique of Christianity* (New York: Columbia University Press, 2014). Anidjar's analysis of the history of Christianity is also the source of my use of the word "mystical" throughout this chapter (see particularly his conceptualization of *corpus mysticum* in relation to the Eucharistic transformation of "community" into the "nation" as an inseparable part of the cerberean formation of nation-state-capital).

one can represent them sensually"[71]—let's say, in our terms today, they become sexy theoretical concepts, tantalizing, but with no real, that is to say consciously imagined, conceptual import.

Philological Orientalism, then, emerges through Herder's reflection on the *planetary* economy of translation, as a sort of *rationally* justifiable slave trade to keep "lively" the overabstracted, philosophized, or more precisely, reified languages of the bourgeois world, and most importantly their traditions of "*fine* prose and *fine* poetry." It mirrors, metaphorically, the *necessity* of manual labor in order to provide the material basis for intellectual labor to be able to continue *separating* itself from the material conditions of its own possibility, that in turn makes the division and compartmentalization of *both* manual and intellectual labor into abstractly organized units possible.[72] The idea of a properly universal reason that was formerly suppressed in the interest of aestheticized national languages thus here returns as that which mediates translational, that is to say transnational, capital.[73] This *conception* of the philological enterprise cannot be considered a German peculiarity. As Aamir Mufti has argued, German Orientalism cannot be conceived of as radically different from the French and British Orientalist traditions, assuming that Germany has been a latecomer to "imperial experience." It has definitely been shaped to certain degrees according to the particular *raison d'état* of the German (linguistic) state. But as the translational exchange relations exemplified in the word choices of both Goethe and the English translators of his "Hegire" demonstrate, "imperial experience" itself was an object of exchange in modern Europe. As Mufti has it, "Modern Orientalism emerged from the very beginning as a continent-wide network and system of relays," and in the eighteenth and nineteenth centuries it should be regarded as a "multiple, but simultaneously singular, and pan-European" enterprise.[74] I would like to further stress, alongside Mufti, that "first of all, 'world literature' is a *concept*."[75] That is to say, the *sensuous image* through which it represents itself as the

---

[71] Herder, *Philosophical Writings*, 37.

[72] See Max Horkheimer and Theodor Adorno's reading of the *Odyssey*, the most philological fragment of their *Dialectic of Enlightenment: Philosophical Fragments*, ed. Gunzelin Schmid Noerr, trans. Edmund Jephcott (Stanford: Stanford University Press, 2002), 35–62. NB the episode of the Sirens' island.

[73] It is also noteworthy that a good part of Herder's celebrated essay on Shakespeare that was originally published in *Von deutscher Art und Kunst* (1773)—a historically important volume cowritten with Goethe and Justus Möser against the reign of French taste—is dedicated to an argument against the Classical ideal of the unity of time and place in drama, which Herder argued was not at all a Greek idea, yet that the French who did not understand their own historical difference from the Greek had invented it. Shakespeare's disregard for the unities of time and place, however, is compared at the crux of that argument with "Mahomet's dream," referring to the narrative of Meʿraj, which demonstrates how the "soul create[s] its own space, world, and time, however and wherever it wishes." This sudden surfacing of "Mahomet's dream" *as a literary example* that defies the principles of French aesthetics, in the middle of an essay on Shakespeare, that is written to establish the right of Germany to its own national literature, points to the *vital* role that translational Orientalist capital played in determining the fate of European rivalries (Johann Gottfried Herder, *Selected Writings on Aesthetics*, trans. Gregory Moore [Princeton: Princeton University Press, 2006], 304–5).

[74] Mufti, *Forget English!*, 66–7.

[75] Ibid., 10.

ideal of a (mystically) unified literary stage on which each nation sings its own songs, cannot, and should not, be mistaken for its material reality; that is, the *real abstract force* that it exerts on *worldly* textual traditions by organizing them into so many "national literatures" as the expressive literary traditions of the world of the nation-states.

To give an aesthetic twist to one of the lines of Mufti's argument throughout *Forget English!*, Orientalist philology, as the condition of possibility of World Literature, is that which *abstractly* organizes the world into a civilizational assembly of fundamentally *partitioned* and *sensibilized* nations, which can then in turn be joined together through exchange relations. Thus, each time we encounter the harmonious image of a global fraternity, we ought to remember that "the *totality* within which we live, and which we can *feel* in each of our social actions, is conditioned not by a direct 'togetherness' encompassing us all, but by the fact that we are *essentially divided* from each other through the *abstract* relationship of exchange."[76] Thus, secondly, to continue with Mufti, World Literature is "fundamentally a concept of exchange, in other words, a concept of bourgeois society" that functions to establish an *abstract* "plane of equivalence" through which not only historically different "practices of writing" become exchangeable as tokens of the same reified object (i.e., "literature"), but also those practices themselves become similar, or better, standardized, through these very abstract relations of exchange.[77] Thus, if that plane of equivalence is not problematized in every study of world literatures, then World Literature as a scholarly (and creative) paradigm functions to mystify the realities of exchange relations in an *essentially* unequal world.[78]

5

Inversions in language are as necessary as asymmetry in painting and dissonance in music.

Herder, out of context

Just like his contemporary Goethe who had to provide an index to help his readers with the "unavoidable foreign words,"[79] Fath-Ali Akhundzadeh (1812–78) too had to preface his *Kamal-od-Dowleh's Letters to Prince Jalal-od-Dowleh* (ca. 1863) with a glossary to "explain [*sharh*]" some words "in the languages of the West [*farangestan*]" that "proved very difficult to translate to an equivalent in the language of Islam [*keh tarjomeh-ye*

---

[76] Theodor W. Adorno, *Introduction to Sociology*, ed. Christoph Gödde, trans. Edmund Jephcott (Stanford: Stanford University Press, 2000), 43. My emphases.

[77] Mufti, *Forget English!*, 10–11. On World Literature as a modality of "standardization," see Mufti's chapter on Auerbach and Said, pp. 203–42.

[78] Herder is commonly read as a figure of "Counter-Enlightenment," yet given the return of abstract calculative reason in his thought when it comes to international trade, we would be better off to read him as a figure of the mythological, and this time also mystical, return of the Enlightenment.

[79] Goethe, *West-East Divan*, 176.

motabeq-e anha dar zaban-e eslam besyar doshvar minomud]." He thus transliterated those words "exactly, into the letters of Islam [*horuf-e eslam*]" and provided a commentary to "inform" his "readers of their original concept [*asl-e mafhum*]." This list of words, alongside some others, also included *literator* ("literature") and *poˈezi* ("poetry"). He defined the first as "all sorts of compositions in prose or in verse [*har now˙ tasnifat ast nasran ya nazman*]," and the latter as

> such writing [*ensha*] that should include the expression [*bayan*] of a person or a people's [*tayefeh*] ways and mores [*ahval va akhlaq*] as it befits them, or that it explains a subject [*matlab*], or that it describes the situation of the natural world [*bar vasf-e owzaˈe alam-e tabiˈat*], in verse and with utmost beauty and effect [*dar kamal-e jowdat va taˈsir*].[80]

That there were no readily available concepts of "literature" and "poetry" in "the language of Islam"—which itself had to be *translated* to "the Persian language" as a national language; and that these concepts were not simply translatable to *adab* and *sheˈr*, and needed to be explained and understood; and also that this was a translational act to establish a philological ("all sorts of compositions") and Romantic ("expression of") concept of "literature" and "poetry" should be evident. What may need emphasizing is that there is *no* Persian literature that is not already World Literature, for the simple fact that there is no Persian *literature*, no matter from what time, which has already not been trans-lated to the universalized Romantic *category* of Literature, or really "poetry," which is understood as the universal language of human race that manifests itself as particular expressions of the numerable and finite national souls of the world—in other words, there is no Persian literature which has not been trans-lated to Literature as a nationally divided, planetary institution.

Casanova reads "the first enlargement of literary space to include the European continent as a whole," as the result of what she calls "The Herderian Revolution." This is because Herder's concepts of language and literature not only provided Germany with the most effective arguments against French literary hegemony, but "the theoretical basis" that he provided soon spread all over Europe and caused the emergence of what Casanova calls "The Herder Effect." Herder's theories provided the *philosophical capital* on which base maybe "the politically dominated territories in Europe" could later on "invent their own solutions to the problem of cultural dependence"; yet contrary to Casanova's claim, such a thing did not happen "elsewhere."[81] In the periphery of world literature, we witness an inverted Herder effect, which causes and furthers cultural dependence. If for Herder the invention and development of a properly national German literature as the way out of the hegemony of French taste and Enlightenment universalism passes through the rejection of bourgeois values and the call to cultivate livestock and shepherds' knowledge, inventing a properly national literature for Akhundzadeh is a necessary condition of "progress" in order to join the "civilized"

---

[80] Fath-Ali Akhundzadeh, *Maktubat*, ed. Baqer Moˈmeni (n.p., 1350/1971), 10–11.
[81] Casanova, *The World Republic of Letters*, 75

(i.e., the bourgeois) world. If, following Michael Löwy and Robert Sayre, we grasp European Romanticism "*in nuce*" as the opposition of "qualitative values ... to the reign of exchange value,"[82] we see a complete inversion of this principle in Iran. If European "Romanticism represents a critique of ... modern capitalist civilization in the name of values and ideals drawn from the past,"[83] Akhundzadeh is at pains to show that despite its present degeneration, the Iranian past is imbued with contemporary values of the progressed bourgeois civilization. He invokes the values of the "national" past, uses Voltaire as a role model, and also calls for "Protestantism [*porotestantizm*] in the religion of Islam" in order to free the Muslim community's time so that they can work more, because they spend too much time praying.[84] For Akhundzadeh, there is no contradiction between the acceptance of Enlightenment universalism and calculative reason, the imitation of French literary models, and the call to invent national literatures. The task of national literature for him is precisely to cultivate bourgeois values.[85]

Conceiving of Persian literature as a national literature becomes possible only through explicit reference to world literature as a bourgeois concept of exchange. This particular conception is evident in one of the most important nationalist histories of Persian literature. Zabihollah Safa opens his monumental *History of Literature in Iran* (1953–91) by situating this literature within the context of world literature, that is, within the context of the world of the nation-states. "Among the old nations of the world," Safa declares in his 1953 preface to the book, "Iranians" are distinguished for having "a continuous literary existence and various beautiful works in different dialects [*lahjeh*]," in all of which

> the light of the creative soul and brilliant Iranian thought is evident and apparent ... Among these innumerable works, many are the most beautiful consequences of the genius of the Iranian race [*natayej-e qariheh-ye nezhad-e irani*], and some may be counted among the best masterpieces of literature and thought in the whole world [*behtarin shahkar-ha-ye adab va fekr dar sarasar-e alam*]. Is there anyone who is not aware of the global value [*arzesh-e jahani*] of Ferdowsi's *Shahnameh*, the *Rubaiyyat* of Khayyam, the *Masnavi* of Mowlavi, and the *ghazal*s of Hafez? And there might be other innovative [*badi'*] works that would be enumerated among these great works should they be presented, as they ought to, to the world's knowledge [*ke agar chonan ke bayad dar ma'raz-e elm va ettela'-e jahaniyan qarar girad dar shomar-e inguneh asar-e bozorg dar-ayad*].[86]

[82] Michael Löwy and Robert Sayre, *Romanticism against the Tide of Modernity*, trans. Catherine Porter (Durham: Duke University Press, 2001), 15.

[83] Ibid., 17.

[84] Akhundzadeh, *Maktubat*, 144.

[85] This is only one in a series of Romantic inversions that I am further discussing in a forthcoming essay on "national allegory."

[86] Zabihollah Safa, *Tarikh-e Adabiyat dar Iran va dar Qalamrow-e Zaban-e Parsi* [*A History of Literature in Iran and in the Territory of the Persian Language*], 15th ed., vol. 1 (Tehran: Ferdows, 1378/1999 [1332/1953]), first page of the author's preface, np.

"Global value" is the highest form of value within the hierarchy of literary value, and its acquisition is predicated on acknowledgment by "the world"—or on its being consecrated by world literary authorities, as Casanova has it. The very worth of national literature is ultimately determined by the planetary economy of translation, which is constitutive of world literature. Future literary growth, even of the "classical" national assets, is dependent on global recognition of (old) innovations. If German literature needed the philological import of "original" literary material to trans-late itself into the space of literary originality and innovation, Persian literature's acquisition of literary value, even on a national level, is dependent on its being imported into the philological process of production and accumulation of translational literary capital (today, its "Persian-studization"), and then again imported back into the national space with added world literary value. That is to say, Hafez, Ferdowsi, and Mowlavi's national value is not at all independent of the world literary value of *Hafiz*, *Firdawsi*, and *Rumi* (think of the importation and exportation of crude oil and gasoline as a point of reference).

Bibliography

Adorno, Theodor W. *Introduction to Sociology*. Ed. Christoph Gödde. Trans. Edmund Jephcott. Stanford: Stanford University Press, 2000.

Akhundzadeh, Fath-Ali. *Maktubat*. Ed. Baqer Mo'meni. n.p., 1351/1971.

Anidjar, Gil. *Blood: A Critique of Christianity*. New York: Columbia University Press, 2014.

Auerbach, Erich. *Time, History, and Literature: Selected Essays of Erich Auerbach*. Ed. James I. Porter. Trans. Jane O. Newman. Princeton: Princeton University Press, 2014.

Baildam, John D. *Paradisal Love: Johann Gottfried Herder and the Song of Songs*. Sheffield: Sheffield Academic Press, 1999.

Casanova, Pascale. *The World Republic of Letters*. Trans. M. B. DeBevoise. Cambridge, MA: Harvard University Press, 2004.

Eckermann, Johann Peter, and Johann Wolfgang von Goethe. *Conversations with Eckermann: Being Appreciations and Criticisms on Many Subjects*. Trans. John Oxenford. New York: M. Walter Dunne, 1901.

Foucault, Michel. *The Order of Things: An Archaeology of the Human Sciences*. New York: Vintage, 1994.

Glissant, Édouard. *Poetics of Relation*. Trans. Betsy Wing. Ann Arbor: University of Michigan Press, 1997.

Goethe, Johann Wolfgang von. *Goethe's Reineke Fox, West-Eastern Divan, and Achilleid*. Trans. Alexander Rogers. London: George Bell & Sons, 1890.

Goethe, Johann Wolfgang von. *West-East Divan: The Poems, with "Notes and Essays": Goethe's Intercultural Dialogues*. Trans. Martin Bidney. Albany: State University of New York Press, 2010.

Goethe, Johann Wolfgang von. *West-Eastern Divan*. Tran. Edward Dowden. London: J. M. Dent & Sons, 1914.

Goethe, Johann Wolfgang von. *West-östlicher Divan*. Stuttgart: Cottaischen Buchhandlung, 1819.

Herder, Johann Gottfried. *Herder: Philosophical Writings*. Trans. Michael N. Forster. Cambridge: Cambridge University Press, 2002.

Herder, Johann Gottfried. *Selected Early Works, 1764–1767 : Addresses, Essays, and Drafts; Fragments on Recent German Literature*. Ed. Ernest A. Menze and Karl Menges. Trans. Ernest A. Menze and Michael Palma. University Park: Pennsylvania State University Press, 1991.

Herder, Johann Gottfried. *Selected Writings on Aesthetics*. Trans. Gregory Moore. Princeton: Princeton University Press, 2006.

Horkheimer, Max, and Theodor W. Adorno. *Dialectic of Enlightenment: Philosophical Fragments*. Ed. Gunzelin Schmid Noerr. Trans. Edmund Jephcott. Stanford: Stanford University Press, 2002.

Karatani, Kojin. *Nation and Aesthetics: On Kant and Freud*. Trans. Jonathan Abel, Darwin Tsen, and Hiroki Yoshikuni. Oxford: Oxford University Press, 2017.

Löwy, Michael, and Robert Sayre. *Romanticism against the Tide of Modernity*. Trans. Catherine Porter. Durham: Duke University Press, 2001.

Mufti, Aamir R. *Forget English!: Orientalisms and World Literatures*. Cambridge, MA: Harvard University Press, 2016.

Olender, Maurice. *The Languages of Paradise: Race, Religion, and Philology in the Nineteenth Century*. Trans. Arthur Goldhammer. Cambridge, MA: Harvard University Press, 1992.

Safa, Zabihollah. *Tarikh-e Adabiyat dar Iran va dar Qalamrow-e Zaban-e Parsi* [*A History of Literature in Iran and in the Territory of the Persian Language*]. 15th ed. 5 vols. Vol. 1. Tehran: Ferdows, 1378/1999.

Said, Edward W. *Orientalism*. London: Penguin, 2003.

Weiss, John. "Introduction." In *Goethe's West-Easterly Divan*, by Johann Wolfgang von Goethe. Trans. John Weiss. Boston: Roberts Brothers, 1877.

Contributors

Mostafa Abedinifard is Assistant Professor without Review of Persian Literary Culture and Civilization in the Department of Asian Studies at the University of British Columbia, Canada. With particular attention to Persian and Iranian literatures and cultures, Mostafa is interested in cultural historiography and comparative literature, focusing on (Global South) critical and literary theory, social justice, critical diversity matters, and Islam. Mostafa's articles have appeared in several refereed journals, such as *Asian Cinema, The British Journal of Middle Eastern Studies, HUMOR: International Journal of Humor Research, Social Semiotics*, and *de genere: Journal of Literary, Postcolonial and Gender Studies*.

Omid Azadibougar is Professor of Comparative Literature and Translation at Hunan Normal University, China. He is the author of *The Persian Novel: Ideology, Fiction and Form in the Periphery* (2014) and *World Literature and Hedayat's Poetics of Modernity* (2020).

Gay Jennifer Breyley is a senior research fellow in the Faculty of Arts at Monash University, Australia, and the convener of the Central and West Asia and Diasporas Research Network. She has published widely in the fields of Iranian Studies, literature, and music.

Olga M. Davidson is a research fellow of the Institute for the Study of Muslim Societies and Civilizations, Boston University, United States. From 1992 to 1997 she was Chair of the Concentration in Islamic and Middle Eastern Studies at Brandeis University, and since 1999 she has been Chair of the Board, Ilex Foundation. Her books, *Poet and Hero in the Persian Book of Kings* (1994) and *Comparative Literature and Classical Persian Poetry* (2000), have been translated into Persian and distributed in Iran. Her papers have appeared in *Bulletin of the Asia Institute* and *Journal of the American Oriental Society*, and in many volumes on Persianate literatures and cultures.

Naghmeh Esmaeilpour is a PhD student at Humboldt University of Berlin in PhD-Net, "Das Wissen der Literatur." She earned both her BA and MA degrees in English Language and Literature in, respectively, 2006 and 2011 from Islamic Azad University, Karaj, Iran. Her work on comparative literature has appeared in *Dehkhoda Persian Language and Literature Quarterly* and *Current Objectives of Postgraduate American Studies*. In 2016, she was a visiting scholar at Harvard University for a semester, and since August 2017 her research has been funded by a scholarship of the

Friedrich-Ebert Foundation. Her research interests are Comparative Literature in the global context with a focus on contemporary Persian Literature, and interdisciplinary study of literature (narrative mobility, transfictionality, and transmediality) in comparison with other art forms such as film, photography, painting, and video games. Persian literature, the effects of (global) media culture on people's lives, literature and film, mobility, and narrative theory.

Alexandra Hoffmann is a PhD candidate in Persian Language and Literature at the University of Chicago, United States. Her dissertation focuses on masculinities and male bodies in Persianate literature from the tenth to the sixteenth century.

Amir Irani-Tehrani is the Persian Program Director at West Point Military Academy's Department of Foreign Languages.

Adineh Khojastehpour is a PhD candidate in Film Studies at the University of New South Wales, Australia. Her current research focuses on the significance of cross-cultural adaptations in the development of resistance strategies in Iranian cinema. Her work on the interdisciplinary relations of literature and cinema has appeared in *Literature/Film Quarterly*.

Sam Lasman is a humanities teaching fellow in the Department of Comparative Literature at the University of Chicago, United States, where he earned his PhD in 2020. His research focuses on speculative fiction in the global Middle Ages, with particular attention to the Islamicate world and Northwestern Europe.

Amy Motlagh is Associate Professor of Comparative Literature and Middle East/ South Asia Studies, and the inaugural Bita Daryabari Presidential Chair in Persian Language and Literature at UC Davis. Motlagh's first book was *Burying the Beloved: Gender, Fiction and Reform in Modern Iran* (Stanford University Press, 2012) and her other publications focus on topics including Iranian cinema, genre and narrative, ideologies of gender and race, and life-writing in the Iranian diaspora. Her translation of Zoya Pirzad's *Yek ruz mandeh beh eyd-e pak* has been published as *The Space Between Us* (Oneworld Publications, 2014).

Navid Naderi is an independent scholar residing in Tehran, Iran. His research is focused on philology, translation, and contemporary Persian literature.

Laetitia Nanquette is Senior Lecturer at the University of New South Wales, Australia. Her first book, *Orientalism versus Occidentalism: Literary and Cultural Imaging between France and Iran Since the Islamic Revolution*, was published in 2013. Her second book, *Iranian Literature after the Islamic Revolution: Production and Circulation in Iran and in the World*, was published in 2021. She regularly travels to Iran for research fieldwork and translates contemporary Persian literary texts.

Marie Ostby is Assistant Professor of English and Global Islamic Studies at Connecticut College, USA. Her research focuses on modern and contemporary Iranian literature and its global circulation. Her current book project, *The Global Genres of Modern Iran: From Travelogues to Twitter*, uses the interwoven modern histories of Persian and Euro-American literature, art, and film to explore how transnational literary exchange under politically fraught circumstances is often mirrored in the crossing of genre boundaries.

Abdulla Rexhepi is Professor of Persian Literature and Islamic Culture at the University of Prishtina, Kosovo. His main areas of interest are Islamic and Persian cultural heritage in the Balkans and Albanian lands. He is the author of *The Prevalence of Persian Literature among Albanians* (2019), a coeditor of *İran Düşünce Tarihi* (2019), a coeditor of *Critical Reading of Text: Modern Hermeneutics of Islamic Reason* (2019), and the author of *Naim Frashëri and Persian Literature* (2020).

Levi Thompson is Assistant Professor of Arabic in the Department of Asian Languages and Civilizations, University of Colorado Boulder, United States. Levi teaches courses on modern Middle Eastern literatures and cultures, and is currently working on a book manuscript tentatively titled *Re-Orienting Modernism: Mapping a Modernist Geography across Arabic and Persian Poetry*. He has published articles in the journals *Middle Eastern Literatures*, *Transnational Literature*, *Alif*, and *College Literature*, and his translations of poetry from the Middle East have appeared in *Jadaliyya*, *Transference*, *Inventory*, and elsewhere.

Amirhossein Vafa is Assistant Professor of English and Comparative Literature at Shiraz University, Iran, and the author of *Recasting American and Persian Literatures* (2016). Amirhossein's recent research has been twofold, but intertwined: to read English Literature as a non-European participant in Anglophone literary studies, and to decolonize the canon of modern Persian/Iranian literature to *unlearn* and *recast* the modern/colonial history of the Middle East region.

Index